Living
with
Endometriosis

Living
with
Endometriosis

How to Cope with the Physical and Emotional Challenges

Kate Weinstein

ADDISON-WESLEY PUBLISHING COMPANY, INC.

Reading, Massachusetts   Menlo Park, California   New York
Don Mills, Ontario   Wokingham, England   Amsterdam   Bonn
Sydney   Singapore   Tokyo   Madrid   San Juan   Paris   Seoul
Milan   Mexico City   Taipei

Weinstein, Kate.
   Living with endometriosis.
   Includes bibliographies and index.
   1. Endometriosis—Popular works. I. Title. [DNLM:
1. Endometriosis—popular works. WP 390 W424L]
RG483.E53W45 1987   618.1'42   86-28779
ISBN 0-201-19810-X

Illustration on pages 56–57 from Fertil Steril 43:351, 1985. Reproduced with permission of the publisher, The
American Fertility Society.

Illustrations © 1987 by Dan Winter

Cover design by Copenhaver Cumpston
Text design by Diana Eames Esterly
Set in 10 point Cheltenham by DEKR Corporation

4 5 6 7 8 9 10 11 12 - DO - 94939291
Fourth printing, April 1991

To my father,
Louis S. Weinstein

Contents

Foreword

Endometriosis is one of the most common gynecologic disorders of the reproductive years, and its incidence appears to be on the increase. It is diagnosed in about 25 percent of abdominal operations performed by gynecologists and is second only to uterine fibroids as the most frequent cause of surgical procedures in premenopausal women. Although seldom life-threatening, endometriosis typically causes severe, progressive, and often incapacitating pain, infertility, repeated hospitalizations and surgeries, and prolonged medical treatments. Yet the symptoms and clinical findings of endometriosis vary from patient to patient and may mimic other gynecologic disorders. This makes office diagnosis difficult and often unreliable. Prior to the advent of laparoscopy, physicians learned to depend on clinical observations and impressions describing physical, psychological, and even racial and socioeconomic characteristics of a "typical patient profile." These observations and impressions, however, were never subjected to rigid scientific scrutiny, and many have been subsequently placed in the realm of myths and misconceptions.

Laparoscopy has greatly improved our diagnostic abilities, especially in the earlier stages of endometriosis. Yet it appears that even laparoscopy may be inadequate for evaluation of the microscopic lesions. Endometriosis, through unknown mechanisms, interferes with the reproductive function of the woman, yet it is the function of the ovaries that stimulates the development and spread of the disease. It is not known why some women acquire endometriosis, but it is generally accepted that its persistence and spread are stimulated by the cyclic secretion of ovarian hormones.

The unknown cause of endometriosis precludes development of curative treatment. All current therapeutic methods offer only a temporary resolution. The only method of treatment that prevents recurrence is hysterectomy with oophorectomy. However, as new strides are being made in almost every corner of the medical field, there are also new developments in the area of endometriosis. New research, especially in the field of reproductive immunology, is especially promising. It is likely that, within the not too distant future, pathophysiology of endometriosis will be clarified and noninvasive diagnostic techniques will become available. This should bring us significantly closer to the development of effective preventive measures and therapeutic techniques.

In the meantime, controversies, contradictions, and disagreements among the medical profession on the subject of endometriosis are not conducive to dissemination of adequate and objective patient information. At a time when the practice of medicine is undergoing rapid changes and patients are playing a larger and more active role in the management of their diseases, there is a clear need for a comprehensive, in-depth review on the subject of endometriosis. Kate Weinstein did an excellent job in this respect. Her book should be easily understandable even to those not familiar with the medical jargon. The review is thorough, clear, and objective and should serve as both a guide and a resource to women who suffer from this disease. Patient histories and quotations enliven the text, making it more personal and appealing. Women suffering from endometriosis should find sections on the emotional aspects and the management of pain and stress especially helpful, since these subjects are seldom covered by physicians who treat endometriosis. The book also contains a wealth of comprehensive information on the physiology of menstruation and the reproductive cycle which healthy women may find educational as well.

W. Paul Dmowski, M.D.
February 1987

Dr. Dmowski is Professor of Obstetrics and Gynecology and Director, Section of Reproductive Endocrinology and Infertility at Rush-Presbyterian-St. Luke's Medical Center in Chicago, Illinois.

Preface

Endometriosis—the presence of endometrial tissue outside of its normal location lining the uterus—remains a word unfamiliar to many, yet its signs, symptoms, and complications have confounded researchers and clinicians for more than a century. Since 1860, when the disease was first described in the medical literature, medical writers and researchers, in several thousand case reports and research studies, have attempted to describe, define, analyze, and demystify this perplexing malady.

Despite this, basic knowledge of endometriosis has advanced little since the term was coined in 1921. Alongside a dearth of facts stands a profusion of myths, misconceptions, and unknowns. Causes and cures continue to elude investigators, and even its chief symptoms—pain and infertility—have yet to be fully explained.

Ultimately, the study of endometriosis has led to virtually only one fact about which all agree: it is a poorly understood disease that has generated considerable speculation and controversy concerning all of its aspects, from its etiology to its treatment.

The conventional wisdom about the disease is derived in large part from clinical observation and impressions handed down from decade to decade without benefit of rigid scientific scrutiny. Hence, the popular and medical literature is riddled with contradiction; researchers try to piece together the puzzle, but many are beginning to conclude that the pieces they have been working with simply don't fit.

As a result, the most basic convictions concerning endometriosis are continually being challenged, if not by scientific method, then by the indisputable experience of women afflicted.

Just as there is little consensus on the part of physicians and researchers concerning the nature and effects of the disease, each woman with endometriosis will tell a different story. There is no "textbook" case, no classic experience of the disease. For some women, the disease poses few difficulties. For others, it thoroughly impairs their ability to live normal, productive, and satisfying lives.

It's tempting to present the research findings as a neatly wrapped package. But endometriosis defies such a presentation. Women with the disease must recognize the controversies and the gaping holes in the research, and realize that there is no unified viewpoint from which to comprehend the disease. To prepare themselves for the uncertainties and challenges that endometriosis may pose, women need to understand that their decisions may have to be based on possibility and probability, the half-known and the unknown. There will not always be satisfactory answers to their questions.

Therefore, to reflect the divergence of medical opinion concerning the nature of the disease, as well as the variety of women's experiences, I have tried to leave intact the ambiguities, the controversies, and the unknowns and to gauge the ways in which they, along with the symptoms and effects of the disease, greatly challenge, and sometimes exhaust, patients' coping abilities.

The contents of this book should not be construed as medical advice nor used in lieu of medical consultation. Medical information is provided to form a background against which the emotional aspects of the disease can be better understood. Treatment options are neither endorsed nor opposed; nor are some of the "alternative" therapies not yet subject to scientific investigation. They, like the more conventional therapies, are options to be carefully investigated and considered in consultation with your health care providers.

Living with Endometriosis provides you with the tools, strategies, and resources you need to increase your ability to cope with the disease. Part 1 sets the stage, with an overview of information on the reproductive system and menstruation and a discussion of some of the myths regarding the latter. Current medical knowledge of endometriosis is provided—its characteristics, development, and prevention; its sites, symptoms, and complications; and finally its diagnosis, description, and classification.

Part 2 takes you through the maze of treatment options, exploring the risks and benefits of each, from aspirin for pain relief to definitive surgery. Part 3, the emotional aspects, guides you through five stages, or phases, of adaptation, from initial crisis through resolution.

Awareness, however, is only the first step. The next is to devise strategies for coping with the various stages of the disease and its problems and challenges: gathering information, building support, managing pain and stress, and simply knowing where and how to ask for help when you need it. These important tools, as well as some alternative therapies, are provided in Part Four. Finally, at the end of the book, are the resources: organizations, publications, and glossaries.

I have addressed this book to women who have, or who suspect they have, endometriosis. My hope is that it will be shared with family, friends, and lovers, as well as with health care practitioners, so that they all may better understand the emotional needs of women with endometriosis.

The experiences of women with endometriosis were culled from (1) responses to 100 questionnaires, designed specifically for this book and sent by the Endometriosis Association to a random sampling of its members; (2) responses to a notice in the Endometriosis Association *Newsletter* requesting contact from members; (3) the correspondence files at the Endometriosis Association headquarters in Milwaukee, Wisconsin; (4) the databank of the Endometriosis Association located at the Medical College of Wisconsin in Milwaukee; (5)

interviews with women who have endometriosis; and (6) interviews with a sampling of association support group leaders, chapter officers, and board members.

Medical and psychological information was drawn from (1) an extensive review of the scientific literature concerning endometriosis and related issues (see Appendix D); (2) professional conferences and symposia; and (3) interviews with gynecologists, infertility specialists and counselors, mental health professionals, sex therapists, and alternative practitioners.

Acknowledgments

Many individuals contributed their time, expertise, suggestions, and support to this manuscript. I'm particularly grateful to the following who consented to be interviewed: Dr. Pierre Asmar, reproductive endocrinologist in private practice in Alexandria, Virginia, advisor to the Washington, D.C. Endometriosis Alliance; Dr. Veasy Buttram, Jr., director of the division of reproductive endocrinology and fertility, Baylor College of Medicine, Houston, president of the American Fertility Society; Dr. Margaret Davis, assistant professor of obstetrics and gynecology, George Washington University Medical Center, Washington, D.C.; Dr. Charles Debrovner, gynecologist in private practice in New York; Dr. W. Paul Dmowski, professor of obstetrics and gynecology, director of reproductive endocrinology and infertility at Rush Medical College, Rush University, Chicago; Dr. Richard Falk, chief of reproductive endocrinology and fertility, Georgetown University Medical School and Columbia Hospital for Women in Washington, D.C.; Dr. Elizabeth Herz, associate professor of obstetrics and gynecology and psychiatry, director of the psychosomatic obstetrics and gynecology program at George Washington University Medical Center; Dr. Laura Hitchcock, psychologist in private practice in Bethesda, Maryland; Dr. Jennifer Jacobs, a Seattle homeopathic physician; Dr. Linda Kames, clinical psychologist and assistant professor of psychology, University of California, Los Angeles; Dr. Milton Kline, director of the Institute for Research in Hypnosis and Psychotherapy, New York; Dr. Burt Littman, assistant professor of obstetrics and gynecology, George Washington University Medical Center; Dr. David Meldrum, associate professor of reproductive endocrinology and chief of female infertility at the UCLA Medical School; Dr. Deborah Metzger, chief resident, Duke University Medical School, Durham, North Carolina; Dr. Suzanne Pratt, gynecologist in private practice in Rome, Georgia; Dr. David Redwine, gynecologist practicing at the Mountain View Women's Clinic in Bend, Oregon; Dr. John Rock, associate professor of obstetrics and gynecology, director of reproductive endocrinology at the Johns Hopkins University School of Medicine, Baltimore; Dr. Andrea Shrednick, a Los Angeles infertility counselor and sex therapist; Catherine Tuerk, a Washington, D.C. therapist; Dr. Anne Ward, gynecologist in private practice in Chicago; Dr. Benny Waxman, professor of obstetrics and gynecology, George Washington University Medical Center; and Wanda Wigfall-Williams, clinical psychologist in private practice in Great Falls, Virginia.

I owe special thanks to Mary Lou Ballweg, president and co-founder of the Endometriosis Association, Milwaukee, Wisconsin; to the staff and volunteers of the Association and to the following members and officers: Linda Barbarotta, Marilyn Beggs, Randy Beggs, Jean Foos, Georgette Gerben, Khristine Lohr, Kate Shaughnessey Low, Suzanne McDonough, Jennifer Jean Yoell, and Joanna Brown; and to Alisa Irving of the Endometriosis Society in London. I'm also grateful for the assistance and information provided by Claudia Dominitz, Medical Center Public Relations, The George Washington University; Mark Stern, News and Information, The National Institutes of Health; the reference staffs at the UCLA Biomedical Library, the National Library of Medicine, and the Dahlgren Library at Georgetown University Medical School; and to the following organizations: the American College of Obstetricians and Gynecologists, the American Fertility Society, the Center for Communications in Infertility, the East West Foundation, Resolve, Inc., Tambrands, Inc., and Winthrop-Breon Laboratories.

I'd also like to thank Tim Moriarity, editor of *Feeling Great*, for giving me the initial opportunity to explore endometriosis in an article from which this manuscript grew; Dan Winter of Emerson Braxton & Co., for providing the illustrations; my editors at Addison-Wesley: Robin Manna, for involving me in the project; Genoa Shepley, for getting me started; and most particularly Cyrisse Jaffee, not only for pushing me across the finish line, but also for her vision, clarity, and sensitivity, which shaped the manuscript, and her vast reserves of patience. I'm also indebted to Perry McIntosh, production supervisor at Addison-Wesley, for extraordinary grace under pressure. I'm continually appreciative of the friends and family members who offered support and encouragement in countless ways, especially: Michelle LaSane; Rick Lesser; James and Mary Proth, Wesley and Irma Schneyer, Herman Silver, Louis Weinstein, Wanda Wigfall-Williams, Laura Wiggins, Peggy Willens, Dr. Lee Winston, Mark, Penne, Katie, and Bo Winston, Helen Zeilberger, Joan Ziemba, and, most certainly not least, Mollie B. Zion.

Finally, to the men and women who shared with me their experiences in hope that others might benefit, I'm grateful.

Note to Readers

In a book written to empower women to take charge of their own health care, and to encourage them in asserting their rights (within a medical system that often neglects those rights), I particularly regret the perpetuation of sexist language. However, since the medical professions continue to be male dominated, and in order to clearly distinguish between doctor and patient while avoiding the cumbersome and repetitious *he/she*, I have used feminine pronouns for patients and masculine pronouns for medical professionals.

Introduction

There is probably no other benign condition in gynecology that has remained so long misunderstood, misdiagnosed, and refractory to effective obliteration as pelvic endometriosis. [1]

To be sure, it is rarely a fatal disease, but rather the great gynecological crippler. [2]

Endometriosis is not yet a household word; still, as many as nine million women may suffer its common consequences: pain, sexual difficulties, menstrual irregularities, and infertility. Despite the fact that it is a leading cause of infertility in women over twenty-five, and the underlying component in as many as half the cases of severe menstrual cramps, endometriosis frequently goes undetected and untreated.

Although theories abound, the precise cause of the disease remains unknown. A variety of treatments—medication, hormonal therapy, conservative surgery—provide little more than a temporary remission of symptoms. Definitive surgery—the removal of the uterus, cervix, fallopian tubes, and ovaries—offers the greatest promise of a permanent cure. Thus, when more conservative treatments fail to bring sustained relief, women severely afflicted by endometriosis must decide whether to continue to live with pain or to forfeit their reproductive organs and the potential for childbearing.

Once the reproductive organs are removed, unless a woman takes replacement hormones, she may face the symptoms of "surgical" menopause: hot flashes, vaginal dryness, osteoporosis, and increased risk of heart disease. And, for some, even definitive surgery is not the end of the line. Although very uncommon, endometriosis can recur or persist following even such radical treatment.

For many women, this "cure" exacts too great a penalty and arouses too many fears. Therefore, to alleviate as much pain as possible, while preserving or attempting to restore their fertility, it is not unusual for women to proceed from one treatment to another, following courses of hormonal therapy with repeated conservative surgery, waiting, hoping, and wondering whether each will be the last.

Faced with these uncertainties, women are reassured that the disease is at least not life threatening. But it can be devastating, not only physically, but emotionally, sexually, and financially as well.

Determined to understand the confounding medical facts and to find a cure, patients and physicians alike often pay little attention to the serious emotional repercussions that occur along the way: that is, the psychological stress that is caused by the disease and its chronicity. In many cases, physicians are unwilling or unable to offer practical coping strategies, and patients are too preoccupied with treatments to deal with the day-to-day problems the disease poses. Beset by pain, disability, anxiety, and fear, often isolated and confused, many women are unable to make critical treatment decisions. They cannot sustain the energy and clear thinking they need to cope with various changes in lifestyle and life goals the disease may bring.

When physicians and other professionals are unable to help with the emotional aspects, they often advise women to "live with it." Seldom, however, do they provide the tools and strategies to do so.

The single most important thing you can do to improve your ability to live with the disease is to face head-on the unpleasant fact most women go to great lengths to avoid: endometriosis will probably be with you for a very long time. It may come and go, it may get better or it may get worse, but it is unlikely that it will disappear completely. Although it seems a dismal and discouraging prospect, this fact actually offers you a measure of control. You are forced to see that you must deal not only with the physiological effects of the disease, but also with its impact on your life plans and goals, because a cure may never come.

As you turn your energies from pursuit of a cure to management of the disease, you soon realize that you are not helpless, that endometriosis needn't always be the focus of your life, that definitive surgery is *not* inevitable, and that there is much you can do to make living with endometriosis easier.

Aptly described as "making the best of a bad bargain,"[3] coping—learning to live with chronic illness with a minimum of that which holistic thinkers term *dis-ease*—means cutting your losses and moving on. It takes an enormous amount of motivation, determination, resources, and support. Frustrations and disappointments are all too common. But as you learn to gather information and make use of coping strategies, you will soon discover that you have been empowered to regain and sustain the energy and clear thinking you need to take charge of your life as you face the continuing challenges of endometriosis.

Living
with
Endometriosis

PART 1

Endometriosis: Medical Aspects

To effectively cope with a disease as puzzling, complex, and unpredictable as endometriosis, women will need many different kinds of information. Those who suspect they have endometriosis need to learn as much as possible about its signs and symptoms as well as the methods by which it is detected. Those who already have been diagnosed and who now approach treatment decisions need to learn more about the ways in which the disease is believed to develop in order to understand the ways in which it is combatted. Whatever stage you are in, it's important to become familiar not only with the facts, but also with the theories and myths associated with endometriosis and to learn to distinguish one from the other. To make appropriate decisions, you need access not to only one point of view or interpretation of the disease, but to a variety of viewpoints. And, in order to understand these various viewpoints, a solid background of fundamental medical information is necessary.

Part 1 provides an overview of the basic medical knowledge concerning endometriosis, drawn from many sources and representing a broad spectrum of opinion. It begins not with endometriosis, however, but with a detailed exploration of reproductive anatomy and physiology. While you may be eager to delve directly into a discussion of endometriosis, realize that a firm grasp of the reproductive cycle is an essential prerequisite to an understanding of the disease. Without this knowledge, you cannot comprehend the rationales behind the various treatments discussed in Part 2 or the complex and mysterious ways in which endometriosis affects fertility.

Chapter 1, therefore, explores the complexities of the female reproductive cycle from menarche—the beginning of the reproductive years, to menopause—the cessation of menstruation and the end of reproductive life. At the same time, this chapter looks into those myths surrounding menstruation and menopause that hinder women's ability to differentiate normal from abnormal characteristics of the cycle.

1

Chapter 2 investigates the nature of endometriosis: what it is and what it is not, who gets it, what its consequences are, how it develops, and how it *may* be prevented. Of particular importance to women who merely suspect that they have endometriosis, Chapter 3 details the sites and symptoms of endometriosis, while Chapter Four illustrates the methods by which the disease is detected and discusses the many obstacles to a rapid and accurate diagnosis.

With this background, you will be able to grasp the various treatment methods discussed in Part 2 and more confidently approach treatment decisions.

1
Menarche to Menopause: The Reproductive Years

MYTHS AND TABOOS

By the time the average childless woman reaches twenty-one she has menstruated more than 100 times, yet probably knows little about the processes involved. Think back to when you first learned about menstruation. At the very least, you were instructed in the use of pads or tampons; perhaps you were told you might need to rest, stay in bed, or limit your activities for a day or two. You were told that your body was changing. Chances are you got the message that those changes would be associated with pain, discomfort, and infirmity. Euphemisms such as "on the rag" and "the curse" reinforced those messages.

If you reached puberty in the 1950s or 1960s you probably were given a pamphlet or shown a film about "becoming a woman" or "the monthly miracle." The facts of reproductive life may have been explained cursorily.

According to the *Tampax Report*, a 1981 survey exploring attitudes toward menstruation, one-third of American women did not know what menstruation was when they first experienced it.[1] Our knowledge of the menstrual cycle is usually scanty from the beginning; moreover, many of us have little opportunity to add to it.

Menstruation is indeed complex, but it is not incomprehensible. The reason women are not taught its intricacies may have to do with primitive menstrual taboos and their lingering influence on the perception of menstruation in our own culture.

In primitive societies throughout the world, menstruation was variously synonymous with shame, magic, mystery, uncleanliness, pollution, power, and destruction. A menstruating woman was believed to be a source of contamination—she could blight crops, sour milk, and cause farm animals to abort. In some cultures she was revered, but in most, whether feared, envied, condemned, or honored, she was in one way or another segregated, relegated to a menstrual hut, or confined to quarters.

3

By the late 1800s and early 1900s, menstruation in Western society came to represent sickness, frailty, and suffering. Barbara Ehrenreich and Deirdre English, in their book, *For Her Own Good: 150 Years of Experts' Advice to Women*, quote the doctors of the day:

We cannot too emphatically urge the importance of regarding these monthly returns as periods of ill health, as days when the ordinary occupations are to be suspended or modified....Long walks, dancing, shopping, riding and parties should be avoided at this time of the month invariably and under all circumstances....

All heavy exercise should be omitted during the menstrual week...a girl should not only retire earlier at this time, but ought to stay out of school from one to three days as the case may be, resting the mind and taking extra hours of rest and sleep. [2]

Soon after, the ideas of Sigmund Freud began to have a profound effect on the ways in which menstruation was perceived. Invalidism associated with menstruation was seen as the manifestation of deep-rooted psychological difficulties, an idea that took hold in this country after World War II. Dysmenorrhea—pain or difficulty associated with menstruation—came to be seen as an unconscious repudiation of femininity or the result of faulty attitudes toward sex. These psychoanalytical theories about women were inexplicably transformed into medical "fact" and used to dismiss those mysterious disorders scientists had not yet been able to explain. The authors of a 1951 medical textbook declared, for example, that "functional dysmenorrhea is not a disease entity; it is a symptom of a personality disorder whose etiology [cause] is unknown."[3] The same authors concluded: "Menstruation is the 'badge of femininity' and the badge may be worn in misery, pain or pride, depending on the attitude of the woman."[4] These views held firm well into the 1970s.

Through the years not only dysmenorrhea but also menopausal distress, infertility, painful intercourse, and, more recently, premenstrual syndrome, have all been subject to this "medicalization" of psychoanalytic speculation. At one time or another all were seen as the result of underlying neuroses related to a woman's rejection of the feminine role, even though it has been shown that these conditions have a physiological basis.

We like to think we live in a society in which such myths and taboos are clearly of another age. However, these misassumptions persist, fueled not so much by what is said but by what is not said.

Feminine hygiene products have been advertised on television since 1972, when a National Broadcasters' Association ban was lifted.[5] Yet menstruation remains a word unfit for prime time. Commercials continue to refer to "that time of the month" or "those difficult days" as they promote products based on security, protection, and discretion. It appears that television, at least in this regard, does imitate life. Even today menstruation is not considered a topic of polite conversation. According to the 1981 *Tampax Report*, two-thirds of men and women believe that menstruation should not be discussed at work or socially, while one-quarter find the subject offensive even in the home. If the idea of modern menstrual taboos seems far-fetched, consider the following findings from the 1981 *Tampax*

Report. They indicate that menstrual taboos and myths continue to shape society's views of this physiological function.[6]

- Fourteen million Americans believe that women, when menstruating, should attempt to stay away from others.
- One-third believe that women's physical activities should be curtailed during menstruation.
- Eighty-seven percent believe that women are particularly emotional while they are menstruating.
- Fifty percent believe that women should not have intercourse during menstruation.
- More than one-quarter believe that women cannot function normally at work while menstruating.
- One-third believe that menstruation affects women's ability to think.
- Twenty-two percent believe that menstrual pain is in women's minds.

Vestiges of the psychoanalytical interpretation of menstrual disorders still contribute to our perception of menstruation. Such concepts have been well-refuted, but they are not easily relinquished. As recently as 1976, medical students, today's gynecologists, were taught that menstrual pain is an emotional contrivance. A popular textbook in 1979 declared that "considerable evidence has been presented to suggest that psychogenic factors are responsible for most of the dysmenorrhea seen today."[7] Another recent textbook suggests that "those with severe pain have a preexisting resentment of their feminine role" and links severe and incapacitating menstrual pain to the "highly strung supersensitive patient."[8]

Menstruation, then, remains hedged by stigma. Out of shame or embarrassment, to avoid subtle public censure, and in fear of being labeled neurotic, women avoid open discussion of menstruation. Furthermore, women are concerned that focusing on menstrual problems may jeopardize the progress now being made toward equality in the workplace.

Thus, from our earliest years, we receive, absorb, and transmit the message that the experience of menstruation—even the word itself—is offensive. (It has even been speculated that "taboo" may be derived from a Polynesian word for menstruation: *tapua.*[9]) Language and culture conspire to cloak a basic physiological function in secrecy and silence. By our own reticence to speak out, we perpetuate these taboos and myths.

Impact of Taboos and Myths

The consequences of these taboos and myths stretch beyond subtle social ostracism and discrimination in the workplace to impinge upon vital issues of reproductive health.

If normal menstruation is spoken of in hushed tones (if at all), then its disorders are even more rarely discussed. Silence creates embarrassment and misunderstanding. Without open discussion, a woman cannot distinguish the normal from the abnormal. She has been conditioned either to accept discomfort accompanying her period, or to suspect an "emotional" problem as the cause of pain.

The mystery surrounding menstruation, then, often obscures the recognition of a disorder, prevents a prompt and accurate diagnosis, and precludes or delays treatment. Poorly understood disorders are still labeled psychogenic by some doctors. These theories not only blame the victim, they inhibit further research by implying that the cause of such disorders is known. Mystery and silence support the taboos, the taboos reinforce ignorance, and ignorance fosters neglect. When this cycle is broken women will be better able to understand the differences between normal and abnormal menstruation and be better equipped to recognize and seek help for problems such as endometriosis.

While it is no doubt important for all women to have an understanding of the menstrual cycle, it is a necessity for women with endometriosis. The story of endometriosis—its symptoms, causes, treatments, and consequences—unfolds against the background of a woman's reproductive life, beginning at menarche and ending at menopause. In order to understand endometriosis, it is important to understand the anatomy and physiology of menstruation, from menarche to menopause. Don't be disheartened by the complexity of the subject. You will be able to grasp at least the basics and you can refer to this chapter during later discussions involving these processes.

REPRODUCTIVE ANATOMY AND PHYSIOLOGY

The Uterus

The uterus, moored in the pelvis by eight ligaments, is located between the bladder and the rectum. A hollow, pear-shaped organ, its primary function is to house and nourish the developing fetus during pregnancy. It is composed of three layers of tissue. The innermost layer, the *endometrium*, rich with blood-supplying arteries, is the soft nesting place and source of nutrients for the fertilized ovum (egg) during pregnancy. The endometrium is itself composed of two layers, a thin undercoating that remains unchanged throughout the menstrual cycle and an outer glandular coat. The latter varies in thickness at different times during the cycle, from approximately 0.5 mm after menstruation to about 5 mm just before menstruation.

The middle layer, the *myometrium*, is the uterine muscle. It contracts during menstruation to expel debris and during pregnancy to facilitate labor.

The outermost layer of the uterus is a sheath of peritoneal tissue. (The *peritoneum* is the membranelike tissue that coats the walls and organs of the abdomen.) (See Figures 1 and 2.)

The Ovaries

Anchored by a ligament above each side of the uterus is an ovary, a small oval organ. Inside each ovary are follicles—pouches containing ova (eggs). The follicles are lined with cells which, when stimulated, produce the hormones that direct ovarian function. Each month one ovary expels a ripe ovum.

Figure 1   Reproductive Anatomy

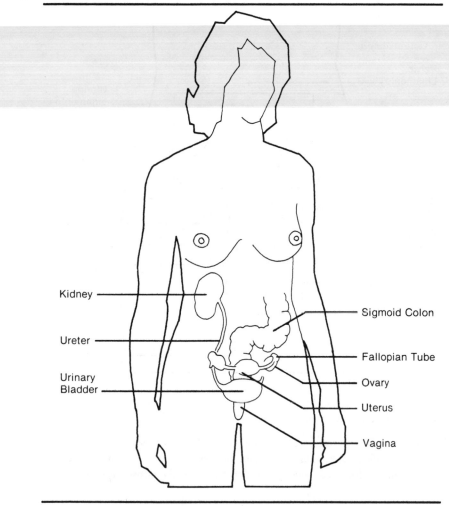

Kidney	Sigmoid Colon
Ureter	Fallopian Tube
Urinary Bladder	Ovary
	Uterus
	Vagina

The Fallopian Tubes

Extending upward from each side of the uppermost portion (the fundus) of the uterus is a fallopian tube, a narrow projection about four inches long that curls toward the ovary. The ends of the tubes are fimbriated (fringed), and these fingerlike ends grasp the expelled ovum and draw it inside the tube, through which it is transported to the uterus.

Figure 2   Detail of Reproductive Anatomy

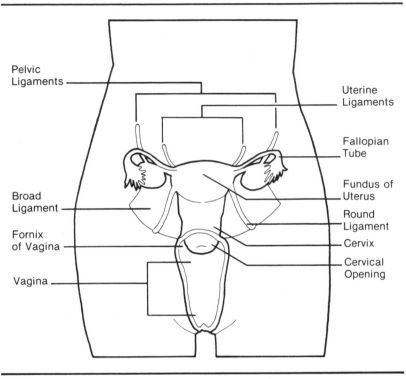

The Hypothalamus

The *hypothalamus* is the portion of the brain that links the nervous and endocrine systems. It transmits and translates messages between the two systems and controls the secretion of hormones from the *pituitary gland* that governs the menstrual cycle.

The Pituitary Gland

The pituitary gland is a pea-sized organ located at the base of the brain and connected to the hypothalamus by a stem. Although sometimes called a master gland, the pituitary simply carries out the orders of the hypothalamus to coordinate the secretion of hormones.

The ovarian hormones. *Estrogen* is a generic name for a variety of hormones which, among many other functions, stimulate the growth of the endometrium. *Progesterone* is the hormone primarily responsible for maturing the endometrium and preparing it to nourish a fertilized ovum.

Gonadotropins.   Gonadotropins are pituitary hormones carried through the blood-stream to stimulate the ovaries (gonads). One of these, *follicle stimulating hormone (FSH)*, promotes the growth of ovarian follicles and leads to the maturation of a ripe ovum. Another, *luteinizing hormone (LH)*, stimulates the ovary to produce its own hormones and instigates ovulation—the expulsion of a mature ovum from the ovary.

Gonadotropin releasing hormones.   Gonadotropin releasing hormones (GnRH) are neurochemical transmitters, or messengers, dispatched by the hypothalamus to order the release of gonadotropins.

The Feedback System

In the years just preceding menarche—the onset of menstruation—the hypothalamus begins to send the messages that set the stage for the elaborate cycle that will be repeated monthly throughout a woman's reproductive years. The other principal players in this drama are the pituitary gland and the ovaries. Together, they are known as the hypothalamic-pituitary-ovarian axis.

The menstrual cycle is governed by an intricate hormonal feedback system—a highly synchronized orchestration of signals and countersignals mediated by the hypothalamus.

For 21 days of each month, the components of this axis prime the body for pregnancy by building a support system to nurture and sustain the fertilized ovum. If conception does not occur, they reverse their efforts and destroy that support system, only to begin rebuilding it again on the twenty-ninth day.

The feedback system is highly complex, yet it is not difficult to understand. Like a Rube Goldberg cartoon of a mechanical contraption which, through an exceedingly contrived series of steps, performs an exceptionally simple function, the entire process seems mystifying. But when you look at the individual parts and their interrelationships, however, the process becomes clear.

The hypothalamus directs the production of the hormones. Hormone levels rise and fall throughout the cycle, inhibiting and stimulating the production of other hormones as they do so. Hormone is a Greek word which means "to urge on." Hormones "urge on" other hormones. But they "urge off" too, that is, they work via both positive and negative feedback.

To understand how feedback works, think of a thermostat. When the temperature drops to a certain point, the change triggers the furnace to generate heat. That's positive feedback. When the temperature rises to the desired level, this change triggers the furnace to shut off. That's negative feedback.

The amount of a particular hormone secretion from a gland can be regulated by the level of another hormone. Just as cold air triggers a thermostat to produce hot air, low levels of one hormone, for example, can, through positive feedback, signal the hypothalamus (the thermostat) to secrete another hormone. Just as the desired level of hot air instructs the thermostat to stop producing more heat, the second hormone, once it's reached a desired level, signals the hypothalamus to stop its secretion (negative feedback). Positive feedback leads to increased secretion of a substance; negative feedback inhibits secretion.

THE PHASES OF THE MENSTRUAL CYCLE

The 28-day cycle is the end result of the extraordinary synchrony of the hypothalamic-pituitary-ovarian axis. It is divided into three phases: the proliferative phase, the luteal phase, and menstruation (bleeding). Ovulation, the expulsion of a ripe ovum from the ovary, separates the proliferative and luteal phases. Although there are normal variations in the length of the cycle as a whole and in the length of each individual phase, the average 28-day cycle could be divided this way:

Days 1–5:   Menstruation
Days 6–13:   Proliferative (or follicular) phase
Day 14:   Ovulation
Days 15–28:   Luteal (or secretory) phase

Menstruation, although commonly referred to as the beginning of the cycle, is actually the culmination of the monthly hormonal ebb and flow. To track the phenomenon chronologically, consider an average cycle as it unfolds from the beginning of the proliferative phase, which sets it in motion, to the climax—menstruation.

The Proliferative Phase

The proliferative (or follicular) phase begins when the hypothalamus reacts to the low levels of estrogen and progesterone that prevail during menstruation. These low levels, through positive feedback, launch the cycle by triggering the hypothalamus to route gonadotropin-releasing hormones to the pituitary gland. The pituitary then releases gonadotropins (hormones that stimulate the gonads). One of those hormones, follicle stimulating hormone (FSH), spurs the growth of the ovarian follicles. It also releases a smaller amount of luteinizing hormone to prod the cells of the follicles to produce estrogen, which also contributes to the development of the follicles.

As the follicles mature and produce more estrogen, the endometrium responds by *proliferating*—swelling with blood and nutrients to form the thick lining that nourishes a fertilized ovum.

At the same time, spurred on by FSH, the growing follicles push toward the outer layer of the ovary. For reasons unknown, one of these, known as the Graffian follicle, outstrips the others in development. Only this follicle will continue to mature, straining the surface of the ovary as it does so.

Meanwhile, the level of estrogen continues to increase, and, through negative feedback, signals the hypothalamus to order a decrease in the production of FSH. On about day 12, the estrogen level peaks and, this time through positive feedback, signals the hypothalamus to dispatch its gonadotropin releasing hormone, which in turn instructs the pituitary to order a surge of luteinizing hormone.

This surge accelerates the growth of the already swollen follicle to the point of rupture. The ovary contracts, propelling the ovum through its outer surface. This process—ovulation—occurs on or about the 14th day before menstrual flow begins (at approximately the middle of a normal 28-day cycle).

The Luteal Phase

The luteal (or secretory) phase follows ovulation. The remnant of the ruptured follicle on the surface of the ovary is transformed by the luteinizing hormone into a different kind of structure called the *corpus luteum* (yellow body). The rising LH levels that brought about ovulation also cause the corpus luteum to release progesterone and estrogen, with progesterone in greater quantity.

Progesterone's main responsibility at this point is to expand upon the work that estrogen began in the previous phase—stimulating the cells of the endometrium to thicken the lining. Progesterone, now in greater quantity than estrogen, stops the cell multiplication and causes the existing endometrial cells to develop. All the while, the high level of progesterone, through negative feedback, is inhibiting the hypothalamus from triggering additional follicle stimulating hormone secretion from the pituitary. Since the follicle has already matured and ejected an ovum, no further stimulation is needed.

After ovulation, the fimbriated end of a fallopian tube grasps the ovum that has been expelled from the follicle and draws it into the tube. There it is propelled by means of pulsing contractions and guided by cilia (hairlike projections) toward the uterus. This trip takes about five days.

If midway during the journey of the ovum through the tube, fertilization (the fusion of the ovum with sperm) occurs, the ovum normally continues its passage to the uterus and implants there in the soft, thick endometrium. This will become the placenta, the embryo's source of nourishment. If fertilization does not occur, the ovum begins to degenerate a day or two after ovulation and is carried out of the body by cervical and vaginal secretions.

Implantation generally takes place on about day 21, seven days after ovulation. The fertilized ovum will secrete human chorionic gonadotropin (HCG)—a hormone resembling luteinizing hormone—which directs the corpus luteum to continue production of estrogen and progesterone to sustain the pregnancy until the placenta is able to produce its own hormones.

If the fallopian tubes have been deformed or blocked by scar tissue resulting from infection or disease, the ovum may be trapped in the tube and forced to burrow into its wall. If this occurs, surgery will be necessary to remove the ectopic (misplaced) pregnancy before its growth ruptures the tubal wall.

If conception has not occurred, the high levels of estrogen and progesterone will inhibit the production of LH. Without LH, or the HCG that would have been produced by a fertilized ovum, the corpus luteum is no longer stimulated to produce hormones and begins to regress by about day 23 or 24. By days 26 to 28, when it has thoroughly regressed, estrogen and progesterone levels plummet.

Without the continued support of estrogen and progesterone, the arteries to the endometrium constrict, cutting off blood and nutrients, and causing the endometrium to deteriorate and break away from the uterine wall.

Bleeding

By day 28, the endometrial debris begins to flow from the uterus through the cervix and exits the body through the vaginal canal. The menstrual cycle begins on day 1 with this discharge of tissue, blood, mucus, and vaginal and cervical secretions. By the end of the flow, the endometrium has shed its bulk and is again only a thin layer coating the inside of the uterus.

During menstruation, the ovary secretes only minimal amounts of estrogen and progesterone. In response to these low levels, the hypothalamus again unleashes its hormone releasing factors; these instruct the pituitary to release FSH to mature another follicle, and the cycle again is set in motion.

Unless interrupted by pregnancy, breast-feeding, or the occurrence or treatment of a menstrual disorder or disease, this cycle will be reenacted monthly from menarche to menopause.

NORMAL CHARACTERISTICS OF THE REPRODUCTIVE YEARS

Menarche

Menarche—the onset of the menstrual function—generally occurs between the ages of twelve and thirteen, although it is not abnormal for it to start as early as ten or as late as fifteen.

At menarche, the menstrual cycle may be somewhat erratic and periods are often anovulatory (without ovulation) for a few months or even years. Since there is much variation in the duration and amount of menstrual flow, in the monthly timing of the cycle, and in the amount and kind of discomfort, once a cycle has stabilized any deviation from one's own normal pattern may signal a problem. However, general guidelines described below will help you determine if what you experience is within a normal range.

The Adult Menstrual Cycle

Duration. The normal interval between periods, according to the *Merck Manual*, is "28 days plus or minus three days for 65 percent of women, with a range of 18 to 40 days; once a menstrual pattern has been established, the variation does not normally exceed five days" (fourteenth edition, 1982, p. 1655). A variety of factors can lead to changes in the duration of the cycle, including illness, a change in lifestyle or environment, and other kinds of emotional stress. Stress stimulates the cerebral cortex to affect the functioning of the hypothalamus which directs the menstrual cycle. There is no reason to worry about a change in the length of your cycle, however, unless it is extreme (for example, less than twenty-one days or more than thirty-five days).

Ovulation.   As ovulation occurs midway in the cycle, a jabbing or aching sensation (known as *mittelschmerz*, or middle pain) may occur in the area of the ovary. At this time a woman may feel a mild ache in her lower back. Unless severe, this is a normal reaction to ovulation.

Flow.   The menstrual flow normally lasts from three to five days, with bleeding characteristically heavier on the second day. Periods as short as two days or as long as eight days are not considered abnormal.

The amount of blood loss varies from 13 to 300 ml, typically 130 ml. This amount of blood, 130 ml, would saturate about seven or eight pads or tampons.

The menstrual blood is characteristically dark red and has a musty odor. Because the endometrium contains an enzyme that breaks down blood clots, the menstrual discharge, unless particularly heavy, is generally free of clots. What appear to be clots may simply be clumps of mucus coated with blood.

Normal cramps.   Childbirth and menstruation are unique in that they are the only physiological functions during which discomfort and pain are commonly believed to be normal. Contrary to popular belief, however, menstrual cramps are not inevitable. Although it is not abnormal to experience some mild and transient discomfort, approximately half of all menstruating women experience no pain accompanying the flow of blood.

Spotting a day or two before the period is not uncommon; its occurrence at other times, however, should be brought to the attention of your gynecologist.

Menopause

Natural menopause—the cessation of the menstrual function—generally occurs between the ages of forty and fifty, most commonly at age forty-eight or forty-nine. During the perimenopause—the time just before and after the menstrual cycle gears down—the ovaries become less responsive to follicle stimulating hormone and luteinizing hormone; consequently, follicles fail to develop and the ovaries no longer expel ova. (The ova, in fact, degenerate.) Furthermore, the ovaries no longer produce significant quantities of estrogen and progesterone. The pituitary increases production of FSH and LH in an attempt to activate the ovaries, but the ovaries continue to be unresponsive. The endometrium is no longer instructed to proliferate, and, with nothing to shed, menstruation ceases. This may be an abrupt process, but more often it is gradual: the menstrual cycles are erratic for a period of months or even years. A woman is not truly postmenopausal until her periods have ceased for at least six months.

Estrogen production doesn't shut down entirely in the postmenopausal woman, however. Although severely curtailed, a certain amount of estrogen remains, as the adrenal glands and the ovaries secrete androgens that can be converted into estrogens. For some women, these other sources of estrogen may be enough to prevent the occurrence of menopausal symptoms. Other women, unless they receive replacement hormones, will over time experience such symptoms as hot flashes; vaginal dryness, atrophy, or infection; irritation of the urinary tract tissues; and, possibly, osteoporosis—the progressive loss of bone mass—all due to diminished levels of estrogen following menopause. Another consequence is an increased risk of heart disease: heart attacks are twice as common in postmenopausal women as in pre-menopausal women. To combat the symptoms and risks associated with menopause, estrogen replacement therapy is often prescribed.

It is not unusual for menopausal women to experience depression, irritability, anxiety, and changing levels of sexual desire and satisfaction. The precise cause remains unclear, but it appears to be in some way linked to hormonal fluctuations as well as to the discomfort and disruption caused by hot flashes and vaginal atrophy. Psychological factors may also contribute to these changes.

Before it became clear that menopausal discomfort and emotional distress often have a physiological basis, all women who experienced these difficulties were said to be neurotic, acting out their fear of aging, bemoaning the loss of their youthful appearance, inconsolate over the end of their childbearing years and their "lost womanhood." Thus, with menopause, the taboos, myths, and misinformation come full circle. Because *some* women do suffer the menopausal symptoms described above, their experiences have come to be viewed as typical. Menopausal women—and, by extension, those who undergo surgical menopause (the removal of the ovaries)—are expected "to have emotional breakdowns, lose their sexual appetites, experience hot flashes, and sprout little mustaches. Their breasts and vaginas are supposed to shrivel up."[10]

Since emotional instability has become the hallmark of the menopausal woman in the popular imagination, she is often the subject of derision and contempt. If she assimilates these beliefs she may begin to see herself as defective, purposeless, sexless, and unattractive because she can no longer bear children. Or she may fear that others see her that way. Ironically, many women begin adulthood ashamed of menstruating and end their reproductive years ashamed of not menstruating.

MENSTRUAL DIFFICULTIES

There are a number of problems associated with menstruation that women need to be aware of. Perhaps the two most troubling are premenstrual syndrome and dysmenorrhea. Others include

Primary amenorrhea	Metrorrhagia
Secondary amenorrhea	Oligomenorrhea
Hypermenorrhea	Polymenorrhea
Hypomenorrhea	(See Glossary for definitions)
Menorrhagia	

Premenstrual Syndrome

During the week or two preceding their period, many women suffer from a constellation of emotional and physical symptoms known as premenstrual syndrome (PMS). No two women experience PMS in quite the same way, and any one woman will experience it differently from month to month. During one cycle, she may have no symptoms; during the next, she may suffer from a combination of complaints. These include:

abdominal bloating	hypoglycemia (low blood sugar)
absentmindedness	irritability
acne	itching
anxiety	joint pain
asthma	lack of coordination
backache	leg cramps
breast tenderness	mood swings
changes in appetite	muscle pain
changes in libido	nausea
constipation	painful varicose veins
craving for sweet or salty foods	panic attacks
crying	rapid heartbeat
depression	sadness
diarrhea	tension
difficulty concentrating	thirst
disorientation	tinnitus (ringing in the ears)
dizziness	urinary discharge
excitability	vaginal discharge
fatigue	visual disturbances
fluid retention	weight gain
headache	

These symptoms were first described in 1931. It is estimated that 40 percent of all women experience at least some of them; nevertheless, until recently, PMS has been largely ignored by the medical professions.

From relative obscurity, PMS has recently become a household word. This transformation has taken place as a result of two issues. The first is based in law. Premenstrual syndrome has been successfully used as a legal defense in cases of murder, a precedent that some feel has broad and frightening implications. The second is economic. As women take their place in the workforce, increased attention has been paid to the amount of downtime attributed to premenstrual syndrome. There is concern that companies may become hesitant to hire women for high-level positions.

Debate continues as to the precise cause and nature of PMS and whether or not it represents a true medical entity. There are those who argue that PMS is primarily a physical disorder tied to monthly hormonal fluctuations; others seek to classify its emotional components as a category of mental illness (called *premenstrual dysphoria*). Still others deny that PMS exists in any fashion.

Medical naysayers in the past attributed PMS symptoms to woman's "natural instability." More recently, many feminists have argued against its existence. They fear that recognition will fuel the argument that women are biologically unfit for the workplace and lay the groundwork for other forms of discrimination. Others argue that only through recognition (although not necessarily as a mental disorder) will research and treatment follow, thus eliminating the cause of discrimination.

Since the symptoms of PMS were first described, researchers have been trying to pinpoint their biological bases. The precise cause or causes of premenstrual syndrome are not well understood; however, theories point to several possible contributing factors:

- an imbalance in the ratio of estrogen to progesterone
- elevated levels of prolactin (a pituitary hormone that stimulates secretion of milk)
- an abnormal metabolism of magnesium or lineolic acid (an essential fatty acid) which might lead to a heightened sensitivity to hormonal changes
- water retention caused by estrogen
- vitamin deficiency
- progesterone deficit, withdrawal, or allergy
- decreased levels of endorphins (the brain's opiates)

Until the mechanisms that trigger PMS symptoms are better understood, research and debate will continue. In the meantime, PMS clinics dot the landscape, dispensing a variety of treatment approaches—some potentially hazardous—including supplemental natural progesterone; oral contraceptives; tranquilizers and antidepressants; vitamin and nutritional therapy; nonsteroidal anti-inflammatory agents; and drugs such as danazol, bromocryptine, and spironolactone.

Some PMS clinics bring needed and welcome relief to many afflicted women; others offer questionable treatment to the desperate and vulnerable. Already incapacitated for perhaps a week or more each month, women with endometriosis are particularly frustrated by premenstrual syndrome. It can increase their physical and emotional downtime to three weeks or more and render them especially vulnerable to the lure of dubious PMS "cures."

Many clinics use a standard approach to PMS, whereas only treatment developed for each woman's unique symptoms is likely to provide relief. For example, progesterone therapy may be appropriate for some women, while other women's symptoms may be adequately controlled through simple changes in diet combined with an exercise regimen.

If you suffer from premenstrual syndrome, learn as much as possible about the symptoms, possible causes, and treatment approaches. Discuss these with your physician before rushing off to a PMS clinic. A variety of publications and organizations offer useful information, such as how to chart your symptoms as a prerequisite to diagnosis and treatment, and how to evaluate treatment centers and their approaches. (For more information about coping with PMS, and for a listing of relevant organizations and publications, see Appendixes B, C, and D.)

Dysmenorrhea

The experience of pain is so subjective that it is often difficult to describe and nearly impossible to quantify. Variations in individual tolerance make it difficult for women and their doctors to differentiate between simple menstrual discomfort and pain that may indicate an underlying disorder.

Since many women experience some sort of menstrual cramping, and since not all such pain is a manifestation of a disease or disorder, the question is, How much pain is too much? For physicians, it's a difficult question to answer, but experts seem to agree that medical intervention is required whenever menstrual pain is severe enough to interfere with normal activities, is not eliminated by over-the-counter analgesics or medications such as Advil or Nuprin, or intensifies from month to month.

As opposed to the discomfort of "normal" cramps, dysmenorrhea describes *severe* pain with menstruation. Researchers estimate that more than half of all women are troubled by dysmenorrhea, and about 10 percent are incapacitated for one to three days each month. Many women fail to report it to their gynecologists. They believe that it's normal for a woman—something they must endure—or that there is no treatment. If your pain worsens or regularly disrupts school, work, sleep, leisure activities, regular exercise, or sexual activity, seek the advice of a gynecologist.

Dysmenorrhea has become synonymous with cramps. However, in addition to severe pain, the term actually refers to a number of symptoms associated with menstruation: nausea, dizziness, vomiting, diarrhea, low backache, headaches, and, in severe cases, fainting.

There are two types of dysmenorrhea: primary (for which there is no apparent organic cause) and secondary (resulting from an organic disorder). Some causes of secondary dysmenorrhea are:

Adenomyosis
Anatomic abnormalities
Endometriosis
Use of an intrauterine device
Ovarian cysts
Pelvic adhesions

Pelvic inflammatory disease and other pelvic infection or inflammation
Tumors
Uterine adhesions, fibroids, and polyps

Secondary dysmenorrhea, although it may, like primary dysmenorrhea, occur shortly after menarche, more commonly occurs later in menstrual life, and often increases with age. The pain, described as dull or grinding, often begins well before menstruation and lasts beyond the flow of blood. It may be localized or diffuse, radiating to the back, rectum, or thighs. (See Chapter 3 for a more extensive discussion of secondary dysmenorrhea as a symptom of endometriosis.)

Primary dysmenorrhea generally begins soon after menarche and tends to lessen with age and childbearing. The pain, which begins with the menstrual flow and lasts for only one or two days, is colicky (sharp and sudden) and usually located in the lower middle abdomen. There are a number of speculations as to the causes of primary dysmenorrhea.

Psychogenic pain.   In the recent past, dysmenorrhea has been treated with analgesics and, in more severe cases, narcotics, tranquilizers, antidepressants, and antispasmodic drugs. No cause-directed treatment was available because pain of this sort was widely believed to originate in the mind. Cramps were believed to represent a neurotic complaint associated with a woman's rejection of her "feminine role." In 1966, half of all gynecologists supported this theory.[11] Consequently, dysmenorrhea was poorly studied and treated. Patients complaining of severe menstrual pain were frequently dismissed with a prescription for a tranquilizer or a referral to a psychiatrist. Although the myth has been well refuted, it is not uncommon for patients today to encounter physicians who continue to attribute menstrual pain to emotional instability.

Cervical dilation.   Some physicians suggest that primary dysmenorrhea may be caused when the cervix dilates to allow menstrual blood to flow into the vaginal canal. Support for this theory comes from the observation that childbirth, which stretches the cervix and thus makes it easier for blood to flow, brings relief from dysmenorrhea. However, it has been observed that cesarean delivery, which does not stretch the cervix, also brings relief, so other factors must be considered. In addition, x-rays show that women with dysmenorrhea are no more likely than those without dysmenorrhea to have narrow cervical openings.[12] Furthermore, women who have cervical stenosis (narrowing of the cervix) don't necessarily experience more menstrual pain. Nevertheless, cervical dilation has been used in an attempt to treat menstrual pain.

Progesterone.   Some researchers point the finger of blame at progesterone, observing that dysmenorrhea occurs only in ovulatory cycles and therefore only with exposure to progesterone. They speculate that excess progesterone may contribute to dysmenorrhea and suggest a treatment regimen of oral contraceptives. Birth control pills prevent ovulation and excessive production of progesterone and therefore diminish dysmenorrhea.

Prostaglandins. Another theory suggests that pain results from uterine contractions which constrict the arteries supplying blood to the uterine muscle. This belief gained credence with the 1957 discovery by British physiologist Dr. V. R. Pickles of substances in the menstrual fluid later identified as prostaglandins—hormonelike substances originating from polyunsaturated essential fatty acids. These substances are known to stimulate the contraction of the uterine muscle that facilitates the expulsion of menstrual fluid.

Prostaglandins are manufactured in all parts of the body, but the endometrium produces the greatest amounts in the female reproductive tract. Two types of prostaglandins known to have an effect on uterine contractility, PGE^2 and PGF^{2A}, have been found in great quantities in the endometrium during the luteal phase of the cycle and in menstrual blood. Researchers have discovered that, not only does the endometrium of women with dysmenorrhea produce greatly increased amounts of prostaglandins, but it produces them seven times faster than in women without dysmenorrhea.[13]

The uterus responds to the presence of these substances by increasing its muscular activity and contracting sharply, causing uterine arteries to constrict and choke the blood flow. It is this increased muscular activity and constriction that are believed responsible for the pain of dysmenorrhea. (In contrast, some believe that prostaglandins dilate these blood vessels, increasing menstrual flow and thereby causing pain.) In addition, prostaglandins may increase the sensitivity of the nerves in the uterus and cervix, further exacerbating menstrual pain.

According to studies by Dr. M. Yusoff Dawood and colleagues, "Most of the production and release of prostaglandins during menstruation occur during the first 48 hours of menstrual flow, thus explaining the occurrence of intense pain during the first or second day of menstruation in primary dysmenorrhea. There is also good correlation between the amount of prostaglandins released in the menstrual fluid per hour and the clinical symptoms of the dysmenorrhea during the first 48 hours of menstruation."[14]

Further support linking menstrual cramps to excess production of prostaglandins comes from observations that intravenous infusions of PGF^{2A} during menstruation result in increased uterine contractions and menstrual pain. High doses also brought about diarrhea, nausea, and irritability.[15] In addition, the fact that medical inhibition of the synthesis of prostaglandins eliminates or significantly relieves menstrual pain supports this theory.

The potential for this medical inhibition was discovered serendipitously. During the 1950s potent drugs used to reduce the inflammation and thus ease the pain of severe arthritis were found to have an interesting side effect: they reduced or eliminated menstrual cramps. It was later discovered that these drugs had prostaglandin-inhibiting qualities. Unfortunately, they had other less welcome side effects as well. Since that time, a number of safer anti-prostaglandin drugs have been developed and are used for the treatment of primary dysmenorrhea. Some of these drugs are available over the counter, so many women have access to relief from primary dysmenorrhea. But, for those suffering from secondary dysmenorrhea, which is often caused by factors other than, or in addition to, prostaglandins, these medications are inconsistently effective.

When anti-prostaglandin drugs fail to bring relief, physicians may suspect secondary, rather than primary, dysmenorrhea—or secondary in addition to primary dysmenorrhea. To further treat primary dysmenorrhea, or to help distinguish it from secondary dysmenorrhea, the physician may, following treatment with prostaglandin inhibitors, attempt to suppress ovulation through the use of low-dose, combined estrogen and progesterone oral contraceptives administered cyclically, three weeks on, one week off. The rationale for this treatment is the observation made earlier that dysmenorrhea accompanies only ovulatory cycles. Birth control pills eliminate ovulation and thus are often effective in relieving menstrual pain.

When this treatment causes symptoms to become worse before they become better, or when it proves ineffective, it increases the suspicion of secondary dysmenorrhea, particularly that caused by endometriosis.

Surrounded by myths and taboos, women's reproductive health has been jeopardized by two seemingly incompatible responses to disorders associated with the menstrual cycle: resignation and denial. Women too readily accept pain as normal, life disruptions caused by "female complaints" as a woman's lot, and emotional or physical distress as a manifestation of psychological deficits. Pain, discomfort, and disequilibrium—from menarche through menopause—are not normal merely because they are commonplace. Cancer is commonplace, yet no one would suggest that it should be endured as a fact of life.

Rather than seek help for painful menstruation, premenstrual symptoms, or menopausal discomfort, women tend to be embarrassed by such conditions, and hide or deny them. Women fear that "female troubles" will be perceived as an Achilles' heel, supporting notions of gender frailty and inferiority. Confronting and debunking the taboos, myths, and misinformation will increase recognition of the problems, stimulate research, and, eventually, help find solutions to very real and debilitating disorders, including endometriosis.

2
What
Is
Endometriosis?

Endometriosis is the presence of endometrial tissue outside its normal location lining the uterus. This ectopic (misplaced) tissue takes the form of lesions, implants, nodules, and cysts. (The word *endometrioma*, usually refers to cysts large enough to be considered tumors.) Individual areas of ectopic endometrium may range in size from microscopic to 10 cm.

Endometriosis typically affects the organs and structures of the pelvis—the ovaries, the surface of the uterus, the uterine ligaments, the cul-de-sac (a deep pouch between the uterus and rectum), the fallopian tubes, the pelvic peritoneum (the lining of the pelvic cavity) and, less typically, the gastrointestinal system. Although cases are rare, the urinary tract, the lower genital tract, and extra-pelvic locations such as the lungs or the limbs can be affected. In isolated cases, it has been found in virtually every organ of the body.

THE CHARACTERISTICS OF ENDOMETRIOSIS

Because endometriosis appears between menarche and menopause, it is believed to depend upon stimulation by ovarian hormones. Like the endometrium itself, ectopic implants respond each month to the cyclic hormonal fluctuations by swelling, bleeding, and breaking apart. Unlike normal endometrium, however, ectopic endometrium and its bloody debris have no means of escape from the body. They remain to inflame surrounding tissue, which leads to the formation of scar tissue and adhesions—bands of filmy or dense fibrous tissue that can spin webs among the pelvic organs, matting them together in unnatural formations that may interfere with normal functioning. When the pelvic cavity is filled with endometriosis and adhesions and the organs are fused and immobilized, the pelvis is said to be "frozen."

Endometriosis ranges from minimal to severe. There may be only a few small lesions on the peritoneum or the ovary, along with some filmy adhesions. Severe cases may involve

21

multiple lesions on the peritoneum, or invasive lesions or cysts as well as dense adhesions that affect the ovaries, fallopian tubes, cul-de-sac, gastrointestinal system, or urinary tract. The majority of cases, however, are mild or moderate.[1]

Regardless of the extent or severity of the disease, a woman afflicted may have no symptoms whatsoever, or she may experience any number of complaints ranging from mild to incapacitating: menstrual pain, generalized pelvic pain, backache, and pain upon intercourse, urination, or defecation. A symptom or cluster of symptoms may accompany the menstrual period itself or persist throughout most or all of the menstrual cycle.

CONSEQUENCES AND COMPLICATIONS OF ENDOMETRIOSIS

Pain and infertility are the major consequences of endometriosis. Pain affects about half of all patients; infertility, approximately 30 to 40 percent. It is presumed, but unproven, that the likelihood of infertility increases with time in patients with endometriosis, compounding the natural decline of fertility in all women with advancing age.

Fatal complications are very rare. When they occur, they may be due to a ruptured endometrioma, an ectopic pregnancy (resulting from endometriosis in the fallopian tubes), or kidney failure (caused by obstruction in the ureter). Bowel obstruction is more common but is generally discovered and surgically corrected before it causes extensive damage. (The complications of endometriosis, along with its common sites and symptoms, are discussed more fully in Chapter 3.)

Endometriosis has been described as a benign cancer. The processes by which it develops share certain characteristics of cancer: it has the capacity to proliferate, to metastasize (spread to distant sites), and to invade and penetrate organs. However, endometriosis, unlike cancer, does not digest or consume the organs and structures it affects; it merely compresses them, pushes them aside, or surrounds them. Malignant transformation of endometriosis is exceptionally rare;[2] cancer has been found in less than 1 percent of women with endometriosis,[3] and in few of those cases has the malignant transformation of endometriosis been demonstrated.[4] In those highly unusual circumstances in which cancer does arise, it is always a low-grade variety known as *adenoacanthoma*, which generally does not spread and is seldom fatal.[5]

WHO GETS ENDOMETRIOSIS?

Endometriosis is generally accepted as one of the most prevalent gynecological diseases experienced by women in their reproductive years. Although it can develop at any age, it has been estimated that 15 to 20 percent of all women between the ages of twenty and thirty-five have the disease.[6] It leads to more surgical procedures in premenopausal women than does any other gynecological disorder except fibroid tumors, and it is responsible for about one-quarter of all abdominal surgeries performed by gynecologists. Endometriosis is also implicated in as many as half of all cases of menstrual cramps. It is the leading cause of infertility in women older than twenty-five. In 1980 it accounted for 570,000 office visits to gynecologists, not including visits to physicians at hospitals, health groups, clinics, or teaching or research facilities.[7]

The actual number of women afflicted with endometriosis is unknown. Because the disease is frequently asymptomatic (without symptoms), and because it can only be diagnosed by laparoscopy (see Appendix A), the only way to determine its true prevalence in the general population would be to laparoscope all women. As a result, estimates by specialists—extrapolations based on the frequency with which endometriosis is observed in specific study populations—range dramatically from 1 to 32 percent of women of childbearing age,[8] with the weight of opinion suggesting 10 to 15 percent—approximately 6 to 9 million.[9]

For decades medical doctrine dictated that endometriosis occurred predominantly in white, childless women in their thirties and forties who belong to the middle and upper strata of society. The "typical patient profile" describes a bright, highly aggressive, ambitious, meticulous, and somewhat obsessive woman who leads a stressful lifestyle and who has deliberately deferred childbearing to pursue education or a career. Endometriosis has been labeled the "rich woman's disease," the "private patient's disease," and most recently the "career woman's disease." Such descriptions are derived largely from presumptions, impressions, clinical correlations, and dogma rather than fact. In reality, not one of these labels has been scientifically validated, and bit by bit research and experience chip away at these stereotypes. As a result of improved diagnostic techniques (see Chapter 4), endometriosis is now found in the entire spectrum of women: adults, teenagers, black, white, rich, poor, mothers, childless women, homemakers, executives. Nevertheless, some of the old stereotypes persist in even the most current medical textbooks and the scientific and lay press.

The only common denominator among women with the disease is that they menstruate. And, while there is clearly no typical endometriosis patient, a recent study indicates that women with menstrual cycles of less than twenty-seven days and menstrual flow of one week or longer are more than twice as likely to develop endometriosis as those with longer cycles and shorter periods of menstrual flow.[10]

HOW DOES ENDOMETRIOSIS DEVELOP?

Apparently no one factor is responsible for all cases of endometriosis. Rather, the disease may develop as a result of several factors. While the true cause or causes of endometriosis remain unknown, there are a number of theories to explain why it develops in susceptible women.

Transplantation: Retrograde Menstruation

The oldest, and still the most widely accepted, explanation for the appearance of endometrium in ectopic locations is Dr. John Sampson's theory of retrograde menstruation, which he formulated in 1921. Dr. Sampson contended that during menstruation a certain amount of menstrual fluid is regurgitated, or forced backward, from the uterus through the fallopian tubes and showered upon the pelvic organs and pelvic lining.

He postulated that in the particles of endometrium contained in the menstrual fluid are cells capable not only of implanting and multiplying on the tissues on which they land, but also of retaining the same functions and response capabilities of the endometrium from which they originate. Thus, as the endometrium thickens each month and discharges its bloody debris cued by hormonal stimulation, so these lesions swell and bleed in response to the same stimulation.

Since 1921, there has been evidence to support Dr. Sampson's theory. Studies in humans and animals have shown that refluxed menstrual fluid can indeed flourish in ectopic sites. The fact that endometriosis most typically strikes the ovaries, which are directly in the path of refluxed menstruation, also tends to support Dr. Sampson's theory. Findings of more recent studies demonstrating an association between particular sites of endometriosis and the position of the uterus are also consistent with this hypothesis. The position of the uterus would determine where refluxed menstrual fluid would collect in the pelvis. Researchers have demonstrated that patients with an anteverted (tipped forward) uterus have a greater incidence of disease in the anterior of the pelvis.[11]

Possibly giving further weight to Dr. Sampson's theory is the purported increase of endometriosis in patients with anatomical anomalies, such as cervical stenosis (narrowing), which prevent or obstruct the free exit of menstrual fluid, coupled with the clinical observation that the disease appears particularly early in women with such structural anomalies. It is not clear, however, that women with endometriosis are more likely to have these abnormalities, or that those with such conditions are actually more prone to develop endometriosis. The following are some anatomical abnormalities and conditions that may contribute to retrograde menstruation:

- *Bicornuate uterus*: a uterus with two horn-shaped branches at the fundus
- *Cervical atresia*: congenital absence of the cervix
- *Cervical stenosis*: a narrowing of the cervix
- *Hematocolpos*: an accumulation of blood in the vagina
- *Hematometra*: an accumulation of blood in the uterus
- *Hematosalpinx*: an accumulation of blood in the fallopian tubes
- *Imperforate hymen*: a condition in which the hymen, a thin membrane that normally only partially closes the vaginal orifice, totally obstructs it
- *Transverse vaginal septum*: a vagina divided lengthwise into two canals by a membranous barrier

The theory of retrograde menstruation still leaves several questions unanswered. For example, it explains the mechanism through which endometrial tissue can be disseminated to ectopic locations, but it does not indicate what causes those tissues to implant and give rise to symptoms in some women and not in others. Virtually all women reflux menstrual fluid through the fallopian tubes, yet only some of them develop endometriosis.[12]

Dr. Sampson believed that inflammation caused by the refluxed menstrual debris "produces a site more amenable" to the implantation of menstrual debris, but did not explain why this irritated tissue proves hospitable for only a fraction of women.

His theory also fails to account for the development of endometriosis in such sites remote from the uterus as the lungs, the lymph nodes, the limbs, and the breasts.

Other Transplantation Theories

Blood and lymph transplantation.   Endometrial tissues metastasize, according to another theory, from the pelvic cavity through the lymphatic and circulatory systems. Viable endometrial cells have been found in the lymphatic system and in the blood vessels. This method of dissemination can explain endometriosis in most sites.

Iatrogenic transplantation.   One explanation for the development of the disease, about which there is no controversy, is iatrogenic (doctor-caused) transplantation—the accidental transference of tissue from the uterus to another site (usually a surgical scar) during pelvic surgery or manipulative procedures of the genital tract: laparotomy, laparoscopy, curettage, episiotomy, cervical cauterization, conization, and amniocentesis (see the Glossary and Appendix A). As a result of improved surgical techniques, it is uncommon today.

Transformation: Coelomic Metaplasia.

A requisite for transplantation of endometrium to ectopic sites is the occurrence of menstruation, for without the endometrium, there is nothing to be transplanted. Yet endometriosis occasionally occurs in the absence of menstruation. At least two case reports describe the existence of the disease in women who have never menstruated. Moreover, although extremely uncommon (only four cases known to date), endometriosis has been observed in the bladders of men who, having undergone removal of the prostate, received long-term treatment with estrogen. While these cases are exceptions, they clearly demonstrate that the disease may occur when there is no endometrium to be refluxed or metastasized. None of the transplantation theories, including retrograde menstruation, can explain these unusual manifestations of the disease.

A possible explanation for these rare occurrences, as well as for most instances of extrapelvic disease, is the theory of coelomic metaplasia, put forth independently by Dr. Ivanoff and Dr. Meyer around the turn of the century. This theory derives from the fact that certain cells, when stimulated, can transform themselves into different kinds of cells. The cells that make up the peritoneum, for example, derive from coelomic epithelium—the cells that line the body cavity of the embryo. Coelomic epithelium is *totipotential*, meaning it has the ability to differentiate into any type of cell. When stimulated, it is capable of transforming itself into endometrial cells. This abnormal cell differentiation is called *metaplasia*.

Dr. Ivanoff and Dr. Meyer suggested that repeated irritation of the coelomic epithelium, perhaps in response to the presence of refluxed menstrual blood, can lead these immature cells to undergo metaplastic changes. This suggestion weds the process of coelomic metaplasia to retrograde menstruation. It was later suggested that hormonal stimulation might trigger the transformation, allowing for the possibility of coelomic transformation in the absence of retrograde menstruation. Although less well defined and supported than transplantation theories, this transformation theory explains most sites of endometriosis.

WHY ARE SOME WOMEN MORE SUSCEPTIBLE THAN OTHERS?

All of the theories above merely suggest mechanisms for the development of the disease in susceptible women. But they all leave unanswered one question: What triggers these responses and why does the ectopic tissue implant, become active, and give rise to symptoms of the disease? One theory is that endometriosis may be a congenital birth defect. Endometrial tissue may already be located outside the uterus at birth, becoming active only after puberty.[13] Two other theories concern heredity and immunology.

Heredity

The possibility of a genetic predisposition to endometriosis was suggested as early as 1943, and more recent studies support this speculation. Research indicates that first-degree relatives of women with endometriosis are more likely to develop the disease, are more severely afflicted, and tend to manifest symptoms earlier than women without affected relatives. Whether this tendency is genetic or the result of certain environmental characteristics shared by family members is a matter of debate. It may be a combination of the two.

Some researchers suggest that family members, particularly siblings, are likely to share socioeconomic factors, similar patterns of delayed childbearing, and professional drive—all factors *presumed* by many to affect a woman's likelihood of developing endometriosis.

Another possibility is that family members share a genetic predisposition toward retrograde menstruation, anatomical abnormalities that may contribute to refluxed menstruation, or hypersensitivity of the coelomic epithelium to irritating substances or hormonal stimulation. But the question remains, What is responsible for this increased sensitivity or for the tendency of refluxed endometrial tissue to implant? Research linking endometriosis to immunologic factors transmitted genetically may provide some convincing answers.

Immunology

According to Dr. W. Paul Dmowski, professor of obstetrics and gynecology and director of reproductive endocrinology and infertility at Rush Medical College of Rush University in Chicago, studies indicate that disorders of two different arms of the immune system may be involved in the development of endometriosis: cell-mediated immunity, in which specific immune cells fight disease; and humoral immunity, in which antibodies are formed to attack antigens.

As mentioned earlier, retrograde menstruation occurs regularly in most women, yet endometriosis develops in only a fraction of them. Studies by Dr. Dmowski and others indicate that migrating endometrial tissues implant only in women with deficient cell-mediated immunity. In women who do not have this deficiency, the transplanted cells are destroyed and prevented from implanting.

The precise nature of the deficiency has yet to be explained, but researchers suggest it may be related to the severity of the disease: "A severe defect, transmitted genetically, ought to be associated with more extensive endometriosis and with onset at an earlier age, while mild immune deficiency would be more likely to cause mild disease later in life."[14] This may explain the presence of extensive disease seen in some teenagers as well as mild disease in women around the time of the menopause, both of which are not readily explained by retrograde menstruation.[15]

Humoral immunity with regard to endometriosis—the development of antibodies against endometrial tissue perceived as antigen—may be a secondary phenomenon, says Dr. Dmowski. This has been suggested by studies in which he and his colleagues revealed that rhesus monkeys with endometriosis respond differently to endometrial antigens than do monkeys without endometriosis.

In addition, prostaglandins—known to affect the contractility of uterine smooth muscle and to result in dysmenorrhea—are produced in reaction to an immune response; it has been speculated that individuals genetically predisposed to endometriosis may also be genetically predisposed to an increased production of prostaglandins.[16]

"If the immune system is involved," says Dr. Dmowski, "the lesions that we see in the pelvis may be just the very surface symptoms of the disease, not the entire picture of the changes that are associated with endometriosis."

Research into the immunological factors that appear to be related to the development of endometriosis have important and promising implications for future treatment of the disease. "Just as one would not treat typhoid fever, for example, by applying medication to the skin lesions, maybe in the future we are not going to treat endometriosis by removing small endometriotic implants, but by treating it systematically," explains Dr. Dmowski.

CAN ENDOMETRIOSIS GET WORSE?

According to the leading theories concerning its development, endometriosis is a progressively spreading disease, increasing in extent with a woman's age. Each month menstruation offers new opportunity for the "seeding" of the pelvic cavity with refluxed endometrium and provides the hormonal stimulus believed to trigger its proliferation. In addition, the debris from ectopic endometrium may spill onto previously unaffected areas and implant there.

A woman with endometriosis is painted a frightening picture of untreated disease running rampant in her pelvis, tying her organs into knots of adhesions and endometriotic lesions. The media feeds this image with dire warnings about the consequences of untreated disease. A recent book warned teenagers that "untreated endometriosis progresses slowly, but it does progress and is one of the leading causes of infertility today."[17] According to a *Time* magazine report, "If anything about endometriosis is clear, it is that once the disease has begun, it will probably get worse."[18]

However, there is little evidence to support such seemingly authoritative conclusions. This is not to say that endometriosis does not progress, but simply that, in the absence of longitudinal studies documenting the natural history of the disease, its progression over time remains unknown. Until such studies shed more light on this area, the notion of the disease as "progressive" remains presumptive, and medical thought will be divided.

"Most of us believe that endometriosis does slowly progress," says Dr. John Rock, associate professor of obstetrics and gynecology and director of reproductive endocrinology at The Johns Hopkins University School of Medicine in Baltimore. "The rate at which it progresses varies from individual to individual, such that some women may have rapid progression of the disease, and in other women it may be a very slow process that really creates no problem over many years."

"I feel that this is a disease that has a chronic, progressive character," agrees Dr. Dmowski. "Some of the lesions may heal, but new ones appear." Certain women, however, he says, might be more prone to developing extensive disease as opposed to mild disease and there may be women in whom very mild disease may remain unchanged for a prolonged period of time.

According to Dr. Burt Littman, assistant professor of obstetrics and gynecology at George Washington University Medical Center's division of reproductive endocrinology and fertility in Washington, D.C., progression does not always occur. "I see women who have severe disease to start with, and despite various treatments, it keeps coming back. On the other hand, I see women who have a couple of spots and they are never bothered by it. I don't know how long they've had it, but I have to assume it is not running rampant. It appears that mild disease may remain mild disease forever."

"When I look at my patient population, those women with the worst disease are the youngest patients," explains Dr. Richard Falk, chief of reproductive endocrinology and fertility at Georgetown University Medical School and Columbia Hospital for Women in Washington, D.C. "The women with big ovarian cysts and a lot of pain and discomfort are not thirty-seven or thirty-eight-year-olds; they're more likely to be twenty-two." He adds, "the thirty-year-old patient who upon laparoscopy is found to have a couple of spots of endometriosis will never end up with severe disease."

Dr. David Redwine, a gynecologist practicing at the Mountain View Women's Clinic in Bend, Oregon, has researched the extent of disease in different age groups from sixteen to fifty-two. His findings duplicate Dr. Falk's experience and indicate that older and younger patients have roughly the same distribution of disease, but the extent of the disease declines with age.[19]

CAN ENDOMETRIOSIS BE PREVENTED?

As an endometriosis patient, you may wonder what can be done to prevent your daughter from developing the disease. As with so many other issues concerning endometriosis, medical opinion is divided on prevention; suggested measures are based only on hunches.

Some physicians believe steps can be taken to discourage the development of endometriosis. Some feel that for susceptible women the disease is inevitable. Others claim it is impossible to prevent a disease if its cause is unknown.

Whether or not a physician believes in prevention is bound to be determined by the credibility he places in the various etiological theories. Those who maintain that genetic factors play a primary role probably will be less inclined to believe that the disease can be prevented to any significant degree. Others, particularly those who believe that endometriosis arises principally from repeated irritation of pelvic tissues by refluxed menstrual debris, suggest that endometriosis is more likely to develop following prolonged periods of uninterrupted ovulation and menstruation. They suggest that any effort to reduce the frequency or amount of retrograde menstruation will lessen a woman's chances of developing endometriosis.

Theories of Prevention

Preventive methods that have been recommended include correction of anatomical abnormalities that may obstruct the menstrual flow; use of cyclic oral contraceptives to lessen the duration and quantity of the menstrual flow; regular exercise programs begun early in life; early and frequent pregnancies to provide prolonged rest from menstruation; avoidance of therapeutic gynecological procedures during menstruation; and avoidance of devices or practices that *may* encourage reflux menstruation, such as tampons or intercourse during menstruation. Until research sheds more light on the nature of the disease, it remains to be seen whether or not these recommendations will contribute to its decline.

Anatomic corrections. Many proponents of Dr. Sampson's theory argue that it is logical to correct any anatomical abnormalities (listed earlier in the chapter) that may obstruct the exit of menstrual fluid from the body and encourage reflux. They recommend that such structural malformations be corrected early in a young woman's life, before she begins to ovulate, even though few women with these conditions will develop endometriosis.[20]

Oral contraceptives. Many physicians recommend that young women use low-dose oral contraceptives on a cyclical basis, beginning shortly after they start to ovulate and continuing until they are ready to conceive. Birth control pills reduce the duration and quantity of the menstrual flow by limiting the growth of the endometrium. Therefore, their use may lessen the likelihood that endometriosis will develop. Oral contraceptives are particularly likely to be recommended for young women with a family history of endometriosis and those with a severely retroverted (tipped backward) or anteverted uterus. Although one study suggests that women who used oral contraceptives for long periods are less likely than others to develop severe disease,[21] another study revealed no protective effect. Moreover, the latter study found an increased risk among women with moderate or severe disease who had used high-dose oral contraceptives (greater than 50 mg).[22] In Chapter 6 the use of contraceptives as treatment for endometriosis is discussed.

Avoidance of procedures.   To avoid encouraging retrograde menstruation, some physicians advocate a cautious attitude toward procedures involving manipulation of the genital tract during or around the time of the menstrual period or shortly following cervical dilation or curettage, particularly procedures that could force menstrual fluid in a retrograde manner. These include:

- tubal insufflation, hysterosalpingography (to determine if the fallopian tubes are open), or any other gynecological procedure that involves the endometrium
- vigorous pelvic examinations
- cryotherapy, cautery, or conization of the cervix
- procedures that abrade or puncture the vagina or vulvar lining
- gynecologic operations in which the uterus is penetrated, such as myomectomies (removal of fibroid tumors)
- plastic surgery

Avoidance of practices and devices.   Many physicians believe that tampons, cervical caps, menstrual sponges, and diaphragms do not contribute to retrograde menstruation. (It's even been suggested that tampons may actually discourage reflux by drawing blood away from the uterus.) Others suggest that women, particularly those with a narrow cervical opening, a tipped uterus, or a family history of endometriosis, avoid their use, at least during the heaviest days of menstrual flow. Although there is no evidence that intercourse or douching during menstruation promotes reflux, some caution against these practices.

Exercise.   Regular strenuous exercise, which reduces estrogen levels and often leads to lighter and less painful periods, appears to offer women protection against endometriosis. According to the findings of a recent study published in the *Journal of the American Medical Association*, women who begin engaging in regular exercise (at least two hours weekly) at an early age (younger than twenty-six) are considerably less likely than others to develop endometriosis. Those activities most likely to exert a protective influence, say the researchers, are conditioning exercises such as jogging or calisthenics.[23] In addition, Dr. Robert Kistner suggests that exercise-induced amenorrhea may prove to inhibit the development of the disease.[24] Check with your physician first, however, before beginning any strenuous exercise regimen.

Pregnancy and childbirth.   Although endometriosis is frequently labeled by doctors as a disease of modern civilization and is *attributed* to delayed childbearing, experts are at odds concerning any preventive effect of early childbearing. On one side are physicians who suggest that endometriosis is seen most often in older infertile women and is therefore associated with delayed childbearing; on the other side are those who claim the disease is seen as frequently in fertile women as well as in increasing numbers of teenagers and that childbearing status is therefore irrelevant. In addition to controversy concerning pregnancy as a preventive measure is debate about pregnancy as a therapeutic measure (see Chapter 7).

Those who blame the later age at which modern women begin their families suggest that long, uninterrupted periods of hormonal cycling and menstruation provide increased opportunity for the seeding of the pelvic cavity with particles of endometrium through retrograde menstruation.

"The more menstrual periods a woman has before she starts trying to have children, the greater the likelihood that she will develop endometriosis," says Dr. Veasy Buttram, Jr., director of the division of reproductive endocrinology and fertility at Houston's Baylor College of Medicine, and president of the American Fertility Society. "Most women in whom we find endometriosis are women who have infertility problems and who have delayed childbearing until their late twenties and early thirties. So you put two and two together and come up with the thought that endometriosis is related to delayed childbearing."

"In the years when women were not delaying childbirth—when they were conceiving at the age of fifteen and sixteen—endometriosis was not a common cause for infertility," explains Dr. Rock. "Now that women are delaying childbearing because of their education and perhaps in some cases their professional careers, endometriosis seems to be more prevalent."

Some suggest that the dilation of the cervix that occurs during childbirth also helps to reduce retrograde menstruation and thereby lessen a woman's chances of developing endometriosis. "The longer women continue to menstruate with a cervix that has never been stretched by a pregnancy, the more likely they are to have some retrograde menstruation and the set-up, at least, for developing endometriosis," says Dr. Charles Debrovner, a gynecologist in private practice in New York. "I do think that women who have had pregnancies early are certainly less likely to get endometriosis later."

According to Dr. Dmowski, however, delayed childbearing has no bearing on whether or not a woman will develop endometriosis. "We have patients who have completed their families, patients who had two or three children and are either using some form of oral contraceptive or who were sterilized and who have endometriosis." During the time the patient has children the appearance of endometriosis may be delayed, he adds, "But once that time period stops, endometriosis develops."

Chicago gynecologist Dr. Anne Ward's experience has led to a similar conclusion: "I have patients who have had three or four children and develop endometriosis. I have people who had babies when they were young and get endometriosis in their thirties." Childbearing status, she says, "doesn't mean anything."

"Most of my patients who are diagnosed with endometriosis have already been pregnant and delivered babies," says Dr. Redwine. "So it is basically a disease of fertile women, not infertile women. It doesn't matter whether you have been pregnant zero times or three times. Pregnancy just doesn't provide any protection at all."

If prolonged periods of uninterrupted ovulation and menstruation do contribute to endometriosis, women could have children early in life and still be subject to prolonged periods of menstruation. According to the logic of the argument, only early and frequent pregnancies will prevent endometriosis—an observation made more than forty years ago by Dr. James Robert Goodall: "Let it be well understood that the development of endometriosis, like that of fibroids, is not restricted to the spinster, nor to the nulliparous [childless] married women, but is also the common affliction of women who have had one or more children followed by a long period of sterility, either physical or self-imposed."[25]

In 1952, Dr. Joe Meigs, who vehemently and moralistically argued in favor of pregnancy as a preventive measure, made a similar observation: "For women to have children and fulfill their reproductive role is physiologically normal; 12 to 14 years of menstrual life without interruption is not. In a woman who is leading a normal, married life, periods may be infrequent."[26]

Given the climate of the 1950s, such a statement is hardly surprising. Yet, in July 1985, in an article in *Surgical Rounds*, the same observation seems shockingly anachronistic: "Pregnancy tends to prevent the development of endometriosis. If a woman becomes pregnant when she is approximately twenty years of age and then has pregnancies at five year intervals up to age thirty- five, there is only a very slim chance that she will ever develop endometriosis."[27]

Currently, there is no hard evidence to support an association between delayed or infrequent childbearing and endometriosis and its related infertility; only time and research will determine the role of childbearing in the prevention of the disease. Nevertheless, many women have come to believe that endometriosis and infertility are the penalties they pay for choosing to delay or preclude childbearing. Women with endometriosis are particularly disturbed and frustrated when pregnancy is encouraged by their doctors even though childbearing is not an option. Some women are too young to take on the responsibilities of parenthood, or are financially unprepared, without partners, or gay.

Until conclusive evidence exists to indicate that childbearing will prevent endometriosis it seems unlikely that women will return to the childbearing patterns of a century ago in the hope that they might prevent the development of a disease that will strike perhaps one in five or one in ten.

3

Sites, Symptoms, and Complications

Symptomatology of endometriosis is consistent only in its inconsistency.[1]

Renee, a twenty-two-year-old law student, had endured severe menstrual cramps since thirteen, when she began to menstruate. On the advice of her gynecologist, she took Tylenol and spent the worst days of her period tethered to a heating pad. In college she became aware that her periods were getting longer and heavier. Sharp, stabbing pain sliced through her abdomen, radiating down her thighs. From several days before until several days after her period she suffered from nausea, diarrhea, backache, and dizziness. From the middle of her cycle until after her period had ended, intercourse caused her to recoil in severe pain. Afterward she bled and ached. In her first year at the university Renee began to miss classes at least three days a month, during which time she was confined to her bed. Weary of the pain and concerned that her schoolwork was deteriorating, Renee consulted another gynecologist, who prescribed a mild narcotic. This medication allowed her to attend class but made her drowsy and muddled her thought. No longer able to tolerate this monthly ordeal, she consulted a specialist at the university medical center who diagnosed endometriosis.

Mari, twenty-five, an active, athletic mother of two had never suffered menstrual discomfort. One evening, shopping with her husband, Mari doubled over and collapsed with sudden, wrenching abdominal pain. Rushed to a nearby emergency room, she was prepared for surgery to remove a suspected ruptured appendix. Awake in the recovery room, she learned that she had endometriosis. Her symptoms had been caused by the rupture of a large ovarian endometrioma.

Jeanne, unlike Renee and Mari, experienced no symptoms whatsoever. Thirty-two and by all accounts in excellent health, she became concerned when, after eighteen months, her attempts to conceive had proved unsuccessful. Jeanne and her husband, Matt, consulted an

33

infertility specialist. After examining Matt and ruling out a male factor, the specialist began a series of tests on Jeanne. Three months into the work-up, after initial tests had uncovered no abnormalities, the doctor performed a laparoscopy. Jeanne was astonished at the diagnosis: moderate endometriosis.

SYMPTOMS AND COMPLICATIONS

As many as one-third of all women with the disease may be asymptomatic; the rest will experience any number of complaints that may or may not be linked to the menstrual cycle.

When symptoms do occur, they are highly variable and inconsistent; a woman may have pain one month but not the next. Symptoms may be vague or specific, mild or acute, intermittent or continuous. They may appear like clockwork at specific times of the month, or they may come and go without warning. They may grow progressively worse or continue at a steady level for years.

Symptoms seldom offer clues as to the location or extent of the disease. A woman with a few tiny spots of endometriosis may suffer excruciating pain, while a woman with severe and extensive disease may be entirely pain-free.

Menstrual pain, pain with intercourse, and infertility occur with sufficient frequency to be labeled a triad of classic complaints. These, as well as several other general symptoms, may prevail to some extent regardless of the location of the disease. There are, however, some symptoms that are site-specific. The sites and symptoms are listed below and will be discussed fully in the remainder of this chapter.

- General symptoms and complications
    dysmenorrhea
    dyspareunia
    infertility
    pelvic pain
    backache
    menstrual disorders
    spontaneous abortion
- Reproductive sites: ovaries, cul-de-sac, ligaments, pelvic peritoneum, surface of the uterus, fallopian tubes
    Symptoms or complications:
    ruptured endometrioma (ovaries)
    ectopic pregnancy (fallopian tubes)
- Gastrointestinal sites: rectosigmoid colon, rectum, rectovaginal septum; small bowel, cecum, appendix, distal ileum
    Symptoms or complications:
    nausea
    vomiting
    abdominal cramping

rectal pain
urgency to defecate
diarrhea
constipation
straining with bowel movements
blood in the stool
low back pain
pain in the area of the umbilicus
sharp gas pains
abdominal bloating
rectal bleeding

- Urinary tract sites: bladder, ureter, kidney, urethra
  Symptoms or complications:
  pain or burning upon urination
  pus or blood in the urine
  urinary urgency, frequency, or retention
  flank pain, possibly radiating toward the groin
  fever
  hypertension
  headache
  tenderness around the kidneys
  excessive fatigue
- Lower genital sites: cervix, vagina, vulva, perineum
- Pulmonary sites: lungs, pleura, diaphragm
  Symptoms or complications:
  coughing of blood or blood-stained sputum
  constricting chest pain
  shoulder pain
  shortness of breath
- Miscellaneous sites: abdomen, umbilicus, sciatic nerve, groin, lymph nodes, spleen, gallbladder, breast, brain, bone, heart
  Symptoms or complications:
  pain in leg, hip, or thigh (sciatic nerve)
  blue bulges in skin, tender to the touch (umbilicus)

Dysmenorrhea

"Sharp shooting pains make me double up."

"My lower abdomen feels like its filled with rocks."

"The terrible stabbing pain begins two weeks before my cycle starts."

"There is such pain and pressure in the vulva and vaginal lips that it feels as if they are going to be pushed right out of my body."

"It feels like your insides are dropping."

Chapter 1 looked at secondary dysmenorrhea as a menstrual disorder. More specifically, it is the most common symptom of endometriosis and affects more than half of all women with the disease. As the descriptions above suggest, it takes many forms. Dysmenorrhea usually refers to menstrual pain itself, but, as mentioned in Chapter 1, it also refers to a syndrome that includes nausea, vomiting, diarrhea, backaches, headaches, dizziness, and fainting. As many as one-third of women who seek help for severe menstrual pain are found to have endometriosis.[2]

The pain associated with endometriosis is seldom described as "cramps." Some of the adjectives that are used are: dull, persistent, deep, achy, burning, stinging, searing, stabbing, grinding, boring, or gnawing.

Pain may be localized or diffuse, in the center of the abdomen, or on one or both sides. In addition, it may radiate to the lower back, the thighs, and the rectum, and it may worsen during defecation or urination. Some women experience significant pain and pressure in the area of the vulva, the vaginal lips, and the pubic bone. The pain may be accompanied by nausea, intestinal cramping, vomiting, diarrhea, constipation, and dizziness.

The pain is likely to begin several days or more before the beginning of the flow, becoming gradually more severe, and possibly lasting throughout the menstrual period or longer. Episodes may increase in duration as the months go by, until finally the pain lasts through all but the days immediately following menstruation.

The mechanisms by which endometriosis causes dysmenorrhea are not thoroughly understood, but it is likely that there are a number of factors. Ectopic endometrium, like normal endometrium, produces prostaglandins, which may contribute to the intensity of uterine contractions and the degree of arterial constrictions which have been shown to affect pain levels. Since the pain of endometriosis is inconsistently responsive to anti-prostaglandin drugs, however, this does not explain all pain resulting from endometriosis. Moreover, pain produced by excess prostaglandin production originates in the uterus with the contraction of the myometrium, whereas endometriosis pain does not originate entirely in the uterus. Other possible explanations for pain are irritation caused by bleeding from the ectopic endometrium, the contortion of the normal pelvic anatomy caused by scar tissue and adhesions, and the pressure resulting from periodic swelling of endometriotic implants or cysts.

Dyspareunia

"I am now afraid to make love with my husband because the pain is often too severe to hide. I have hidden my tears, but after two years, it's more and more difficult."

"I would have painful intercourse for six months, and then none for three months, then pain again for four months. The pain was very inconsistent and very severe; it would radiate up to my shoulder blades."

Dyspareunia, which means pain or difficulty with intercourse, is a common symptom of endometriosis. Like dysmenorrhea, it is variable and unpredictable.

Dyspareunia is emotionally devastating as well as physically excruciating. The intrusion of pain into the sexual bond tears tragically at relationships. It erodes a woman's sexual self-esteem, inspiring in her feelings of inadequacy and insecurity, while at the same time placing a burden of guilt upon her partner, which can lead to impotence. Like infertility, dyspareunia is a shared problem, yet it is often difficult for many women to talk about, even with their partners. When a source of pleasure and an expression of intimacy and affection becomes an exercise in pain, communication can break down. Sometimes, the damage to the relationship is irreparable.

It's difficult, too, for some women to discuss sex with their physicians. This may account in part for the conflicting reports concerning the prevalence of dyspareunia as a symptom of endometriosis. Reports do suggest, however, that from 12 to 75 percent of patients experience pain upon intercourse.

Dyspareunia is often associated with disease of the cul-de-sac, the uterosacral ligaments, the rectovaginal septum, the ovaries, the vagina, and the cervix, although the degree of pain is not necessarily related to the severity of disease in these locations.

Painful intercourse may occur with deep-thrust penetration, during which the penis jars or stretches surfaces involved with endometriosis. In a woman with ovarian endometriomas, penetration may compress the cysts, particularly when they are matted to the broad ligament or adherent to lower recesses of the cul-de-sac.

In addition, trauma to endometriotic implants may lead to spot bleeding following penetration, and a woman may experience a deep aching for some time after intercourse.

Penetration may cause only mild, transient discomfort in some instances; in others it becomes an exercise in agony, so intercourse becomes impossible. Dyspareunia may interfere with or preclude sexual relations during menstruation only, during menstruation and ovulation, or from ovulation through menstruation.

For an unfortunate few, intercourse always brings pain, regardless of the time of the month. In those cases, especially when a woman's disease predates her first sexual experience, it's often difficult to imagine intercourse without pain. "I always had dyspareunia," says Lena, now thirty-one. "I thought it was normal." Rosa, twenty-nine, was diagnosed with endometriosis at seventeen. "I only recently realized that other women enjoy being penetrated. To me, it feels just like a knife."

Although generally associated with deep-thrust penetration, pain may also occur with orgasm. For Margaret, orgasm is accompanied by "squeezing, bearing-down, labor-like pains." Lauri, on the other hand, says, "Orgasm leaves me with a congested, bloated feeling that takes a long time to dissipate."

Infertility

Many women will not experience any symptoms of endometriosis other than an inability to conceive. In fact, approximately 30 to 40 percent of women with endometriosis are infertile, as opposed to 15 percent of the general population of women. Of all infertile women, more than one-third have endometriosis. (Infertility, its causes and treatments, is addressed in Chapter 10.)

Pelvic Pain and Backache

"Sometimes I can't sit, and other times I can't stand up straight."

"When I sit, I feel as if my insides are being pushed up."

"It's a constant pulling pain on my right ovary to the right side of my pelvic wall."

"The pain seemed to be in my tailbone. It was so severe I thought I'd broken it."

Another complaint associated with endometriosis is generalized pelvic pain not necessarily linked to the menstrual period. Women often feel pelvic discomfort when sitting in certain positions or when executing certain movements or sudden actions. This type of pain is often described as a tugging sensation—the feeling that the pelvic organs are being dragged, pulled, or sharply yanked. This pain may result from tension or traction on the pelvic organs as a result of adhesions or scar tissues stretching between them.

As much as 31 percent of women with endometriosis report sacral backache accompanying menstruation or ovulation. It may be mild, or severe enough to prevent normal activity.

Menstrual Irregularities

In Chapter 1 menstrual disorders were discussed. Premenstrual spotting, excessively heavy bleeding, and cycles and menstrual flow that are too short or too long (see list of disorders in Chapter 1) occur in about 35 percent of patients with endometriosis, but it is likely that not all of these irregularities are caused by the disease. These are also common symptoms of polyps or fibroids, which may coexist with endometriosis; when these conditions are taken into consideration, menstrual irregularities as a result of endometriosis may occur in about 18 percent of women with the disease.[3]

Spontaneous Abortion

An association between endometriosis and an increased incidence of spontaneous abortion (miscarriage) has been observed by some researchers. Studies reveal miscarriage rates of 10 to 52 percent in women who conceive prior to diagnosis or treatment of endometriosis.[4] Rates are higher for women with mild, as opposed to moderate or severe, endometriosis. Spontaneous abortions usually occur between one and three years prior to diagnosis. Following surgery, the rate falls to about 10 percent—not a significant difference when compared against the rate for women without endometriosis. In light of these statistics, many physicians look upon a history of spontaneous abortion as potentially symptomatic of endometriosis. Other studies, however, fail to demonstrate a clear association. They suggest that all women, with or without endometriosis, experience a similar rate of spontaneous abortion.

COMMON SITES

The Ovaries

The ovaries are the most common site of endometriosis, affected in approximately half the total number of patients. In response to refluxed menstruation (or some other as yet unknown stimuli), cystic tissue surrounds the ovary, forming an endometrioma. When the endometrioma is filled with dark, old blood it is called a "chocolate cyst." Although ovarian disease is very often without symptoms, reduced circulation to the ovary as a result of inflammation may lead to spot bleeding before or after the menstrual cycle.

Ruptured endometrioma.   Ovarian lesions and endometriomas are very often painless. They may swell unnoticed until they rupture, producing acute symptoms that demand immediate emergency surgery.

A rupture is most likely to occur around the time of menstruation, during pregnancy, or toward the end of hormonal therapy that simulates pregnancy, but it can take place at any time. The cyclic swelling of the endometrioma may cause it to burst and splash its irritating contents upon the peritoneum and pelvic organs, triggering an inflammatory response by which scar tissue forms over the remnants of the cyst, possibly binding the ovary to adjacent structures. Moreover, a rupture can lead to peritonitis—a potentially fatal, acute inflammation of the peritoneum characterized by intense abdominal pain, constipation or diarrhea, vomiting, and fever.

The symptoms of a ruptured endometrioma—sudden sharp abdominal pain, abdominal distention, collapse, and shock—are similar to those of appendicitis or ectopic pregnancy, so it's important to keep in mind the possibility of a ruptured endometrioma when these acute abdominal symptoms occur.

The Cul-de-Sac

The cul-de-sac (or Pouch of Douglas), a deep gulch between the uterus and the rectum, is the lowest point in the pelvic cavity (see Figure 3). As a reservoir for pelvic fluids it is a very common site of endometriosis. Menstrual debris refluxed through the tubes pools in the cul-de-sac. Disease of the cul-de-sac may produce generalized symptoms, lead to intestinal complaints, and, as noted earlier, contribute to dyspareunia.

The Uterine Ligaments

Eight uterine ligaments moor the uterus in place between the bladder and the rectum: two broad, two uterosacral, and two round ligaments, as well as a posterior and an anterior ligament. Of these, the broad and uterosacral ligaments are more commonly affected with endometriosis, the latter contributing to dyspareunia.

Figure 3   Common Sites of Endometriosis

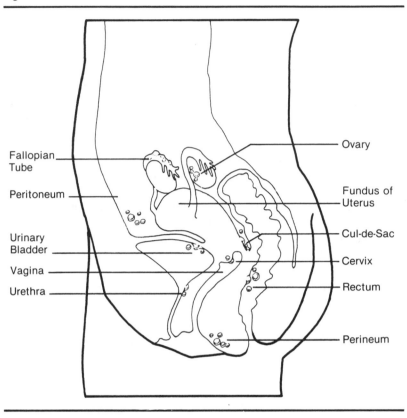

The Fallopian Tube — Ovary — Peritoneum — Fundus of Uterus — Urinary Bladder — Cul-de-Sac — Vagina — Cervix — Urethra — Rectum — Perineum

The Fallopian Tubes

Disease of the fallopian tubes is often painless. Lesions and adhesions generally occur on the outside of the tubes and are often superficial with no effect on tubal function. Less commonly, however, these implants and adhesions are significant enough to cause a kinking or an obstruction of the tubes.

Ectopic pregnancy.   A tubal ectopic pregnancy, a potential consequence of endometriosis affecting the fallopian tubes, is the implantation of a fertilized egg inside the wall of the tube. Tubal pregnancy always requires emergency surgery; if left untreated it is usually fatal.

The symptoms of an ectopic pregnancy include spot bleeding and cramping after a missed period, followed by increased bleeding and pain. The pain and pressure, due to the gradual growth of the egg and the resulting distention of the tube, may be great enough to signal a woman to consult a physician, but the tube may rupture suddenly as well, leading to hemorrhage, shock, and collapse. This is most likely to occur six to eight weeks into the pregnancy.

LESS COMMON SITES AND SYMPTOMS

Gastrointestinal Tract

Gastrointestinal endometriosis affects as much as 37 percent of women with endometriosis. It may lead to partial or complete blockage of the bowel—the most common severe complication of the disease.[5]

The most common site of gastrointestinal disease is the rectosigmoid colon (part of the large bowel), followed by the rectovaginal septum, the small bowel, the rectum, the cecum, the appendix, and the distal ileum. (See Figure 4.)

The bowel is composed of an outer layer called the *serosa*, a middle layer called the *muscularis*, and an inner layer called the *mucosa*. When endometriosis affects the bowel, it is generally confined to the outside layers, growing only from the outside in, and only rarely affecting the inner mucosa. Most of the damage arises from the inflammation and adhesions surrounding the lesions, rather than from the lesions themselves.

Partial obstruction in the large bowel occurs as a result of scar tissue and adhesions circling and constricting the bowel. It is less common for the large bowel to be completely obstructed. Complete obstruction is more likely to occur in the small bowel and is usually caused by the kinking of the bowel wall around lesions and adhesions.

Gastrointestinal lesions often produce complaints that are commonly mistaken for signs of a malignancy. This occasionally leads to unnecessary radical surgery. Therefore, be alert to the following symptoms occurring during menstruation only or throughout the cycle, worsening at menstruation: nausea, vomiting, lower abdominal cramping, rectal pain, diarrhea, constipation, urgency to evacuate bowel, tenesmus (straining with bowel movements), hematochezia (blood in the stool), pain in the lower back or tailbone, pain in the area of the umbilicus, sharp gas pains, and abdominal bloating. Although very uncommon, rectal bleeding may occur. If the appendix is involved, symptoms may mimic those of acute or chronic appendicitis with pain in the lower right abdomen.

Urinary Tract and Kidney

Although involvement of the urinary tract is rare, affecting only 1 percent of women with endometriosis,[6] it can lead to permanent kidney damage—the most serious complication of the disease. However, disease of the urinary tract most commonly strikes the bladder, followed by the ureter, the tissues in and around the kidneys, and the urethra (see Figure 5).[7]

Figure 4   Gastrointestinal Sites of Endometriosis

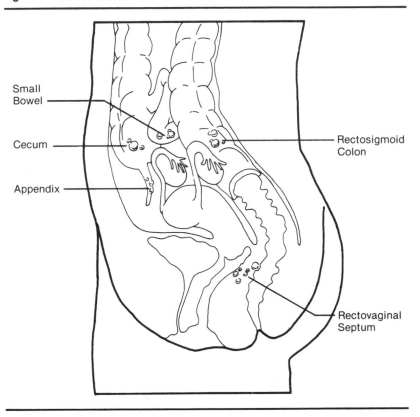

Small
Bowel

Cecum

Appendix

Rectosigmoid
Colon

Rectovaginal
Septum

Among the potential consequences of urinary tract endometriosis are blockage of the ureter, leading to hydronephrosis (the distention of the pelvis and kidney with urine) and loss of kidney function. With tragic results, extensive disease can obstruct the ureters and lead to irreversible kidney damage without a sign. As a result, diagnosis is frequently impossible until significant destruction has occurred, causing 30 percent of patients with ureteral disease to lose a kidney.[8]

When symptoms do occur, they are often mild and vague. The following symptoms can be caused by a number of other problems, but when they occur or worsen during menstruation they may indicate endometriosis of the urinary tract and should be investigated without delay: pyuria (pus in the urine), dysuria (pain or burning upon urination), flank pain possibly radiating toward the groin, hematuria (blood in the urine), fever, and urinary frequency, urgency, or retention. Hypertension, headache, tenderness around the kidneys, and excessive fatigue may be symptoms of advanced ureteral disease.

Figure 5   Urinary Tract Endometriosis

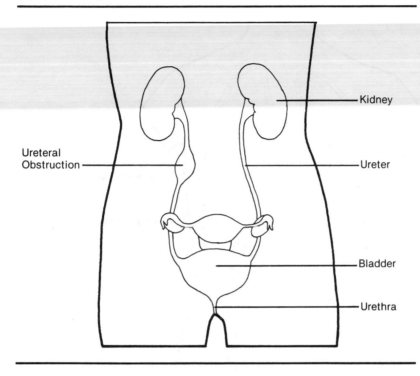

Lower Genital Tract

Endometriosis of the lower genital tract may result from the accidental transplantation of endometrial tissue during surgical or therapeutic procedures, or, it's been suggested, from the spread of lesions in the area of the cul-de-sac. Lesions in the lower genital tract, which may be visible during physical examination as red or blue raised lesions, can cause pain with intercourse and bleeding and swelling during menstruation.

Pulmonary

Pulmonary endometriosis is a rare manifestation of the disease (see Figure 6). It may involve the lungs, pleura (membrane lining the lungs and the chest cavity), or diaphragm (the muscle and membrane partition separating the abdominal cavity from the thoracic or chest cavity).

Symptoms of pulmonary endometriosis occurring typically at the time of menstruation include coughing up blood or blood-stained sputum, the accumulation of air or gas in the

Figure 6   Extrapelvie Sites of Endometriosis

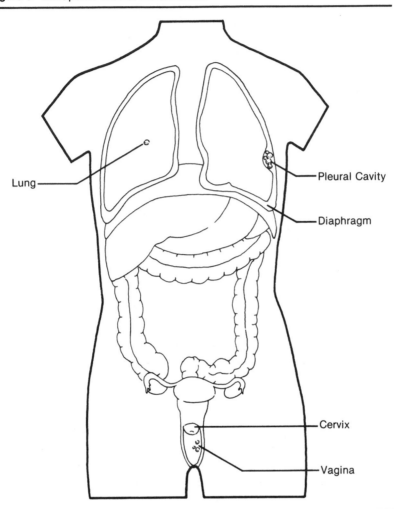

chest cavity, constricting chest pain, shoulder pain, and shortness of breath. In addition, testing may reveal a pulmonary nodule or a collection of blood in the chest cavity.

When gastrointestinal, urinary tract, or pulmonary endometriosis is suspected, your doctor may order special diagnostic tests to rule out the possibility of a malignancy, or to help locate and determine the extent of endometriotic involvement. These tests are described in Appendix A.

Abdomen, Leg, and Groin

Endometriosis resulting from surgical procedures in the abdomen also may appear about the time of menstruation as small blue bulges in the area of the umbilicus and in surgical scars. They may be tender to the touch and may produce bleeding if they swell and break through the surface of the skin.

Pain in the leg or the hip radiating down the leg may be indicative of endometriosis of the sciatic nerve and the area surrounding it, or may suggest endometriosis of the inguinal area (the groin).

CONDITIONS WITH SIMILAR SYMPTOMS

Endometriosis, because its symptoms can be inconsistent and nonspecific, easily masquerades as other diseases or disorders such as the following (see Glossary for definitions):

adenomyosis	gonorrhea
appendicitis	inflammatory bowel disease (IBD)
benign ovarian cysts	irritable bowel syndrome
bowel obstruction	ovarian cancer
colon cancer	pelvic inflammatory disease (PID)
diverticulitis	primary dysmenorrhea
ectopic pregnancy	salpingitis isthmica nodosa
fibroid tumors	

4

Diagnosis, Description, and Classification

We see only what we look for; we look for only what we know.[1]

Patients are accustomed to rapid diagnoses. A quick blood test, a physical exam, an x-ray are often all that is needed to confirm a disease. But the road to a diagnosis of endometriosis is fraught with obstacles, and it is not uncommon for a woman to see a number of doctors over a period of months or even years before being diagnosed.

You may turn first to your family doctor for help. Unfortunately, it is likely that he is less familiar with the symptoms of endometriosis and less able to interpret findings than a gynecologist or reproductive endocrinologist. If he fails to diagnose you, you may become disenchanted. You may consult another general practitioner, and another, before making an appointment with a specialist. Your choice of doctor, therefore, will influence the speed and accuracy with which you are diagnosed (see Chapter 16 for information on evaluating and choosing a doctor).

Even gynecologists may not rapidly diagnose the disease. They are not uniformly trained to detect endometriosis, and some are not as informed as others on research and development in the field. Even the best-trained, most vigilant gynecologist finds diagnosis difficult when symptoms are vague.

The number one problem is that there is no simple, accurate, noninvasive technique for diagnosing endometriosis. Symptoms may suggest a diagnosis, and examination may heighten the suspicion, but a definitive diagnosis requires direct visualization through laparoscopy and confirmation by biopsy of excised endometriotic tissue.

The methods and procedures for selecting patients for laparoscopy involve a certain amount of guesswork and intuition. Many women experience symptoms that can be caused by endometriosis yet do not have the disease. Based on clinical evidence alone, it's often difficult to decide who needs further investigation. "Everybody has a different tolerance for pain, and what incapacitates one woman, another woman might not give any thought to," explains Dr. Littman. But physicians are as reluctant to perform surgery when it may not be absolutely necessary as patients are to undergo the procedure. "I would have to err on the side of assuming that if the woman is incapacitated, she needs to be investigated." There's an old proverb in medicine, says Dr. Littman: if you don't take out enough normal appendixes, you're not doing enough appendectomies. "It is probably the same case with endometriosis: some normal women are probably going to have to be laparoscoped to find everybody that's got the disease." But the aggressiveness with which dysmenorrhea or dyspareunia is investigated varies among doctors.

If your symptoms are vague, and if the physical examination uncovers nothing out of the ordinary, your physician may want to keep an eye on you for a period of time and perhaps treat your symptoms (Chapters 5 and 6) before scheduling a surgical diagnostic procedure (Chapter 8). The initial consultation and physical examination, therefore, is a yardstick by which your doctor can determine whether or not further investigation is warranted.

MEDICAL HISTORY AND CONSULTATION

Your physician will investigate your medical history as well as your current symptoms. To minimize your chances of undergoing possibly unnecessary diagnostic surgery yet maximize your chances of being completely evaluated, it is vital that you be as thorough as possible in detailing your symptoms.

Your physician will want to distinguish between primary and secondary dysmenorrhea, for example (see Chapters 1 and 3). If menstrual pain is one of your complaints, be prepared to answer the following questions:

- At what age did you begin to menstruate?
- Are your periods regular? How long do they last?
- How heavy is the flow? How many pads or tampons does it require?
- Do you bleed between periods?
- When did your pain begin?
- Has it gotten worse?
- Do you experience any pain between periods?
- Where is the pain?
- At what point in the menstrual cycle does the pain begin? How long does it last?
- What kind of pain is it? (dull, aching, cramping, stabbing, grinding, etc.)
- Is the pain in one spot or is it diffuse?
- Is the pain accompanied by any other symptoms such as nausea, diarrhea, vomiting, dizziness, or pain on urination or defecation? Do they occur only during menstruation?
- Have you had to curtail your activities?

- Have you taken any medication for the pain? What kind? How effective was it?
- Does anyone in your family experience severe menstrual cramps or other pelvic pain?

Write down your answers to these questions beforehand, along with any questions you may have. Keep a chart of symptoms and record them regularly, even after you have been diagnosed. This helps the doctor determine the effectiveness of the chosen treatment.

Some women are reluctant to discuss dyspareunia. However, symptoms relating to intercourse can provide important clues. Does pain occur with penetration, with orgasm, during menstruation only, at ovulation, from ovulation through menstruation, or throughout the cycle? Include this information on your chart. It may be an unpleasant reminder, but it will help you pinpoint the stage at which you experience pain. Similarly, a woman may think her backache or leg pain is insignificant; but, when considered in light of other symptoms, it may indicate endometriosis. Be sure to report these symptoms to your doctor.

PHYSICAL EXAMINATION

The examination usually consists of a general inspection, followed by an inspection of the external genitalia, the internal reproductive organs, and the rectum. While many women are familiar with this sequence of events, it may be frightening to a young teenager experiencing it for the first time. Knowing what to expect will relieve some of your anxiety.

Different doctors have different techniques. Ask your doctor to explain the procedure and describe what it will feel like. It is usually quick and normally painless, although an infection or other disorder may produce some tenderness as the doctor probes involved areas.

You are usually asked to provide urine and blood samples before the pelvic examination. The nurse or physician will take your temperature and blood pressure and evaluate your respiration, listening to your heart and lungs. The physician will then palpate your abdomen and your flanks to detect any masses. He will search for tenderness in the abdominal organs or the kidneys and will examine your breasts.

For the pelvic examination, you will recline on your back on the examining table, legs spread, knees bent, and feet in the stirrups at the end of the table. Your doctor begins by examining the external genitalia—the vulva, the clitoris, and the labia—for signs of irritation or infection. Endometriosis of the vulva or perineum, although relatively uncommon, may be visible at this time. If the doctor observes the characteristic red, blue, or black raised lesions in these areas he may want to perform a biopsy. Before moving on to the speculum examination, the gynecologist will insert a finger into the vagina to detect any enlargement of the two Bartholin's glands just inside the vaginal opening and will look for any irritation in the area of the urethra. He then inserts the speculum, an instrument that opens the vagina to provide a view of the cervix. (The insertion is painless, but, if you are anxious, muscle tension may make the insertion uncomfortable.) At this time he may use a cotton swab or a wooden spatula to take a Pap smear or sample of any unusual or excessive discharge. He then searches for endometriotic lesions of the cervix and vagina.

Figure 7   Pelvic Examination; Rectovaginal Examination

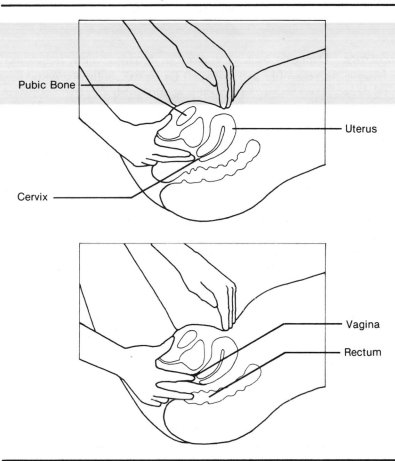

Pubic Bone

Uterus

Cervix

Vagina

Rectum

Your doctor then removes the speculum and performs a bimanual examination (see Figure 7). Inserting two fingers into your vagina, he places the fingers of his other hand on your abdomen so that he can feel between both hands the shape, size, and configuration of the pelvic organs, as well as any unusual growths or tenderness.

Finally, he performs a rectovaginal examination similar to the pelvic, but with the index finger of one hand in the vagina and the middle finger in the rectum. He uses his other hand to feel the abdomen.

Findings

The examination may not uncover anything conclusive. However, it will provide the physician with enough clues to investigate further. For example, he may discover enlarged ovaries and other abnormalities. Enlargement of the ovaries or fallopian tubes is sometimes present in patients with moderate to severe endometriosis. Congenital abnormalities may be discovered upon physical examination. Other findings include nodularity and uterine displacement.

Nodularity.   During the bimanual examination the physician may feel nodules in the posterior fornix of the vagina (the part that meets the cervix), on the uterosacral ligaments, or in the cul-de-sac. These nodules are evident in approximately 25 percent of patients with mild, 30 percent with moderate, and 50 percent with severe, endometriosis.[2] The physician may also feel cystic lesions of the ovaries that may be tender to the touch. Experts caution, however, that nodularity does not necessarily indicate endometriosis. Nodules and cysts may result from other conditions, but their presence does increase suspicion of endometriosis and indicate more aggressive investigation. On the other hand, in patients who *do* have endometriosis, nodules may be too small or too inaccessible to be felt during the pelvic examination.

Uterine displacement.   During the bimanual examination the physician can detect whether or not the uterus is in its normal position tilting slightly forward in the pelvis. The normally positioned uterus has a range of movement that can be tested. Extensive endometriotic involvement of the cul-de-sac may anchor or freeze the uterus into an abnormal position—often called a tipped uterus—tilted either too far backward (retroversion) or too far forward (anteversion). A retroverted uterus, possibly caused by disease in the posterior cul-de-sac, is present in about 42 to 46 percent of women with endometriosis.[3] (These figures are not much higher than those that reflect incidence in the general population.[4]) An anteverted uterus, possibly from endometriosis of the anterior cul-de-sac, is found in approximately 20 percent.[5] In addition, the abnormal position of the uterus may be more extreme; it may be anteflexed or retroflexed—meaning bending abnormally in one direction or another (see Figure 8). Displacement may also be due to disease of the uterine ligaments and associated adhesions.

Retroversion of the uterus is like the chicken and the egg. Which came first? Does it predispose a woman to retrograde menstruation, thereby causing the disease, or is it a result of scarring in the area of the cul-de-sac, which fixes the uterus permanently in this position? The latter is known to occur; the former is believed possible.

Lack of Findings

If there are no abnormal findings, your doctor may schedule another examination to take place during, or just before, your next menstrual period. Another may be scheduled at a different point in the month so that he can detect any changes that may occur throughout the cycle.

If your symptoms are not severe, your doctor may decide on medication. You may be given prostaglandin inhibiting drugs such as Motrin, Anaprox, or Ponstel (see Chapter 5). These help to rule out primary dysmenorrhea; that is, if you do not respond, the likelihood of endometriosis is increased. Before scheduling a laparoscopy, your doctor may prescribe

Figure 8 Normal and Abnormal Positions of the Uterus

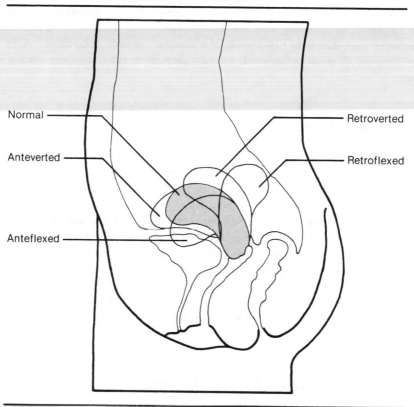

Normal — Retroverted

Anteverted — Retroflexed

Anteflexed —

oral contraceptives to be taken cyclically, three weeks on and one week off (see Chapters 5 and 6). If, while on oral contraceptives, you find that your symptoms initially worsen, the suspicion of endometriosis is heightened, and you will probably be scheduled for laparoscopy.

Remember, at this point these medications are essentially for diagnosis, not treatment. Follow-up examinations must determine their effectiveness. If symptoms are severe, and if nodules, for example, are found, it's important to investigate further without delay, not only to treat the endometriosis but to rule out malignancy.

In some cases, following physical examination, and without confirmation of endometriosis by laparoscopy, physicians recommend hormonal treatment. However, most experts advise against any treatment modality other than prostaglandin inhibiting drugs or birth control pills before diagnosis.

In one study of 140 adolescents, laparoscoped to determine the cause of chronic pelvic pain, endometriosis was found in 34 percent.[6] Treatment, if based on a presumptive diagnosis, would have been unnecessary, inappropriate, and perhaps risky for 66 percent. If a malignancy has not been ruled out, and if hormone therapy involving estrogen is used either to provide symptomatic relief from dysmenorrhea or to treat suspected endometriosis, the estrogen can enhance the development of a cancerous growth. If hormone therapy based on presumptive diagnosis is suggested, carefully consider its risks. You may want a second opinion.

LAPAROSCOPY

When symptoms are severe, when findings during clinical examination suggest endometriosis, or when prostaglandin inhibitors or birth control pills do not adequately address the symptoms, you most likely will be scheduled for laparoscopy (see Figure 9). For a complete description of this procedure, see Appendix A.

Traditionally a diagnostic tool, the laparoscope is used increasingly to treat the disease at the time of diagnosis. A well-equipped, well-trained surgeon can remove much of the visible endometriosis by excising it, cauterizing it with electric current, or vaporizing it with the laser during the laparoscopy (see Chapter 8).

During laparoscopy endometriosis may or may not be readily apparent to the surgeon. Whether or not he detects it may be determined by his ability to recognize the variety of forms the disease may take. Be sure you know beforehand whether or not the procedure is strictly diagnostic.

LESIONS, CYSTS, AND ADHESIONS

In its early stages endometriosis is typically described as small, superficial, red or blue lesions called mulberry, raspberry, or blueberry spots. In later stages it appears as brown or blue-black "powderburn" lesions. The size varies: small spots or patches of spots, palpable nodules that invade the host tissue, or large fluid-filled cysts. Cysts filled with dark, old blood are known as "chocolate cysts."

Leakage from lesions and cysts leads to the formation of scar tissue or webs of adhesions that may plaster the ovaries to the broad ligament, the surface of the uterus, or the cul-de-sac. It may distort other pelvic organs such as the bowel or ureter, even if they are not directly affected with endometriotic lesions (see Figure 10).

This is the "classic" description of the disease. Some researchers claim it's a misleading and incomplete picture. Because gynecologists have been trained to look primarily for mulberry spots, powderburn lesions, and chocolate cysts, the disease is often overlooked when these telltale signs are not seen.

Dr. Redwine researched different visual manifestations of the disease and found that the native endometriotic lesion is a clear papule that may change in appearance over time, evolving into the more familiar classic black powderburn lesion as patients age.[7] "When you

Figure 9 Laparoscopy

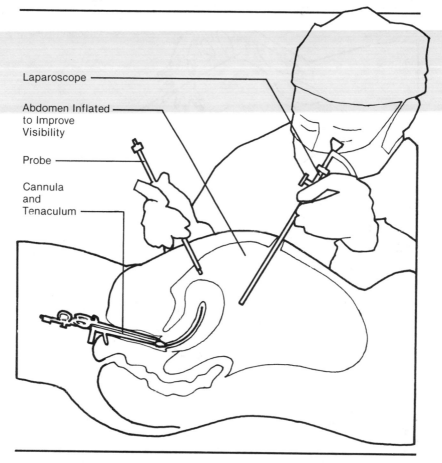

Laparoscope

Abdomen Inflated
to Improve
Visibility

Probe

Cannula
and
Tenaculum

add up the various visual manifestations of the disease and compare them against the classic, textbook appearance," says Dr. Redwine, "the black powderburn implant may actually be in the minority."

"I think we are just now starting to understand that endometriosis can have a variety of forms," says Dr. Rock. "It can, in fact, be microscopic, where one can't even see it. It can be subperitoneal, so that you are unable to appreciate its presence. I would not be surprised if there are other forms of its presentation." When in doubt, he explains, "the key is to perform a biopsy so that you know if indeed it is or is not endometriosis." A biopsy of several endometriotic lesions and cysts is normally done at the time of the laparoscopy to confirm a diagnosis based on the visual appearance of the disease.

Figure 10   Adhesions

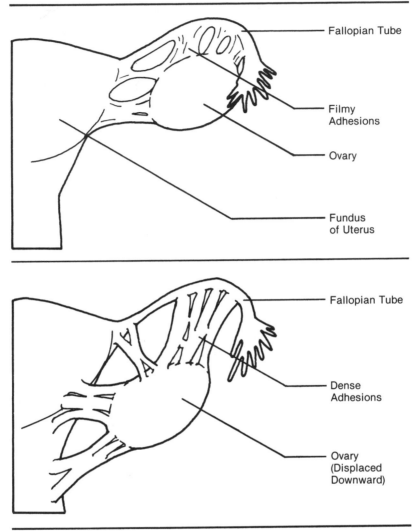

Fallopian Tube

Filmy
Adhesions

Ovary

Fundus
of Uterus

Fallopian Tube

Dense
Adhesions

Ovary
(Displaced
Downward)

"We can take a biopsy from the peritoneum that looks perfectly normal, and under the microscope this is going to show endometriotic lesions," explain Dr. Dmowski. "So some lesions—minimal lesions—may not necessarily be visible, or may not be visible to a laparoscopist who is not experienced in looking for the lesions."

In addition, says Dr. Dmowski, visualization at laparoscopy is not always possible because endometriosis may be in locations that are obscured from the surgeon's vision. "Lesions are frequently in the ovarian fossa (a pouch, on the posterior of the broad ligament, that contains the ovary), which is not readily detectable. Lesions deep in the cul-de-sac may be covered by adhesions."

CLASSIFICATION OF ENDOMETRIOSIS

During laparoscopy, the degree—that is, the extent and severity—of the disease is determined. This classification by degree of disease permits physicians and researchers to gauge the effectiveness of various treatments in terms of symptomatic relief, pregnancy rates, and recurrences. Classification also documents the level of disease so that physicians can chart its progression during future surgical procedures.

The surgeon will diagram the extent of disease. He notes the location, amount, and size of all endometriotic lesions and adhesions on prepared diagrams. In some cases photographs are taken and videotapes are made. This information is then graded on a point system, based on criteria established by a committee of the American Fertility Society, to determine the degree of disease.

The first classification scheme for endometriosis was developed in 1973; since that time the criteria have been revised and refined three times in efforts to arrive at a more precise method for documenting the extent of disease. As of 1985 the classification scheme details the nature of four categories or stages of disease: minimal, mild, moderate, and severe (see Figure 11).

LAPAROTOMY, ULTRASOUND, AND OTHER DIAGNOSTIC PROCEDURES

Laparotomy, primarily a therapeutic procedure (see Chapter 8 and Appendix A), may be required in rare cases when laparoscopy and biopsy fail to provide a definite diagnosis. During laparotomy biopsies are taken of lesions of the bowel, urinary tract, and other areas of suspected endometriotic involvement, usually when a malignancy must be ruled out.

Another procedure used to help detect endometriosis is ultrasound. Its usefulness is limited, however. Ultrasound can demonstrate the presence of a growth, but not the nature of that growth. According to Dr. Charles W. Hohler, vice-president of the American Institute of Ultrasound in Bethesda, Maryland, "With pelvic ultrasound, endometriosis presents a very broad spectrum and the appearance is usually not specific." He adds that lesions can be very difficult to differentiate from malignancies or from pelvic inflammatory disease.[8]

Figure 11   Classification Scheme

Revised American Fertility Society Classification of Endometriosis: 1985

The American Fertility Society*†

Birmingham, Alabama

Patient's Name _____   Date_____

Stage I (Minimal) · 1-5	Laparoscopy_____ Laparotomy_____ Photography_____
Stage II (Mild) · 6-15	Recommended Treatment_____
Stage III (Moderate) · 16-40	
Stage IV (Severe) · >40	
Total_____	Prognosis_____

		<1cm	1-3cm	>3cm
PERITONEUM	**ENDOMETRIOSIS**			
	Superficial	1	2	4
	Deep	2	4	6
OVARY	R Superficial	1	2	4
	Deep	4	16	20
	L Superficial	1	2	4
	Deep	4	16	20
	POSTERIOR CULDESAC OBLITERATION	Partial		Complete
		4		40

		<1/3 Enclosure	1-3-2-3 Enclosure	>2-3 Enclosure
	ADHESIONS			
OVARY	R Filmy	1	2	4
	Dense	4	8	16
	L Filmy	1	2	4
	Dense	4	8	16
TUBE	R Filmy	1	2	4
	Dense	4*	8*	16
	L Filmy	1	2	4
	Dense	4*	8*	16

*If the fimbriated end of the fallopian tube is completely enclosed, change the point assignment to 16.

Additional Endometriosis: _____   Associated Pathology: _____

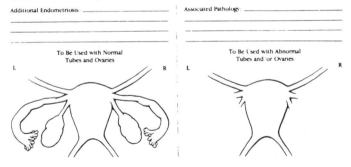

To Be Used with Normal Tubes and Ovaries

To Be Used with Abnormal Tubes and/or Ovaries

*Drafted by a committee composed of William C. Andrews. Veasy C. Buttram. Jr., S. Jan Behrman, Erskine Carmichael. Melvin R. Cohen, Paul Dmowski, R. Donald Eward, David S. Guzick, Howard W. Jones. Jr., Robert W. Kistner, John C. Weed, Charles B. Hammond, and Herbert H. Thomas and approved by the Board of Directors of The American Fertility Society on November 3, 1984.

†Padded reprint forms are available from The American Fertility Society, 2131 Magnolia Avenue, Suite 201, Birmingham, Alabama 35256.

Figure 11 Classification Scheme

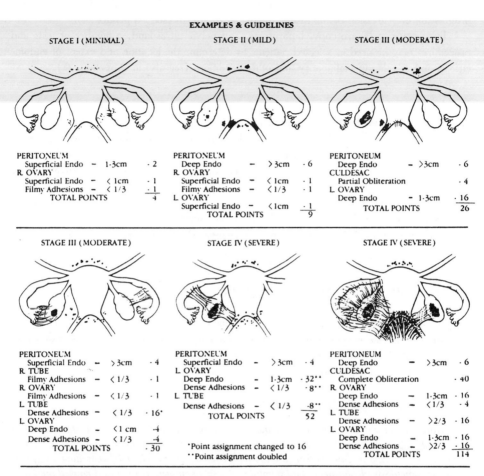

EXAMPLES & GUIDELINES

STAGE I (MINIMAL)

PERITONEUM
Superficial Endo – 1-3cm   · 2
R. OVARY
Superficial Endo – < 1cm   · 1
Filmy Adhesions – < 1/3   · 1
TOTAL POINTS   4

STAGE II (MILD)

PERITONEUM
Deep Endo – >3cm   · 6
R. OVARY
Superficial Endo – < 1cm   · 1
Filmy Adhesions – < 1/3   · 1
L. OVARY
Superficial Endo – < 1cm   · 1
TOTAL POINTS   9

STAGE III (MODERATE)

PERITONEUM
Deep Endo – >3cm   · 6
CULDESAC
Partial Obliteration   · 4
L. OVARY
Deep Endo – 1-3cm   · 16
TOTAL POINTS   26

STAGE III (MODERATE)

PERITONEUM
Superficial Endo – >3cm   · 4
R. TUBE
Filmy Adhesions – < 1/3   · 1
R. OVARY
Filmy Adhesions – < 1/3   · 1
L. TUBE
Dense Adhesions – < 1/3   · 16*
L. OVARY
Deep Endo – <1 cm   -4
Dense Adhesions – < 1/3   -4
TOTAL POINTS   · 30

STAGE IV (SEVERE)

PERITONEUM
Superficial Endo – >3cm   · 4
L. OVARY
Deep Endo – 1-3cm   · 32**
Dense Adhesions – < 1/3   · 8**
L. TUBE
Dense Adhesions – < 1/3   -8**
TOTAL POINTS   52

*Point assignment changed to 16
**Point assignment doubled

STAGE IV (SEVERE)

PERITONEUM
Deep Endo – >3cm   · 6
CULDESAC
Complete Obliteration   · 40
R. OVARY
Deep Endo – 1-3cm   · 16
Dense Adhesions – < 1/3   · 4
L. TUBE
Dense Adhesions – >2/3   · 16
L. OVARY
Deep Endo – 1-3cm   · 16
Dense Adhesions – >2/3   · 16
TOTAL POINTS   114

Determination of the stage or degree of endometrial involvement is based on a weighted point system. Distribution of points has been arbitrarily determined and may require further revision or refinement as knowledge of the disease increases.

To ensure complete evaluation, inspection of the pelvis in a clockwise or counterclockwise fashion is encouraged. Number, size and location of endometrial implants, plaques, endometriomas and/or adhesions are noted. For example, five separate 0.5cm superficial implants on the peritoneum (2.5 cm total) would be assigned 2 points. (The surface of the uterus should be considered peritoneum.) The severity of the endometriosis or adhesions should be assigned the highest score only for peritoneum, ovary, tube or culdesac. For example, a 4cm superficial and a 2cm deep implant of the peritoneum should be given a score of 6 (not 8). A 4cm

deep endometrioma of the ovary associated with more than 3cm of superficial disease should be scored 20 (not 24).

In those patients with only one adenexa, points applied to disease of the remaining tube and ovary should be multipled by two. **Points assigned may be circled and totaled. Aggregation of points indicates stage of disease (minimal, mild, moderate, or severe).

The presence of endometriosis of the bowel, urinary tract, fallopian tube, vagina, cervix, skin etc., should be documented under "additional endometriosis." Other pathology such as tubal occlusion, leiomyomata, uterine anomaly, etc., should be documented under "associated pathology." All pathology should be depicted as specifically as possible on the sketch of pelvic organs, and means of observation (laparoscopy or laparotomy) should be noted.

Pelvic ultrasound, however, may help suggest the need for further investigation. Once endometriosis is confirmed, pelvic ultrasound can be used during follow-up to document progression or regression of the disease following treatment (see Appendix A).

In addition to laparoscopy, laparotomy, and pelvic ultrasound, a number of tests and procedures may be used in selected patients to determine the location and extent of endometriosis and to rule out malignancy and other conditions (see also in Appendix A).

- *Breast:* mammography
- *Chest:* CT scan, lung biopsy, thoracentesis and pleural biopsy, x-ray
- *Gastrointestinal tract:* colonoscopy, sigmoidoscopy and biopsy, upper and lower GI series
- *Genital (reproductive) tract:* biopsy, cervical conization, colposcopy, CT scan, culdocentesis, D & C, endometrial biopsy, hysterosalpingography, hysteroscopy, lymph node biopsy
- *Sciatic nerve:* CT scan
- *Skin, muscle, scars, umbilicus, limbs, groin:* excisional biopsy
- *Urinary tract and kidney:* cystoscopy and biopsy, IVP, renography

ROADBLOCKS TO DIAGNOSIS

As mentioned earlier, endometriosis is frequently mistaken for other conditions. Not only are there limitations in diagnostic methods, there are many other roadblocks to diagnosis as well—obstacles created not only by stereotyping and medical ignorance but also by the vagueness or lack of symptoms and the mythology surrounding menstrual pain.

Asymptomatic Endometriosis

"In March I noticed a large mass on the left side of my abdomen. Within three weeks I underwent surgery to remove a huge cyst on my left ovary and fallopian tube as well as part of the remaining ovary. Fortunately, the lab report ruled out cancer, but I was diagnosed with severe endometriosis. I had never had painful periods. They were regular and caused only mild cramps. There seems to be no resurgence, but I wonder if the disease which crept up on me so silently the first time will do so again without any pain or symptoms at all."

An obvious problem is that endometriosis is frequently asymptomatic and, at present, can only be diagnosed through exploratory surgery. There is, however, some hope that in the future endometriosis may be detected through a simple blood test.

CA-125.   Researchers have discovered that patients with advanced endometriosis have higher blood levels of CA-125, a cell surface protein, than women without the disease. Testing for CA-125 levels has its limits, however. It cannot replace laparoscopy as a diagnostic method for all cases of endometriosis. The test is not sensitive enough to detect many cases of mild disease; and elevated CA-125 levels have been discovered in pregnant women and women with other conditions such as ovarian cancer and pelvic inflammatory disease.[9] This test can be useful in another way, however. CA-125 levels decline following treatment. Therefore, the blood test may be helpful in tracking the effectiveness of treatment.

Until a more specific noninvasive test is developed, remember that diagnosis of endometriosis is not an exact science. For an expedient, accurate diagnosis, seek out a doctor who is highly experienced with endometriosis (see Chapter 16).

The Myth of the Typical Patient

"It never occurred to me that I might have endometriosis. After all, I'm not a working woman, and I've never been under much stress."

"I suffered for ten years before being diagnosed, all because I was "too young' for endometriosis."

"My gynecologist said it was very unlikely that I had endometriosis because I had had two children and it was basically a disease of childless women. He said a laparoscopy really wasn't necessary. Two doctors and eight months later I had a laparoscopy. It revealed moderate endometriosis."

"After countless courses of antibiotics, and lots of unnecessary bedrest for pelvic inflammatory disease—all with no results—I asked my doctor if I might have endometriosis. He advised me to leave the diagnosing to him. Besides, he said, black women seldom get that disease. I saw a specialist. He was astonished. "Nobody still believes that,' he said. He scheduled a laparoscopy, which revealed endometriosis."

Women learn from newspapers and magazines, doctors and medical textbooks, just who is at risk for endometriosis. As explained in Chapter 2, the disease has long been thought to affect primarily white, older, childless, career women. If a woman doesn't fit this profile, despite her symptoms, she reassures herself that "it's just cramps." Doctors often fail to suspect and investigate endometriosis in women who don't fit the profile.

Black women, for example, were seldom considered candidates for endometriosis. "I've seen circumstances where two patients had identical symptoms and findings," recalls Dr. Dmowski. "A black woman might be diagnosed with pelvic inflammatory disease and treated with antibiotics, while a white woman would be diagnosed with endometriosis and treated with whatever methods were available."

Similarly, teenagers are often overlooked, as are fertile women. Explains Dr. Redwine, "People are honing in on the infertile woman when they look for endometriosis patients, and they often ignore fertile women or diagnose them as having something else."

Professional Ignorance

"I had a sharp shooting pain across my stomach. My doctor told me it was gas."

"During my period I had severe cramping, nausea and vomiting, the urgent need to void urine and feces, diarrhea, hot sweats, and chills. In the emergency room they told me I had the flu.

After about eighteen months the symptoms disappeared, until an endometrioma burst and I was admitted for surgery."

"My doctor said I was acting like a baby and that I had a low threshold of pain."

"Every day I would double up with pain and cramps. Sometimes I would vomit and get diarrhea. It took three years until I could find a doctor to take me seriously."

"I had very heavy periods and severe cramps. Four doctors—all gynecologists—gave me muscle relaxers. I started getting severe aches in my side to the point where I couldn't walk any more. A new specialist said it was just an ovarian cyst. Four months later I had to have emergency surgery."

"My first doctor said it couldn't be endometriosis because he couldn't feel anything during the pelvic examination."

"I always had painful cramps during menstruation. I took Darvon from the time I was sixteen. At twenty-four I switched to Tylenol 3 with Codeine. I was constipated always and had terrible pain with intercourse. The doctors never told me they thought there was a problem. At twenty-six, when the pain got worse with intercourse, I began to look for reasons."

Not all family physicians, internists, and gynecologists can detect endometriosis. They may see few cases of endometriosis and do not always recognize its symptoms. A woman's first concern should be her doctor's awareness of the outward signs and symptoms of the disease. Her next concern should be his ability to recognize the disease during laparoscopy.

A physician who performs a laparoscopy may not be experienced enough to interpret the findings. Dr. Dmowski finds endometriosis daily in patients who were laparoscoped by doctors who did not detect the disease. "Unless the laparoscopist is experienced," he says, "it is difficult sometimes to make a correct diagnosis."

If a doctor selects only "typical patients" for laparoscopy and is aware of only the typical powderburn implant, lack of diagnosis or misdiagnosis is likely. "Doctors are looking for the wrong patients in their practices to take to laparoscopy," explains Dr. Redwine. "And when they get to laparoscopy, they are looking for the wrong thing. So they have two chances to miss the patient with disease."

The Mythology of Menstrual Pain

"I suffered with the symptoms of endometriosis for many years, but I didn't know that I wasn't normal. I always thought that if my periods were regular, nothing could be wrong."

"After years of being told I "just had cramps,' when in fact I had excruciating pain, and still do, I found out I had endometriosis."

"Six months ago my doctor told me she felt I might have endometriosis. Until that moment I had never even heard the word, let alone did I have any idea what it was. I only knew that for at least two weeks out of every month I was miserable. For several days I would have cramps so bad that it was difficult to function. My other doctors told me pain was normal."

"When something happens to us, we think that everybody experiences the same thing, because we look at the world through our feelings," says Dr. Deborah Metzger, chief resident at Duke University Medical School in Durham, North Carolina. "So when a woman is incapacitated by cramps, she thinks all women are incapacitated by cramps." As a result, women seldom discuss menstrual pain with their gynecologists. And few doctors taking gynecological histories ask a woman if she has pain and how severe it is.

"I think I've had endometriosis since I was twelve. I had terrible cramps, but my mother said she had cramps when she was my age and I was just blowing it out of proportion."

"Many times I required bedrest with hot water bottles and over-the-counter painkillers, which were ineffective. I sometimes had to leave school, or not attend at all when my symptoms were severe. When I reported my difficulties to my mother, she told me that seeing a doctor would not help, since her doctor had told her when she had similar problems that "there was nothing that could be done.' So, believing him, she coped the best she could and encouraged me to do the same. 'You'll just have to try to learn to live with it. It's a part of being a woman.' "

Dr. Suzanne Pratt, a gynecologist in private practice in Rome, Georgia, speculates that many women whose mothers taught them that menstrual pain is normal may have had mothers with unrecognized and untreated endometriosis. "The patient feels that she has menstrual cramps because every woman in her family had them and that was the normal state of affairs."

Not only do women start out believing that pain is normal, they also come to believe that *increasing* pain is normal. The human body, explains Dr. Redwine, gets used to pain. A woman with dysmenorrhea, he says, "frequently puts up with a little more pain, a little more time off work, a little more time under the heating pad, a little more time in the bathtub, a little more wine to help the pain. She puts up with a little bit by a little bit over the months or years, and by the time she finally comes to the doctor, she may be walking on her hands and knees. She may be really debilitated, but she's gotten used to it. And you can see it at a glance, because she's got lines in her face and has a drawn expression. She just doesn't look healthy. When you ask how she's doing, she says she's okay, that she has a little pain. When you start to question her about it, you find that she's hurting maybe fifteen days out of the month—50 percent of her life! It's been so long since she's felt good, she's forgotten what it's like."

The Legacy of Freud: Psychogenic Pain

"I guess I always felt guilty for having so much pain and discomfort; I think I always saw myself as a weakling for not tolerating pain better than I did."

"My mother called me neurotic, but she was never fond of female weaknesses. The school nurse said I overexaggerated."

"I was told to have counseling by a doctor who said my menstrual cramps and pain with intercourse were a result of childhood training and that I needed professional help to get those ideas out of my head. I was nineteen at the time, newly married, and deperately needing medical attention. I questioned my self-worth and wondered if he could be right."

"After being told repeatedly that there was no physical cause for my pain or infertility, I began to believe I imagined the pain. I was embarrassed and uncomfortable telling doctors about the pain because the result was always the same—a pat on the arm: "You're fine, relax.' The pain continued and became worse. I made an appointment for a check-up. I gathered all my nerve and tried one more time to tell the gynecologist how I felt. She examined me, said she felt something in my uterus, and announced that I was pregnant. The pregnancy test was negative. She sent me home, saying that the problem was probably hormones and would correct itself. The pain continued and five months later I made an appointment with an infertility specialist. Before the appointment I had decided that if he found no cause for the pain and infertility, I would consult a psychiatrist. He found a polyp, adhesions, and endometriosis. The pain was real. Now, medication may treat the endometriosis, but I still have to deal with the bitterness."

"I spent five frustrating and painful years going to highly recommended specialists complaining of severe pain on intercourse. Each and every one wanted me to relax more, to take Valium, or try different coital positions."

"I thought I was imagining the pain. I was told that so often I started to believe it until it got so bad I couldn't walk."

Physicians trained to view menstrual pain as emotional may tell a woman with undiagnosed endometriosis that there is no physical cause for her pain. Sometimes they prescribe a tranquilizer, or they may refer her to a psychiatrist. Specialists bristle at the assertion that any gynecologist in this day and age would suggest a psychogenic cause for dysmenorrhea but, until very recently, this appears to have been the rule rather than the exception. Approximately 70 percent of the women surveyed for this book had been told at some point in their quest for diagnosis that there was no physical cause for their pain. Dr. Linda Kames is an assistant professor of psychology at UCLA and a clinical psychologist who works with endometriosis patients in the Pelvic Pain Program at UCLA's Pain Management Center. She says that almost every patient she sees there had been told that the pain was only in her head.

Patients raised on this notion feel guilty or hypochondriacal and therefore are hesitant to discuss their menstrual pain. And, because symptoms are not visible (a woman with severe disease may appear perfectly healthy), friends and family may be unsympathetic. Meanwhile, a very real physical condition goes undiagnosed and untreated, leading to private fears and anxieties about what could be wrong.

You know your body best. Listen to its messages and investigate the cause of new or increasing pain. If your doctor fails to take your complaints seriously, don't be intimidated; never resign yourself to pain. Search until you find a knowledgeable doctor who will work with you for an accurate diagnosis.

PART 2

Treatment Options and Outcomes

Although in recent decades doctors have initiated a variety of surgical and medical approaches to treating endometriosis, no cause-directed therapy exists. Nor can any be developed until the cause of endometriosis is determined.

Therefore, doctors treat symptoms and aim to suppress disease. Medications, since they are not curative, are considered effective only insofar as they are able to induce regression of existing implants, suppress further development, provide relief from pain, and increase the likelihood of conception.

Conservative surgical approaches strive to remove all areas of endometriosis through excision, electric cautery, and laser vaporization. However, complete success is virtually impossible, since the disease is frequently microscopic.

Following medication or conservative surgery, endometriosis typically recurs within, or persists for, an unpredictable length of time. Unless the disease or its symptoms are extremely severe, a repeated course of medication or additional conservative surgery will see most women through until menopause, allowing approximately half of them to conceive. At menopause, the natural output of ovarian hormones may bring relief.

But, when endometriosis threatens the vital organs or when prolonged pain drastically impairs the quality of life, the only hope rests with definitive surgery—that is, total hysterectomy with bilateral salpingo-oophorectomy: the removal of the uterus, cervix, and ovaries. Because removal of the ovaries eliminates a woman's major source of estrogen, it creates a "surgical menopause." This is often accompanied by symptoms of estrogen deficiency—hot flashes, vaginal dryness—as well as an increased risk of osteoporosis and heart disease. Following definitive surgery, most women are given replacement estrogen to counter these symptoms and reduce or eliminate risks such as these.

While hysterectomy alone (removal of the uterus only) sometimes results in permanent eradication of endometriosis, continued hormonal stimulation from the ovaries more often reactivates any microscopic or inaccessible disease remaining. And, when replacement estrogens are taken to ameliorate menopausal symptoms following definitive surgery, endometriosis can persist, albeit infrequently.

For most women, definitive surgery or hysterectomy is unacceptable. A woman uninterested in having children may choose to relinquish her reproductive organs with little regret in order to restore the quality of her life. But most, particularly those who strongly desire a child, will go to great lengths and undergo an assortment of treatments, to avoid definitive surgery.

As a result, many women face treatment decisions again and again. Choices involve considerations of age, degree of symptoms, tolerance for medication, feelings about surgery, and feelings about childbearing. Decisions also depend on the philosophy, experience, biases, and skills of the physician.

Recognize that there *are* options and realize that only you can decide what is best for you. To do so, you need to understand fully the range of options, the risks, the possibilities, the consequences, and the outlook for the future.

To provide you with information upon which to base these decisions, Part 2 reviews, but does not evaluate or recommend, the most common courses of treatment. Only you, in consultation with your doctor, can decide which best meets your needs and affords the most relief from pain, and which, for those of you who want children, offers the most hope.

5

Expectant Approach to Symptomatic Relief

Expectant therapy for symptomatic relief refers to a period of observation and minimal medical intervention that includes regular follow-ups to monitor possible progression of endometriosis. It is a wait-and-see approach, also used in diagnosis, as discussed in Chapter 4. Generally reserved for patients with superficial disease and mild symptoms, it is usually recommended for young women who have no immediate desire to conceive and for older women nearing menopause.

Expectant management of symptoms may involve mild analgesics, nonsteroidal anti-inflammatory agents (NSAIAs), and, less commonly and less desirably, narcotics, tranquilizers, and antidepressants. Keep in mind that an expectant approach treats the *symptoms* of the disease, not the disease itself. These medications may improve your general well-being, but they have no effect at all on the extent of the disease.

Although this chapter explores medications for pain relief, drugs are only one option and, arguably, not the best. If you are experiencing chronic pain, remember that medicine alone has its limitations. Try to regard your pain as a problem to be solved. There may be more than one solution and, to find the best possible answer, you may have to look beyond the obvious.

Chronic pain can be all-encompassing: it can cause fatigue, depression, despair, insomnia, and irritability. It can influence your relationships, undermine your sex life, impair your work performance, and prevent you from taking part in pleasurable activities. Your reaction to these losses may cause you further stress and agitation, which in turn can exacerbate your pain.

Taking a pill is a relatively simple act. Pain medications may reduce your discomfort but seldom bring full relief, because they do not help you deal with the cumulative effects of pain on your life and your lifestyle. A more effective approach to pain relief is to devise a comprehensive strategy that will encompass improving your general health, learning to reduce

65

stress, recognizing the subtle ways in which pain affects your daily life, exploring your emotional reactions to pain and its effect upon your life, and learning ways you can help to minimize the impact of pain.

You may want to explore "alternative" or complementary therapies, such as acupuncture, biofeedback, or relaxation training (see Chapter 18). When pain has had a profound effect on your life, counseling may also be useful, not only to help you sort out your emotional response to pain, but also to increase your ability to develop coping strategies (see Chapter 17).

MEDICATION GUIDELINES

According to a recent survey by the Food and Drug Administration, 70 percent of respondents whose prescriptions had been filled within the preceding two weeks reported that their doctors said nothing about precautions, side effects, or proper dosages. Ninety percent never asked their doctor or pharmacist about the effect of the medications.[1]

Before taking any drug, whether prescription or over-the-counter (OTC), ask your physician these questions:

1. What is the generic name of the drug? Brand name?
2. What is its purpose?
3. What is the proper dosage? What is the best way to take it?
4. How long should I continue to take it? When can I expect results?
5. Are there any contraindications that may apply to me?
6. Does the drug interact with any foods or alcoholic beverages or other medications?
7. Is the drug photosensitive? (That is, does exposure to sunlight produce an untoward reaction?)
8. Will my mental acuity or physical coordination be affected in any way? Is it safe to drive, to operate machinery, to perform other dangerous or demanding tasks?
9. What are the common side effects? How can I reduce the likelihood of experiencing them?
10. Are there any serious adverse reactions, allergic responses, toxicity? Any risks? What are the warning signs, if any?
11. Is any special monitoring or follow-up necessary?
12. Is the drug safe during pregnancy or breastfeeding?
13. Is the drug habit-forming?

You may, if you wish, obtain a manufacturer's package insert which contains this information. Or, if you want more details, consult the most recent edition of the *Physicians' Desk Reference.*

Keep in mind that OTC medications are *not* harmless. Before taking any OTC drug, check with your doctor. Ask the same questions and heed the same precautions and guidelines as you would when taking prescription drugs.

CHARACTERISTICS OF ALL DRUGS

Side Effects and Risks

Side effects refer to adverse reactions that, although unpleasant, are generally not hazardous. *All* drugs have side effects, even aspirin.

Get all the information on the side effects of the medications you are taking. Some physicians are afraid they may alarm their patients, so they are reluctant to fully inform them. And some patients don't ask. Providing information about side effects is not intended to frighten, but to forewarn. A common complaint among women taking medications for endometriosis is that they could easily have tolerated side effects if only they had known what to expect and had been reassured that their reactions were not unusual, unexpected, or dangerous. In many cases patients have discontinued treatment because they were not fully informed about the extent of possible side effects.

Remember, although the list of side effects may be formidable, each side effect may affect only a fraction of users. You may experience none at all, or you may experience several. Be sure to inform your doctor about any and all reactions you have.

Many side effects are transient and diminish or disappear in time. Many others can be reduced or eliminated by reducing the dosage. (Be sure to consult your doctor before altering any dosages.) Virtually all side effects will disappear if you discontinue the drug. If you are concerned about possible side effects, discuss your fears with your doctor before you rule out any drug that may bring significant relief. The side effects must be weighed against the potential benefits.

All drug users incur some risks. But, like side effects, risks must be weighed against possible benefits. Generally, the benefits are worth the very small risk of serious repercussions. Decide what risks you are willing to accept only after you have enough information to make a wise decision. In the sections below on specific kinds of medications, risks (unlike side effects) refer to a serious adverse reaction. In most cases, however, serious consequences and complications are the exception, not the rule.

Allergies

A drug allergy is a negative reaction to a medication that follows prior exposure to that drug or a similar substance. Allergic responses are less common than side effects. Some can be extremely serious. Mild allergic reactions include itching, wheals, hives, or rashes. A more serious reaction is wheezing or shortness of breath. The most hazardous of all is an *anaphylactic reaction.* Mild anaphylactic reactions are characterized by hives and itching. In severe cases shortness of breath (a result of swelling of the larynx and constriction of bronchial passages) and sudden loss of consciousness can occur (the latter known as anaphylactic shock). An anaphylactic reaction develops rapidly and, if not treated immediately, can lead to death. Learn to recognize the symptoms of an allergic response; be sure to inform your doctor of any allergies you may have to drugs, foods, or other substances *before* you take any medication.

Avoiding Drug Problems

Keep a written record of your drug use, including both the generic and the brand name, the dosage, the duration of use, any side effects, and the effectiveness. In this way you will avoid unnecessary problems with drugs later on.

NONNARCOTIC ANALGESICS

Mild analgesics, often available over the counter, are nonaddicting drugs used to relieve mild to moderate pain. The most widely used in the treatment of dysmenorrhea, and possibly the least effective, are aspirin, acetaminophen, and combination products that may include aspirin, acetaminophen, caffeine, and other substances.

Aspirin and Other Salicylates

Aspirin belongs to a class of drugs called *salicylates*. Although the ways in which aspirin relieves pain are not fully understood, it appears that it acts directly on the site of injury or inflammation as well as upon the hypothalamus to alter the transmission of pain impulses. In addition, it blocks the synthesis of prostaglandins, implicated in the pain of dysmenorrhea. Aspirin, therefore, is both an analgesic and an NSAIA (see below). In normal doses it is the least potent NSAIA and therefore often less effective against dysmenorrhea than other NSAIAs.

Side effects.   Aspirin interferes with blood clotting. Therefore, it can cause you to bruise and bleed more easily. Other common side effects, often dose related, involve the gastrointestinal tract and include stomach upset, bleeding from the stomach lining, blood in the stools, nausea, and vomiting. Gastrointestinal distress may be minimized by taking either regular aspirin with food, milk, or a large glass of water, or buffered aspirin, which contains antacids and similar substances. Specially coated aspirin also reduces stomach upset, but, due to the coating, takes longer to relieve pain. Other salicylates (Arthropan, Disalcid, Mono-Gesic, Magan, Trilisate) are less likely to cause stomach upset, gastrointestinal disturbances, and bleeding from the stomach lining. Ask your doctor which type is best for you.

Other side effects of aspirin include tinnitus (buzzing or ringing in the ears) and hearing loss. They often can be eliminated quickly by reducing the dosage. Some mild reactions (including skin rash, hives, itching, and nasal inflammation, polyps, and discharge) are relatively uncommon. They are more likely to occur in individuals who have asthma, hay fever, or preexisting nasal polyps. A strong allergy may lead to bronchial spasm or anaphylactic reaction.

Risks.   Aspirin, in large doses, or with long-term use, may cause stomach ulcers, excessive blood loss from the lining of the stomach, anemia, the development of a hypersensitivity to aspirin, and liver and kidney damage.

Contraindications.   Aspirin and other salicylates are contraindicated in individuals who are hypersensitive to these medications.

Precautions.   Aspirin should be used only under the direction of a doctor if you have peptic ulcers or kidney or liver impairment or if you use anticoagulant drugs. Diabetics requiring oral medication should also consult their physicians. Remember, aspirin is not innocuous: overdose can be serious. Use aspirin with the same caution you would other drugs and pay particular attention to information about its interaction with other drugs. Never take more than the recommended dosage, except on the advice of your physician. Discontinue use and contact your doctor if you experience any of the following: rapid and difficult breathing, excessive fatigue, hearing disturbances, nausea, vomiting, diarrhea, blood or black coloration in the stools, wheezing, rashes, or hives.

Acetaminophen

Acetaminophen, sometimes called an aspirin substitute, works principally at the site of injury, possibly by blocking the production of prostaglandins. Acetaminophen does not, like aspirin, lead to gastrointestinal complaints or affect bleeding. It has no serious side effects. However, it has no significant anti-inflammatory effects, either. Therefore, it is less effective than other drugs against dysmenorrhea.

Risks.   High doses, or long-term use of even a small dose, can result in anemia or kidney or liver damage. The risk of liver damage is exacerbated by excessive consumption of alcohol. It has been speculated that combining acetaminophen and aspirin may increase the risk of kidney damage—a point to keep in mind when considering the combination drugs described below.

Contraindications.   Acetaminophen is contraindicated in individuals who have had an allergic reaction to it.

Precautions. Acetaminophen should be used with special care and only under the guidance of your doctor if you have liver or kidney impairment. Mild allergies produce a skin rash or hives; severe reactions may result in an anaphylactic reaction or a swelling of the vocal cords.

Acetaminophen is a common ingredient in many OTC medications, so you may be taking more of it than you (or your doctor) realize. Be sure your doctor knows about *all* the medications you are taking. That way he can monitor your total intake of acetaminophen. If acetaminophen does not provide adequate relief, resist the temptation to take larger or more frequent doses. Your physician may recommend something stronger instead.

Acetaminophen should not be used in combination with alcohol, barbiturates, or epilepsy, antianxiety, or anticoagulant drugs. In addition, oral contraceptives may reduce the effectiveness of acetaminophen.

Combination Products

Many OTC products for relief from dysmenorrhea are combinations of drugs such as aspirin and acetaminophen. Other substances are often included: caffeine, antihistamines, and diuretics. Combination products have not been shown to be more effective than aspirin or acetaminophen alone. Check the individual ingredients listed below to determine contraindications, side effects, and precautions.

Cope: buffered aspirin, caffeine
Femcaps: acetaminophen, caffeine, ephedrine sulfate, atropine sulfate
Midol: aspirin, caffeine, cinnamedrine
Mobigesic: magnesium salicylate, phenyltoloxamine
Pamprin: acetaminophen, pamabrom, pyrilamine maleate
Pamprin Maximum Cramp Relief Formula: acetaminophen, pamabrom, pyrilamine maleate
Premesin: acetaminophen, pamabrom, pyrilamine maleate
Sunril Premenstrual: acetaminophen, pamabrom, pyrilamine maleate
Trendar: acetaminophen, pamabrom

NONSTEROIDAL ANTI-INFLAMMATORY AGENTS

Anti-inflammatory agents relieve pain and inflammation by blocking the synthesis of prostaglandins (see·Chapter 1). They are effective against the pain of dysmenorrhea caused by endometriosis in as many as 80 percent of women. The effects, however, are inconsistent. Pain relief may be incomplete because the pain of endometriosis appears to involve other factors in addition to prostaglandins.

Nevertheless, in one study of the effectiveness of NSAIAs against moderate to severe pain caused by endometriosis, 83 percent of patients obtained complete or substantial relief with no significant side effects when treated with an NSAIA called naproxen sodium, as opposed to 41 percent treated with placebos. The normal activities of women taking naproxen sodium were less likely to be disrupted by pain than were those of women treated with placebos. No significant side effects were reported in the study.[2]

A variety of NSAIAs, originally developed to treat severe arthritis, have been approved for the treatment of dysmenorrhea. Of these, only ibuprofen (Advil or Nuprin) is available without a prescription.

Ibuprofen (Motrin, Rufin)
Mefanamic acid (Ponstel)
Naproxen (Naprosyn)
Naproxen sodium (Anaprox)

NSAIAs effective in the treatment of mild to moderate pain (though not specifically for dysmenorrhea) are

Fenoprofen calcium (Nalfon, Nalfon 200)
Diflunisal (Dolobid)

Sometimes prescribed for patients with dysmenorrhea, although approved only for arthritis, is a group of drugs that are an undesirable form of treatment for most women with dysmenorrhea. They have a higher incidence of severe side effects that are sometimes dangerous.

Indomethacin (Indocin, Indocin 200)
Tolmetin sodium (Tolectin)
Meclofenamate sodium (Meclomen)
Piroxicam (Feldene)
Sulindac (Clinoril)
Phenylbutazone (Azolid, Butazolidin, Phenylbutazone)

Finding an NSAIA that will relieve your symptoms may be a matter of trial and error. Although most NSAIAs approved for dysmenorrhea are equally effective, you may respond to one but not another. For you, one may produce side effects, another may not. If an NSAIA is ineffective, or if you have a bad reaction, ask your doctor to prescribe another. Don't give up if the first one you try fails to ease your pain.

Side Effects

There are many side effects, but most are associated with regular use of these drugs (for arthritis). For relief of dysmenorrhea, however, intermittent use (a few days a month) produces only minimal side effects which often can be eliminated, or at least diminished, by reducing the dosage. A mild allergy to NSAIAs may cause itching or a rash; a strong allergic reaction, on the other hand, may bring on an asthma attack or serious anaphylactic reaction. Women allergic to aspirin are more likely to be allergic to NSAIAs as well. General side effects are:

abdominal pain	heart palpitations
anemia	hepatitis
anorexia	inflammation of the lining of the mouth and
bleeding, prolonged	tongue
blood in the urine	insomnia
bronchial spasms	irritability
chest pain	nasal congestion
constipation and diarrhea	nausea and vomiting
depression	pain upon urination
dizziness, vertigo, and lightheadedness	rapid heartbeat
drowsiness	skin discoloration, eruptions, rashes, and
fluid retention	itching
gastrointestinal bleeding	sweating
hair loss	swelling of arms or legs
headache	thirst
hearing disorders (tinnitus)	ulcers, aggravated
heartburn and indigestion	vision disturbances

For additional side effects, consult the *Physicians' Desk Reference*, check the manufacturer's package insert, or ask your physician or pharmacist.

Contraindications and Precautions

NSAIAs may cause peptic ulcers or gastrointestinal bleeding as well as liver and kidney damage. They are contraindicated for individuals who have had a previous allergic reaction to NSAIAs or aspirin: an asthma attack, inflamed nasal passages, wheals or hives, itching, or a drop in blood pressure.

NSAIAs should be used with caution in individuals with kidney or liver disease, fluid retention, or a history of gastrointestinal lesions. Furthermore, NSAIAs should be used only for relief of transient pain. If dysmenorrhea persists throughout the cycle, the advisability of regular use of these prostaglandin inhibitors is questionable. More aggressive treatment is probably necessary.

Prostaglandin inhibitors may cause liver or kidney damage. Be alert for the signs of kidney damage: increased or decreased amount or frequency of urination, change in color of urine, and back pain. Also watch for signs of liver damage: sore throat, fever, bruising easily, and jaundice. Moreover, never take different kinds of NSAIAs together, unless directed to do so by your physician.

ORAL CONTRACEPTIVES

As explained in Chapter 1, dysmenorrhea tends to occur only with exposure to progesterone during ovulatory cycles. Oral contraceptives administered cyclically reduce progesterone production, which results in a thinner endometrium; therefore, they may suppress endometriosis and prevent its progression. (See Chapter 2.) This is still only speculation. However, it has been demonstrated that women with mild endometriosis have spent more time on oral contraceptives prior to its diagnosis than have women with severe endometriosis.[3] Side effects and risks associated with oral contraceptives are discussed in Chapter 6.

NARCOTICS

When mild analgesics and NSAIAs are ineffective, a potent narcotic pain reliever is sometimes prescribed. Narcotic analgesics include morphine, codeine, opium, opium derivatives, and similar synthetic substances. These powerful drugs work by reducing the transmission of pain impulses and by altering your perception of pain and your emotional response to it.

If your pain is that severe, or if it persists beyond menstruation, you should consider aggressive treatment of the disease itself, rather than simply trying to control your symptoms with narcotics.

Some of the more commonly prescribed narcotics and their ingredients are

Anacin with Codeine #3:   codeine
Empirin #2, #3, and #4:   codeine
Tylenol #1, #2, #3:   codeine
Darvocet-N, Darvon, Darvon-N, Darvon Compound: propoxyphene
Wygesic: propoxyphene
Percodan, Percocet: oxycodone
Tylox: oxycodone
Demerol: meperidene

Tolerance and Dependence

Many people are uneasy about narcotic use because they fear drug dependence, but often they confuse dependence with tolerance. Drug tolerance means that the body becomes accustomed to regular use of a particular drug and consequently is less responsive to that drug. In order to sustain the same level of relief from pain, a patient may require larger or more frequent doses. However, the patient can stop taking the drug without any ill effect except the return of pain; she is not dependent on the drug physically or emotionally. Continued use of increasing doses, however, may lead to physical or emotional dependence.

Psychological dependence (habituation), in contrast, is an emotional response—an overwhelming desire for a drug for its ability to produce euphoria and diminish emotional distress.

Physical dependence (addiction) may result from tolerance or psychological dependence if a drug is used in greater amounts or is administered with increasing frequency. The body accommodates itself to the regular use of the narcotic. Body chemistry is altered by the drug to the degree that the body needs the influence of the drug in order to function normally. If the drug is withdrawn after several weeks of regular use, the body must readjust, and withdrawal symptoms, both physical and emotional, occur.

The point to be understood here, however, is that both addiction and tolerance are associated with continuous, rather than occasional, use of a drug. Therefore, neither is likely to occur as a result of narcotics used only several days a month for dysmenorrhea. A history of drug or alcohol abuse strongly indicates a likelihood of becoming psychologically dependent. If you are, or were, dependent on a drug, and if non-narcotic analgesics fail to control you pain, discuss it honestly with your physician, who may be able to suggest an alternative.

Side Effects, Risks, and Precautions

Narcotics may produce nausea or vomiting, which, if severe, will be treated with drugs called antiemetics. Constipation, another common side effect, may require the use of a laxative. Other side effects include drowsiness, dizziness, difficulty concentrating, and euphoria (elevated mood) and dysphoria (negative mood). Many narcotics contain aspirin or acetaminophen and therefore produce the side effects associated with those drugs as well. Additional side effects are

anaphylaxis	heart rate changes
anorexia	insomnia
blood pressure changes	lethargy
depressed respiration	reduced libido
breathing difficulties	sedation
dizziness, lightheadedness, and fainting	skin rashes, hives, and itching
dry mouth	temperature changes
excitability and delirium	urinary retention
fluid retention	wheezing
headache	

Two major risks can occur with any narcotic: dependency, as discussed above, and overdose, which can be fatal. Ask your doctor about the specific risks of any narcotic he may prescribe. Follow his instructions precisely. Pay special attention to information concerning food, drug, and alcohol interactions. If the dosage prescribed is ineffective, consult your doctor. Never increase the dosage or take additional medications simultaneously on your own.

ANTIDEPRESSANTS AND ANTIANXIETY MEDICATIONS

Chronic pain results in stress, anxiety, and depression. These in turn exacerbate the pain. An insidious cycle develops; pain leads to increased tension and despair, which results in still more pain, which generates greater depression, and so on. To make matters worse, any of these elements may contribute to sleeplessness, which further aggravates the pain and the anxiety. The cycle has the effect of a whirlpool, pulling patients under, despite all their efforts to hold their ground. To break this cycle, some doctors prescribe antidepressants such as Elavil, or antianxiety medications (tranquilizers) such as Valium, Librium, Ativan, and Paxipam.

These drugs have great potential for misuse and abuse. However, under certain circumstances, and when used with care under the guidance of your physician, they can significantly reduce tension, depression, and pain. They reduce the emotional component of pain and allow the patient to take constructive measures against physical discomfort. Unfortunately, they are sometimes prescribed by doctors who believe that pelvic pain is a manifestation of emotional stress or instability (see Chapter 4). If your doctor recommends antidepressants or antianxiety agents, be sure they are intended to complement, not replace, a comprehensive approach to the management of pain. In addition, be aware that antidepressants and antianxiety agents are intended to be used for a limited amount of time; long-term use can prove hazardous. Clearly, misuse is serious, so pay special attention to information concerning interactions, and follow your doctor's instructions. Contraindications, side effects, risks, and precautions depend on the specific drug prescribed. Ask your physician or consult the *Physicians' Desk Reference.*

With an expectant approach to the management of symptoms related to endometriosis, follow-up is especially important. Schedule regular appointments with your doctor so he can determine the effectiveness of the approach and monitor your condition. If this approach does not adequately relieve your symptoms, or if your condition worsens, hormonal treatment is usually the next step.

6

Hormonal Treatment: Suppression

Many physicians initially prefer hormonal therapy, the most popular treatment for all but the most severe cases of endometriosis today. Because endometriosis often regresses during pregnancy and menopause, hormone treatment chemically replicates the hormonal environment that prevails during those states.

The rationale for the use of hormones is that ectopic endometrium, in theory, functions in a manner similar to normal endometrium; therefore it should respond to hormonal stimulation in a similar fashion. If the hormonal environment of pregnancy or menopause leads to a regression or atrophy of the endometrium, then a simulation of that hormonal milieu should produce the same results in the ectopic endometrium.

In practice, however, endometriosis responds inconsistently to hormonal treatment. Some women experience symptomatic relief and regression of the disease, others do not respond at all, and a minority worsen.

Like pregnancy and menopause, hormonal treatments do not cure endometriosis. The benefits of suppression and regression are temporary, and the disease typically persists when treatments are suspended. To extend the period of remission, physicians often advise those patients who do not wish to conceive immediately to follow hormone regimens with the cyclical use of oral contraceptives. Those who do want children, however, are typically advised to try to conceive as soon as possible after treatment. If endometriosis persists following hormonal treatment, patients may be given a second or even a third course of hormonal therapy. If these are ineffective, surgery is usually suggested.

Even though they don't cure endometriosis, hormones are used to provide symptomatic relief, to cause regression and thereby enhance fertility, and to suppress progression of endometriosis in women who, although they may have no immediate desire for childbearing, want to forestall surgery. In addition, hormones are used as a precursor or follow-up to surgery and to treat recurrences.

76

ANDROGENS

Androgens are male hormones that, when given to females, inhibit the release of gonadotropins and prevent the secretion of follicle stimulating hormone (FSH) and luteinizing hormone (LH). As you recall from Chapter 1, without FSH and LH, ovulation does not take place, and the endometrium is not instructed to proliferate.

Androgens, in the form of testosterone or methyltestosterone, are administered sublingually (under the tongue), generally in doses of 5 to 10 mg daily for six months. Androgens have produced symptomatic improvement in patients with endometriosis; however, following discontinuance, recurrence of symptoms is often swift. These pregnancy rates of 11 to 19 percent are not considered impressive.[1] Furthermore, androgen treatment does not consistently block ovulation, so pregnancy during treatment is possible, and fetal abnormalities may occur. Androgen treatment can produce potentially irreversible masculinizing side effects, such as hirsutism (excessive hair growth), hoarseness, deepening of the voice, reduced breast size, and enlargement of the clitoris.

Androgens have been used to treat endometriosis for decades and are still used by some doctors. But, with the advent of more effective and less problematic treatments, their use has fallen out of favor and they are prescribed less commonly today.

ESTROGENS

Synthetic estrogens, one of the earliest treatments of endometriosis, were first used in 1948 to simulate the hormonal environment of pregnancy. Doses of estrogens such as DES (diethylstilbestrol), beginning at 1 mg and adjusted upward to as high as 400 mg a day for three to nine months, brought about relief of symptoms in most patients. It effectively halted the progression of the disease and resulted in a 25 percent pregnancy rate. But 27 percent of women experienced a recurrence of symptoms at an average of eighteen months later.[2] Multiple and sometimes severe side effects included severe nausea, breakthrough bleeding, weight gain, breast tenderness, vaginal discharge, anaplastic endometrial hyperplasia, and uterine hemorrhage. DES has subsequently been shown to increase a user's risk of vaginal, cervical, and breast cancers and to produce reproductive tract abnormalities in the sons and daughters of women who took the drug. In the wake of these devastating consequences, estrogen regimens, like androgens, have been discarded in favor of newer treatments.

PSEUDOPREGNANCY: ESTROGEN/PROGESTERONE ORAL CONTRACEPTIVES

The continuous use of estrogen/progestogen oral contraceptives was once the first line of treatment for women with endometriosis. It has since taken a backseat to newer treatments but is still prescribed by many physicians today.

Dr. Robert Kistner, a gynecologist in Boston who pioneered the use of combination therapy for endometriosis in 1958, called the regimen "pseudopregnancy." It was designed to simulate the hormonal status achieved by pregnancy—a state dominated by increased blood levels of progesterone and estrogen.

Combination therapy works by inhibiting the hypothalamic-pituitary axis, thereby halting the cyclic stimulation of the endometrium and eliminating ovulation and menstruation. Just as the proliferation of the endometrium is suppressed, the growth of ectopic endometrium is prevented, thereby reducing the potential for swelling, bleeding, and inflammation.

Estrogen/progestogen oral contraceptives include the following

Brevicon	Norlestrin
Demulen 1/35	Norlestrin FE
Demulen 1/50	Ortho-Novum 1/35
Enovid 5 mg	Ortho-Novum 1/50
Enovid 10 mg	Ortho-Novum 7/7/7
Loestrin	Ortho-Novum 10/11
Lo/Ovral	Ortho-Novum 2 mg
Modicon	Ovcon-35, 50
Nordette	Ovral
Norinyl 1 + 35	Ovulen
Norinyl 1 + 50	Tri-Norinyl
Norinyl 2 mg	Trephasil

Dosage and Administration

Although there are many combination pills, Enovid is the most widely used in the treatment of endometriosis. When used for contraception, combination pills are taken for three weeks each month, followed by one pill-free week. As treatment for endometriosis, however, they are taken every day without interruption. The dosage is normally a 5 or 10 mg tablet taken daily, beginning on the fifth day of the menstrual cycle and continuing for two weeks or until breakthrough bleeding occurs. At the end of every two weeks or each new episode of breakthrough bleeding, the daily dosage is increased by 5 or 10 mg until the total dose is 20 mg a day. If breakthrough bleeding occurs, the total daily dose may be raised as high as 40 mg a day. Treatment may continue for six to twelve months, and, upon discontinuance, ovulation and menstruation generally resume in four to eight weeks.

Relief, Regression, and Recurrence

Pseudopregnancy offers relief from dysmenorrhea and pelvic pain in more than 80 percent of patients,[3] about half experiencing partial and half complete amelioration of symptoms. Pseudopregnancy produces an initial proliferation and softening of ectopic endometrium in the first weeks or even months of therapy. During that period many women experience an initial aggravation of symptoms. For most, symptomatic relief follows; for some, aggravation continues. In addition, this initial growth and softening can lead to a spontaneous rupture of an endometrioma and the subsequent spread of disease as the contents are spilled into the pelvic cavity.

Resolution of endometriosis following pseudopregnancy is variable and incomplete. Objective improvement occurs in 30 to 50 percent of patients treated.[4]

Recurrence rates are not well established, but are said to range between 16[5] and 62[6] percent of patients. Rates are highest in the first year following treatment.

Pregnancy

Although pregnancy rates following pseudopregnancy are said to fall between 20 to 50 percent,[7] the effects on fertility are not well documented. It appears that combination therapy is not promising when compared against other hormonal or surgical methods.

Side Effects and Risks

Common side effects—severe enough to cause many women to discontinue treatment—include:

bleeding between periods	rash
breast tenderness	vaginal discharge
candidiasis (yeast infections)	vomiting
headaches	weight gain
nausea	

Less common side effects include:

acne	dizziness
aggravation of myopia or astigmatism	fluid retention
appetite changes	galactorrhea
abdominal pain	hyperglycemia
anorexia	intolerance to contact lenses
bowel constriction	jaundice
bloating	libido changes
cervical erosion	pancreatitis (inflammation of the pancreas)
constipation	seborrhea
depression	skin discoloration/redness, rash, oiliness
diarrhea	worsening of migraines or asthma

If you experience any of these effects during pseudopregnancy therapy, contact your doctor to see if a change in dosage would help.

The formation of blood clots is a serious risk associated with the use of oral contraceptives. They can occur in the limbs, lungs, brain, heart, eyes, and abdomen, as well as elsewhere in the body, and can lead to stroke, heart attack, or pulmonary embolism (a clot that travels to the lungs)—all of which can be fatal. Although extremely rare, this is the most common serious adverse reaction. The risk increases with age and may persist even after the pill is stopped.

If accidentally taken during an unsuspected pregnancy, birth defects may occur. Other risks include enlargement of fibroid tumors, gallbladder disease, hypertension, liver tumors that may rupture and bleed, and vision disorders.

It has been suggested, but not confirmed, that the estrogen in oral contraceptives may increase the risk of breast and certain genital cancers. Research findings have been contradictory. Most researchers believe there is no evidence of increased risk. It has also been suggested that the use of oral contraceptives may decrease one's risk of developing ovarian and endometrial cancers.

Contraindications and Precautions

Combined oral contraceptives are contraindicated for women who smoke and for women over forty. They should not be used by those who have

- known or suspected cancer of the breast (past or present)
- known or suspected estrogen-dependent neoplasia
- benign or malignant liver tumors (past or present) that developed during the use of oral contraceptives or other estrogen- containing products
- a history of stroke, heart attack, or chest pain upon exertion
- thrombophlebitis or thromboembolic (blood clots or clotting) disorders (past or present)
- undiagnosed abnormal genital bleeding

Combination therapy should be used with caution by patients with the following conditions. Frequent monitoring is mandatory.

asthma	jaundice
diabetes	kidney, heart, or gallbladder disease
fibroid tumors	lupus
high cholesterol levels	mental depression
history of epilepsy	metabolic bone disease
hypertension	migraines

Discontinue the pill and contact your doctor immediately if you experience any of the following reactions during pseudopregnancy therapy:

breast lumps	severe leg or chest pain
coughing of blood	severe or persistent pain in the abdomen

difficulty breathing	swelling of hands or feet
dizziness or fainting	vaginal bleeding or discharge
jaundice	vision or speech disturbances
severe depression	vomiting
severe headaches	weakness, numbness, or pain in the arm or leg

As mentioned earlier, estrogen may increase one's risk of developing breast cancer and certain genital cancers. Therefore, women with a family history of such cancers, as well as those who have cystic breasts or who have had abnormal mammograms, should be monitored closely: breast exams and pap tests should be done every six months.

Cigarette smoking increases the risks of cardiovascular side effects. This risk is especially pronounced in women older than thirty-five and in those who smoke more than fifteen cigarettes a day. If you take oral contraceptives, don't smoke!

Advantages and Disadvantages

Pseudopregnancy therapy is inexpensive. Moreover, suppression is useful in "buying time" before pregnancy or surgery, and it avoids the risks of surgery.

On the other hand, side effects are more severe, more common, and more hazardous than those of most other currently used hormonal therapies. The softened ectopic endometrium that may result can lead to a rupture of endometriomas. In sum, benefits are temporary, recurrence rates high, regression incomplete, and response variable.

PSEUDOMENOPAUSE: DANAZOL

Danazol is a synthetic androgen (a derivative of the male hormone testosterone). Today it is the staple in the treatment of mild and moderate endometriosis. Although it frequently produces unpleasant and occasionally severe side effects, it effectively reduces symptoms and produces a temporary regression of pelvic and extrapelvic lesions in many women.

Synthesized at the Sterling-Winthrop Research Institute in 1963, danazol was first used to treat endometriosis by Dr. Robert Greenblatt and colleagues in 1971. In their study of more than forty patients they observed symptomatic improvement in more than 90 percent. Evidence of regression was seen in more than 50 percent.[8] Since that time, danazol has been studied extensively. It was given FDA approval for the treatment of endometriosis in 1976. Danazol is marketed in the United States under the brand name Danocrine, and in Canada it is sold as Cyclomen.

Danazol is believed to work on several levels. Essentially it throws a wrench into the feedback mechanism described in Chapter 1. The proliferation and subsequent shedding of the endometrium is the end result of communication between components of the hypothalamic-pituitary-ovarian axis. Danazol circumvents the pituitary's production of gonadotropins. Follicle stimulating hormone (FSH) and luteinizing hormone (LH) are suppressed, preventing ovulation and the increased production of progesterone. As a result, levels of both estrogen and progesterone remain consistently low, and the uterine and ectopic endometrium are not stimulated to proliferate. Since there is no endometrial buildup, there is no debris to be shed, and menstruation does not occur. Similarly, since the growth of ectopic endometrium is suppressed, there is no bleeding or inflammation to produce symptoms.

Thus, danazol is known as an antigonadotropin, and the regimen is called pseudomenopause, because it simulates the very low levels of estrogen that characterize menopause.

But danazol does more than inhibit the production of gonadotropins; it is thought to work directly at the site of endometriotic lesions to cause regression. In addition, danazol may diminish the synthesis of prostaglandins by ectopic endometrium and may also have some effect on the immune system, suppressing some of the antibody formation observed in women with endometriosis.[9]

Dosage and Administration

Since danazol has not been shown to be safe during pregnancy, it's important that treatment be started at the beginning of the cycle to rule out an unsuspected pregnancy. Danazol treatment normally eliminates ovulation and menstruation, but women are advised to use a barrier-type contraceptive throughout treatment.

Dosage of danazol is a matter of some controversy. Until recently, the standard dosage of danazol was 800 mg per day, administered in a dose of 200 mg four times daily, beginning on day 1 of the menstrual cycle. Researchers have been investigating the effectiveness of lower doses, from 100 to 600 mg per day, but results have been somewhat contradictory. Studies suggest that lower doses appear to be less consistently successful at inhibiting ovulation and menstruation and thus lead to a less complete regression of disease. Nevertheless, many of these studies suggest that doses of less than 400 mg per day may be adequate in mild cases, doses of 400 mg per day may be sufficient for most cases, and doses of up to 800 mg a day may be necessary for many cases of moderate, and most cases of severe, disease.

Danazol's effectiveness appears to be related to its ability to create amenorrhea— evidence of ovarian suppression and anovulation. As a result, many physicians now recommend starting danazol at 800 mg per day, followed by a reduction to the lowest dose at which amenorrhea can be maintained. Conversely, others advocate an initial dose of 400 mg daily, to be increased if breakthrough bleeding occurs. Since side effects appear to be somewhat dose-related, the effort to find the lowest dose at which amenorrhea can be maintained may improve tolerance of the drug. In addition, since danazol is very expensive, lower doses can significantly reduce the cost of treatment.

The length of danazol treatment, which depends upon the severity of the disease, generally ranges from three to nine months. For patients with mild disease and no endometriomas, three to four months of treatment are required; for patients with moderate endometriosis and small endometriomas, six to nine months. Severe endometriosis, particularly when large endometriomas and dense adhesions are present, is usually only partially responsive to danazol treatment. It often must be eradicated surgically following pseudomenopause.[10]

Treatment may be continued longer unless side effects prove too severe. (Danazol has been used for as long as thirty-six months with no substantial increase in side effects.)[11] Menstruation and ovulation usually cease by the second month of treatment and resume promptly, generally within four to six weeks, following discontinuation of treatment.

Relief, Regression, and Recurrence

Relief of symptoms, experienced by more than 90 percent of women,[12] is often swift and marked, usually occurring in the first month of treatment. According to some studies, danazol is more effective in relieving dysmenorrhea than dyspareunia, possibly because nodularity in the rectovaginal septum and uterosacral ligaments (see Chapter 4), which often gives rise to dyspareunia, is frequently unresponsive to danazol.

Regression of lesions, as observed upon second-look laparoscopy (see Chapter 4), has been noted in 70 to 95 percent.[13] Danazol effectively eradicates small lesions and implants and may shrink, but does not eliminate, large endometriomas.[14] It is also ineffective against preexisting adhesions and scar tissue. Danazol, therefore, is most effective in cases of mild and moderate disease, and seldom effective in cases of severe disease, especially when ovarian endometriomas, dense adhesions, tubal occlusion, and rectovaginal nodularity are present.

Some physicians caution patients to wait one complete cycle before trying to conceive. Fetal death has been reported by some investigators when conception occurred in the first month following treatment.[15] Others see no evidence of danger and suggest patients attempt to conceive immediately.

Rates of recurrence reported in the medical literature range from 10 to 60 percent. The average time between the end of treatment and recurrence is fifteen months. Women who conceived following treatment, however, have half the recurrence rate and a much longer average time until recurrence.[16] In one study, recurrence has been associated with the severity of the disease; severe disease may recur twice as often as minimal disease.

Recurrent or persistent disease may be treated with additional courses of danazol. However, experts caution that, if the disease fails to resolve or recurs early, other approaches should be considered.[17]

Pregnancy

Pregnancy rates following danazol treatment range from about 40 to 83 percent.[18] Rates are generally higher than those achieved with pseudopregnancy and comparable to those following expectant therapy. Reports comparing conception rates following danazol to rates following conservative surgery for women with mild or moderate endometriosis have been somewhat contradictory: some suggest comparable results, while others give an edge to conservative surgery. Reports concerning the effect of varying dosages on conception rates are inconclusive. Conception most commonly takes place within six months following discontinuation of treatment.

Side Effects and Risks

The side effects of danazol, *some of which* are experienced by about 85 percent of women, are as follows:

- Androgenic effects
    acne
    clitoral growth (rare)
    decrease in breast size
    deepening of the voice
    fluid retention
    mild hirsutism
    oiliness of hair or skin
    weight gain (usually less than ten pounds)

- Hypoestrogenic effects
    hot flashes
    irritability
    mood swings
    nervousness
    sweating
    vaginitis (itching, dryness, burning, bleeding)

- Hepatic effects
    jaundice
    liver dysfunction

- Allergic effects
    nasal congestion (rare)
    skin rashes

- Central nervous system effects
    anxiety
    burning or tingling in the limbs (rare)
    changes in appetite
    chills
    depression
    dizziness
    fatigue
    headache
    nervousness
    sleep disorders
    weakness

tremor
visual disturbances

- Gastrointestinal effects
  constipation
  gastroenteritis (inflammation of the stomach and intestines)
  nausea
  vomiting

- Musculoskeletal effects
  joint lock-up
  joint swelling
  muscle spasms and cramps
  pain in back, legs, or neck

- Genitourinary effects
  hematuria (blood in the urine) (rare)

- Other effects
  abnormal glucose tolerance test and increased insulin needs in diabetics
  carpal tunnel syndrome (compression of median nerve in the wrist causing pain,
     tingling, or numbness in the fingers or arm)
  increased blood pressure
  hair loss
  pelvic pain (rare)

Side effects related to the drug's hypoestrogenic effect normally cease upon discontinuation of therapy; side effects related to the drug's androgenic properties, however, may be
irreversible, even after discontinuing treatment. Therefore, if you take danazol, monitor
yourself for androgenic side effects and report any such changes to your physician so that he
may adjust the dosage.

Many of these side effects are related to fluid retention, and some women have found
relief by decreasing or eliminating their salt intake or by using diuretics. If you experience
side effects, ask your doctor if diuretics would be appropriate for you. In addition, muscle
cramps may be alleviated somewhat by increasing your consumption of foods containing
potassium. Lubricants and certain medicated douches can help to relieve vaginal dryness.

It has been suggested that the side effects may be somewhat dose-related, but studies
have produced contradictory results; some show no difference in side effects at low and high
doses, while others suggest that side effects are diminished with lower doses.

Reactions to the drug vary from woman to woman. Some sing its praises while others
are less charitable.

"Danazol brought on a severe rash. After cutting the dose in half, I was fine for a few months, but then I felt I was on "speed'. I couldn't sleep, was never tired, didn't eat, and felt very jumpy."

"I've been taking the drug now for six months and it has been quite effective. The doctor can no longer feel anything during a pelvic exam and the pain has been almost completely eliminated. I have had some side effects, none serious. The worst has been weight gain of about ten pounds."

In addition to the discomfort brought about by the side effects themselves, there may be a certain psychosocial impact associated with some of these effects. Acne, weight gain, hirsutism, and decrease in breast size, for example, can be damaging to a woman's self-image, self-esteem, and feelings about femininity, which in many instances have already been eroded by chronic disease, sexual difficulties, and infertility.

"Taking danazol makes me feel less feminine, like an "it'."

"Being on danazol means no periods, which makes me feel less feminine, but it's worth it because it relieves the pain."

"I feel fat and ugly and I haven't been able to lose all the weight I gained from danazol. This has been a burden. After being thin and attractive, it's hard to handle. No one, not even my husband, believes the weight gain is from treatment. Exercising is helping a little, but my self-image is in trouble."

Although these side effects and their emotional component can be troublesome, some physicians feel that their colleagues overstate the negative aspects. Says Dr. Dmowski, "The potential side effects should be viewed in the context of the benefits of the drug." Overestimation of these side effects, he claims, tends to frighten patients into taking medications or undergoing therapies that actually may be more hazardous for them.

Although the risks of long-term use of danazol are unknown, therapeutic use for endometriosis sometimes causes the following temporary effects:

changes in liver function	exacerbation of diabetes and alteration of insulin
jaundice	requirements
hepatitis	worsening of epilepsy, migraine, heart or kidney function

Contraindications and Precautions

Danazol should not be used by patients with undiagnosed abnormal genital bleeding, who are pregnant or breastfeeding, or who have serious liver, kidney, or heart impairments.

Since some androgenic side effects may not be reversible, monitor yourself for signs of viralization (development of masculine characteristics), such as increased hair growth or a deeper voice. To monitor effects on the liver, periodic liver function tests should be performed at follow-up exams. Women with epilepsy, migraines, or impaired heart or kidney function should be monitored carefully.

Danazol increases the effects of anticoagulants (blood-thinning drugs), which can cause hemorrhage. Patients taking these medications require careful monitoring and follow-up.

Although it is unlikely that pregnancy will occur while on danazol therapy, use a barrier method of contraception, since danazol has not been proven safe for use during pregnancy.

Advantages and Disadvantages

Danazol avoids the risks and expenses of surgery and can be useful in "buying time" before surgery is needed. It provides a quick return of menstrual function, which is important for women eager to conceive and, when used preoperatively it may facilitate surgery. Danazol treatment may result in pregnancy rates comparable to those following conservative surgery.

Danazol provides better symptomatic relief and regression of disease than pseudopregnancy. It offers a greater likelihood of conception, with less hazardous side effects.

Danazol is very expensive, however. One month's treatment can cost $275, and insurance reimbursement is inconsistent. Furthermore, benefits are temporary and recurrences frequent. The length of treatment, moreover, is a drawback for women eager to conceive.

While danazol often leads to the regression of small lesions and implants, it has little effect on large endometriomas, dense adhesions, and tubal occlusion. Patients with this type of involvement will likely require conservative surgery.

Danozol's long-term effects are unknown.

PROGESTINS

Progestins (or progestogens)—synthetic forms of progesterone that inhibit gonadotropin secretion—are commonly used by women who, for one reason or another, cannot tolerate other hormonal treatments. The following progestins are available.

Medroxyprogesterone acetate: Amen, Curretab, Depo-Provera, Provera
Norethindrone: Micronor, Norlutin, Nor-QD
Norethindrone acetate: Aygestin, Norlutate

Dosage and Administration

Although no longer approved by the FDA for the treatment of endometriosis, medroxyprogesterone acetate (MPA) is the most commonly prescribed progestin. Administered orally, it is known as Provera, and is generally given in doses of 30 mg daily (10 mg three times a day) for three to twelve months. The dosage may be increased if breakthrough bleeding occurs and reduced again once the bleeding stops. When administered through a long-acting injection, MPA is known as Depo-Provera. Dosages are generally 100 to 200 mg injected intramuscularly every two weeks for two or three months, followed by 200 to 400 mg injected every month for up to a year.

Relief, Regression, and Recurrence

Symptomatic improvement has been reported in 57 to 96 percent of patients.[19] Regression has been observed in 40 to 60 percent. Recurrences have occurred in 9 to 40 percent of women.[20]

Pregnancy

Pregnancy occurs in 5 to 90 percent, with an average of approximately 50 percent.[21] However, since the resumption of menstrual function is delayed, progestin therapy is an unlikely first choice for women desiring to conceive.

Side Effects and Risks

Since many side effects of estrogen-progesterone therapy are caused by estrogen, side effects from progestin therapy are less severe and generally well tolerated. The most common include breakthrough bleeding, edema (water retention), weight gain, and acne, and these are sometimes controlled by the addition of Delestrogen, an estrogen. Other side effects are listed below:

abdominal cramps	hyperglycemia
acne	jaundice
breakthrough bleeding	lethargy
breast enlargement, tenderness, or secretion	migraine
candidiasis	nausea
decreased libido	rash
depression	skin discoloration
dizziness	vaginal discharge
fluid retention	vomiting
hives	weight gain

With Depo-Provera, soreness or infection at the site of injection may occur.

The following risks have been associated with the use of progestins:

altered glucose tolerance	fibroids
birth defects (if taken accidentally during unsuspected pregnancy)	hypertension
	pulmonary embolism
changes in lipid metabolism	thrombophlebitis
edema	

The use of Depo-Provera in laboratory animals has been linked to the development of breast nodules and malignancies and to uterine cancer; and there is some concern as to whether or not a woman's risk of endometrial or breast cancer is increased through use of this drug. In addition, use of Depo-Provera is associated with a delay of months or even years in the resumption of menstrual function and ovulation. Less commonly, menstrual function may never resume, rendering women sterile.

Contraindications and Precautions

Progestin therapy is contraindicated in individuals who smoke cigarettes, who have a history of breast or genital cancers, a history of thromboembolic disorders (blood clots, stroke), severe liver disease, and undiagnosed abnormal vaginal bleeding.

Women with the following conditions should be monitored regularly during progestin therapy:

asthma	mental illness
diabetes	migraines
heart disease	seizures

Patients on progestin therapy should get regular Pap tests and breast exams and should perform breast self-examination monthly. If you experience any of the following, discontinue the drug and contact your doctor:

fainting or blackout	sudden weakness or paralysis of any part of the body
migraines	
pain or tenderness in the thigh or leg	swelling of the foot, ankle, or leg
severe dizziness	visual disturbances (blurred vision, double vision, flashing lights)
speech impairments	

Advantages and Disadvantages

Progestin therapy is a useful alternative for women with contraindications to oral contraceptives or danazol. Its side effects are generally mild and tolerable, and it is less expensive than danazol therapy.

The delay in menstrual function return is a particularly distressing factor for women eager to conceive. When Provera is used, menstrual function may take as long as a year to resume. When Depo-Provera, the injectable form, is used, menstrual function may never resume. Consider that, with the use of Depo-Provera, you cannot simply stop taking the medication if side effects or adverse reactions occur, since it has been injected and its effects are long-acting.

MEDICAL OOPHORECTOMY: GnRH ANALOGUES

The newest weapons in the hormonal arsenal against endometriosis are the promising gonadotropin-releasing hormone (GnRH) analogues, which have been in experimental use for more than five years. GnRH analogues (also known as luteinizing hormone-releasing hormone analogues, or LH-RH) are drugs similar in chemical structure to the naturally occurring gonadotropin-releasing hormone. There are two types of analogues—antagonists and agonists. They are being investigated as a possible form of contraception, as well as for the treatment of prostatic cancer, fibrocystic breast disease, premenstrual syndrome, precocious puberty, hirsutism, acne, and infertility. Although antagonists may be used increasingly for endometriosis, to date research has centered on the use of agonists.

As explained in Chapter 1, gonadotropin-releasing hormone, produced by the hypothalamus, triggers the secretion of the pituitary gonadotropin hormones—follicle stimulating hormone (FSH) and luteinizing hormone (LH)—which in turn regulate the secretion of ovarian hormones and control ovulation and menstruation.

Surprisingly, the administration of GnRH agonists—superpotent derivatives of GnRH—suppresses the release of FSH and LH and therefore inhibits ovulation and menstruation. GnRH agonists work in the following way. Normally, FSH and LH are released by the pituitary gland following pulsatile spurts of naturally occurring GnRH. Researchers have discovered that the continuous (non-pulsatile) administration of a GnRH agonist desensitizes the pituitary gland and leads, paradoxically, to the suppression of FSH and LH. Without these hormones, the ovaries are not instructed to secrete their hormones, ovulation does not occur, the endometrium does not proliferate, and, consequently, menstruation does not occur.

When administered by subcutaneous injection or nasal spray in doses of 500 to 1000 mg daily for up to six months, GnRH agonists have reduced the levels of ovarian hormones to levels found in women who have undergone surgical menopause—levels two to four times lower than those achieved with danazol. Upon discontinuation of treatment, ovulation and menstruation resume promptly.

Currently, GnRH analogues, although marketed for the treatment of prostatic cancer, generally are available only to those endometriosis patients participating in research studies. However, they are expected to be on the market in several years, pending FDA approval of their use for endometriosis.

Administration

In studies to date, GnRH agonists are administered primarily by subcutaneous injection. Nasal sprays have also been investigated, but nasal routes require much larger amounts of the drug. So far, a pill form has not been developed because the hormone would be digested before it could act. While a variety of methods, such as transdermal patches, are being researched, the most likely form of administration in the future is a sustained-release biodegradable implant with a fixed duration of action.

Relief, Regression, and Recurrence

Doses of 600 to 1200 mg a day for six to twelve months have brought prompt and near-complete symptomatic relief to women with endometriosis. Studies have shown a significant decrease in symptoms by the fourth week of treatment and maximal relief by the twelfth week. In most cases, complete regression of visible implants has been confirmed by laparoscopy following treatment: but microscopic studies reveal the presence of inactive residual disease.[22] Like danazol, GnRH agonists are more effective against superficial disease than against endometriomas and have no effect on preexisting adhesions and scar tissue.

Although treatment with GnRH agonists is too new to provide precise information about recurrence rates, it appears that the agonists, like other treatments, do not cure endometriosis but may effect temporary remissions. However, long-term treatment with minimal side effects may provide long-lasting relief.

Pregnancy rates associated with GnRH agonist treatment have not yet been established.

Side Effects and Risks

Hot flashes, headaches, and vaginal dryness, the most common effects associated with GnRH agonist treatment, are related to estrogen deficiency and may be controlled in the future with hormone replacement therapy.[23] Other side effects include breakthrough bleeding, decreased libido, mild breast swelling or tenderness, mild depression, and some swelling and inflammation at the injection site.

Some researchers have observed a decrease in bone mass, but effect on bone mass has not been thoroughly assessed. Other long-term effects are unknown, but it *appears* that treatment with GnRH agonists is a safe and well-tolerated therapeutic approach.

Advantages, Disadvantages, and Prognosis

When compared to danazol, GnRH agonists result in fewer and less severe side effects. The quick return of ovulation and menstruation is advantageous for women eager to conceive, and treatment can be expected to be less costly than danazol.

Like other hormonal treatments, GnRH agonists do not cure endometriosis, but effect temporary remissions. Like danazol, GnRH agonists appear to be ineffective in resolving large ovarian endometriomas and do not resolve preexisting adhesions and scar tissue. The risk of osteoporosis associated with long-term use needs further investigation.

Although GnRH agonists appear to have great potential in the treatment of endometriosis, much has yet to be learned. Animal research suggests that complete suppression of ovarian hormone levels may not be necessary to obtain symptomatic relief and regression of disease. Further investigation of the effects of partial suppression on humans is needed. Continued research, ongoing at a number of institutions across the country, is attempting to ascertain long-term effects, the likelihood of recurrences, effects on fertility, the best administration routes and dosages, potential side effects, and advantages and disadvantages over currently available hormonal treatments.

AFTER HORMONE THERAPY

Following hormone therapy, patients interested in childbearing are generally advised to conceive. Those who want to postpone childbearing are often advised to start using oral contraceptives cyclically. Sometimes infertility patients will be laparoscoped again to determine the effectiveness of treatment and the outlook for pregnancy. When symptoms persist following treatment, another course of hormone therapy, a different hormone therapy, or surgery may be advised.

7

Pregnancy as Therapy

"My doctor told me the cure was pregnancy, which I'm not prepared for, and didn't plan on—ever."

"The thing I found most frustrating was my doctor telling me to get pregnant—and I'm single."

"The pain of endometriosis lasted until the fourth month of my pregnancy and there was a great deal of pain during labor. By the time the baby was weaned, the endometriosis returned full force."

"My gynecologist suggested that I should try to achieve a pregnancy as soon as I can since this may help my condition. This has put a terrible strain on my husband and me to make a decision about having a family."

"After my pregnancy, my uterus was enlarged and endometriosis covered one ovary. When my baby was less than a year old, I had to have the ovary removed, since I now had family responsibilities and could not function with so much pain."

If a prescribed drug fails to bring relief, you can try something else. If your endometriosis persists after an operation, you will have faced the risks of surgery, and you will have a scar. But if you follow the advice still given by many doctors and have a baby to "cure" endometriosis, chances are you will have a baby...and endometriosis.

If having a baby is part of your life plan, and if you are emotionally, financially, and socially prepared for parenthood, it's reasonable to consider pregnancy. Otherwise, it's a high price to pay, since pregnancy seldom cures endometriosis. Nevertheless, many doctors advise it. With so much at stake, however, you need to differentiate between advice based on impression and speculation and a knowledgeable, thoughtful recommendation based on fact—or, at the very least, compelling evidence.

93

The idea that endometriosis may be "cured" by pregnancy appears to derive from the observation made by Dr. Joe Meigs in 1922 that the disease occurs more often in childless women. Putting aside the argument that many childless women with endometriosis are probably infertile as a result of the disease, Dr. Meigs suggested that endometriosis is often arrested during pregnancy and breastfeeding. These conditions lead the endometriotic cysts to shrink. However, he also indicated that after pregnancy and breastfeeding the cysts "begin to grow again much later in life" than they would have otherwise. He surmised that repeated pregnancies would keep the cysts small.[1]

In 1924, not long after this observation, Dr. John Sampson agreed that pregnancy "*may possibly* retard the future development" of endometriosis or "even cause the retrogression of any implants already present."[2]

These and other early reports on the benefits of pregnancy clearly were based on speculation. In 1943, for example, Dr. James Goodall suggested that early and frequent pregnancy *may* protect against endometriosis, but he warned that his position was based on opinion, belief, and impression rather than fact.[3] He also noted that his hypothesis could only be validated by "statistical studies," of which there were none. (There are still none today.)

Jumping ahead a decade, in 1952, Dr. Meigs concluded: "The best medical treatment for endometriosis is pregnancy. During pregnancy growth ceases and *occasionally*, during lactation, activity is absent." Interestingly, nowhere, in neither his early or later report, does he suggest that pregacy cures the condition; in both, he clearly indicates that endometriosis will persist after pregnancy. Dr. Meigs, himself an ardent proponent of preventive and therapeutic pregnancy, prefaced his views by observing that "the proof of the contention may be lacking but the trend always seems to be in that direction."[4]

Nevertheless, from these early equivocal observations arose the misconception that pregnancy and endometriosis are incompatible, and pregnancy, ever since, has been touted as a cure for the disease.

But, in fact, research dating back three decades indicates that pregnancy and endometriosis can, and frequently do, coexist. Moreover, it may forestall, but does not prevent, recurrent or persistent disease.

In 1965, Drs. Janet McArthur and Howard Ulfelder reviewed published case reports concerning the effect of pregnancy on endometriosis. Of fourteen cases in one report reviewed, only three patients experienced a loss or decrease of pain with pregnancy, while two reported an increase. Overall, in the total of twenty-four cases reviewed, endometriotic lesions tended to expand during the first trimester of pregnancy and regress during the second and third. However, upon follow-up, disappearance of endometriosis was the exception; persistent disease was the rule. The authors concluded:

The vagaries in the response of endometriotic implants to the hormonal stimulation of pregnancy parallel the variability which has been noted during the nonpregnant state in response to therapy with estrogens, androgens, and progestogens.... The impression that pregnancy exerts a consistent curative effect upon endometriosis is not supported by a critical analysis of the reported cases, and appears to be ill-founded.[5]

Twelve years later Dr. Leslie Walton reviewed the records of fifty pregnant women diagnosed with endometriosis at one hospital from 1970 to 1975. Of the fifty patients, twenty-eight had one or two previous pregnancies, eighteen had three to five pregnancies, and four had six to eight pregnancies. Twenty-two patients were more than nine years beyond their last pregnancy, nearly half were not more than five years beyond and half were less than two years beyond. After pregnancy, the sites and symptoms of endometriosis were unchanged. Dr. Walton concluded, "endometriosis retards the process of conception, but conception does not retard the progress of the disease."[6]

When pregnancy *is* beneficial, the period of benefit may last seven years or more; but, cautions one expert, "It should not be expected to last much beyond the duration of one or two ovulatory cycles after the resumption of menstruation, particularly in women who have inherited a propensity to develop endometriosis."[7]

Not only is pregnancy often only fleetingly beneficial, but it does not consistently provide relief: sometimes it worsens the disease. Endometriosis can progress during pregnancy, enlarging and softening endometriomas, posing the risk of rupture and the possibility of fatal hemorrhage. Dr. Brooks Ranney writes, "We have palpated cul-de-sac endometriomas which enlarge each month during pregnancy."[8] He also points out that patients have developed intestinal obstructions requiring cesarean section and surgical resection of endometriosis two weeks before term.

Despite the ambiguity of the early reports and subsequent evidence suggesting that the beneficial effects of pregnancy are temporary, gynecology textbooks as well as popular books and articles extol the curative value of pregnancy, with little indication of the transient nature of relief. In Walker's *Combined Textbook* of 1976, for example, the authors state: "It is well known that pregnancy has the effect of curing endometriosis but the mechanism of this is obscure."[9] Little wonder, then, that physicians, although less frequently than in past years, continue to "prescribe" pregnancy as treatment for their patients with endometriosis.

Apart from the questionable beneficial effects of pregnancy upon endometriosis, one problem is obvious. Many women inclined to consider pregnancy as a "cure" for endometriosis cannot conceive *because of* the disease. But there are other less obvious problems as well.

As observed in Chapter 2, many women advised to have a child for "therapeutic purposes" are single, gay, financially or emotionally unprepared for parenthood, too young, or any combination of the above. But these women are extremely vulnerable at this time and will do almost anything, short of definitive surgery, to end their pain. Even those with no inclination toward motherhood may attempt to conceive. A single woman may enlist a friend, or search for a candidate to father her child; she may investigate artificial insemination with donor sperm, even though she knows single motherhood may create financial and social hardships. Or she may begin to look for a mate and make choices she would not have made otherwise.

To further confuse the issue, women with endometriosis are often advised to become pregnant in order to insure against future infertility. Since the likelihood of infertility is presumed (but not proven) to increase the longer one has endometriosis, patients are advised to conceive as early as possible, because later may be too late. It's a gamble: wait until you are ready to conceive and run the risk of not being able to do so; or rearrange your life plans and attempt it earlier, since you might be infertile later.

Lisa was twenty-three when her endometriosis was diagnosed. In several months she planned to marry Mark, twenty-four. Both Lisa and Mark wanted children very much, but not then. Mark was getting started in his career, and Lisa had just finished college. Her doctor suggested they attempt a pregnancy. It might cure her disease. Besides, he said, if she and Mark wanted children, there was no time to spare. They tried to imagine a future without children; they also tried to imagine themselves coping with a child so early in their marriage.

"The problem for me was that nobody could tell me what our chances were. We had totally different plans. We weren't even going to think about having a child for at least five years. I'd love to postpone it until all the factors are right, but it's a time bomb. The longer I wait, the harder it's going to be, and the more I'm going to hurt. It's hard to think about having a child for medicinal purposes. We want children, but we're just not ready now and I don't think it would be fair to the child or to us. On the other hand, if I can't have children, I want to know now, so I can take whatever drastic measures are necessary to stop the pain and bring my life back to normal. We feel torn between wanting to have a child when we're not emotionally or financially prepared, and the possibility of never being able to have children. There's the possibility that I can't even get pregnant. And if I can, there's a higher risk of ectopic pregnancy and miscarriage. And after all that, will I be able to handle a miscarriage? And there's the fear of recurrence after pregnancy. I see myself with an infant, and imagine myself sick again. Will I have the energy to enjoy and take care of my baby?"

Pregnancy cannot be prescribed. Only you can decide what risks you are willing to take. If endometriosis forces you to make an untimely decision, be clear about your needs and goals. If having a child is very important to you, it may make sense to consider rearranging your timetable to accommodate a family earlier in life than you had planned. It's vital, however, that you do not make major life decisions from a vantage point clouded by weakness, confusion, pain, or the hope that somehow your health will benefit from such decisions. Pregnancy and childbirth will definitely make you a parent, but won't necessarily free you of endometriosis.

8
Surgical Treatment

There are several surgical approaches to the treatment of endometriosis, ranging from extremely conservative—the removal of superficial disease during laparoscopy, to radical—the partial or complete removal of the reproductive organs.

When it comes to surgery, terminology is used loosely, blurring the distinction between conservative and radical. To a certain extent, one surgeon's "conservative" may be another's "radical." To some, a conservative operation is any procedure that retains the patient's reproductive ability. To others, it represents any operation, including hysterectomy, that leaves intact at least part of one ovary so that the natural production of hormones is not impaired. Likewise, the meaning of radical surgery varies: some consider hysterectomy alone radical surgery; others reserve the term for operations in which all the reproductive organs are removed. To clarify, three types of surgery—conservative, hysterectomy, and definitive—are discussed below.

- *Conservative surgery* refers to procedures in which lesions, implants, cysts, and associated adhesions are removed. The uterus and at least one ovary and fallopian tube are retained.
- *Hysterectomy* refers to operations in which all visible and accessible lesions, implants, cysts, and adhesions are removed, as are the uterus and cervix. Although an oophorectomy may also be done, at least part of one ovary is retained—enough to allow continued production of hormones and avoid the symptoms and risks associated with surgical menopause. This procedure is often called a *total hysterectomy*.
- *Definitive surgery* is considered a cure for endometriosis. It refers to hysterectomy with bilateral salpingo-oophorectomy—the removal of the uterus, cervix, and both ovaries and fallopian tubes, as well as any lesions, implants, cysts, and adhesions found on the remaining pelvic organs and structures (see Appendix A). Also known as "castration"

or "pelvic cleanout," definitive surgery creates a surgical menopause. It is followed by the rapid onset of menopausal symptoms such as hot flashes and an increased risk of heart disease and osteoporosis.

CONSERVATIVE SURGERY: THERAPEUTIC LAPAROSCOPY AND LAPAROTOMY

In the last several decades the pendulum of popularity has swung back and forth between a medical and a surgical approach to the treatment of endometriosis. When disease is severe or extensive, particularly when large endometriomas or dense adhesions are present, most experts agree that surgery is the appropriate course of action. But, for minimal to moderate disease, physicians remain divided: some, insisting that all but the most severe cases should be treated medically, reserve surgery as a last resort. Others believe that most disease is best eradicated surgically at the outset.

Currently, conservative surgery is usually performed on women with

- moderate to severe disease
- large endometriomas and dense adhesions typically unresponsive to medical treatment
- large bilateral ovarian endometriomas
- severe symptoms that do not respond to expectant or hormonal therapy
- contraindications to hormonal treatment
- a desire to conceive immediately
- infertility complicated by factors other than endometriosis that are better corrected surgically

The immediate goals of the surgeon are: to remove as much visible endometriosis and adhesions as possible; to restore normal pelvic anatomy (if distorted by disease, or if congenital abnormalities exist); and to do everything possible to minimize the formation of adhesions postoperatively. He ultimately aims to provide his patient with the greatest pain relief possible and to preserve and enhance her fertility, increasing the likelihood of conception if she wants to bear a child.

A considerable amount of conservative surgery can be accomplished at the time of diagnostic laparoscopy, discussed in Chapter 4. Therapeutic laparoscopy (called operative laparoscopy by physicians) is a procedure often reserved for patients with mild to moderate disease. When disease is severe, particularly when there are dense adhesions, large bilateral ovarian endometriomas, extensive disease of the cul-de-sac, or severe bowel or urinary tract disease, laparotomy is usually required (discussed in detail later in this section; see also Appendix A).

With your consent, laparotomy can often be performed immediately following diagnostic laparoscopy. That way, you are saved the additional expense, risk, and recuperation period of a second operation, as well as a second experience with general anesthesia. More typically, though, laparotomy is performed six to eight weeks later. Prior to the refinement of laparoscopic instrumentation, traditional conservative surgery required laparotomy. Today, with laser technology, and the increased experience and ability of surgeons to use such technology, most endometriosis patients can be treated (some say, *should* be treated) through the laparoscope at the time of diagnosis. Laparotomy remains the primary surgical approach to the disease, however.

Therapeutic Laparoscopy

Doctors disagree about the indications and limitations of therapeutic laparoscopy. Some physicians believe that endometriosis should be eradicated routinely to the extent possible at the time of diagnostic laparoscopy whenever the surgeon has the training and skill to do so. Others argue against laparoscopic treatment. They suggest it treats only "the tip of the iceberg"[1] and risks damaging healthy tissue, major blood vessels, and vital organs.

Many doctors limit therapeutic laparoscopy to patients with minimal to mild disease; some, mild to moderate cases. Others will laparoscopically treat patients with severe and extensive disease—even women with large ovarian endometriomas up to 1 cm; others draw the line at 3 cms; still others set no limit on size. A few will treat implants in the cul-de-sac during therapeutic laparoscopy; many insist that such implants be dealt with only during laparotomy. Most agree, however, that therapeutic laparoscopy is unlikely to be useful when the patient has dense adhesions that completely distort the pelvic anatomy.

The basic procedure for therapeutic laparoscopy is the same as that for diagnostic laparoscopy. (Laparoscopy is described in detail in Appendix A.) Once the abdomen is inflated with gas, a laparoscope is inserted into a small incision near the navel. An instrument to steady or manipulate the abdominal organs (to increase visibility) is inserted into a second incision. Additional punctures allow accessory instruments to be inserted into the abdominal cavity. When adjacent organs are removed from harm's way, implants, small endometriomas, and adhesions can be excised, cauterized with electrical current, or vaporized with the laser.

Risks.   The risks and complications of therapeutic laparoscopy are the same as those of diagnostic laparoscopy (see Chapter 4 and Appendix A). With cautery, however, there is the additional risk of burning tissues that underlie or are adjacent to endometriotic implants and injuring the bowel, bladder, ureters, fallopian tubes, or pelvic peritoneum.

Advantages.   If during diagnostic laparoscopy it becomes clear that you require further surgery, there are practical advantages in having it done then, rather than undergoing a laparotomy later: one surgical procedure instead of two; one hospital visit; one bill to pay; one recuperation period.

While laparotomy is major surgery, laparoscopy is minor surgery and associated with fewer risks. You will spend less time on the operating table, reducing the risk of complications associated with general anesthesia. Postsurgical pain and swelling are reduced and recovery time is shorter. Normally, you will leave the hospital within twenty-four hours and can resume normal activities within seventy-two hours. Recovery is complete within a week. Laparotomy, on the other hand, requires a hospital stay of nearly one week and as much as a month for full recovery.

Laparoscopic Cautery

Today, laser laparoscopy (see below), uses flexible fiberoptics that allow a laser beam to be delivered through the laparoscope to the site of disease. Prior to the development of laser technology, however, therapeutic laparoscopy was limited to the cauterization of implants by electrical current. It resulted in complete pain relief in as many as 63 percent of patients[2] and pregnancy rates of about 59 percent.[3]

But cautery can be risky. Tissues surrounding and underlying the lesions can be injured. When the surgeon cauterizes endometriotic lesions, he has no way of gauging precisely how much tissue he is actually destroying. If he underestimates the depth of tissue destruction, diseased tissue will remain. If he overestimates, he will destroy healthy tissue as well. This is a particularly important consideration when working in the delicate areas of the bowel, bladder, and ureter, where burns can have serious consequences. Cautery may also cause uncontrolled bleeding; furthermore, postoperative adhesions may develop. Cautery is still used, but many gynecologists favor the laser for its safety, precision, and versatility.

Laser Laparoscopy

Laser is an acronym for light amplification by stimulated emission of radiation. It describes a technology that converts electrical energy into light energy. Three types of lasers—the carbon dioxide (CO_2), the argon, and the YAG—are used to treat endometriosis. All can be transmitted through the laparoscope to vaporize or coagulate tissue; but the versatile carbon dioxide laser is the most widely used in gynecological surgery, particularly for endometriosis. The CO_2 laser vaporizes tissue (turns it into water).

To perform a laser laparoscopy, the surgeon can view the pelvic cavity in either of two ways—directly through the laparoscope or on a video monitor. In the latter procedure, videolaseroscopy (see Appendix A), the laparoscope is equipped with a miniature video camera. The surgeon magnifies the image of the abdominal cavity onto a video monitor. Areas of endometriosis that might have been missed with the laparoscope alone can be detected.

Once the instruments are in place, the surgeon views the pelvic cavity, determines the location and extent of endometriosis, and, with the laser, vaporizes superficial implants and endometriomas.

A procedure called *uterine suspension* may be performed during laser laparoscopy. Uterine ligaments are shortened or repositioned to hold the uterus up and out of the cul-de-sac and to prevent the formation of adhesions.

At this time, a laser neurectomy—the severing of nerves—can be performed to provide relief for patients with severe dysmenorrhea. Nerve fibers that transmit pain are concentrated in the uterosacral ligaments at the point where they meet the posterior cervix. These ligaments can easily be removed or severed by the laser.

Laser eradication of endometriosis has a number of significant advantages over cautery. Diseased tissues can be precisely attacked without damaging surrounding or underlying tissues. Using the laser, the gynecologist can safely vaporize lesions and implants on or around the ureter, bladder, bowel, and fallopian tubes. In addition, the laser coagulates blood vessels. This reduces bleeding, which improves the surgeon's visibility, and eliminates the need for suturing. At the same time, the laser cuts down the risk of postoperative infection because the heat it generates destroys bacteria. And, since laser vaporization leaves little debris, the likelihood of scar tissue and postoperative adhesions is significantly reduced.

Laser surgery is a significant advance in the treatment of endometriosis. Unfortunately, not all patients will have access to it. Unlike cautery, which requires little additional instrumentation or expense, laser equipment is not affordable for many hospitals.

Pregnancy rates. About 59 percent of patients who try to conceive achieve pregnancy following laser laparoscopy. Although not yet well established, these rates can be expected to improve as gynecologists become increasingly proficient with laser procedures.[4]

Laser laparoscopy has a special advantage for many infertile women: they may consider pregnancy soon after the procedure. They don't have to spend six months on hormonal therapy or wait until after major surgery.

Should You Undergo Therapeutic Laparoscopy?

Despite its advantages, many gynecologists do not use the laparoscope to treat endometriosis. Some find the procedure unnecessary or controversial. According to one specialist, however, the only reason for not routinely removing disease through laparoscopy when feasible is a surgeon's lack of experience with the procedure.

According to Dr. Buttram, if a physician is trained to treat endometriosis at the time of diagnostic laparoscopy, "there is no rhyme or reason why it shouldn't be done. To perform a laparoscopy on a woman, to find endometriosis and not be able to deal with it at that time to the extent possible, is irresponsible," he says. "In today's age, every gynecologist should have that ability."

Unfortunately, they do not. Therapeutic laparoscopy, particularly when the laser is used, is a highly specialized skill. Not all gynecologists are equipped, and few have the extensive training they need for proficient use of the laser. Your decision, therefore, will be determined to a large degree by your choice of doctor—his preferences, experience, and training. For this reason, find the best possible doctor *before* you undergo diagnostic laparoscopy. For example, consult a reproductive endocrinologist, who has more experience. (See Chapter 16 for more information on choosing a doctor.)

After Therapeutic Laparoscopy

Following the operation you will have several options. If most or all of the endometriosis was removed, patients who wish to do so can attempt to conceive without further treatment. Others who do not may be advised to take oral contraceptives cyclically (three weeks on, one week off) to reduce the likelihood of recurrence. As mentioned in Chapter 6, it has not been demonstrated that use of oral contraceptives prevents the development or recurrence of endometriosis. Still, many physicians believe it at least decreases the risk.

Sometimes a surgeon is unable to remove all visible endometriosis during laparoscopy. He may then recommend a course of hormonal therapy, followed by the cyclic use of birth control pills, or pregnancy, if you wish it. If severe symptoms occur or persist, laparotomy may be necessary.

Laparotomy

The fallopian tubes may be occluded, or there may be additional infertility factors that require surgical treatment. Severe and extensive disease often affects the cul-de-sac, the gastrointestinal tract, or the urinary tract. Under these conditions, or when severe disease persists or recurs following therapeutic laparoscopy, laparotomy is usually performed.

Preoperative medical therapy.   Hormonal therapy, usually danazol, is often used in combination with conservative surgery, either preoperatively or postoperatively (see below). Danazol may be used preoperatively for two to six months to reduce the amount of disease that must be removed during surgery and to inhibit the development of postsurgical adhesions.

Surgical techniques.   The surgeon performing the operation may use traditional surgical techniques (excision) combined with cautery, laser vaporization (discussed earlier), or microsurgery. Strictly speaking, the term microsurgery refers to the use of optical loupes or microscopes for magnification of the surgical field. Sometimes it implies the use of particularly fine, sharp operating tools, extremely small, nonirritating sutures, and special salt solutions (to keep tissues continually moistened to prevent them from drying out with exposure to air). Often, however, it describes a surgical philosophy dictating particularly delicate and meticulous handling of tissues.

Before proceeding, your surgeon may or may not dilate your cervix, depending on his beliefs concerning the origin of endometriosis and whether or not it can be prevented. As explained in Chapter 2, the flow of menstrual blood through a tight cervical opening is believed to cause dysmenorrhea and to encourage retrograde menstruation. Cervical dilation reduces the possibility of menstrual reflux and perhaps reduces dysmenorrhea. It is likely to be performed by surgeons who strongly support the theory of retrograde menstruation. Dilation of the cervix also facilitates insertion of instruments during the operation.

The surgeon's aim is first to remove superficial lesions, implants, cysts, and ovarian endometriomas. Resection (partial removal) of the ovary is sometimes necessary, as is correction of uterine displacement and any anatomical abnormality that may contribute to reflux menstruation. Coexisting disease such as a fibroid tumor is removed, and the pelvic organs and structures are freed from adhesions.

The surgeon makes a small incision (usually about four inches) across the abdomen (just above the pubic hairline) and searches the pelvis to assess the location and extent of disease, and to determine the necessary procedures and their sequence. Before destroying endometriotic lesions and implants, however, he often has to cut or vaporize adhesions that have fused the uterus and ovaries to other organs, obscuring underlying disease.

Ovarian disease. Superficial lesions and implants on the ovaries (as well as on the pelvic peritoneum) are generally scraped, cauterized, or vaporized. When there is no danger of impairing the blood supply to the ovaries, endometriomas are excised and the ovary is resected if necessary, leaving as much healthy tissue as possible. When one ovary and fallopian tube are severely diseased, but the other ovary and tube are normal or can easily be repaired, the surgeon may remove, rather than attempt to repair, the diseased organs on one side, or he may resect both ovaries. (Oophorectomy is the removal of the ovary; salpingectomy is the removal of the tube.) It is still possible for a woman to conceive, even if one ovary and two-thirds of the other have been removed. Conception can take place with only a tiny piece of ovary remaining. When both ovaries are irreparably damaged, definitive surgery—a total hysterectomy with bilateral salpingo-oophorectomy—probably will be performed (see below).

Fallopian tubes. During conservative surgery, dye injected into the fallopian tubes allows the surgeon to see whether or not the tubes are blocked by endometriosis or adhesions. If they are occluded, which is uncommon, complicated microsurgical reconstruction (tuboplasty) or removal of the tube (salpingectomy) may be necessary. If tubal lesions are superficial, they can be removed through cauterization or vaporization.

Bowel and bladder disease. Small implants on the bowel or bladder are excised only if there is no danger of damage to the underlying organs. If there is, the lesions are left, to be treated postsurgically with hormone therapy. Surgical correction of bowel obstruction—usually a bowel resection—may be performed during the laparotomy or handled separately in a subsequent operation, depending on the severity of the problem and the preference of the surgeon.

Cul-de-sac and uterosacral ligaments. Superficial lesions on the cul-de-sac and uterosacral ligaments are vaporized or cauterized. More invasive lesions are excised.

Uterine suspension. Although sometimes performed routinely, a uterine suspension is usually part of a conservative operation if the uterus is retroverted or retroflexed and if the cul-de-sac is filled with adhesions. Adhesions in the cul-de-sac may immobilize the uterus and plaster the ovaries to the uterus, the cul-de-sac, or the sigmoid colon. A uterine suspension is performed by tightening or shortening the uterosacral ligaments and/or the round ligaments so that they hold the uterus and ovaries up and out of the cul-de-sac. This procedure is performed to reduce the likelihood of menstrual reflux and the development of postoperative adhesions and to help minimize dyspareunia.

Presacral and uterosacral neurectomies. The presacral nerves transmit pain messages to the brain. A presacral neurectomy is performed to relieve dysmenorrhea or to prevent its development should endometriosis recur after surgery. The presacral nerve filaments affect the contractility of the smooth muscle of the uterus. Remember, prostaglandins influence the contractility of the uterine smooth muscle, and ectopic endometrium produces prostaglandins. A presacral neurectomy may be performed, then, to eliminate or minimize the effect of prostaglandins on the smooth muscle and thereby relieve pain.

Presacral neurectomy brings relief from dysmenorrhea to 75 to 85 percent of women, but it is only effective in preventing midline abdominal pain—that is, pain in the center of the abdomen originating in the uterus. It has no effect on ovarian pain or pain resulting from the tugging of adhesions on the pelvic organs.

The presacral neurectomy is a somewhat controversial procedure. For some gynecologists, it's a routine part of any conservative operation for endometriosis. Others are concerned that it increases a patient's chances of developing postoperative adhesions and therefore will not include it under any circumstances. Some limit the practice to patients with very severe dysmenorrhea.

There are two additional drawbacks to this procedure. First, the neurectomy may lead to difficulty in emptying the bowel and bladder for some time following surgery and to chronic postoperative constipation. Second, since the presacral neurectomy affects the contractility of the smooth muscle of the uterus, it may affect your perception of pain during pregnancy when the muscle contracts during labor. During the first stages of labor, you may not feel contractions. While this may sound like a blessing at first, consider that those early contractions signal the onset of labor. If you miss your cue, you may not be able to accurately gauge the stages of labor. It's important, therefore, if you plan to have a child, to know your surgeon's philosophy on presacral neurectomy ahead of time. You may want to get a second opinion.

A similar procedure, the uterosacral neurectomy, involves severing and repositioning the uterosacral ligaments to reduce dysmenorrhea and dyspareunia.

Appendectomy. Some surgeons routinely remove the appendix during laparotomy for endometriosis; others, only if it appears to be diseased. Endometriosis on the appendix is often not visible during laparotomy. According to one report, 38 percent of apparently normal appendices removed and examined microscopically were found to be involved with endometriosis.[5]

Myomectomy.   Since fibroid tumors of the uterus coexist with endometriosis in about 15 percent of patients, myomectomy—the removal of a fibroid—is a frequent part of conservative surgery for endometriosis.

Medications.   Corticosteroids, antihistamines, and antibiotics are commonly given before, during, and after surgery to reduce the risk of infection and postoperative adhesions.

Effectiveness, Recurrence, and Pregnancy Rates

Conservative surgery appears to bring more effective and long-lasting pain relief than hormonal therapy.[6] Unfortunately, however, as with medical treatment, recurrences are common and reoperation often necessary. It's not entirely clear whether reported "recurrences" are areas of newly developed disease or a proliferation of disease missed during surgery. Disease can be microscopic, impossible to detect and remove at surgery. Some surgeons are unable to recognize areas of endometriosis that do not match the "textbook" appearance. Consequently, areas of endometriosis can be left behind.

Recurrence rates reported vary tremendously, from as low as 2 percent to as high as 41 percent. In one study of 801 patients treated surgically, 15 percent experienced symptoms of recurrent or persistent disease. The severity of disease seems to have little bearing on recurrence rates, although more severe disease may be more difficult to eradicate completely and may increase the likelihood of a second, or even a third, operation. A pregnancy after surgery may delay (but not necessarily prevent) recurrences.[7]

Pregnancy rates are generally equal to or higher than those following medical therapy. Rates reported in the medical literature range from 13 to 94 percent, most clustering between 55 and 65 percent.[8] About 60 to 75 percent of women with mild disease, 36 to 74 percent with moderate disease, and 0 to 48 percent with severe disease will conceive following conservative surgery,[9] with most pregnancies occurring within eighteen months.[10]

The prognosis for conception following a second operation may be reduced. According to one study, only 12 percent of patients conceived following second conservative surgery; an equal number required definitive surgery.[11] In another study, however, 47 percent of infertility patients with recurrent endometriosis conceived after a second operation. In that study, 20 percent of patients requiring a second operation subsequently required a third.[12]

Combination Therapy: Danazol and Conservative Surgery

Hormonal therapy, usually danazol, combined with surgical treatment, has become popular, especially in cases of severe disease. Before an operation it facilitates surgery; after surgery it suppresses any residual disease and reduces adhesions. Like most other treatment regimens, combination therapy is controversial: some doctors advocate only preoperative hormones; others, only postoperative; and still others no hormones at all.

Preoperative danazol.   Preoperative danazol therapy makes surgery easier, reduces the size and number of lesions and implants, and inhibits the development of postoperative adhesions. Dosages vary from 400 to 800 mg daily; length of use is from two to six months.

Some surgeons believe that preoperative use of danazol may improve the outlook for conception after surgery. In some studies a dose of 800 mg daily has been found to result in a 10 to 15 percent increase in pregnancy rates for moderate, and in some cases severe, disease,[13] with no increase for mild disease; in other studies its influence on fertility has been negligible.[14]

Postoperative danazol.   Danazol therapy may follow conservative surgery, especially in patients with severe or widespread disease, and when there is residual endometriosis that could not be removed at surgery. It may be useful, say some proponents, in suppressing microscopic disease that could not be detected or removed.[15]

In one study, fifty-eight patients were treated immediately after surgery with danazol. Pregnancy rates, followed for at least fifteen months, were higher for combination therapy than for surgery alone: 64 percent, 64 percent, and 67 percent respectively for mild, moderate, and severe disease, as opposed to 57, 54, and 36 percent. However, the higher rate is significant for patients with severe disease only.[16] One drawback is that conception must be delayed for up to six months. Studies show that most conceptions occur in the six-month period immediately following surgery.[17]

Second-Look Laparoscopy

Laparoscopy is sometimes repeated following therapeutic laparoscopy or laparotomy to evaluate the success of the surgery and to assess the need for additional treatment. During a second procedure, any adhesions that may have developed postoperatively can be destroyed, and any areas of persistent or recurrent endometriosis cauterized or vaporized. In addition, the likelihood of pregnancy can be determined.

If numerous adhesions and recurrent or persistent disease are revealed, a second operation may be indicated.

WHEN CONSERVATIVE SURGERY IS NOT ENOUGH: HYSTERECTOMY OR DEFINITIVE SURGERY

Conservative surgery is likely to be inadequate and some type of radical surgery is often necessary or recommended when

- endometriosis of the ureter poses a serious hazard to kidney function
- endometriosis and adhesions may lead to irreparable bowel obstruction
- the intestines are plastered to the uterus or ovaries
- the rectovaginal septum is deeply involved with endometriosis
- large, refractory, bilateral ovarian endometriomas and adhesions may rupture

- a woman with no plans for childbearing experiences severe symptoms that persist following medical therapy and one or more conservative operations
- a woman, with or without plans for childbearing and despite conservative operations experiences symptoms so severe and incapacitating that the quality of her life is intolerable

Except when vital organs are jeopardized or when it appears that endometriomas might rupture, hysterectomy or definitive surgery for endometriosis is seldom absolutely necessary and rarely must be performed at the discretion of the surgeon without the patient's knowledge. Most often, it is, and should be, your choice.

When vital organs are at risk, the consequences of not having radical surgery may be fatal. In all other circumstances the consequences are generally limited to a continuation of symptoms or perhaps a progression of disease. When symptoms continue to be severe and refractory to conservative treatment, you may have to make a very difficult decision between a drastically diminished quality of life with continued intractable pain and the loss of your reproductive organs and your ability to bear children.

Many women suffer for years. They undergo one operation after another, living on pain medication to avoid radical surgery at all costs. Perhaps they are unwilling to relinquish the possibility of pregnancy. Some may feel they will forfeit their femininity, their sexuality, their "womanness." Others are concerned about menopausal symptoms and the long-term effects of replacement hormones. Some are afraid they are being pushed unnecessarily into an irrevocable decision.

On the other hand, many doctors, despite rumors to the contrary, are extremely reluctant to subject a woman, particularly a younger woman who has not had children, to radical surgery, however eager she may be. A woman often must plead for definitive surgery. Often she sees it as her only chance to regain control over her life.

"After a lot of consultation with my gynecologist, I scheduled myself for a hysterectomy. I was tired of it all and wanted some painless days to live. The gynecologist objected. He even consulted my former gynecologist, and she, too, objected. They didn't think I should have the surgery because, at thirty-five, I was too young and had no children. That was not a concern to me. I had suffered too long and I wanted no more of it."

It is seldom an easy decision, even if you have completed your family or have no interest in future childbearing. Your doctor cannot determine your needs, your priorities, or your level of tolerance for pain and life disruption. Only you can—at your own pace, along with adequate information on the procedures and their effects, the consequences, and the alternatives.

Women who face definitive surgery must consider more than the medical aspects of the procedure and its physical consequences. They must also come to terms with the emotional, psychological, and social components: fears concerning risks and complications of surgery, feelings toward loss of childbearing ability, changes in body image, feminine self-image and sexual response; and the reaction of family, friends, and lovers. If you are ready, willing, perhaps even eager, to face definitive surgery, consider the adjustments you will have to make. Preparing for them can help you assimilate the changes you may face. (For information about the procedures, their risks and complications, see Appendix A. Some useful publications are listed in Appendix B. Emotional repercussions and decision-making strategies are explored in Part Three.)

What Are the Effects of Hysterectomy?

If you undergo hysterectomy, you will continue to ovulate, but you will no longer menstruate or be able to bear children. Generally, unless the blood supply to the ovaries is impaired by endometriosis or by surgery, the ovaries continue to produce hormones. Therefore, you will not suffer symptoms of estrogen deficiency until you reach menopause, when the output of ovarian hormones declines gradually. If, however, the blood supply is traumatized, ovarian function may be compromised, and some of the symptoms of surgical menopause may occur (see Chapter 9). A woman whose ovaries have been retained, yet who has some symptoms of surgical menopause, may be experiencing ovarian failure. By having her FSH levels checked she can determine whether her ovaries are functioning. If they are not, she will want to consider the effects of diminished estrogen and determine whether or not to try hormone replacement therapy or explore some other means of dealing with menopausal symptoms.

What Are the Effects of Definitive Surgery?

The effects of definitive surgery will be discussed in detail in the following chapter. In brief, a hysterectomy with bilateral salpingo-oophorectomy brings on a surgical menopause. The most significant source of estrogen is cut off and symptoms of estrogen withdrawal occur, principally hot flashes and vaginal atrophy. Since the withdrawal of estrogen is so sudden and drastic, as opposed to the gradual decline of natural menopause, symptoms are often swift and severe. Hot flashes may begin immediately after surgery, while vaginal atrophy may not occur for months or even years. The loss of vaginal lubrication and the thinning of the vaginal lining may lead to irritation, infection, and pain and bleeding during or after intercourse.

Surgical menopause increases the risk of heart disease. Additionally, osteoporosis may develop. This progressive thinning of bone can lead to fractures with serious consequences. To counter these symptoms and risks, most women will be advised to take replacement hormones which have risks of their own, including the possible reactivation of any residual endometriosis.

Should the Ovaries Be Removed?

Before you agree to radical surgery, discuss with your surgeon his philosophy and practices concerning oophorectomy. Some physicians base their decision on whether to retain or remove the ovaries on the extent of disease and the patient's age. They favor removal if you have severe disease or are within a decade of menopause. Others routinely perform oophorectomies. Some will discuss the pros and cons and seek your opinion; others will not.

Remember, a procedure with such serious repercussions, unless absolutely medically indicated, must be carefully considered, based upon your needs, feelings, and preferences.

Definitive surgery, as opposed to hysterectomy alone, is widely considered essential when

- the ovaries are severely diseased
- the blood supply to the ovaries is impaired or threatened by surgery
- less than one third of only one ovary can be saved
- the bowel, bladder, or ureter are at risk

Other situations will be less clear-cut and your decision—made in consultation with your doctor—will be more a matter of preference than medical necessity. Perhaps your symptoms are severe but your ovaries are healthy. Or your ovaries, although involved with endometriosis, can be resected without endangering their blood supply. Removing the uterus alone will eliminate the source of both the ectopic endometrium and much of your pain. When combined with the removal of all other areas of endometriosis in the pelvis, it generally results in complete symptomatic relief. However, symptoms may recur later.

There are many factors to consider when determining whether or not to remove the ovaries when a hysterectomy is performed. They are covered in numerous publications listed in Appendix C. Here, however, the overriding concern is whether or not the retention of the ovaries will lead to a recurrence of the symptoms of endometriosis following surgery.

"Two months after conservative surgery, the pain returned and got more severe. By the fifth month, I was put on danazol for three months, after which I had my uterus and one ovary removed. I still have pain on the side where my other ovary remains and I continue to have bowel and bladder trouble."

Simply put, by keeping your ovaries, you avoid the risks and discomforts of surgical menopause and eliminate the need for replacement estrogen. On the other hand, your healthy ovaries will continue to produce those hormones upon which endometriosis thrives, and you run the risk of persistent disease and subsequent oophorectomy. How great a risk is a matter of considerable controversy. If all or most areas of endometriosis are removed, a recurrence of symptoms is unlikely.

If, however, areas of endometriosis remain, because either they were not visible or accessible or removal was impossible, continued hormonal output is likely to reactivate residual disease and give rise to symptoms. Even a tiny piece of ovarian tissue may produce this effect.

According to some experts, the likelihood of persistence is slim. Others note that endometriosis can be microscopic. The surgeon can only remove what he can see. If you gamble against the possibility of recurrence, the odds will be against you. "It's probably incorrect to say that endometriosis recurs," says Dr. Rock. "I think there is evidence now that it is persistent, that you are never able to get rid of all endometriosis, that in fact microscopic disease is present. With time and stimulation of estrogen from the ovary it may become proliferative. There is a recurrence of symptoms, rather than a recurrence of disease, because the disease was never fully eradicated."

The statistics are equally confounding. Some studies suggest a risk of less than 1 percent. Others indicate that, if the ovaries are preserved, a second, definitive operation will be necessary about 85 percent of the time.[18]

Many women, particularly those far from menopause are willing to take this risk in order to avoid surgical menopause.

"I felt I was taking a calculated risk by electing to keep the left ovary, but that it was worth it. For four years afterward I was asymptomatic. Then, I started feeling cramps, pulling sensations, and problems with pain upon sitting, standing, or with any kind of exertion."

A compromise.   To reduce the likelihood of persistent disease, some surgeons will remove all but a part of one ovary. This allows a woman to produce her own hormones and avoid surgical menopause. The patient undergoes danazol therapy for at least six months postoperatively to suppress residual disease. It's still a gamble, but some believe such a compromise reduces the likelihood that symptoms will recur.

AFTER DEFINITIVE SURGERY: HORMONE REPLACEMENT THERAPY

Once the ovaries are removed, patients usually receive replacement hormones to ward off menopausal symptoms and risks. Will those hormones stimulate residual endometriosis? If so, is the risk of persistent or recurrent disease comparable to that resulting from a woman's own hormones? Many women fear it is, but experts claim that preserving the ovaries is associated with a much higher rate of persistent disease than that associated with the removal of the ovaries, whether or not replacement hormones are given.

Some experts suggest a slightly increased risk of recurrent symptoms after definitive surgery if replacement hormones are given. Others suggest the recurrence occurs in approximately 1 to 3 percent following definitive surgery, with or without replacement therapy.[19]

Many experts believe estrogen replacement therapy (ERT) is safer than relying on the ovaries' own estrogen because if symptoms do recur, ERT can easily be controlled or discontinued. This is preferable to an additional operation to remove the remaining ovaries. Replacement therapy can be withheld for four to six months to starve the ectopic endometrium and eliminate symptoms.[20] (See Chapter 9 for a full discussion of ERT.)

"I feel as if I'm trapped in pain and I've gone as far as I can go."

"I thought endometriosis was behind me, but now, on estrogen replacement therapy, I still have painful intercourse and my doctor feels that undetected sites of endometriosis have been "fueled' by the estrogen."

If symptoms persist following surgery and hormone replacement, many physicians will take patients off estrogen therapy, prescribe medroxyprogesterone acetate or another progestogen for up to six months, and then start estrogen therapy again. Others switch patients from estrogen replacement to low-dose estrogen/progesterone oral contraceptives or Depo-Provera. The problem can be avoided by postponing estrogen replacement for a few weeks, perhaps up to a year. This allows any residual disease to regress. Some doctors prescribe danazol, progestins, or low-dose estrogen/progesterone oral contraceptives to facilitate regression.

Many women produce enough estrogens from other sources to keep menopausal symptoms at bay. Others need to experiment with alternative methods for managing symptoms. Danazol and, to a lesser degree, progestins afford significant relief for many women. None, however, reduces the risk of osteoporosis (see Chapter 9) or heart disease; but most physicians say the risk is insignificant if ERT is postponed for a limited time. There are women, though, who try postponing ERT and yet are still troubled by menopausal symptoms. Despite increased risk of persistent disease, they find those symptoms are too uncomfortable and too disruptive. They are willing to resume ERT and take their chances.

"I started hormone replacement therapy about three days postoperatively because of the depression and the hot flashes. I could not stop crying. The flashes were terrible. I know some people recommend waiting for six months to start hormone replacement, but I couldn't get through three days."

Again, the choice is yours. You have little to lose by trying to go without replacement therapy for a period of time. If symptoms are too bothersome, you can always change your mind.

9

Surgical Menopause: After Definitive Surgery

Total abdominal hysterectomy with bilateral salpingo-oophorectomy results in a premature, or "surgical," menopause. In natural menopause, a woman's hormone levels decrease slowly and changes take place over a period of years. For the younger woman who undergoes surgical menopause, the changes are sudden and often dramatic. Some occur immediately after surgery. Surgical menopause requires an adjustment to these profound changes in hormone levels. For some women it may also require a certain amount of psychological adaptation.

HOT FLASHES AND NIGHT SWEATS

A hot flash (or flush) is just as the name suggests: a sudden wave of heat radiating through the upper torso and face. It affects approximately 75 to 85 percent of women after natural menopause and 37 to 50 percent after surgical menopause.[1] The flashes are not dangerous, but they can be severe, debilitating, and, for some, embarrassing.

Hot flashes may begin immediately after surgery. They are often preceded by awareness that the flash is coming. Seconds later a surge of heat washes across your face and neck and possibly your chest. Infrequently your whole body is diffused with heat. Flashes, perhaps accompanied by sweating, redness in the face, dizziness, rapid heartbeat and/or palpitations, headache, and a tingling sensation in the extremities, head, or entire body, generally end as quickly as they begin. They usually last for only several minutes, less commonly for half an hour to an hour. Women often report a chilling sensation after the flush subsides.

The number of flashes varies from once or twice a week to several times a day or more. Sleep may bring no relief. The nocturnal counterpart of hot flashes are night sweats, which may cause you to wake up, short of breath, in a pool of perspiration. The repeated interruption of sleep contributes to the irritability and depression so often reported by postmenopausal women.

Flashes may be aggravated by hot weather, hot drinks (particularly coffee and tea), stressful situations, cigarettes, and alcohol.

Treatment

Hot flashes are believed to be caused by estrogen withdrawal; once estrogen reaches a stable low level, which can take years, the flashes taper off. The most common treatment, therefore, is estrogen replacement therapy (ERT), which is effective in about 90 percent of patients.[2]

Since estrogen replacement is associated with the development of uterine cancer, doctors add progestins to the estrogen regimen to eliminate that risk. With progestin, the regimen is known as hormone replacement therapy, or HRT. The terms HRT and ERT are commonly but incorrectly used interchangeably. When discussing the risks and benefits of replacement therapy with your doctor, make sure you know whether he is talking about ERT or HRT. Here, ERT refers to estrogen preparations only; HRT refers to combination estrogen-progestin therapy. Progestins alone have been used to treat hot flashes, but not only are they less effective than estrogen alone or estrogens combined with progestins, but they are ineffective against other, more serious menopausal symptoms.

Danazol is also effective in treating hot flashes. In one study, women experiencing vasomotor symptoms following surgical menopause found relief within one to twenty-eight days of treatment with danazol. After discontinuance, hot flashes were less severe or absent entirely.[3] Danazol is especially useful against hot flashes in women with residual endometriosis after surgery, because it controls flashes and suppresses remaining disease as well.

Other drugs used to treat hot flashes include Bellergal and Catapres. These have significant side effects and disadvantages, however, and, like danazol and progestins alone, they do not address other symptoms of menopausal distress.

Hot flashes, although uncomfortable, even intolerable, are not a threat to health. Thus, treatment to alleviate flashes is, or should be, a personal choice, based on your own level of tolerance for discomfort. You may choose to wait out the flashes; or you may want to try to decrease their impact through alternative approachs such as vitamin therapy, biofeedback, or herbs. (Publications with useful information about alternative remedies for hot flashes and other menopausal symptoms are listed in Appendix C.)

VAGINAL ATROPHY

Following hysterectomy and oophorectomy the vagina becomes shorter and smaller and its tissues less pliable. Vaginal atrophy—not as hideous as the word suggests—is the thinning, drying, and loss of elasticity and muscle tone of the vaginal walls. Atrophy may develop slowly, noticeable only after months, even years, following surgery. Lubrication is diminished and occurs more slowly, so intercourse may lead to irritation. This in turn may cause inflammation, burning, bleeding, tenderness, itching, and pain. This inflamed and irritated tissue invites bacteria. To make matters worse, the pH balance of the vagina becomes less acidic following surgery, making the vagina still more vulnerable to germs and infection. Vaginitis may result. These changes may lead to a profound deterioration in sexual desire, comfort, and pleasure.

Treatment

The standard treatment is ERT, but several alternatives have been used successfully. Lubricants relieve irritation, reduce susceptibility to infection, and diminish the discomfort of intercourse. Frequent intercourse helps maintain the muscle tone of the vaginal lining and increases lubrication. Masturbation or penetration with manual dilators may serve the same purpose. Some women have found vitamins, vitamin oils, herbs, and dietary changes helpful as well. (See Appendix C for sources of information.)

URINARY TRACT CHANGES

Declining estrogen levels cause the epithelial lining to deteriorate. This leads to decreased bladder control and to bladder infections; burning and irritation upon urination may result, and the urethra may become inflamed. Estrogen replacement therapy can help eliminate urinary symptoms, and antibiotics to fight infection may also be required. Alternatively, Kegel exercises—the repetitive contraction of the muscles controlling the vagina and bladder—help many women maintain muscle tone (see Appendix C).

CHANGES IN SEXUAL INTEREST AND RESPONSE

In countless lay and scientific publications, on talk shows and behind closed doors, in doctors' offices and at home, doctors, therapists, researchers, and the recipients of hysterectomies and oophorectomies have clashed over two questions: (1) Does the level of sexual desire change following definitive surgery? and (2) If so, are these changes induced by physiological or psychosocial factors? Typically, physicians are accused of denying or downplaying these changes; patients are accused of exaggerating them.

Certain studies reveal that a significant number of women experience less sexual interest and satisfaction following surgery than their counterparts with intact reproductive organs; other studies reveal no such differences. Cogent arguments link sexual changes to reduced hormone levels affecting both the brain and the reproductive anatomy; equally compelling arguments suggest that such changes may reflect a woman's emotional response to surgery and altered perceptions of her femininity and social roles.

The fact is, a significant number of women following surgery *do* experience varying degrees of changes in sexual interest and response. These are not always negative, however. Some women, freed from the pain of endometriosis and the constraints of birth control, engage in sexual activity with renewed interest and vitality and with vastly greater comfort and pleasure. Others find they no longer become aroused, or they become aroused less easily.

Decline in libido may result from a number of factors. After oophorectomy, levels of androgens—hormones with known effects on the libido—decline. Although the adrenal glands continue to produce these hormones, the elimination of ovarian androgens may reduce sexual interest. For some women, androgen therapy (testosterone) is helpful in restoring sexual desire. In addition, in ways not fully understood, decreased estrogen appears to have some relationship to the libido, although estrogen replacement alone generally does not affect sexual desire. Studies show, however, that a combination of estrogen and androgen increases sexual desire. [4]

Apart from hormone levels and vaginal atrophy, other factors may contribute to a deterioration in the sexual experience: an altered body image; a loss of self-esteem, particularly in women who equate womanhood and femininity with the ability to reproduce; and concern about a sexual partner's reaction to your surgery. Also, sexual problems that existed before surgery may be exacerbated by, and become fused with, those difficulties described above.

EMOTIONAL CHANGES

Some women report varying degrees of depression, irritability, anxiety, mood swings, and lethargy following surgery; for some it may be mild and transient; for others, severe and persistent. Sometimes emotional changes may not occur for some time after surgery. On the other hand, there are those who experience an increased sense of emotional well-being following surgery.

Emotional changes, like sexual changes, have long been thought to be purely psychological reactions to surgery. Psychosocial factors may contribute to emotional distress following definitive surgery, but evidence suggests that hormones play a role in this emotional reaction, although the nature of that role remains unclear, and these feelings are generally unchanged by estrogen therapy.

The fact that some women experience emotional distress following surgery doesn't mean that you will respond similarly. On the other hand, if you find yourself depressed, you needn't feel that your reaction is unusual, that you are intrinsically less able to cope than others, or that you do not deserve support, assistance, or treatment.

OSTEOPOROSIS

A more hazardous consequence of estrogen loss is osteoporosis, a progressive loss of bone density leading to backache, bones that can fracture easily, and a "dowager's hump." The earlier you reach menopause, natural or surgical, the more you are at risk. It's estimated that 25 percent of women after natural menopause, and as much as 50 percent of women whose ovaries have been removed, will develop osteoporosis if they do not take replacement estrogen.[5] The risk is believed to be higher for women whose ovaries are removed before the age of forty-five.[6]

It may be difficult to appreciate the seriousness of a problem that may or may not affect you at some distant point in time, especially when you are preoccupied with the many other difficulties posed by endometriosis and its treatment. Moreover, compared with your other concerns, a fracture may seem insignificant.

However, bone loss is truly a threat to life and limb. When bone mass is severely deteriorated, fractures of the spine, wrist, or hip can occur spontaneously, without any mechanical stress or injury. These fractures occur in one in four postmenopausal women by the age of sixty-five, and the consequences can be deadly. Approximately 200,000 hip fractures occur each year, the majority of which are linked to osteoporosis; between 15 and 30 percent of those who suffer such fractures will die from associated complications.[7] And spinal (or crush) fractures, which result from the compression of spinal vertebrae, lead to severe back pain, reduction in height, disability, and the emotional devastation that accompanies pain and disfigurement.

The section below concerns the use of estrogen replacement therapy to prevent osteoporosis following surgical menopause. However, *all* women need to learn as much as possible about osteoporosis. Osteoporosis cannot be reversed; it can only be arrested. Therefore, prevention is essential. A natural method of prevention is a diet rich in calcium combined with regular weight-bearing exercise. Calcium supplements may be taken as well. Whatever your age, and whether or not you have undergone surgical menopause, by taking steps now to increase and maintain your bone mass, you can help avoid serious problems later in life. There are several organizations and publications that will help you assess and minimize the risk of developing osteoporosis. These resources can guide you in devising a diet and exercise plan (see Appendixes B and C).

Estrogen Replacement Therapy for Osteoporosis

Estrogen plays a significant role in remodeling bone; its absence increases loss of calcium and contributes to osteoporosis. Doses of at least 0.625 mg of conjugated estrogens have been shown to be effective in reducing bone loss; but higher doses, which may be hazardous, offer no additional bone-preserving benefits and carry additional risks.

Replacement estrogen to relieve symptoms such as hot flashes and vaginal atrophy can be started as needed and tapered off or eliminated once symptoms subside. However, for women who have experienced natural menopause, estrogen therapy, to be effective against osteoporosis, must start within three years of the menopause and continue until about age sixty-five, when bone loss slows. After surgical menopause, many women are advised to begin replacement therapy sooner and to continue it for a longer period. Studies show, for example, that women who take estrogen therapy for four years, and no therapy the following four years, lose the same amount of bone as women who were never on replacement estrogen.

Although it is not known how long replacement therapy is necessary after surgical menopause, some physicians suggest it must be a lifetime commitment.

About half of women who undergo surgical menopause will develop osteoporosis. For some, natural preventive measures may stem the risk. Nevertheless, there is no reliable way to detect bone loss until the damage is done. Therefore, most physicians believe that if you have lost your ovaries, you have no alternative as effective as estrogen replacement therapy. The medical consensus is that replacement estrogen is essential and its risks and discomfort do not equal the risks of osteoporosis.

If you decide to forego estrogen replacement after weighing your risk factors for osteoporosis, or if for any reason you cannot undergo replacement therapy, it is especially important that you minimize the risks, watch your diet, supplement your calcium intake if necessary, and get regular weight-bearing exercise to prevent as much bone loss as possible. Again, consult your physician before beginning any program of strenuous exercise. (Estrogen replacement therapy is discussed more fully below.)

INCREASED RISK OF HEART DISEASE

Women who reach natural menopause and women who experience surgical menopause are at an increased risk of heart disease, including hypertension, arteriosclerosis (hardening of the arteries), and heart attack, if they do not take replacement estrogen. (Some suggest that hysterectomy alone may slightly increase the risk, but the evidence is sketchy and contradictory.)

As with other symptoms and risks accompanying menopause, cardiovascular hazards are associated with low estrogen levels. Estrogen lowers blood levels of low-density lipoproteins, which increase the risk of heart disease. Levels of high-density lipoprotein, known to decrease the risk of heart disease, are raised by estrogen. So, cardiovascular risks provide yet another reason why you may be prescribed replacement estrogen.

ESTROGEN REPLACEMENT THERAPY

Few women's health care issues (except possibly endometriosis itself) have been the subject of as much vitriolic debate, misunderstanding, fear, and controversy as that of estrogen replacement following natural or surgical menopause.

In the 1940s Premarin—the leading estrogen used for replacement therapy—was widely used, although many competitors were vying for a share of the market. By 1947 researchers were pointing to estrogen's ability to cause overstimulation and resulting overgrowth of the uterine lining, which might progress to cancer. Research brought into question the often careless and unnecessary use of estrogens in postmenopausal women.[8] As information came to light about estrogen's harmful effect upon the uterine lining, the wholesale use of Premarin declined.

Then, in 1966, Dr. Robert Wilson published the now notorious book, *Feminine Forever*. In it he hawked estrogen as a "youth pill" that would banish what he called the horrible "living decay" of menopause. With estrogen, he preached, women would be "forever young."[9] American women, believing Dr. Wilson's magic potion was good-for-whatever-ails-you, beseeched their doctors to prescribe estrogen, often years before menopause, and prescriptions for Premarin soared. Others were equally strong in praising estrogen. Although estrogen has no effect whatsoever on the aging process, Dr. Wilson's propaganda, and extensive advertising by the manufacturers of Premarin, helped make it the fifth best-selling drug in the United States. More than six million women took it.

By the 1970s more information on estrogen and endometrial cancer surfaced. In December of 1976 the *New England Journal of Medicine* published the first of several articles offering conclusive findings revealing a five- to fourteen-fold increase in endometrial cancer among users of replacement estrogen over non-users.[10]

When these sobering reports made the headlines, the honeymoon, for many estrogen users, was over. The cancer scare was fueled by subsequent studies duplicating the original findings and women became increasingly fearful. Soon reports of possible association of estrogen use and breast cancer began to filter out and prescriptions for estrogen plummeted further.

Recently attention has centered on the hazards of DES, estrogen replacement, anabolic steroids, and high-dose oral contraceptives. The public is now wary not only of estrogens but hormones of any kind. Since both the benefits and hazards of estrogen have been subject to exaggerated claims, patients today are often ambivalent about its use.

The final word is not in. The long-term safety of ERT remains unknown, and it may be years before scientists provide unequivocal evidence of its benefits and risks. In the meantime, most physicians believe that, for most menopausal women, and particularly for younger women who have undergone surgical menopause, the benefits far outweigh the risks.

To feel comfortable about taking replacement hormones, and to make informed decisions, consider and weigh the risks and benefits for yourself. The choice is yours. Some women are given replacement estrogen in the hospital following surgery without being consulted beforehand. Discuss hormone therapy with your doctor *before* surgery.

Increased incidence of uterine cancer, gallbladder disease, and possibly breast cancer are serious concerns. For women with endometriosis there is a third concern—whether or not ERT will duplicate the hormonal environment in which endometriosis flourished in the first place.

Effectiveness

Estrogen replacement therapy has been shown to be effective in treating hot flashes, osteoporosis, urinary symptoms, vaginal atrophy, vaginitis, and vulvitis. Although sometimes prescribed by physicians or requested by patients to combat irritability or depression, there is no evidence that it is effective for this purpose. However, it does relieve physical distress and sleeplessness associated with hot flashes and thereby may improve psychological well-being. Some estrogen products contain antidepressants, tranquilizers, or sedatives. Many women are unaware of this and so believe estrogen itself has a profound effect on their emotional state. It does not. Nor does it prevent or delay the aging process.

Risks

It is difficult to clearly delineate the risks associated with ERT because studies have looked principally at estrogens in oral contraceptives and at combined estrogen and progesterone. Estrogens used for replacement therapy are usually natural rather than synthetic and dosages are much lower. They mimic the body's own premenopausal levels of these hormones. Dosages for contraception are significantly higher. It is, says one physician, like comparing apples and oranges.

Different types of estrogen may be used for hormone replacement. The most widely used, and some say the safest, are the natural, conjugated estrogens, not the synthetic estrogens used in oral contraceptives. Because the doses are low and the estrogen is natural, explains Dr. Margaret Davis of The George Washington University Medical Center, replacement estrogens have much less effect on the liver than the estrogens and dosages used in the birth control pill; and it is the liver where most of the complications of the pill can be traced. Consequently, explains Dr. Davis, "The very real problems seen in a small number of women on birth control pills—hypertension or venous thrombosis, for example—we don't see as problems in menopausal women on replacement therapy."

Risk of endometrial cancer. If you have had a hysterectomy, you are obviously not at risk of developing uterine cancer. If, however, your uterus remains intact and you experience ovarian failure, ERT may be prescribed, so you should be aware of its hazards.

Studies demonstrate that women taking estrogen (without progestin) are five to ten times more likely to develop endometrial (or uterine) cancer than women who do not. The risk appears to be associated with doses of higher than 1.25 mg taken for two years or more. Studies suggest there is no increased risk with dosages of 0.625 mg—the minimum required to prevent osteoporosis—and no increased risk when progesterone is added to the hormone regimen.

As you may recall from Chapter 1, one job of estrogen is to stimulate the growth of the uterine lining. Progesterone is responsible for opposing and limiting that growth. When replacement estrogens are unopposed by progesterone, the endometrium is continually instructed to proliferate. If endometrial growth is not held in check by progesterone, hyperplasia—excessive growth—may develop. Hyperplasia is a precancerous condition that may progress to uterine cancer. By adding progestins to the replacement estrogen, the endometrium is shed each month and therefore cannot overdevelop.

Risk of breast cancer. Shortly after studies documenting a relationship between estrogen and uterine cancer appeared, speculation turned toward a similar link to breast cancer, but the research has been highly contradictory. Various studies demonstrate a small increased risk of breast cancer in humans; others indicate no increased risk at all. Some even suggest a decreased risk.

Those studies pointing to an increase in breast cancer among ERT users link that increase to the duration and dosage of estrogen use. Rather than cause breast cancer, replacement estrogen may stimulate the growth of existing undetected cancer.

Many experts now believe there is no real evidence of an increased risk of breast cancer at dosages prescribed for replacement therapy.[11] They concede, however, that there may be a hazard at higher doses, so it makes sense to work with your doctor to determine the lowest dose possible to produce the desired effect. To be safe, if you have a history of breast cancer, don't use estrogen. Use extra caution, and be particularly vigilant about monthly breast self-examinations and regular monitoring, if you

- have a history of uterine cancer or benign breast lumps
- have a family history of breast cancer
- have had no pregnancies or a first pregnancy after thirty
- are obese
- use DES
- had your first menstrual period before twelve, or menopause after fifty-five

Progestins.   As research linked uterine cancer with estrogen replacement therapy and more attention was paid to a possible increased risk of breast cancer, most experts advocated the addition of a progestin for ten to thirteen days to estrogen replacement regimens. Additional progestins are known to modify the risk of uterine cancer, and because they may also protect against the development of breast cancer, they are usually recommended, even for women who have had hysterectomies and are not at risk for uterine cancer.

While estrogen replacement therapy is known to increase the risk of endometrial cancer, fewer women will die from such cancer than will die from complications arising from osteoporosis. Although research findings are contradictory, most experts suggest that when progestins are added to the estrogen regimen for at least ten days a month, there is no increased cancer risk. There is a risk with estrogen alone, but that is no longer the customary treatment program.

Risk of gallbladder disease.   Women who take ERT are two to three times more likely than nonusers to develop gallbladder disease requiring surgical intervention.[12] It is not known whether or not adding progestins decreases the risk.

Risk of heart disease.   Unlike estrogen used for contraception, low doses of estrogen to treat menopausal symptoms have not been associated with an increased risk of hypertension, heart attack, or stroke.[13] To the contrary, evidence suggests it helps prevent heart disease by reducing blood levels of low density lipoproteins, and increasing levels of high density lipoproteins. This is important to remember when considering estrogen replacement therapy. While there may be a danger of developing cancer as a result of estrogen therapy unopposed by progesterone, heart disease leads to far more deaths in women of all ages than does breast and uterine cancer combined.[14]

Some researchers believe that women who have a history of hypertension, heart attack, or stroke, or who are already high-risk candidates for heart disease (those who smoke, are obese, or have high cholesterol levels) are at increased risk with estrogen use. It is not yet known whether or not the addition of progestins nullifies the heart-protective effects of estrogen.

Thromboembolic disorders.   Estrogens used for contraception increase the risk of thrombophlebitis, embolism, and stroke. These disorders have not been observed in women using the natural, conjugated estrogens in the low doses recommended for menopausal symptoms.[15] Some studies even show a decreased risk.[16] But again, women with a prior history of thromboembolic disorders and those with existing risks factors should not use estrogen, for it may increase the likelihood of these disorders. What effect progestins may have is not yet clear.

Dosage and Administration

Doses of oral estrogens range from 0.3 to 3.0 mg. For most women, the standard accepted dosage for menopausal symptoms is between 0.3 to 0.625 mg of conjugated estrogens given from day 1 to day 25 of each month.

Natural estrogens given orally are

 conjugated estrogens: Premarin
 esterified estrogen: Estratab, Menest
 esterified estrogen with librium: Menrium
 estropipate: Ogen
 estradiol: Estrace

Synthetic estrogens given orally are

 ethynyl estradiol: Estinyl, Feminone
 chlorotrianisene: Tace
 DES
 quinestrol: Estrovis

Estrogen replacement hormones administered as vaginal creams are

 conjugated estrogen: Premarin
 dienestrol: DV, Estraguard, Ortho Dienestrol
 estropipate: Ogen
 estradiol: Estrace

DES (diethylstilbestrol) is administered as a vaginal suppository.

Hormones can also be administered by injection, subcutaneous implant, transdermal patch, in vaginal creams and suppositories, and as a wafer under the tongue.

When progestin is included in the regimen, it is given for at least ten days, usually days 16 through 25. Typically, 5 to 10 mg of medroxyprogesterone acetate are used. This and other progestins are listed here.

medroxyprogesterone acetate: Provera, Amen, Curretab
megestrol acetate: Megace
norethindrone: Norlutin
norethindrone acetate: Norlutate, Aygestin, Micronor, Nor Q-D
norgestrel: Overette

Contraindications, precautions, and side effects of progestins are discussed in Chapter 6.

When to Begin ERT or HRT

Many women are advised—or elect—to postpone estrogen replacement for a few weeks to as long as a year after surgery. This provides time for residual disease to fully regress, and it reduces the likelihood of a resurgence of endometriosis. Physicians differ in how they view the timing of replacement therapy. Some routinely begin therapy immediately after surgery, some wait several days, some six weeks, and others as long as six months to a year. The decision may be arbitrary, or may depend on the amount of endometriosis believed to remain after surgery. Before surgery, talk with your doctor about his preferences and yours with respect to the timing of hormone replacement.

Contraindications and Precautions

Replacement estrogen should not be taken by women with

- active thrombophlebitis or thromboembolic disorders
- acute liver disease
- history of thrombophlebitis, thrombosis, or thromboembolic disorders associated with previous estrogen use
- known or suspected cancer of the breast (except for patients specifically being treated with estrogens for such cancer)
- known or suspected estrogen-dependent tumors
- undiagnosed abnormal vaginal bleeding

Estrogen replacement may sometimes be used, with caution and frequent monitoring, in women who smoke, as well as those with

asthma
blood disorders
bone disease
cerebral vascular disorders
coronary artery disease
diabetes
epilepsy
fibroid tumors
gallbladder disease
heart impairment

history or family history of breast or uterine cancer,
   fibrocystic breast disease, breast nodules, or
   abnormal mammograms
history of depression
hypertension
liver impairment
migraines
obesity
severe varicose veins

Side Effects

Common side effects of estrogen replacement therapy, particularly when the dose is too high, are fluid retention, weight gain, leg cramps, headaches, nausea and vomiting, enlargement of fibroid tumors, and breast tenderness, enlargement, or secretion. Women who have had jaundice may experience it again while using replacement estrogens. Less common side effects are

abdominal cramps
bloating
breakthrough bleeding
candidiasis
cervical discharge
change in libido
cystitis

depression
dysmenorrhea
hair loss or excessive hair growth
intolerance to contact lenses
migraines
PMS-type symptoms
spotty skin discoloration

Many of these side effects can be reduced or eliminated by decreasing the dosage. (Ask your doctor before changing your dose.)

Should You Take Replacement Hormones?

Whether or not to take replacement hormones is a personal choice. It must be based on an assessment of your risks and a realistic appraisal of the pros and cons. It's difficult to make a decision when the data concerning hazards are so contradictory. There are alternative methods of eliminating hot flushes and reducing the discomfort of vaginal atrophy, but currently none provides adequate protection against osteoporosis or heart disease. Therefore, experts overwhelmingly agree that hormone replacement is essential for women whose ovaries have been removed. The risks associated with prolonged estrogen deficiency are far greater than the threat of recurrence of endometriosis or any risk associated with the use of replacement hormones. If you decide against hormone therapy, seek alternative remedies for troubling symptoms. Learn as much as possible about natural methods of preventing osteoporosis (see Appendix C).

If you decide to take replacement hormones, have a comprehensive physical examination first. Be sure it includes a complete medical history, breast exam, blood pressure check, vaginal smear (to reveal estrogen levels), blood and urine analyses, and a Pap smear. If you have had a hysterectomy, a Pap smear of the vaginal cuff can be done. If you have not had your uterus removed, an endometrial biopsy is generally necessary before you begin therapy. This rules out the possibility of a cancerous or precancerous condition. (The biopsy is not necessary with HRT.) Depending on your age and medical history, you may be advised to have a mammogram first. Be sure your doctor is aware of any conditions requiring monitoring, as well as any medications you are taking, to avoid drug interactions. See your doctor about a month later so he can adjust the dosage. To avoid problems and side effects, work with your doctor to find the lowest dose possible to achieve the necessary results.

It's especially important to have regular Pap tests, breast exams, and blood pressure checks while using replacement estrogen. Some physicians suggest regular check-ups every three to six months. Others say an annual check-up is sufficient. In addition, perform a breast self-examination each month (see Appendix A). If your uterus has not been removed, an endometrial biopsy may be necessary annually.

Report side effects to your doctor. Be especially alert to the following:

abdominal pain	leg pain
abnormal vaginal bleeding	pain, numbness, or swelling in the calves or
breast lumps	buttocks
change in color of urine or stools	severe headaches
chest pain	severe or persistent cough
coughing of blood	sudden shortness of breath
depression	swelling of hands or feet
faintness or dizziness	visual disturbances
jaundice (yellowing of white of	
eyes or skin	

Replacement therapy is a long-term commitment, and its effects are not completely known. Increased attention to the known risks and potential hazards of hormone replacement therapy will lead to further research. Try to stay current with research findings (see Chapter 16 and Appendix D).

10

Infertility and Its Treatment

"It's hard to separate the endometriosis from the infertility. Each month, my hopes and expectations rise as I await the time when my menstrual period should begin. Will I get pregnant this time? Did my last surgery and drug therapy combination work? Then, as the cramps, pain, and period start, I simultaneously experience the reality of endometriosis and the pain of infertility."

The challenges of endometriosis—both physical and emotional—are difficult. Perhaps the most difficult for many women are those associated with infertility. Treatment is arduous, and it arouses feelings that are complex and often overwhelming. To understand infertility, its treatment, and its emotional ramifications, you will need a great deal of information, guidance, and support. This chapter explores the medical aspects of infertility. Chapter 14 addresses some of the difficulties involved in resolving the crisis of infertility. The issues are extensive and far-reaching, and adequate coverage is beyond the scope of this book. Fortunately, however, there are a variety of excellent resources on the subject (see Appendixes B and C).

ENDOMETRIOSIS AND INFERTILITY

Infertility is usually defined as the inability to conceive after a year of unprotected intercourse. But infertility means more than that. It also means an inability to carry to term a live infant. Thus infertility refers to miscarriage, ectopic pregnancy, and stillbirth. As opposed to sterility, the absolute and permanent inability to conceive or carry a child to term, infertility suggests hope and often results from factors that can be corrected. A woman with primary infertility has never conceived; secondary infertility occurs in women whose fertility has already been demonstrated.

Approximately 30 to 40 percent of women with endometriosis are infertile, as opposed to about 15 percent of the general population. Women with endometriosis are said to be 20 times more likely to be infertile than those without,[1] and endometriosis is the most common cause for infertility in women older than twenty-five. Of all infertile women, more than one-third are said to have endometriosis. Often, infertility associated with endometriosis is secondary; following treatment, more than half will conceive, and most will deliver a healthy infant.

Possible Causes

When severe disease and adhesions produce anatomic distortions that thwart the mechanisms of conception—expulsion of the ripe ovum, fertilization, transport of the ovum through the tube to the uterus, and implantation—there is clearly a direct connection between endometriosis and infertility.

What is less clear is the relationship between infertility and *mild* disease in which the reproductive anatomy is *not* impaired. Women with untreated mild disease achieve pregnancy at rates similar to those who are treated, so some researchers believe that infertility in women with mild disease is coincidental; others are convinced that even mild disease may interfere with a woman's ability to conceive.

Infertility associated with mild endometriosis is probably the result of more than one factor, including impediments to sexual relations, ovulation, transport of the ovum, fertilization, and implantation. In addition, prostaglandins are implicated.

Sexual relations.   Avoidance of, or infrequent, intercourse, or inadequate penile penetration due to dyspareunia, obviously contribute to infertility. Dyspareunia, along with the fear and tension it can provoke, may cause muscle spasms which can affect the functioning of the fallopian tubes.

Anovulation.   Failure to ovulate is not uncommon in women with endometriosis. Whether it is caused by endometriosis, or is coincidental, is not yet known.

Luteinized unruptured follicle (LUF) syndrome.   This describes an ovarian follicle that has been stimulated by luteinizing hormone to produce progesterone yet fails to rupture and expel the ovum. Basal body temperature charts, endometrial biopsies, and plasma progesterone level tests may indicate that ovulation has occurred because progesterone levels are normal, yet the ovum has not been released from the ovarian follicle. Prostaglandins have been implicated in preventing the release of the ovum (see below). Studies to determine whether the incidence of LUF syndrome is increased in women with endometriosis have been contradictory.

Transport of the ovum.   Irritation from the ectopic endometrium and increased prostaglandins may result in decreased activity of the smooth muscle of the uterus and the tubes. This prevents transport of the ovum from the ovary to the uterus. Increased muscle activity may cause the ovum to reach the uterus before the lining is ready to sustain a pregnancy.

Macrophages.   The irritation and inflammation produced either by retrograde menstruation or by the debris of ectopic endometrium lead to an immune reaction—the formation of wandering scavenger, or clean-up, cells called *macrophages*. The macrophages recognize the ectopic endometrium—or its secretions—as foreign material and, in destroying the foreign invaders, destroy sperm cells as well. These macrophages, once present in the pelvic cavity of women with endometriosis, may release substances that negatively affect corpus luteum function, ovum transport, and fertilization and thereby interfere with fertility. Some studies indicate that the number of pelvic macrophages is increased in the peritoneal fluid and fallopian tubes of these women.

Reduced sperm motility.   Prostaglandins may diminish sperm motility and prevent the merger of sperm and ovum.

Luteal phase defects.   As you will recall from Chapter 1, the luteal phase— normally the last fourteen days of the reproductive cycle—is dominated by the corpus luteum's production of progesterone, which sustains the fertilized egg. When the luteal phase is too short—that is, when the corpus luteum begins to degenerate too quickly, not enough progesterone is produced. Or progesterone is not produced for a long enough time to fully prepare the uterine lining for implantation. Luteal phase defects may be more common in women with endometriosis, but studies have been contradictory.

Excessive uterine contractility.   Prostaglandins may produce excessive uterine contractility, which may interfere with the implantation of the fertilized ovum in the uterine lining.

Autoimmune responses.   Autoantibodies may be formed in response to substances secreted by the ectopic endometrium. This immune response may be weak or strong. If it is strong, the autoantibodies may prevent implantation or cause the uterus to reject the implanted embryo, thus causing spontaneous abortion in women with endometriosis.

Prostaglandins.   Ectopic endometrium secretes prostaglandins, which affect a variety of mechanisms associated with conception: the expulsion of the ovum, tubal motility, corpus luteum function, sperm motility, and the contractility of the uterus, which may affect implantation. Increased levels of prostaglandins can explain most of the impediments to fertility noted above. It also explains the increased incidence of spontaneous abortion noted by some researchers in women with even minimal disease who manage to conceive. There may be an association between infertility and high levels of prostaglandins in the peritoneal fluid, but findings are, to date, extremely contradictory.

PROGNOSIS FOR PREGNANCY

Although the location of endometriosis generally has no bearing on one's ability to conceive, the severity of the disease does. Women with severe disease are less responsive to treatment; the most significant factor seems to be the presence of dense adhesions in the area of the ovaries and fallopian tubes. In addition, women with severe tubal disease, particularly those who require complex surgery to unblock the tubes, are at an increased risk for an ectopic pregnancy.

Several studies link an increased incidence of spontaneous abortion, especially in mild disease, to untreated endometriosis. (Once the disease is treated, rates return to normal.) Others fail to confirm this finding. They suggest that the incidence of spontaneous abortion in women with endometriosis is not too different from that in the general population of women.

TREATMENT FOR ENDOMETRIOSIS-RELATED INFERTILITY

Choice of treatment depends on the location and severity of disease, age, and whether or not there are additional infertility factors. In general, women with moderate disease without dense adhesions and large endometriomas are treated medically or by therapeutic laparoscopy, perhaps followed by hormone therapy. Those with more severe disease and adhesions generally undergo conservative surgery during laparotomy. Some patients benefit from combination therapy with danazol pre- or postoperatively. Following treatment, if attempts to conceive are unsuccessful, additional fertility factors may be investigated and treated, and further treatment of the endometriosis may be necessary.

For patients with mild disease and no obvious impediments to fertility, approaches to treatment differ. It depends on whether or not the physician believes the mild endometriosis is responsible for the infertility. Those who do treat their patients in the same way they treat symptomatic patients unconcerned with childbearing, that is, with therapeutic laparoscopy and/or hormone therapy. Others point to studies that indicate that women with untreated mild endometriosis conceive just as readily as those who are treated. They recommend an expectant approach (see Chapter 5). Some physicians treat additional factors such as anovulation, luteal phase defects, and LUF syndrome first and allow the patient to conceive. Others prefer to treat the endometriosis first and see if conception occurs.

The Expectant Approach

An expectant or "wait and see" approach to infertility in patients with mild endometriosis involves ruling out male factors and detecting and correcting any additional female factors (see below) while treating mild symptoms with analgesics or prostaglandin inhibitors (shown by some researchers to increase the likelihood of pregnancy). Several studies have demonstrated that patients managed with expectant treatment conceive at rates equal to or better than those of women treated with medicine or by surgery.

One advantage is that the couple can attempt to conceive immediately, without waiting the six months necessary for medical therapy, and without exposing the woman to the side effects of medical therapy or the risks of surgery. There is a disadvantage, however. According to some studies, more spontaneous abortions are apt to occur before the disease is treated. Other studies, as noted above, have found no significant increase in spontaneous abortions in patients with endometriosis. In fact, there seems to be more, or just as many, spontaneous abortions in treated, as opposed to untreated, patients.[2]

Expectant therapy for women with mild disease has produced pregnancy rates of 31 to 75 percent. When anovulation is corrected, rates increase to 62 to 72 percent.

Most physicians limit the length of time that an infertile patient with mild disease will be managed expectantly before the endometriosis itself is treated. Some allow a patient six months to conceive, others one year, and still others as long as eighteen months, depending on the patient's age.

Male factors.   A man may not produce enough sperm to fertilize an ovum, or he may not produce enough sperm that are normally shaped and capable of moving through and surviving the woman's cervical mucus. Sperm insufficiency or inadequacy needs to be detected and corrected in an expectant approach to treatment (see below). The causes of male infertility are structural, genetic, and hormonal disorders, infections, sexually transmitted disease, and exposure to radiation.

Female factors.   There are a number of female factors other than endometriosis to be detected and corrected in an expectant approach. Their treatment is discussed more fully below.

- adhesions and scarring, which block the tubes, from present or previous infection or disease (pelvic inflammatory disease)
- anatomic or genetic abnormalities
- anovulation
- cervical factors, which prevent passage of sperm to the uterus, such as hostile or impassable cervical mucus, stenosis, and infection
- hormonal imbalances or deficiency caused by under- or overactive thyroid or adrenal glands

- infection from sexually transmitted diseases (gonorrhea, syphilis, T-Mycoplasma, and Chlamydia)
- luteal phase defects, resulting in insufficient progesterone, which renders the endometrium unprepared for implantation and sustenance of the fertilized ovum
- ovarian failure (the premature depletion of the ovaries' egg supply)

INVESTIGATING INFERTILITY: THE WORK-UP

The infertility work-up allows the specialist to pinpoint the above factors, as well as problems in sexual technique, so that appropriate treatment may begin. The work-up itself, the diagnostic tests, additional factors for infertility and their treatment, how to cope with the emotional strain of the work-up, as well as the diagnosis and treatment of male factor infertility are all covered in detail in numerous publications listed in Appendix C. Appendix B also refers you to organizations that provide not only information but emotional support as well. Included are networks of individuals who have gone through—or are going through—the same difficult pursuit and whose experience and solidarity can be invaluable. The infertility work-up is expensive, confusing, emotionally draining, all-consuming, and life disrupting. Make every effort to learn as much as possible beforehand.

Finding the Right Medical Treatment

Infertility investigations are sometimes carried out by a family physician or a gynecologist. Many women prefer, however, a specialist known as a reproductive endocrinologist—a gynecologist with additional training and certification in the area of infertility. Comprehensive care is also provided in clinics or centers that specialize in infertility. These clinics use a team approach to problems of infertility. The staff usually includes, in addition to a reproductive endocrinologist, other specialists (including a urologist to diagnose and treat male factors) as well as counselors, sex therapists, psychologists, and social workers. Some centers insist on counseling as a routine part of the work-up. When counseling is optional, couples are often reluctant to take advantage of the help of a trained therapist. They believe they will be able to cope with the work-up and with the effect infertility will have on their lives. Unfortunately, they often realize too late that infertility, its diagnosis and treatment, is nothing short of a life crisis, one they are ill prepared to meet. Counseling helps prepare you for the challenges to come. It assists you in making difficult decisions, offers you the perspective of experience, and guides you in supporting your partner.

Beginning the Work-Up

A woman with known endometriosis may begin an infertility investigation when she has difficulty conceiving after treatment, for endometriosis, or when her disease is mild enough not to warrant treatment. Then other factors, both male and female, must be ruled out or discovered and treated.

Many women seeking help for infertility are introduced to the word *endometriosis* for the first time. These asymptomatic and unsuspecting women are frequently surprised by the diagnosis.

Endometriosis may be diagnosed before or during the work-up. Either way, this tedious, emotionally taxing and aptly termed process is more or less the same for everyone. Only the timing and sequence of the individual tests are likely to change. For the infertile woman who has not yet been diagnosed with endometriosis, the work-up generally begins only after the couple has attempted to achieve pregnancy for one year. However, for a woman who has already been diagnosed and treated for endometriosis yet is unable to conceive, or a woman who is older than thirty, the process may begin much sooner.

Initial consultation. Together, you and your partner meet with the infertility specialist to discuss the procedure and schedule initial tests. Complete medical, sexual, and reproductive histories will be taken, and both you and your partner will have a complete physical examination. The diagnostic tests are usually done in the order below. The sequence, however, depends on your own situation, the findings of previous tests, and the preferences of the specialist.

Semen analysis. The quantity and quality of sperm must first be determined. Following two days without sexual activity, your partner will ejaculate sperm into a sterile container for microscopic examination. If it is normal, there is no further testing, and the rest of the work-up will focus on you.

Test of hormone levels. A series of blood tests measure your levels of such hormones as FSH, LH, prolactin, testosterone, and androgen.

Basal body temperature charting: detecting and pinpointing ovulation. The specialist will first determine whether or not you are ovulating, approximately when you ovulate, and how long your luteal phase lasts. Each morning before you get out of bed you will take your temperature and record it on a prepared chart. Progesterone, produced only after ovulation, is thermogenic, meaning it produces heat and thus raises your body temperature. If ovulation occurs, your chart will show a slight elevation of temperature just after ovulation. Your temperature will remain elevated until just before your period. Ovulation is also tested by determination of levels of progesterone in the blood.

Postcoital test. Once ovulation is established and an approximate time determined, you will be scheduled for a postcoital test. The purpose of this test is to evaluate the quality of the cervical mucus and the ability of sperm to penetrate, bypass, and survive it. At ovulation the cervical mucus becomes thin and watery so that sperm can penetrate. If the mucus is still too thick, sperm cannot get through to the uterus. This painless test is performed just before ovulation is believed to occur. You will be instructed to have intercourse within twelve hours before your appointment and not to bathe or douche. A sample of cervical mucus is taken to determine, under the microscope, the number and motility of sperm cells. Depending on the findings, you may be asked to repeat the test to ensure that it is performed before ovulation has occurred. (See Appendix A.)

Endometrial biopsy.   A tiny piece of endometrial tissue is examined several days before menstruation to determine whether or not you are producing enough progesterone to permit implantation and sustenance of the fertilized ovum in the uterine lining. (See Appendix A.)

Hysterosalpingography.   The uterus and tubes are x-rayed between menstruation and ovulation to determine the shape and contour of the uterus, and whether or not the tubes are open. The specialist tries to visualize any adhesions that may be surrounding the opening of the tubes. The procedure follows a pelvic examination. (See Appendix A.)

Laparoscopy.   This procedure is done between menstruation and ovulation to evaluate the reproductive anatomy. If you have not previously been diagnosed with endometriosis, it is only at this point in the work-up that the disease can be confirmed. Even if you have been previously laparoscoped and diagnosed with endometriosis, the procedure may be repeated to assess progression or evaluate the results of previous therapy and destroy adhesions. Minor abnormalities can be corrected and the disease cauterized or vaporized. The surgeon will determine if the tubes are patent by injecting blue dye into the uterus through the cervical opening to see if it emerges from the fimbriated ends of the fallopian tubes. (See Appendix A.)

Hysteroscopy.   At the time of laparoscopy the surgeon will visualize the uterine cavity and examine it for growths, abnormalities, and adhesions. (See Appendix A.)

Ultrasound.   At some point during the work-up a sonogram of the abdomen may be recommended to determine the shape and size of the uterus.

Treatment of Male and Female Infertility

As mentioned earlier, in the treatment of infertility, both male factors and additional female factors must be detected and corrected. Treatment of male factor infertility is often more difficult and less successful than treatment of female factor infertility. It involves the administration of hormones or antibiotics and/or surgery to correct structural problems. For diagnosis and treatment, men generally need to consult a urologist. Female infertility factors may be treated in the following ways.

Anovulation.   Ovulation may be induced in women with patent tubes by using drugs such as clomiphene citrate (Clomid or Serophene) or with human menopausal gonadotropin (Pergonal). Injections of human chorionic gonadotropin (HCG) (A.P.L., Profasi HP, or

Pregnyl) help it along. In women who produce an excess of prolactin, ovulation may be induced with a drug called bromocriptine (Parlodel). A newer method of inducing ovulation involves GnRH analogues.

Luteal phase defects.   Clomiphene citrate, HCG, natural progesterone injections or vaginal suppositories, and injections of a drug called Delalutin are all used to treat luteal phase defects.

Cervical and other factors.   Problems with cervical mucus are treated with hormones, douches that alter the acidity of the mucus, drugs to liquefy the mucus, or estrogen therapy during the first half of the cycle. When cervical factors cannot be overcome, the specialist may suggest artificial insemination—injecting sperm directly into the uterus to bypass the cervical mucus. Hormonal imbalances and problems with the thyroid or adrenal glands are treated medically, and surgery may be necessary not only to treat endometriosis, but to correct anatomic abnormalities, unblock tubes, and remove adhesions. The treatment of infections varies depending on their types. There is no treatment for ovarian failure.

CIRCUMVENTING INFERTILITY

When medical and surgical attempts to overcome infertility prove fruitless, couples may want to explore in vitro fertilization/embryo transfer and gamete intrafallopian transfer. These techniques do not correct infertility but circumvent it.

These are promising options for many women with endometriosis, but they are physically and emotionally arduous and pose a considerable challenge for the infertile couple. The procedures are extremely expensive ($2000 to $8000 per attempt) and seldom covered by insurance. Not everyone is accepted, and institutions providing these services often have stringent criteria as well as long waiting lists. Finally, not all who try these techniques will achieve pregnancy; in fact, most will not.

Couples need to be well informed about all aspects and repercussions of the procedures—physical, emotional, financial, and social. They must enter the programs, not without hope, but with a realistic assessment of their chances. They should understand that they may need to explore other avenues to parenthood such as adoption or surrogate motherhood.

In Vitro Fertilization/Embryo Transfer (IVF/ET)

In vitro fertilization/embryo transfer is an option for infertile women who have healthy ovaries but whose fallopian tubes have been removed or are damaged. IVF/ET, performed at approximately 120 centers in the United States, has resulted in the birth of more than 1000 babies. Results are excellent for women with mild and moderate disease who are unable to achieve pregnancy following traditional treatments for endometriosis.

Normally, conception occurs in the fallopian tube. In IVF, conception occurs in a glass laboratory dish. Ova are surgically removed and combined with sperm from a woman's husband or a donor. Once fertilization occurs and the ova are incubated, they are transferred to the uterus.

IVF/ET is usually reserved for women who are not good candidates for surgical correction of the tubes or who had surgical correction but did not achieve pregnancy after at least one year. Criteria for acceptance in IVF/ET programs vary. Sometimes a woman must be under forty and married. She must have at least one accessible ovary not involved with scar tissue or adhesions. If her husband's sperm, rather than donor sperm, are to be used, a normal sperm count must be demonstrated. Occasionally couples are required to undergo psychological counseling and testing. They should be emotionally prepared to cope with the stress that typically accompanies the procedure.

Once selected as a candidate, you are given fertility drugs (clomiphene citrate or human menopausal gonadotropin, with or without human chorionic gonadotropin) to mature multiple ovarian follicles, usually on days 3 to 7 of your menstrual cycle. By about day 8 to 10, daily monitoring will begin to track the progress of the maturing follicles and pinpoint ovulation. You will be instructed to chart your basal body temperature. Then you will be monitored daily by abdominal ultrasound to track the maturation of the follicles. Cervical mucus will be checked to help determine the approach of ovulation, and daily blood samples taken to evaluate the hormonal changes associated with the various stages of follicular development.

When this daily monitoring indicates optimal conditions, an injection of human chorionic gonadotropin will cause ovulation to occur approximately thirty-six hours later. A laparoscopy to retrieve ova will be scheduled to take place thirty-four to thirty-six hours after the injection of HCG. A long needle inserted into the abdominal incision will pierce all ripe follicles and aspirate as many ova as possible (usually one to three). Mature ova retrieved will be placed in a culture dish with the sperm. The dish will then be placed in an incubator for approximately 36 hours to allow development and cell division. If during incubation the embryo develops normally, you and your husband will be called to the hospital for embryo transfer approximately two days after the laparoscopy.

The embryos will be inserted through a catheter into your uterus. After bedrest lasting from several hours up to two days you will be discharged and instructed in the use of progesterone to support a pregnancy. Within ten days to two weeks you will know whether or not pregnancy has occurred. IVF/ET is successful in approximately 20 percent of women, although about one-quarter of the pregnancies do not reach term. When the first attempt is unsuccessful, additional attempts are often made.

Continued research and experimentation in IVF/ET has resulted in two simplified versions that eliminate the need for general anesthesia and surgery to retrieve ova. Transvaginal IVF uses the high-frequency vibrations produced by ultrasound to image the abdomen and guide the placement of the needle through the vaginal wall. A similar technique, transabdominal IVF, employs the same principles, but the ova are retrieved through a needle inserted in the bladder or urethra. These nonsurgical techniques are quicker, often less expensive, less risky, and more comfortable. They are new, however, and so not yet performed at all IVF centers.

Gamete Intrafallopian Transfer (GIFT)

Another less complex and less expensive type of in vitro fertilization—the GIFT technique—may soon be available. IVF/ET is appropriate for women with damaged fallopian tubes. The GIFT procedure, on the other hand, provides hope for women whose fallopian tubes are intact but who nevertheless are infertile as a consequence of unknown factors associated with endometriosis, male factors, problems with cervical mucus, immunological problems, or luteinized unruptured follicle syndrome.

The GIFT procedure is basically similar to IVF up to the point where the ova are retrieved. But the ova, instead of being mixed with sperm in a culture dish and dividing in an incubator, are loaded in a catheter with sperm obtained earlier and are inserted through the laparoscope (immediately following the laparoscopic retrieval of the ova) in the fimbrial opening of the fallopian tube. Once in the tube, sperm and ova mingle just as they would following intercourse. Fertilization occurs more or less naturally.

In a very small study group, GIFT has achieved about a 25 to 30 percent pregnancy rate. Since the procedure is new, however, its availability is limited. Research continuing at centers worldwide should lead to greater access to GIFT in the coming years.

When infertility treatments do not result in pregnancy, there are other paths to parenthood, such as adoption and surrogate motherhood. These are addressed in Chapter 16.

PART 3

Emotional Aspects

"*The simple everyday rules that govern the way we act are changed for the sick. Though their world and ours look the same, sound the same, are the same, the rules are different, as in a science fiction story in which an alien from another planet invades an earthman's body and takes over. Nobody can tell because to all appearances the earthling is still the same, and thereby hangs the danger.*"[1]

We tend to think of sickness as germs and viruses—foreign entities to be eradicated. But there are actually two components to sickness: *disease*, which concerns abnormal physiological processes involving cells, tissues, and organs; and *dis-ease*, the crisis and the malaise caused by disease. Dis-ease is the cumulative stress involved in attempting to meet the challenges of disease and the failure to resolve or adapt to disruption and loss.

Disease is usually observable through analysis of body fluids, x-rays, biopsies, and other medical tests. You are aware of disease through your physical symptoms. Dis-ease is not necessarily visible, is almost impossible to measure, and may be unrecognized or misunderstood by both physicians and patients.

For women whose symptoms are mild, who are unaffected or unconcerned by infertility, and for whom treatment adequately controls endometriosis, there may be little dis-ease. For others, endometriosis may pose multiple crises, the effects of which radiate like the spokes of a wheel, piercing all areas of their lives.

While Parts 1 and 2 have been concerned with physical disease, Part 3 explores how physical, psychological, and social elements interweave to create the dis-ease that endometriosis may cause. Keep in mind that Part Three raises *potential* problems experienced by women with severe endometriosis. Many women will never face these difficulties. It's important, however, that you be aware of the possible emotional consequences, so that you can guard against them.

11

Dis-ease:
An Overview

"I know I must accept the fact that endometriosis is going to change the rest of my life and that it will prevent me from doing everything I wanted to do. Endometriosis is a lot more than just a physical disease."

"I drink now more than I used to. I worry a lot. I think I'm getting an ulcer. I don't think I'm coping very well."

"I have tried very hard to keep my sense of humor during these years, but it gets tougher and tougher. There are periods of time when I just can't put on that happy face any more."

"The disease is not only rotting away at my insides. It plays tricks on your mind and your sanity. I feel like it's almost a test to see how strong I am, but I'm not that strong and I feel like I'm fighting a losing battle. My social life is a thing of the past. I can't make plans for more than one day at a time. It's more than just sleepless nights and endless crying. When the pain gets too bad for the pain pills to work, I have to go to the emergency room where they give me a shot of Demerol and send me home."

"I used to have a good sex life...no problems having orgasms and no pain. During the past year things have changed drastically. I started getting severe shooting pains, burning, and numbness during sex. What used to take five minutes to have an orgasm now takes 15 minutes and the feeling is not as intense. My boyfriend and I are greatly discouraged because we know how good our lovemaking used to be. Now I don't even want to be touched for the fear of the pain."

"I know more about myself as a result of endometriosis than I ever knew before, both physically and emotionally."

"Learning to live with pain is a profound lesson. It's made me more sympathetic. I'm much less agitated about things that really don't matter."

"I try to be more flexible and make no long-range plans. I try not to let endometriosis or infertility become the most important thing in my life."

The traditional medical approach to endometriosis focuses on the suppression of symptoms and often ignores the dis-ease that results from disease. The typical patient's approach is to search for a cure. Particularly for women with infertility or severe pain, the constant pursuit of pregnancy or an as yet nonexistent cure keeps the focus on disease and away from dis-ease. "When I get cured," you may think, "things will be better." "I don't have time to worry about other issues now, I'm looking for a cure." "All I want is to get pregnant, so I'll live with the pain as long as it takes." You may not develop coping strategies to deal with the kinds of issues, losses, and disruptions that continue to confront you daily, seriously diminishing the quality of your life.

You may spend the majority of your hours in pain, going from one treatment to another, enduring side effects, facing consequences of these treatments and worrying about the future. You may have little time or energy left to engage in normal activities. Your social world may begin to slip away as you are preoccupied with your disease or unable to take part as a result of pain and fatigue. Your work may suffer or you may begin to fear reprisals for poor job performance or excessive sick leave. Infertility and diminished or deteriorated sexual activity may strain your intimate relationships. You may feel guilty about the burdens you think you are placing on friends, family members, or your mate. You may fear the reaction of future partners toward your potential infertility or difficulties with sex. You may even try to find a mate to test your fertility. Whether single or married, fertile or infertile, you may begin to feel defective, not wholly a woman. Together, these changes erode your body image, your self-image, and your self-esteem.

In addition to these fears, concerns, and difficulties, you may experience treatment failures or disease recurrences. This overwhelming combination can leave you feeling helpless and ineffectual, convinced that your situation is hopeless. Anger, depression, and despair result. Initially, you may be unable to see how thoroughly your life has become engulfed by endometriosis or infertility. Then, you may find that you cannot extricate yourself from the role that sickness or infertility has cast you in, or you no longer have the motivation and the optimism to try. You have forgotten what your "normal" life was like.

If you put your life on hold while pursuing a cure yet ignore the emotional toll, you can lose in two respects. You are unlikely to find a cure, but you are likely to sacrifice your present activities, pleasures, and goals to the search. Your days will be dominated by disease as well as dis-ease.

The diagnosis of a chronic disease, for most, is a passport to a foreign territory. There's no way to know what's around the bend, what challenges lie ahead. Nevertheless, you may feel that you are uniquely unprepared, unable to cope, somehow weaker or less adequate than others because you can't easily integrate the experience of illness into your life. It's normal to feel confused, frightened, and overwhelmed. Without contact with other women with endometriosis, you may not know what is normal or abnormal. Perhaps you wonder if you are overreacting.

The emotional repercussions of endometriosis will vary according to the individual, depending on the severity of disease; the frequency, rapidity and virulence with which it recurs; and the degree to which it disrupts one's life and goals. The way you handle it depends on your personality, your family history, your style of coping, and other factors.

It is helpful to know that most individuals perceive chronic illness as a crisis. In response to the threat, they go through a somewhat predictable series of stages, or phases, of adaptation. Women with endometriosis are no exception, but they may go through these stages more than once, since they face multiple crises and multiple losses, each of which must be resolved. The five stages below have been described and delineated somewhat differently by various theorists. The concepts are basically similar, however, and apply equally to issues of pain, infertility, and hysterectomy.

The initial stage is *crisis*, in which you become aware of a threat to your well-being. As symptoms begin to interfere with your daily activities you try to track down the cause of the problem. It's a period of anxiety and uncertainty that leads eventually to diagnosis. Then the threat is identified and given a name. The next stage is *reaction to diagnosis*. This period of absorption is characterized by shock, disbelief, fear, and anxiety.

Fear sometimes transforms initial disbelief into full-fledged denial. Most women, though, soon emerge from this stage and take action to minimize the threat, gather information, and tend to the details of treatment. In this third stage of *mobilization*, daily life is dominated by disorder, disequilibrium, and efforts to understand and control the disease. During this period you may feel out of control, overwhelmed by the demands placed upon you. The rest of your life has been put on hold while you try to cope with symptoms and attend to treatment.

When treatments prove ineffective, or only temporarily effective, and the chronicity of the disease becomes increasingly apparent, the full weight of emotional loss sinks in. Since disease and dis-ease involve losses of many kinds, in the next stage, *grieving*, you may experience reactions similar to those identified by Elisabeth Kübler-Ross in relation to death and dying: anxiety, anger, guilt, and depression. Grief is the bridge to resolution. Without working through losses, you cannot move forward. If you acknowledge your losses and allow yourself to grieve, however, you can take the necessary steps toward the final stage of reorganization or resolution.

For some, the last stage, *resolution*, is dominated by an extremely difficult task: weighing the diminished quality of your life as a result of endometriosis against your desire to maintain your childbearing ability or retain your reproductive organs. At this time, you may consciously and willfully (as opposed to passively) decide to live with the disease, learning to adapt to the illness and minimize its impact, or you may opt for definitive surgery and cope with any changes it brings.

The aim of either option is to move from helplessness and passive suffering toward equilibrium. The tasks of resolution are several: develop practical strategies for dealing with the medical experience; minimize your losses and disruptions; grieve for those that can't be eliminated; restore or redefine your social roles; repair battered relationships; and prepare for recurrences and setbacks.

Family members and mates go through similar stages. This is because endometriosis affects them as well. They need help in coping with the changes and their own sense of helplessness. They, too, may need to work through denial, anger, and depression, and they also need to grieve for losses they incur as a result of your illness. Unfortunately, it is unlikely that you and they will go through the various stages at the same time. The discrepancies may increase the tension you feel.

The five stages are normal, necessary steps in coping with the diagnosis and emotional repercussions of a chronic illness. Different individuals pass through different stages in different sequences; sometimes the stages overlap. You may go through them more than once. But dis-ease produces isolation, so sometimes individuals have the impression that their reactions are unique, that they are the only ones who have gone through this. It's helpful to recognize that others have faced similar stages and feelings.

Part 3 offers a brief guide to these phases of adaptation, from diagnosis to resolution. Although each woman journeys along her own route, each looks forward to the same outcome—resolution. Learning to recognize the stages and the signposts along the way will help you realize that you are not a sole traveler. You may be able to navigate the shortest route to resolution, avoiding common pitfalls, distractions, and detours along the way.

12

From Diagnosis to Treatment

"I felt that deep down my husband, my friends, and my employer were all quite skeptical about whether I was ill or simply a hypochondriac."

"Before diagnostic laparoscopy, I didn't know what the possibilities might be. My doctor didn't tell me what findings he anticipated. It's very frightening not knowing what to expect."

The emotional repercussions of illness begin with the onset of symptoms. When symptoms erupt suddenly and dramatically, they tend to be accompanied by rapidly escalating anxiety. When they are vague, or develop slowly, as is more often the case with endometriosis, anxiety builds gradually. Nagging suspicions are harder and harder to ignore.

Actually, the anxiety is useful. It leads you to seek medical care. Unfortunately, it may take months, or even years, before symptoms and anxieties are compelling enough to motivate you to see a doctor. Even then diagnosis may not be immediately forthcoming. As discussed in Chapter 4, there are many difficulties involved in detecting endometriosis.

THE STRESS OF UNCERTAINTY

Prolonged uncertainty is a great stressor. When you do not know the cause of pain or other symptoms, your mind tends to cast relentlessly over the possibilities. Preoccupied with what might be, you fall prey to anxieties both rational and irrational. In his book, *The Clay Pedestal*, Dr. Thomas Preston writes: "The most frightening and intolerable condition of sickness is to have no explanation of the cause, as this means not knowing how bad the illness is, how long it will last, how to combat it, and whether it is contagious."[1]

Without a diagnosis, you have, or may believe you have, no legitimate claim to pain, no logical recourse. You wonder, "Is it all in my head?" You begin to doubt that there really is a physical problem. Others may reinforce this fear by also expressing doubt, or by accusing you of malingering or of playing for sympathy. Your pain may come and go; it may last for only a few days each month. You may show no outward signs of disability and look perfectly healthy. It's often difficult, therefore, for others to accept that anything is truly wrong.

Frustrated and angry with doctors who cannot help you, with friends and family who don't seem to take you seriously, you must also deal with the symptoms themselves: the continuing pain, the discomfort of intercourse, and infertility. Pain can disrupt your work, but employers may not be very understanding. Pain can also prevent you from taking part in leisure activities. You may be accused of exaggerating normal aches and pains to avoid social obligations. The emotional wear-and-tear may cause you to withdraw still further.

The doubt expressed by others can be humiliating, frustrating, and fatiguing. Feeling defeated and demoralized, you may begin to ignore or minimize your symptoms. You may stop searching for the cause of your discomfort, telling yourself nothing's really wrong.

In *We Are Not Alone: Learning to Live with Chronic Illness*, author Sefra Kobin Pitzele best describes the results of this self-doubt: "As time goes on, feeling bad—and feeling bad about not feeling well—becomes normal for us, and we forget what it feels like to be healthy. As our confidence in our own judgment erodes still further, we depend more and more on the judgment of those people who seem to have grown numb to our complaints. Before long, we don't know what to believe."

If you convince yourself that nothing is wrong, your denial will prevent you from getting adequate professional care or learning methods of self-care, and you will continue to suffer the consequences of the disease. Trust your instincts. Develop the assertiveness you need to pursue the best possible medical care. You know your body best. If you feel that something is wrong, insist on the most logical medical route to take, and be as persistent as you need to be.

DIAGNOSTIC PROCEDURES

As much as you might want to know what is causing your symptoms, the prospect of a surgical diagnostic procedure is likely to provoke considerable anxiety. If you are young and otherwise in good health, you have probably never faced surgery. Perhaps you have never been admitted to a hospital. Often a physician will not, or cannot, tell you what he expects to find. Perhaps he is unsure, or does not want to alarm you unnecessarily. Yet many women are far more alarmed by not knowing what to expect. They worry, "Is it fatal?" "Is it cancer?" They wonder if they will awaken from surgery with all their organs intact.

On the other hand, faced with diagnostic surgery, you may get cold feet and renew earlier doubts: "Am I blowing this out of proportion?" "What if there really is nothing wrong and I subject myself to surgery? Is it really worth the risk and the expense to find out?"

Ultimately, some will be too frightened or reluctant to proceed, preferring to live with the symptoms and the unknown. Others will delay the procedure until symptoms are intolerable. The idea of exploratory surgery can be frightening. Even more troubling, however, is the possibility that a potentially progressive condition that can drastically impair your health and fertility will go undetected and untreated. Don't let fears prevent you from following through with necessary diagnostic measures. If apprehension causes you to hesitate or procrastinate, gathering information will ease your anxiety. Ask your doctor or nurse to fully explain laparoscopy—what it entails, how it feels, what are the risks, and what can be expected in terms of recuperation and follow-up. Insist on a clear explanation of what the findings may be. For further reassurance, talk to other women who have been through it. (See Appendixes A and C for a list of publications that fully describe diagnostic and surgical procedures.) Contact the Endometriosis Association (see Appendix B). It can provide you with information and put you in touch with women who will share their experiences with you.

AFTER DIAGNOSIS

Often, women who have a difficult time getting diagnosed feel both angry and vindicated when they at last learn they have endometriosis.[1] This sets the stage for a troubled relationship with their doctor and those who doubted they were truly ill. If you find yourself angry at doctors because they could not diagnose you quickly, or wounded by friends and family who doubted you, try to acknowledge and work through your feelings. Anger can simmer into resentment or hostility and alienate those whose advice, trust, and support are vital to your recovery.

Other women are relieved to finally hear the word endometriosis: They have a "legitimate" name for their condition. Recognition of the disease process implies hope. But this euphoria doesn't last, for soon they begin to comprehend the reality of the disease and must face the challenges of coping.[2]

Disbelief

Serious or chronic illness is a fact of life. Yet we tend to believe it only strikes others. Especially when we are young we believe that we are indestructible, invulnerable, and inviolable. It shakes us when our faith in our own bodies is betrayed.

If you have had little difficulty obtaining a diagnosis, you may feel astounded to learn that you have a disease. The condition is totally unfamiliar to you, and the unwieldiness and gravity of the name seem ominous.

The way the news is delivered often affects the way it is received. This, of course, will depend on the extent and severity of your disease and the style, philosophy, and communication skills of your physician. If you are told you have an incurable chronic disease that, although it may be treated in a variety of ways, can be permanently eradicated only by definitive surgery, you will be understandably alarmed, perhaps numb, unable to take it all in. You may believe that definitive surgery is inevitable. If, on the other hand, you are told you have a disease that is unpredictable, that tends to be recurrent, and if you are reassured that treatments, resources, and coping strategies are available to you, that in the majority of cases definitive surgery is *not* necessary, your shock and anxiety will be minimized. Finally, if you are *not* told of the recurrent nature of endometriosis, but merely offered a treatment plan, your initial response may be mild and you may approach treatment with an optimistic attitude that you will be cured. Should the disease recur, however, you will likely become increasingly frustrated, resenting the fact that you were not prepared for the possibility of persistent disease following treatment.

Fear

Initial reactions of relief, disbelief, and shock generally give way to a variety of fears and anxieties. Many questions running through your mind will compete for your attention. If recently diagnosed and informed about the unpredictability and recalcitrant nature of endometriosis, you may become preoccupied with the long-term consequences: Will I be able to have children? Will I need a hysterectomy? Will the pain ever end? Can endometriosis lead to cancer? Will there be recurrences? What will happen if I don't get treatment? Will it get worse? If I have a daughter, will I pass this on to her?

In addition there will be the fear of further tests and treatments. It is the rare individual who feels no anxiety when faced with unfamiliar medical tests or therapeutic procedures. When medical treatment is advised, anxiety over side effects as well as long-term effects of the medications, is normal. A woman approaching treatment may fear the hospital experience, surgery and its risks and complications, and even doctors and technicians whose job it is to poke and probe. It is not unusual to fear pain, mutilation, dependency, loss of bodily function, and even death.

These and other fears may help you or hurt you, depending on your reactions to them. They may motivate you to seek information and develop strategies for coping, or they may cause you to feel overwhelmed and to retreat into denial. If your fears, anxieties, and feelings of loss of control are too threatening or overwhelming, you may consciously or unconsciously try to push them away and ignore them, choosing instead to deny the reality of the situation.

It is often helpful to realize that your fears gain strength in numbers. They are more formidable when united, and less threatening when you break them down and look at them individually. Confront your fears; look first at those that are most threatening. Imagine your worst fears coming true and think about how you would respond. Then look at those fears again. Write them down. Talk about them with someone you trust. Ask yourself which are realistic.

Many of your worst fears derive from a lack of information. Determine what facts you need to reduce or eliminate them. Although it may be difficult to absorb information in the moments immediately following diagnosis, the more information you receive soon after, the less likely you are to feel stunned, alone, overwhelmed, and helpless. A lack of such information gives substance to your greatest fears and leaves you feeling bewildered and isolated. Doctors can help by providing clear information and resources, by encouraging questions, and by offering support and guidance. Don't expect your doctor, however, to anticipate all your fears and understand all your information needs. Speak up. Ask questions and state concerns. Again, it may be helpful at this point to talk to others who have been through this stage and who can help you put your fears in perspective.

For those anxieties that remain, ask yourself which you can do something about and which you cannot. While it can be tremendously helpful not to dwell on things that you cannot change, it can also be unproductive to ignore aspects of the disease that are painful or that frighten you. Often by facing those feelings and taking action you can reduce the anxiety that accompanies a diagnosis. It is only by facing your fears in this way that you can begin to take action against them.

Denial

"I often wonder, why me? Sometimes I throw myself into my work and my studies. I've even tried drinking more to relax and forget. Once it was so important to be as educated as possible about my health. Now I don't even want to know the grim facts. Statistics about miscarriage and infertility just depress me."

Denial is an unconscious refuge from realities that are overwhelmingly threatening. Individuals protect themselves from a given situation by creating a sort of cushion or emotional distance between themselves and the full weight of the situation. By negating the reality of the circumstance, they allow themselves to absorb and accept new and frightening information at their own pace.

Denial can be useful and protective to a point, but when it is prolonged, it stands in the way of treatment and recovery. Unfortunately, since denial is an unconscious defense, you may not realize that you are affected by it. Similarly, you cannot be forced out of it until you are ready. Overzealous attempts to draw you out of this stage may force you to burrow your head still deeper in the sand.

One step in helping the process along may be to recognize the different forms denial may take, since it can go unrecognized. Since you have made the effort to read a book about endometriosis, you have already come a long way in facing the realities of the disease and your need for information and action. But you may be denying other aspects of the disease. It's also possible to face the disease squarely at one point yet retreat into denial later when the going gets tougher. Denial, in varying degrees, may resurface many times in many forms during the course of your illness. There are at least three types.

Refusing to face the fact that you have a disease. This represents a complete denial of the reality of disease and illness and a failure to accept or fully absorb the diagnosis. "This can't happen to me," you may say. "There must be a mistake." You may feel overwhelmed and you try to push it out of your mind, thinking that if you ignore it it will go away. It won't. Denial may cause you to reject information and fail to face treatment, retreating in inactivity, avoidance, and procrastination. "Refusing to take steps in the decision-making process and to face up to needed medical treatment or surgery only prolongs the fear and stress," says Mary Lou Ballweg, president and co-founder of the Endometriosis Association.

Refusing to face all the facts about the disease.

You may acknowledge the presence of endometriosis, but refuse to accept the implications of the diagnosis—that the disease is chronic and may persist until menopause; that treatment may be only temporarily effective; that your fertility may be jeopardized. If you are informed that the disease frequently recurs following treatment, you may insist that you will be the exception, that *you* will be cured. You may vigilantly seek information, trying one treatment after another. When treatments don't work, you may blame your doctor, thinking the next doctor will know or help more. You will try anything and everything that offers a promise of hope. Doctors who try to be overly optimistic can reinforce this kind of denial. So can family members and friends who try to offer you a brighter outlook.

According to Mary Lou Ballweg, "Many women contact the Endometriosis Association searching for just one piece of information: they think they just need a good doctor or they just want to know the best treatment for infertility. They often fail to see, or do not wish to see, the bigger picture—that endometriosis is usually something that will affect their lives for many years. Lots of good information will be needed as well as a continuing line of communication with others struggling with the disease for the emotional support it takes to cope with this frustrating disease."

Refusing to face the feelings.

You acknowledge the disease and its chronicity, but you refuse to believe that you will be affected by it. You insist on acting as if nothing is happening, determined that the disease will not affect you, refusing to admit that it causes you emotional difficulty. You consider this a positive attitude: by denying the negative, you hope to become invulnerable and remain unscathed. Many women take this approach, but, ultimately, few are helped by it, because it causes them to sidestep important issues and to bury their feelings. Pretending that pain or infertility are not concerns keeps women from taking action and working toward a resolution of their feelings.

Similarly, you may refuse to accept that your feelings about having a disease, or your feelings about symptoms, affect the course of your illness. Not only does this stance allow you to ignore the issues, it takes a vast expenditure of energy—energy that can more appropriately be harnessed in an effort to cope in a healthier manner.

Other typical reactions to the diagnosis of chronic illness—feelings of self-pity, guilt, victimization, wish-fulfillment fantasizing, and bargaining—contribute to denial. They focus attention away from present reality and the challenges of the disease.

"I've never been sick before, and I've always tried to take care of myself and stay fit. Why should I be in so much pain?"

Unjust punishment: self-pity.   As women begin to process the news about their illness they begin to search for reasons, for some sort of cosmic purpose, pattern, or meaning. You may feel singled out, chosen to bear a burden of illness. You ask yourself, "Why me? What did I do to deserve this?" When you can find no answer, you may conclude that life is cruel and unfair. This inability to see or accept the randomness of illness frequently leads to self-pity.

It's natural to feel sorry for yourself. The danger is in becoming so immersed in self-pity that you focus all your attention away from coping. Cursing the unfairness of life is a normal stage of the dis-ease process, but it's one that must be resolved before meaningful rehabilitation can occur. Try not to berate yourself for indulging in a little self-pity. At the same time, try to acknowledge that you have not been singled out or selected to suffer; illness is not a punishment and wellness a reward. Remember that although feelings of self-pity may never completely disappear, they will lessen as you learn mechanisms for coping with the disease.

"I was told that the cause of this disease is from being nervous and worrying all the time, which I do."

"I should have listened to my parents and my husband when they told me I should worry about a career after I had my children. They said I was being selfish and that I'd be sorry one day. Now, with the pain and the infertility, I guess they were right."

Just punishment: guilt.   Unlike individuals who view illness as the result of unknown, external forces, others readily take responsibility for sickness and see it as a punishment for some real or imaginary, past or present misdeed or fault. They conclude that they have been selected to be ill to atone for their wrongdoings. The trap, in this instance, is that when a woman believes her illness is deserved, she may relinquish all efforts at coping. Instead she is willing to pay the penalty she believes she owes. It's a dangerous and self-destructive denial response that seriously impedes recovery.

Popular misconceptions about endometriosis contribute to the guilt experienced by most individuals with chronic illnesses. For instance, the "career woman's disease" is a misnomer that potently reinforces guilt. It suggests that endometriosis is the price a woman pays for pursuing a career or delaying childbearing. "If I'd gotten married sooner and settled down to raise children, I wouldn't be in pain," many women think. Friends, family, and even your mate may contribute to guilt, suggesting, "You made your choice, now you must live with it." Whether or not delayed childbearing affects the development of endometriosis is not known. If you had had children early, perhaps you wouldn't have gotten endometriosis and perhaps you would. But that is really beside the point. You cannot dwell on what you might have done. You made the decisions that were right for you at the time with the information available to you. Even if it is confirmed at some point that delayed childbearing contributes to the development of endometriosis, early childbearing is not an issue that can be negotiated and planned as a preventive measure.

Another popular, although totally unproven, assumption is that endometriosis is caused by stress, or by certain personality traits. This leads women to believe that they are responsible for the development of their disease. "If only I hadn't worked so hard, maybe this wouldn't have happened." "If I could handle my problems better, I wouldn't be sick now." Although there is much evidence to suggest that all illnesses are *influenced* and *moderated* by stress, there is absolutely none to suggest that endometriosis is *caused* by stress or fostered by certain personality traits.

Guilt also surrounds issues of infertility. Infertile women are particularly prone to internalize guilt, especially if they used birth control or had an abortion in younger years. Infertility, they believe, is a penalty for "defying nature." As a result, feelings of blame surface easily, particularly when careers took precedence over childbearing.

Assess the reality of the situation. Is your illness or infertility any fault of your own? Could you have done things differently? If you look realistically for answers, you will begin to see that your guilt is unfounded, unnecessary. Says Dr. Andrea Shrednick, a Los Angeles therapist specializing in marital, emotional, and sexual aspects of infertility, "You can't dwell on what you think you could have or should have or would have done, because you wouldn't have, couldn't have, and shouldn't have. You have to go forward."

Blaming others: victimization. Less commonly, a woman may blame someone else who, she believes, contributed to her illness. If, for example, her mother had endometriosis, she may hold her responsible for passing on the disease. Others, aware that endometriosis is *attributed* to delayed childbearing, may blame a mate who insisted on waiting until later in life to have children. Women who believe that stress has caused the disease may blame a difficult boss. Acknowledge your feelings, but again try to recognize that not only are they inappropriate—that is, no one caused you to develop a disease—but also they are not helpful. In fact, they probably add stress to relationships that are already strained.

"If only I can have a baby, I'll give up my career forever."

"If I have to be sick, why can't it be some other condition? I'd trade endometriosis for arthritis in a minute. That would be much easier to handle."

Wish-fulfillment fantasies and bargaining. Wish-fulfillment fantasies are a preoccupation with the unrealistic hope that the disease will disappear, that one will awaken to find it was all a mistake, a bad dream. Instead of merely wishing, some women attempt to negotiate a different outcome through prayer or bargaining—offering a set of terms in exchange for a reprieve from destiny or intervention by a supreme power. Wish-fulfillment fantasies, like self-pity, guilt, and victimization, divert energy and attention away from dealing with the realities of illness.

COPING

Instead of wishing for what was, raging at the unfairness of life, fixing blame on others, or taking on the mantle of guilt, turn your attention and energy toward solutions. Begin to say, "The problem exists. I wish it didn't, but I can't change that. I can, however, change my reaction to it." Instead of simply feeling sorry for yourself, ask, "What am I going to do about it? What options are available to me? What are the steps I need to take?" This attitude will lead you to feel more in control and less helpless and demoralized.

Similarly, try not to be lured by the false power of "positive thinking" to pull you through. Positive thinking is not a cure-all. In fact, it can deny the reality of your feelings and relieve you of the responsibility to take charge. Instead of saying, "By eliminating negative thoughts, I won't be affected by this," try to express all your feelings. Then take positive action. Perhaps you now feel that there is nothing you can do to help yourself. But strategies and resources are available to you. As you learn more, and as you continue to act, your negative feelings will decrease.

13

The Treatment Phase: Disruption and Disorder

Once you have absorbed the impact of the diagnosis, you must turn your attention to treatment options, making decisions, and following through. Although this sounds simple, deciding on treatment is exceedingly difficult and highly stressful for most women. Consequently, the treatment phase is often characterized by disruption, confusion, disorder, and disequilibrium throughout its five common stages.

THE FIVE STAGES OF TREATMENT

Initial Disruption

First comes disruption caused by the symptoms and by the need to find adequate medical care, schedule appointments and tests, and so on. It can be difficult during this stage to meet the day-to-day demands of education, career, and family life. Often, leisure activities are curtailed and other pursuits postponed because you are preoccupied with symptoms, collecting information, and the implications of treatment decisions. You may feel overwhelmed, helpless. Your life seems out of control. This disruption typically intensifies throughout the other stages of the treatment phase.

Decision Making: Treatment Dilemmas

Often with illness there are no treatment options. Even when there are, choices may not be terribly difficult or stressful because life goals are not on the line. Mistakes can be rectified. With endometriosis, however, there are many treatment avenues, and results are hard to predict. Unless the endometriosis is life threatening, just which treatment is right

151

under a particular set of circumstances is largely a matter of opinion. Yet treatments affect comfort, productivity, sexuality, relationships, quality of life, and potential for childbearing. A woman with untested fertility may be ambivalent about pregnancy, or she may have no immediate plans but wants children some day. She is forced to make many decisions: should she run the risk that endometriosis *may* affect her future fertility and opt for treatments that *might* suppress the disease until she is ready to conceive? Or should she rearrange her life plans, accelerate major decisions, opt for treatments that enhance her ability to conceive, and attempt pregnancy immediately? Her future seems to hang on each decision. It's little wonder, then, that a woman finds the decision-making stage particularly confusing, frightening, and stressful.

The course of treatment for women with endometriosis is usually determined in one of three ways: (1) the doctor firmly dictates the treatment method; (2) the doctor offers options, but the patient abdicates responsibility and defers to her doctor's judgment; or (3) the doctor and patient work together to reach decisions. Each has its own drawbacks. Distress comes from perceiving that you have no choices, no control over your situation. It also arises from having so many choices that you are overwhelmed, almost paralyzed by all the implications.

Lack of choices.   Following diagnosis, a woman usually turns to her doctor to tell her what to do. Having been taught early on to respect medical authority without question, she is accustomed to accepting his advice and reluctant to challenge it. He seems to have all the answers, and she gratefully clings to his promise of relief. This attitude exacerbates her helplessness, confusion, and anger. It is accentuated by a lack of information about the disease and the choices of treatment, and by a lack of assertiveness.

Abdicating responsibility.   Sometimes a doctor *does* offer choices, but the patient does not know how to respond. She wants a cure and so is shaken by a doctor who offers no easy answers. Says Mary Lou Ballweg, women who let their doctors make all their decisions are often looking for someone to blame when results are unsuccessful. This increases dependency and lessens self-esteem.

Too many choices.   Faced with a bewildering array of options, a woman realizes that each decision may radically alter her lifestyle, future, and emotional equilibrium. In this instance, stress results from an inability to look objectively at all the options and set priorities.

Following Through: Living with Treatments

Once the decision is made, a woman must contend with the difficulties each type of treatment causes—the side effects of medical therapy, the interruptions caused by hospitalization and recovery from surgery, or the disruption and emotional strain of an infertility work-up and the therapies for enhancing fertility.

Waiting and Worrying: Monitoring the Results of Treatment

After treatment a woman waits, worries, and wonders: What next? Will treatment bring results? When treatments are initially successful, it's often difficult to trust the results. Will the pain return? Will I get pregnant next month? Because she knows recurrences are likely, she may find it hard to resume previous activities even when she feels well.

Persistence and Recurrence: The Treatment Carousel

Often, when initial treatment is not successful, when symptoms return quickly, a woman may go through these five phases again and again as she undergoes treatment after treatment. She must repeat the phases of decision-making, treatment, contending with side effects and consequences, relief, recurrence, frustration, and so on. Her daily life and long-range plans are transformed into a treatment carousel. Each time she goes around, the brass ring—relief, cure, or pregnancy—seems even farther from reach.

Some women can't seem to slow down, move ahead, or get off the carousel. They stay on because it seems worth it if pregnancy can be achieved or radical surgery avoided. Says Dr. Metzger, "The desperation of wanting to try anything sometimes clouds judgment. Patients will go through operations that have such low probability of success and will submit to anything to be fertile or avoid hysterectomy." The day-to-day consequences of living with continuing symptoms are discussed in Chapter 14. Chapters 15 and 16 outline the steps women must take to regain control over their lives—to get off the treatment carousel.

CASE HISTORIES

Women usually must face these difficult stages during their teen years through their early thirties—particularly significant and formative periods in their lives. These are prime times for molding life plans and realizing aspirations; working toward attaining goals and indulging in the pleasures and satisfactions they bring. But endometriosis and its treatment can sabotage those plans and goals in a variety of subtle—and not-so-subtle—ways.

Although there is no "typical" endometriosis patient or course of the disease, the following case histories of six women illustrate various issues that arise—reactions to initial symptoms, difficulties reaching diagnosis, making decisions, the doctor-patient relationship, coping with pain, and the different "treatment carousels." Keep in mind that each case is unique; the sequence of events may or may not occur in your particular situation.

Adrien

From the time Adrien began to menstruate, at age thirteen, she had experienced menstrual cramps. She got by with aspirin and a heating pad, as her mother had done. Although the cramping gradually increased over the years, Adrien did not seek medical help.

In junior high, Adrien was already making plans for college. She would need a scholarship, and so she studied hard to maintain a high grade-point average. She would need a part-time job while in high school to save money for college. In the meantime she spent three afternoons a week as a volunteer aide at a local resident school for hearing-impaired children. Yet she managed to maintain an active social life.

At sixteen, Adrien was hired as a part-time paid assistant at the resident school. Her menstrual pain had by now become too severe to ignore. It interfered with her responsibilities at work, her school activities, and her social life. Her supervisor arranged for Adrien to make up for her absences by working extra hours on days when she felt well. Her teachers, however, were less sympathetic. After many missed classes and exams, Adrien was forced to give up her job so she could concentrate on her studies.

Her gynecologist assured her that menstrual pain was not unusual and advised her to take over-the-counter pain relievers. For at least two days a month, despite medication, she was virtually incapacitated. Nausea and diarrhea preceded her periods, and severe pain made walking or standing difficult. She never knew when her period would begin and was often embarrassed by its sudden onset. Sometimes bleeding was so excessive she couldn't leave the house. It was getting more and more difficult to keep up with school and friends and Adrien began to withdraw.

Another gynecologist prescribed anti-prostaglandins. After six months the pain worsened. A pelvic exam revealed no nodules or uterine displacement, so the doctor was reluctant to perform a laparoscopy. Instead he prescribed oral contraceptives. But the pain did not subside; in fact it got worse. Finally, he scheduled a laparoscopy. After diagnosing endometriosis he told Adrien that she had two choices: danazol, or hysterectomy. He suggested that danazol, followed by oral contraceptives, might keep her symptoms at bay until she was ready to have a child, which might relieve the pain. He advised her to reconsider college and give thought to having children early in life. Her fertility might be impaired later on, and a hysterectomy, he believed, would ultimately be necessary.

"I was only eighteen and still a virgin. I didn't even have a boyfriend. I never heard of endometriosis and suddenly I was being told, not only that I might lose my organs, but that I might never have children if I didn't rearrange all my plans and give up my dreams of a career."

Adrien's parents advised her to seek a second opinion. The consulting doctor said her condition was indeed severe but could be managed with conservative but aggressive measures. He recommended six months of danazol, followed by conservative surgery.

Adrien was optimistic. The danazol brought some relief, but she was troubled by side effects. She gained almost fifteen pounds and developed oily skin, acne, and dark facial hair. She already felt different from other teenagers because of her symptoms. The added self-consciousness about her appearance caused even more isolation.

"I withdrew from some of my friends and sometimes avoided family gatherings. I'm sorry now that I told so many people, because they just don't understand. Sometimes they're so insensi-

tive— they want to know how I could have "picked up' something like this. I feel like some kind of freak."

The surgery was scheduled for the summer. Following her recovery Adrien began her last year of high school. Midway into the second semester the pain returned. Her nausea and gastrointestinal symptoms were worse than ever. Another laparoscopy revealed persistent endometriosis and dense adhesions. Her doctor scheduled additional tests, including an IVP and a barium enema which indicated that her bowel was significantly affected by endometriosis. He recommended another conservative operation. Adrien stayed home for seven weeks following surgery. During this time her friends graduated from high school.

For nearly a year and a half Adrien was relatively pain-free and able to repeat her courses and graduate. Slowly, though, the pain returned. She no longer felt confident about her plans for college. She lost her chance at a scholarship and could not save money since she had to quit her job. Her medical care was so costly that her parents could provide only a small part of her college expenses. She would have to work in order to pay for her education. Fearful that recurring pain would once again cause her to leave school, she began to consider a hysterectomy.

"I can't go on this way. I feel suspended in pain for one or two weeks each month, always having to make changes in plans. I find I don't live in the present as much. I worry about the future and how little control I have over it. I can function when I feel well, but then the disease comes back. I have to deal with the issues all over again, just when I thought I was finally beyond it."

Her parents advised her to try another conservative operation. Three doctors have recommended definitive surgery. She wonders how she will feel after a total hysterectomy, knowing she will never have children. Without her uterus, she imagines she will no longer be feminine. She is certain that no one will ever want to marry her. For now, she has decided to live with the pain a while longer.

Linda

Linda is thirty-two, married, and a former copyeditor at a Chicago newspaper. She has been in treatment for endometriosis and infertility for seven years. Her symptoms— primarily a persistent dull ache in her lower abdomen—began when she started to menstruate at eleven. Between thirteen and eighteen she had had several episodes of severe pain. At the emergency room she was given a prescription for a painkiller and sent home. Linda's first pelvic exam at nineteen indicated no abnormalities, nor did her second—a premarital exam at twenty. Three years of birth control pills taken to prevent conception had shortened her periods and eliminated her pain, but when she discontinued them so that she could conceive, her cramps returned. For two years she was unable to conceive, so she consulted an infertility specialist. After Linda and her husband underwent a battery of infertility tests, Linda entered the hospital for a laparoscopy.

"I thought I was prepared for surgery. I had read about the procedure and talked with my doctor. He had told me what to expect, but, looking back, I had failed to prepare myself emotionally for the actual experience. I got to the outpatient clinic late that morning, shaking, sweaty, extremely nervous and anxious. By the time my papers were processed I was in a panic. I knew I needed to talk to someone other than my husband. Fortunately, I was blessed with a very understanding nurse. She explained the procedure in a very caring way and assured me that she was available for support if I should need it. Even with her reassurances, I remained apprehensive. Would there be much pain?"

Laparoscopy confirmed mild endometriosis and the doctor carefully explained the disease to Linda. She read what she could about endometriosis and infertility and concluded that surgery might be her best option. Her doctor suggested danazol instead. After careful consideration she began a six-month course of danazol therapy. During that time she experienced numerous side effects: weight gain, fluid retention, hot flashes, vaginal dryness, decreased breast size, fatigue, acne, severe muscle spasms in her left arm, and dark hair growth on her upper thighs. Most troubling, however, were the mood swings, depression, severe headaches, and irritability.

"My husband was doubly patient with me when I was on danazol, but it was difficult. I flew off the handle at the smallest provocation. We knew the drug was responsible for my behavior, but we chose to continue because we hoped it would bring about a pregnancy."

After completing a six-month course of danazol, Linda's first menstrual period was a crushing blow. The pain was the worst she had ever experienced. At the emergency room she was given an injection of Demerol, a narcotic painkiller. Soon after she began to experience severe pain in the area of her right ovary. She took Anaprox or Motrin regularly, but they helped little. The pain continued and after eight months the doctor suggested another laparoscopy to see if the disease had recurred. He discovered an endometrioma on her ovary and performed a laparotomy that day. The ovary was saved, and there were no other traces of the disease. Linda was released from the hospital six days later. She took danazol for one month postoperatively.

"Our hopes were somewhat raised because the doctor said there was an 80- to 90-percent chance that I would conceive."

But Linda did not conceive. Within eighteen months her symptoms had recurred. A third laparoscopy revealed extensive endometriosis and severe adhesions.

"I was crushed. My emotions were at an all-time low. The doctor told me that if I were to have a second major operation my chances of conceiving were "next to zero.' I was terribly depressed and despondent and didn't know what to do."

Linda considered GnRH treatment. She had heard of a study at the National Institutes of Health comparing danazol and GnRH treatment, but was unable to participate. Instead, she chose laser surgery. Following six weeks of preoperative danazol, she underwent her second major operation. The surgeon, highly experienced in the use of the laser, discussed all aspects of the procedure with Linda. She spent only three days in the hospital, but her recovery lasted for four weeks. She wasn't healing well.

She took danazol again for six weeks following her second operation. But her symptoms continued. She had to reconsider her options. She could stay on danazol and face the side effects as well as symptoms. Surgery might bring temporary relief, but how often could she be operated on? She again considered GnRH treatment.

GnRH was not approved for the treatment of endometriosis. Nonetheless, her doctor ordered injections postoperatively for six weeks. Linda was pleased with the results. There was no bloating or weight gain, only some swelling and inflammation at the injection site. But by the third week she began to develop frequent, severe hot flashes and night sweats, which resulted in insomnia, weakness, and fatigue. For the duration of the GnRH treatment, her doctor prescribed Provera to minimize the flashes; the new medication caused nausea early in the morning and late at night. Linda stopped treatment and spent another four weeks on danazol.

After seven years, five operations, and repeated hormonal therapy, Linda is still experiencing pain.

"Sometimes I have to cancel activities when the pain becomes too severe. Intercourse is still painful at midcycle for several days and then again just before I menstruate. My husband is understanding and tries to be careful during intercourse. But we try not to avoid it, especially when I might be ovulating. We still hope for a pregnancy. It's hard to believe how much endometriosis has affected my life. Sometimes I think I will never be mentally or physically well again. I feel exhausted. Some days it's hard to concentrate. I can't remember simple things. My mind wanders.

"Having to take my temperature first thing every morning is a terrible way to start the day because it reminds me that I haven't conceived—again. And the nights aren't much better. Each time we make love we're also reminded of our failure to conceive. Sex has less and less to do with love and everything to do with making a baby. We chart our attempts and feel like we're getting 'demerits.' The strain is horrible. So is waiting between treatments. Each time I hope maybe this time it will work. In between, I want to change careers, move, go back to school, and become a mother, but I'm stuck 'on hold.' Everyone else seems to be getting on with life.

"Not only have I had to wait to get into an infertility treatment program, but I've had to rearrange my entire schedule once accepted. It takes weeks to just get an appointment, and then the doctor is usually running late. I've spent hours in waiting rooms. And it's difficult to talk to friends about infertility, so we see people less.

"I've tried just about everything available for treatment. My short term goal is to be optimistic and not expect too much. But my long term goal is to avoid hysterectomy so I can have a baby. People wonder why I'm willing to go through all this. I'm thirty-two and I won't give up until I'm forty, even if it means going through a laparoscopy every seventeen months. Am I crazy? Probably, but I'm just not willing to give up my dream of being a mother."

Joan

At twenty-six Joan was married and in her first year of a graduate business program. She planned to work as a junior financial planner before thinking about raising a family. At twenty she had begun to notice frequent, dull pain and tenderness in her pelvic area unassociated with menstruation. She had stomachaches daily and severe cramps every few months. Soon after, her periods became prolonged and the pain became sharper, especially during intercourse. Sometimes orgasms were painful. Her gynecologist felt nodules and observed that her uterus was tilted backward. Suspecting endometriosis, he scheduled Joan for a laparoscopy. Two visible implants were removed, one on the left uterosacral ligament, the other on the back of her uterus. He then suggested that a pregnancy would keep the disease at bay for several years. Infertility was likely if she waited too long. She should become pregnant as soon as possible, he advised. Joan protested. She and her husband, Andrew, were just getting started in their careers. They were not financially equipped, not ready to have a baby. All she wanted was relief from the pain. Her doctor prescribed a six-month regimen of danazol, but strongly cautioned Joan to reconsider.

Joan has been taking danazol for nearly five months. It has effectively relieved her pain with only minimal side effects. Her doctor can no longer feel any growths. Still, his warning runs through her mind.

"It's very difficult to think that I may have trouble conceiving someday. The pressure to have a baby, ready or not, is always with us. Several women we know have had hysterectomies because of endometriosis. It makes us realize how real this threat is. We always expected to have children, but we never thought we would have to make such an important decision so soon."

Joan and Andrew have decided to try to conceive. They hope it's not too late.

"I'll have to drop out of school for now, which means that money will be tight for some years to come. But we're just too frightened to wait."

Margaret

Margaret is a freelance graphic designer. Her husband, Mark, is a carpenter. They have a daughter from Margaret's previous marriage, and they had hoped to have another child.

Last year Margaret underwent definitive surgery for endometriosis. Earlier, when she was twenty-five, she had experienced breakthrough bleeding, pelvic pain, constipation, dyspareunia, and pain with bowel movements. Her gynecologist then told her not to worry— her symptoms were related to stress. So she tried to relax but the symptoms got worse.

"I had to stop working. And even though I couldn't afford it, I sometimes had to hire someone to help care for my daughter."

Margaret then visited a gynecologist who was highly recommended. Laparoscopy revealed endometriosis on the ovaries and in the rectovaginal septum, and the doctor recommended treatment with danazol. It was expensive and neither Margaret nor Mark had medical insurance, but there seemed to be no alternative. The danazol caused increased facial hair growth and oily skin. Margaret felt unfeminine. Before long her doctor took her off danazol because it aggravated her migraine headaches. Instead, he prescribed Provera, but the headaches continued, along with depression, bloating, decreased sex drive, and reduced circulation. She always felt cold. Provera also caused her to be irritable, and her moods created tension in her marriage.

Margaret's doctor suggested pregnancy, but intercourse was now too painful. A specialist performed another laparoscopy. Her disease was extremely severe, and he said that a hysterectomy would be necessary. But Margaret still hoped to have another child. The specialist then suggested conservative surgery instead. He couldn't guarantee, though, that she would be free of pain.

"I was barely functioning, taking two Percodan every six hours. But it did nothing for the pain, so I decided to go ahead with the operation. The doctor kept saying that I might have to have a hysterectomy. I was afraid I'd wake up with all my reproductive organs gone."

In the hospital following surgery Margaret was relieved that a hysterectomy had not been done. But her relief was short lived.

"My doctor hardly spent any time talking to me. He did tell me that I'd probably never be able to have children. There I was in the maternity ward, surrounded by crying babies. I really needed to talk to someone. I asked the nurse if there was any sort of support person I could talk to. She said no. Until that point I really thought that Mark and I would have a baby some day. Nobody really understood that this was the worst shock of my life. I cried for days."

Less than three months later the pain returned full force. The doctor said there was no alternative. Definitive surgery would be necessary. But Margaret's decision did not come easily.

"My parents fought me every step of the way. I suppose they wanted to be grandparents again. I was concerned about Mark. He very much wanted a child. Although he was very supportive, I wondered what would happen to our relationship. How would he feel later? Would he still find me desirable? Less than a year into a marriage with a man I deeply loved, I wondered if we would still have a future together."

With Mark's understanding and encouragement Margaret finally consented to a hysterectomy. She knew she could no longer tolerate a life of pain. Moreover, Margaret didn't want her daughter to grow up with an invalid mother.

"Fighting pain while raising a child is terribly fatiguing. I had to miss out on school plays and helping her with her homework. Also, I needed to earn money. I started to freelance because I couldn't hold down a full-time job. After the second surgery I couldn't even take care of the

few clients I had. I tried to keep up, because I was afraid of developing a reputation for unreliability. But each time I increased my level of activity, the pain got worse. I was depressed by the thought of a hysterectomy, but I didn't see any way out of it."

Margaret's bowel was severely involved with endometriosis, and her ureter was also at risk. The doctor strongly advised Margaret to consent to bilateral salpingo-oophorectomy. He explained to her the nature of surgical menopause. Margaret recalls how she felt after surgery.

"I had to deal with surgical castration, hot flashes, vaginal atrophy, and the loss of my libido. For a while estrogen replacement therapy helped counter the severe menopausal symptoms. But it caused the pain to return."

Even after definitive surgery Margaret had not seen the last of endometriosis.

"It's been a long road for me. I'm twenty-seven years old, and I'm no longer like my contemporaries. I'm losing bits and pieces of myself, and I'm fighting for my emotional survival."

Deborah

Deborah was diagnosed in 1981 and put on danazol immediately. After two weeks she broke out in a severe rash. Her gynecologist then prescribed birth control pills to be taken daily to eliminate her periods. About a year later her pain returned. Another laparoscopy was performed and no endometriosis was visible. Her doctor ordered an IVP and barium enema; nothing abnormal was found.

A specialist recommended a third laparoscopy. He didn't want to rely on another doctor's observations. Although he could see no endometriosis, a biopsy indicated the presence of microscopic disease. He suggested trying danazol again, this time cutting the dosage in half. Deborah was fine for a few months, but then reported that she felt like she was "on speed." She couldn't sleep, was never tired, didn't eat, and was very jumpy. Her doctor decreased the dosage again and suggested she try taking the pills at different times. The reaction continued, however, so she discontinued danazol and went back to birth control pills.

By the end of the following year she was still living on pain pills. During a fourth laparoscopy a small amount of endometriosis was treated with the laser. Although the doctor removed all visible traces, he was not optimistic. Indeed, after the pain of surgery wore off, the pain of endometriosis remained. The doctor then suggested a presacral neurectomy. However, he said, Deborah first had to undergo a complete psychiatric evaluation.

"I was extremely annoyed at first, but he held his ground. The psychiatrist said the pain was real, not in my head, but he strongly objected to surgery, suggesting drug therapy instead. For a couple of weeks I kept mulling over in my mind whether or not I should just have the hysterectomy and to hell with motherhood. But then I opted for the neurectomy. The neurectomy

was worse than my wildest imagination. After four minor surgeries this was my first major, and nobody could have prepared me for the pain. The first two days I was on morphine, then Demerol. I felt like a meat cleaver had gone through my insides. It took about six to eight weeks before I started to feel like myself again."

After surgery Deborah was relieved to discover that she had no more pain. She had been told that the operation would relieve her of pain for five to ten years at least, but after sixteen months the pain returned. She tried to ignore it, but it slowly got worse. The doctor suggested she stay on birth control pills all the time. This worked for a while, but then the pain returned.

Deborah talked with a gynecologist about a hysterectomy. He suggested she have another laparoscopy—her fifth—before he could determine what to do. The operation revealed a few small spots of endometriosis and a few filmy adhesions. These he cauterized, but the pain persisted. He referred her to a metabolism specialist. This doctor suggested that the pain was due to a gastrointestinal disorder, but he ordered blood tests to rule out a metabolic problem. The test results were normal, and he advised her to go to a gastroenterologist. "Another doctor, another $300," she recalls. After an initial examination and more blood and urine tests, the gastroenterologist sent her for a barium enema—her third—which also revealed no abnormalities. He concluded that her pain was the result of endometriosis.

"Two specialists, and two separate opinions. I don't know what to do. I can try to get into a GnRH program. I can live with pain and take drugs, or get a hysterectomy. I have to think about work, too. I can't go on with these interruptions. My employer is understanding, but after six operations even the most understanding boss isn't too thrilled. So far, in deciding on treatment, my role has been passive. I desperately wanted a cure so I did what the doctors told me to do. No one ever talked to me about the pros and cons. Now I don't know how much more I can take. Doctors don't prepare you for these frustrations. They always assume success. It always seems like they don't have time for you, they're always in too much of a hurry to answer your questions. Sometimes I just get tired of fighting the inevitable. Other times I know I can't live with myself if I don't fight. If I give up now I'll regret it. That's what keeps me going."

Leah

Leah recently turned thirty-four. She has been in treatment for endometriosis for more than eight years. By the time she was diagnosed she had already been experiencing pelvic pain, menstrual cramps, and severely painful bowel movements and other gastrointestinal symptoms for nine years. Since her first sexual experience when she was twenty, intercourse has been painful. Despite her symptoms, she managed to finish college and get her law degree. Shortly before diagnosis she had started her first job with a nonprofit, public interest group in Washington—a position with long hours and little pay.

After diagnosis, Leah, then twenty-five, was advised by her doctor to become pregnant. She laughed at first, musing on the absurdity of this advice in light of her lifestyle. Her work kept her busy ten hours a day. Each night she collapsed in pain. She had little time for a social life and hadn't dated for nearly a year. The last time she had intercourse she was in so much pain she had to go to the hospital for an injection of Demerol. She told the doctor that pregnancy was unlikely and asked about alternatives. He suggested birth control pills. But she had been taking birth control pills for contraception since she was twenty. They had not relieved her pain. Leah doubted the doctor's advice and consulted another gynecologist. This doctor started her on preoperative danazol therapy and scheduled her for a laparotomy two months later.

During the laparotomy the gynecologist found severe and extensive endometriosis, with significant involvement of the bowel, rectum, cul-de-sac, and rectovaginal septum. He scraped the rectum and removed as much endometriosis as possible, suspended her uterus, and placed her on danazol for two months postoperatively.

Three months later Leah was taken to the hospital following excruciating abdominal pain. Three and a half feet of small intestine, which had been obstructed by adhesions, were removed. During the operation the surgeon also removed her appendix and suspended her uterus. She was fine for nine months, but then the pain returned. Her gynecologist performed a proctoscopy and found that her rectum was obstructed by endometriosis and scar tissue.

During Leah's third major operation, a third uterine suspension was performed, and the rectal scar tissue was removed. Again Leah was put on danazol, but the pain returned. She consulted a different gynecologist. He scheduled another laparoscopy and another proctoscopy. He diagnosed very severe endometriosis and strongly recommended hysterectomy.

Totally opposed, Leah continued to take danazol, saw another doctor, and had a third proctoscopy. This time three large spots of endometriosis were found in the rectum. The doctor recommended she have a proctoscopy every three months and sent her for ultrasound, which revealed that one ovary was surrounded by disease. He advised her to continue on danazol for six months more. At the end of that period she continued to be in pain, although not as intense as before, and tests showed little regression of the disease. Ultimately, this second gynecologist agreed with the first. A hysterectomy would be necessary.

Like Adrien and Linda, Leah cannot bring herself to consent to surgery, but she admits that she may soon have to.

"I don't know how long I can be a slave to pain. It has gotten to the point where my life revolves around endometriosis. It's getting harder and harder to work, and I worry about not being able to support myself and about the expense. It's difficult holding down my job. After so much time off I've already been put on probation and refused a raise. If I lose my job I won't have medical insurance. I'm afraid I won't be able to get another job. I can't see going through this indefinitely, especially not alone. I would like to have a loving supportive person in my life, but I still fear being hurt, being rejected. I can't show affection because I don't feel good about myself. I don't think any man could feel good about me. Sometimes I meet a man

I might like to get involved with, but I withdraw. I never know when I should mention my problems—painful intercourse, possible infertility, or hysterectomy. What would he say? Do I wait until we get serious, or tell him right away? He might leave me. I wish I could just talk to someone about what I am feeling. I have met other women who have endometriosis and struggle like I do, but they have husbands or lovers to turn to. I've tried talking to my parents for advice and support, but they don't understand. They say it's just female trouble. I'm terrified by the thought of a hysterectomy. Not having a hysterectomy terrifies me too. But if I can't have a relationship, a baby, a career, what's left for me?"

COPING

Because endometriosis tends to be a chronic disease, women must learn skills to cope with repeated treatments. Many women find that slowing down helps them make better decisions. In addition, learning to manage pain or side effects and to deal with disappointment or other emotional consequences are ways of coping more successfully with the illness.

Slow Down

Distress during treatment comes from the sense of urgency women feel about having to make decisions quickly and wisely. But few situations require immediate action. Steps can be taken one at a time to help you minimize the disruption and confusion and cope with the effects of treatment. These tasks are described below and more fully in Chapter 16.

Take control.   Accept the responsibility for making your own decisions in regard to your own health care. Often women do not realize until late in treatment the implications and repercussions of their decisions. Your choices affect your entire future and thus must be your own. Once you accept that responsibility, you can take additional steps to reduce the disruptions and to improve your ability to make decisions.

Focus.   Slow down long enough to clarify your problems and needs. Then determine what information you need to make decisions and to bring about solutions. Women often see their doctors initially when they are feeling miserable. They are afraid, in pain, and under stress. It's not the time to discuss options, make treatment decisions, or take important steps. Most women have a time during their cycle when they feel relatively well. That's the time to schedule an appointment with your doctor to discuss plans.

Gather information.   Collect the facts you need to make an informed decision. Take advantage of all resources. Of the cases described above, Leah was the only woman profiled to stop and learn more about the disease and its treatment options. The others entered treatment with little understanding of endometriosis. They remained dependent and confused.

Get the best possible care.   Your first doctor, often your family doctor, is not necessarily the best person to manage your treatment. It's vital that you take enough time and expend enough energy in finding the right doctor. Choose one who is well informed, one with whom you can form a productive partnership.

Improve your general health.   Pay attention to rest, diet, and exercise. Not only will it improve your ability to tolerate treatment, it will also increase your energy and your ability to think clearly. You will be better able to make reasoned decisions.

Be assertive.   Being assertive is difficult enough for many women under the best of circumstances. When your priorities are vague, when you are in pain, stressed, and fatigued, it becomes even more of a challenge to stand up for your rights and state your needs. Being assertive is crucial in coping with all stages of endometriosis, especially treatment.

Be decisive.   Even with adequate information and an assertive attitude, decision making is not easy. In fact, it is a skill that many individuals never acquire. Take time to learn more about the steps involved in overcoming indecisiveness and in making reasoned choices.

Restore your emotional equilibrium.   When you fight physical disability emotions seem irrelevant. But studies point to how important emotions are, both during the course of illness and afterward. Don't ignore your emotions. Take steps to learn skills for dealing with confusing and destructive feelings. Build an emotional support network. Resolve to get professional help if necessary.

Learn to manage pain and stress.   None of the six women above considered pain or stress management. Yet learning how to cope with pain and its emotional components is probably the single most important step you can take. Energy devoted to pain and stress management makes decision making less difficult. The effects of treatment are less devastating. Some women, through self-help and professional guidance, significantly decrease their need for medical treatment.

Side Effects

Side effects of medical therapy can be physical, psychosocial, and emotional. Many can't be avoided. Remind yourself that they are time-limited and that you must weigh their discomfort against the symptoms of the disease itself. Try at the same time to keep potential benefits in focus.

Always report side effects to your doctor. He may be able to reduce them by decreasing the dosage or by other means. Nurses often have helpful suggestions, too.

Surgery and the Hospital Experience

You may have little control over the side effects of medications. There is, however, a great deal you can do to decrease the stress of surgery and to eliminate some of the difficulties of the hospital experience.

Prepare emotionally. Unless it's an emergency, you will have enough time to get used to the idea of surgery, to prepare yourself practically and emotionally. Numerous studies demonstrate that patients who receive adequate preparation, information, and support pre-operatively recuperate faster and with fewer complications than those who do not. In addition, they have a shorter hospital stay and less pre- and postoperative anxiety, depression, and need for pain medications. Knowledge reduces anxiety and the feeling of helplessness.

Many hospitals provide extensive patient education programs before admission. Generally, these programs include information packets, an explanation of hospital routines and procedures, and sources of support available. Films may be shown on what to expect concerning your surgery. There may be a guided tour of the operating room followed by an opportunity to ask questions. Before entering the hospital, call and ask if a patient education program is available. If not, you will have to work a little harder to get the information you need. Ask questions of your doctors, nurses, and anesthesiologist. Get in touch with others who have gone through the procedure. Ask to see the operating room. Find out just what the procedure involves, from the time you are admitted until your release. Ask what equipment and instruments look like, feel like, and sound like. Find out ahead of time what support the hospital provides.

Prepare physically. Surgery is extremely taxing. Get adequate rest and relaxation and improve your general health before you go into the hospital.

Plan for pain management. Your recovery will be more comfortable if you prepare for it. Before you enter the hospital, begin learning techniques to manage pain and reduce stress. Anxiety contributes to pain; any effort you make to reduce anxiety will decrease your pain. Investigate techniques such as meditation, biofeedback, and self-hypnosis (see Chapter 17).

At-home preparation. Generally, patients are admitted the evening before surgery. They then begin a series of routine preparatory tasks and tests. Often you can do many of the preoperative procedures—enemas, taking medication, and cleansing—at home where you are more comfortable. Ask your doctor if there is anything you can do at home, before you enter the hospital. Many routine preoperative tests can be done before admission on an outpatient basis. Reducing the number of tasks you must face in the hospital will not only increase your comfort, it may shorten your hospital stay.

Locate sources of support.   You may need someone to talk to about unexpected concerns. Often support is available, but patients are unaware of it or do not know how to ask for it. Before you are admitted, ask where to turn for help, what personnel are available for support.

Learn to relax.   Take along a portable tape player and headset; supply yourself with relaxation tapes and soothing music. They will reduce your anxiety and blot out hospital sounds that may be unpleasant, disruptive, or frightening.

Prepare for recovery.   Consider what your needs during recovery will be. Take steps before surgery to ensure that those needs—shopping, cleaning, cooking—can be met. Ask a friend for help. Learn about the risks and complications of surgery and quickly report problems to your doctor. If you are unaccustomed to quiet activity, plan ahead to fill the time you must spend resting in bed. Think about the books you have been meaning to read, the videotapes you have always wanted to see. Arrange ahead of time for visitors, but pace yourself. Keep visits short if they are tiring. Begin to plan how to resume your activities. But take it slowly. Again, pace yourself. Don't try to do too much too soon.

Infertility

To reduce the stress of the infertility investigation and subsequent treatment, gather as much information and support as possible, and as soon as possible. Contact Resolve; request a bibliography of publications concerning infertility (see also Appendix C). Get a list of fact sheets. Find out if there is a support group in your area. If not, consider starting one of your own. Ask for guidelines and suggestions. You may want to consider counseling early in the work-up. It helps you to cope with feelings and anxieties and aids in communication with your spouse. Infertility specialists and clinics sometimes employ counselors, but patients may be unaware of it. If counseling is unavailable, ask the specialist to refer you to someone trained in helping individuals cope with concerns related to infertility. Also, contact Resolve, The American Fertility Society, or the Endometriosis Association. (See Appendix B for the addresses of these organizations.)

14

Living with Continuing Symptoms: Lives on Hold

When treatment fails, when endometriosis recurs, the disruptions and problems continue, and women must reevaluate their treatment decisions. At the same time they must contend with the everyday reality of continuing symptoms—pain, infertility, and sexual difficulties. Chapter 13 covered disruption caused by initial symptoms and treatment. This chapter explores the pattern of emotional response that often occurs when women continue to live with symptoms.

THE PAIN CYCLE

"I know the pain is here to stay. It is just too awful to bear. I can't go on living this way."

"It's so frustrating for the pain to keep coming back month after month. It's hard to explain to my son why I only want to lie on the sofa with a heating pad."

When pain is not adequately controlled by treatment or recurs after repeated treatment, a pattern often emerges. Physical pain leads to anxiety and stress. Stress leads to increased pain as a result of physiological reactions such as muscle tension. Stress also can cause insomnia, which increases pain and anxiety. Pain, anxiety, and stress also contribute to depression, which exacerbates pain still further. All these feelings combine to produce an overwhelming sense of hopelessness, helplessness, and despair. The pattern is not linear but circular. It's difficult to tell which feeling leads to which, or where one emotion stops and another begins (see Figure 12).

167

Figure 12   The Pain Cycle

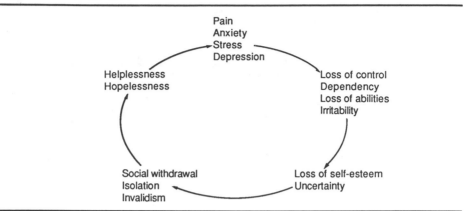

Individuals facing pain typically look only at the root of the problem—the source of the physical pain. As a result they fail to understand the complex ways pain affects them. It's important to understand how your emotions compound your pain. Try to recognize these emotions when they surface and then take steps to eliminate, or at least control, them.

Anxiety and Stress

Dr. Kames points out that individuals start to worry whether or not their pain is going to get worse each day. "Will I have to cancel my plans? What if I have an attack in a public place?" Soon they begin to anticipate. "When will the next attack come? Will it get worse? Will the pain ever go away? Can I live with this forever?"

Anxiety over pain is coupled with the stress of having a disease, having to make difficult decisions, having one's life disrupted, having to undergo treatment. This stress, bolstered by the memory and anticipation of pain, is perceived by the brain as a threat, and the body tenses in order to either fight or flee the source of the stress. Even though you can in actuality neither fight nor flee, physiological changes take place: shallow breathing, muscle tension, increased heartbeat, insomnia. All intensify pain and fatigue. The following are all symptoms of stress: loss of appetite, irritability, panic, muscle aches, cold hands or feet, rapid heartbeat, difficulty breathing, difficulty concentrating, insomnia and other sleep disorders, unusual behavior, frequent colds or infections, gastrointestinal disorders, headaches, and indifference. Stress management techniques, described in Chapter 17, teach you how to recognize your stressors, modify your reactions, and change your behavior.

Depression

Depression is characterized by sadness, guilt, anxiety, lethargy, pessimism, and hopelessness. It is also associated with sleeping disorders and changes in appetite and weight. Depression may be fleeting or prolonged and may range from mild to severe. If it is mild, you may cry a lot, feel sad, demoralized, fatigued, and listless. If it is severe, you may feel an overwhelming despair and hopelessness, or you may have suicidal thoughts. Depressed individuals sometimes lose interest in all their activities. They are unable to feel pleasure or pain and they view everything negatively. They feel that their situation will never improve, that they are powerless to bring about change, and that their problems are due to their own inferiority or shortcomings. The following is a list of symptoms of depression:

agitation	indecisiveness
anxiety	inferiority feelings
apathy, inertia, and lethargy	insomnia and other sleep disturbances
appetite changes	lack of attention to appearance
attention-seeking	lack of interest in previously enjoyable activities
changes in sexual appetite	mood swings
crying or inability to cry	negativity and negative self-image
fatigue	passivity
guilt	pessimism
hopeless or helpless feelings	sadness
inability to concentrate	suicidal thoughts
inability to set goals	weight changes

"Depression can easily develop when you are just physically tired of battling pain," says clinical psychologist Wanda Wigfall-Williams of Great Falls, Virginia. "If you get up in the morning and for the next three or four hours you are dealing with massive pain, you are going to be depressed. You are going to be tired. You are not going to be able to get on top of whatever it is you do for your life's work. You are not going to be able to deal with yourself or your mate or your children."

Depression lowers one's threshold of pain and thereby increases the perception of pain. This in turn leads to greater anxiety and further depression and despair, which increase both the intensity and the duration of pain. According to one study, for example, depressed patients are more likely to report constant, rather than intermittent, pain. When the depression is treated, the perception of pain is reduced.[1]

Depression is difficult to combat on your own. The best approach is to take part in a comprehensive pain management program (see Appendix E). Such programs address both the causes and manifestations of pain and pain's emotional components. Below are some additional ways to help dispel depression. (See Appendix C for more sources of self-help techniques.)

Express your feelings.   Talk with understanding friends and family members. Investigate support groups. They will provide you with an accepting atmosphere in which to vent your feelings. It is only by acknowledging your feelings that you can begin to change them.

Increase your control.   Depression may result not only from pain, but from the loss of control associated with pain. Control can be increased by gathering information and making decisions, which also increase self-esteem (see Chapter 16).

Avoid isolation.   Isolation contributes to depression. Social activities, on the other hand, draw you away from self-absorption. Plan regular activities. At first you won't feel like spending time with others. But taking action—any action—helps relieve depression.

Exercise.   Physical activity is a well-known antidote for depression. Numerous studies demonstrate that depressed individuals who begin and maintain a regular exercise program are able to considerably reduce, even eliminate, their depression. Start slowly with anything you can do comfortably, then gradually increase your level of activity. This will be difficult if you are depressed, so set a schedule and try to follow it regularly, whether or not you feel like it.

Set goals.   Feelings of inferiority, ineffectuality, and helplessness contribute to depression. To counter these feelings, set small goals and develop strategies for attaining them. Your sense of achievement will motivate you to set more goals and increase your activity. Be sure you don't set goals that are too high. Unrealistic goals set you up for failure. Be flexible and modify your goals. Otherwise you will see your inability to carry through as a sign of incompetence, a confirmation of your helplessness.

Seek help.   Finally, recognize that you may not be able to cope with depression on your own. Much depression is the result of distorted thinking, so it is helpful to consult a therapist who can provide an objective viewpoint. He or she can help you perceive the mistakes in your thought processes. In addition, many books provide strategies for correcting distorted perceptions. (See Chapter 16 and Appendix B.)

THE PAIN LIFESTYLE

If the cycle of stress, anxiety, and depression is not broken, a lifestyle of pain and isolation develops (see Figure 13). Pain colors all aspects of your daily life. You feel trapped. Its presence, or your anticipation of it, becomes all-consuming. The world beyond blurs as it grows increasingly distant. In her book, *Stop Hurting! Start Living!*, Jane Whitbread explains, "Pain reflexes trigger more far-reaching responses, with ever more complex effects upon your life, until pain is controlling. Pain dominates the character, the

Figure 23 The Pain Lifestyle

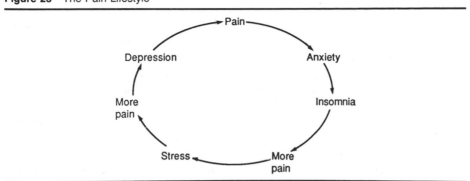

quality, the entire nature of your existence. The life of pain becomes so habitual that you forget that it is abnormal. You can no longer remember what your life was like. You may become so deeply immersed in habits of pain and suffering that you really cannot recognize this description." Consider the following elements of the pain lifestyle.

Diminished Ability to Meet Responsibilities

Pain makes it physically difficult to work. You may find you have to stay home more and more. Even when you are able to get out of bed and go to work, your performance may be impaired by fatigue, poor concentration, and the effects of pain medications. You worry about your job. If unemployed, you fear you will never be hired if you are honest about your illness and frequent absences. You may find you can no longer spend much time with your children. You are unable to clean or shop. Responsibilities provide a considerable measure of self-esteem. They define your social roles. Without them, you depend on others and your sense of self-worth suffers.

Losing Control

"The biggest problem emotionally for a woman with chronic pain is that it feels like her body is being taken over," explains Dr. Kames. "You feel like you don't have *any* control." The unpredictability of pain, coupled with the uncertainty of treatment, makes many women believe that nothing they can do will improve the situation. This loss of control affects different women differently, says Atlanta therapist Marilyn Beggs. "Some will feel a need to rein in every aspect of their lives, becoming highly structured to restore some semblance of control. They begin to do a lot of list-making. Others will give up all pretension of control and will make impulsive changes in many aspects of their lives. They say, "I don't have any control anyway, so why not?' "

Withdrawing

Decreased self-esteem, lost energy, diminished physical ability, and anxiety over pain's unpredictability may cause you to shun social activities. You may isolate yourself from friends and family, withdrawing into a world of your own. Isolation often occurs when pain begins to interrupt events and activities. You cancel plans at the last minute and soon you are afraid to make commitments. You stop participating, not because you are in pain, but because you anticipate and fear pain. You are embarrassed, fearful that friends won't understand, but you are tired of explaining. It seems as if you have nothing to offer anyone, because you are so preoccupied with your own condition. You may feel that you have become a burden to others, and they are tired of listening to you. You're afraid that no one can depend on you any longer. It's difficult to hear about their activities and achievements when your own life is suspended.

Isolation means lack of intimacy with others. This, coupled with an inability to indulge in previously pleasurable pastimes and satisfying tasks, further erodes your self-esteem. It arouses anger and leads to increased depression, pushing you still deeper into your own private world. The "normal" world slips away. You have nothing to replace it with but your own thoughts about pain and illness.

Withdrawal is hard on your friends and family. It strains relationships when you most need support and understanding. Others sorely feel the loss of your company. They may feel guilty if they carry on without you, and you feel guilty if they give up their activities. It's important that you encourage your friends and family members to continue with their activities. Try to help them express their feelings, too.

Most women have certain periods when they feel relatively well. Try to schedule your activities during those times, but don't try to do too much at once. Perhaps you used to enjoy walking for an hour a day. Instead of eliminating such a vigorous outing, walk for ten or twenty minutes. If dinner with friends is too taxing, arrange to meet briefly for dessert.

Communication prevents isolation. "Family members really need to be kept apprised," says Dr. Kames. "People have a tendency to want to protect their families and not let them know how much they are hurting or how many problems there are. And then they don't get any support." It is important to express your needs, but try not to let your needs become the focus of every conversation.

Isolation

Withdrawal is self-imposed. Isolation, on the other hand, results when others withdraw from you. It may be too difficult for them to observe your pain. They sense you are uncomfortable, but they feel helpless and don't know what to say. Perhaps you have avoided their company, canceled plans numerous times with no explanation. They may feel you are not interested in their company. You feel disappointed, slighted when friends and family ignore your feelings. They may not want to talk about your pain, and you may interpret this as a lack of concern. More often, though, it's that those close to you are denying your disease. Like you, they need time to adjust. Express your own feelings as honestly as you can, but try to understand those of others and realize that they, too, need to go through stages similar to those that you have been through. They need some time to adjust before they can be more supportive. You can share what you are experiencing and ask for help. Be specific. Let others know *how* you want to be helped.

Invalidism

Those close to you may find it very difficult to watch you suffer. But they try to be helpful. They are solicitous of you and begin to take on your responsibilities. They encourage you to "take it easy," discouraging you from participating in activities that you really are capable of. Their overprotectiveness can actually increase your pain. Despite the comfort or relief, you may unconsciously begin to depend on your pain for this increased attention. So you feel increasingly helpless, even useless. You take on the role of invalid, and it chips away at your self-esteem. Finally, although family and friends may offer to take on additional responsibilities, they may begin to feel resentful, and soon you have problems with your relationships. Talk to them about it. Tell them that you understand their motives and appreciate their thoughtfulness, but it's not helpful to you. Explain how they can help by listening, by encouraging you to do as much for yourself as possible, by providing positive feedback to counter your negative self-image. Sharing the information in this book may also help to open lines of communication.

Surrendering to Invalidism

Unable to carry out your responsibilities, withdrawing, and soliciting attention from others are all behaviors that arose from a very real impairment. But sometimes we fall back on these behaviors even when they are no longer appropriate. We surrender to invalidism or the sick role. We take comfort in the increased attention. Pain becomes an excuse to withdraw from responsibilities and situations.

It's hard to believe that one can gain from pain. But sick role behavior is unconscious. Realize that this unconscious seeking of rewards may actually increase your pain. Try to be aware of any unintentional benefits you are getting from your pain. Differentiate between those times when you avoid situations or tasks because you truly are in pain and those when pain has simply become an habitual excuse.

Loss of Assertiveness

It's hard when you're in pain to make others realize that there are certain times when you will be unavailable, unable to meet their expectations. Because you don't look ill, often they do not understand. They may be unsympathetic to pain that comes and goes. They don't realize that *all* your days are colored by the anticipation of pain and the stress it provokes. Pain and illness may cause you to feel invalid. You question your usefulness and dependability, and push yourself to keep up appearances. You may find it hard to say no to others' requests or to ask for help when you need it. As a result you may become anxious, angry, and resentful, and again you withdraw.

BREAKING THE PAIN CYCLE

A comprehensive approach to pain management combines relaxation training with psychological counseling. It is the most effective way to break the cycle of pain, stress, anxiety, and depression and to counter the feelings of helplessness and hopelessness it promotes (see Chapter 17). Support groups allow you to ventilate your feelings and observe others doing the same. You and they share similar feelings. Psychological counseling, particularly by therapists who use behavioral and/or cognitive techniques, can effectively correct distorted perceptions, replacing anxiety-provoking behaviors with more constructive responses (see Chapter 16).

INFERTILITY

Chapter 13 sketched the disruption and confusion created by the threat of infertility and the infertility work-up. In this section the feelings associated with the experience of being infertile are addressed. Emotional reactions to infertility are highly complex and a full explanation is beyond the scope of this book. Read as much as possible about infertility and talk to others who have dealt with it. Nothing will eliminate the pain of infertility, but the more you understand the experience, the better you will cope with the feelings it engenders. (See also Appendixes B and C for further resources and publications.)

Like chronic illness, infertility is a crisis—a potentially devastating situation. Surprised and unprepared, couples may deny what is happening. When endometriosis is present, the potential for infertility is also a crisis. Once shock and disbelief subsides, individuals are left to reevaluate their lifestyles and reappraise their goals. Can they accommodate a child earlier than anticipated? Those with known infertility must endure the continuing stress of treatment, face their feelings about their partners' responses, and the often hurtful reactions of friends and family.

Potential Infertility

Fertility can never be taken for granted. The potential for infertility exists for all women, particularly as they age. But most need not contend with it until they try—and fail—to conceive. Catherine Tuerk is a therapist specializing in infertility and issues related to gynecological disorders in Washington, D.C. She says, "One of the things that is psychologically difficult for endometriosis patients is that no one can tell them that they are unfertile until their reproductive ability is tested. They may or may not be able to conceive, but they will never know until they try." Typically, a doctor tells a patient with endometriosis, "The longer you wait, the more likely you are to be infertile." Women feel pressured to test their fertility, even though they are unsure or unprepared. Couples may feel angry, out of control, under pressure to make an important decision about something they are not even sure they want. They need to take enough time to explore their feelings and look at all of the issues involved. It is often helpful to talk to other couples, join support groups, and see an infertility therapist.

The issues involved are even more confusing and frustrating for adolescents. They must often face those problems without the support and comfort of an understanding partner. It's especially difficult for adolescents with endometriosis to reconcile their feelings about possible infertility. Self-identity and future plans are typical dilemmas. These now feel even more troublesome. Adolescents feel set apart from their peers. Their emotional and social development can be affected, as may be the course of educational and career goals. They may be deprived of a sense of choice, a flexibility, concerning the future. It also puts their sexuality into sharp focus, which may be embarrassing and confusing. Parents of younger patients should arrange for a sympathetic physician or counselor to help the adolescent cope with all of these feelings.

Potential infertility also poses additional problems for the single woman. "She may feel a lot of pressure to marry, to have children and test her fertility," says Catherine Tuerk. She may actively search for a partner with whom she can try to have children, ignoring the other needs she may have in a relationship. She may even enlist a friend or a stranger, or she may investigate in vitro fertilization or artificial insemination by donor. Counseling can often help single women determine priorities and deal with their feelings.

Actual Infertility

As with pain, infertility arouses intense feelings of loss of control, leading to anger and depression. Anxiety and agitation lead to the stress reactions described earlier: muscle tension, sleeplessness, and difficulty concentrating. Problems arise between partners—conflicting responses, isolation and secrecy, and alienation.

Conflicting responses. Fertility represents different things to different people. Faced with this crisis, a man and a woman may respond differently. These differences increase the strain as the two struggle to understand each other's coping style. A woman, for example, might become obsessed with infertility, continually expressing her shock and sadness. Her partner may withhold his feelings. He believes that if he reveals his pain, hers will intensify. A man who perhaps typically responds to crises by taking action may realize he is powerless to alter this situation. He may try to listen and to be supportive, but eventually he may withdraw emotionally. "Men tend to protect their wives and to use denial as a coping mechanism," explains Catherine Tuerk. "It's common," agrees Dr. Andrea Shrednick, "for men to think, "If I let her know how bad I feel, she'll feel worse.' " But it's a strategy that usually backfires, leaving each partner isolated and confused.

A man's silence and withdrawal may confuse, anger, and sadden the woman, because she interprets it as lack of interest. She may be deeply hurt, because she feels he doesn't care as much as she.[2] He, on the other hand, must face the turmoil of his own emotions alone, afraid to reveal his feelings. Just when they need each other's support, due to the disparity between their coping styles they are left isolated, unable to help each other.

Typically, arguments ensue, based largely on misunderstandings and assumptions. "Couples argue about feelings because they make assumptions about what the other person's feelings mean, do not like the assumptions, and so try to change the other's feelings," writes Patricia Mahlstedt.[3]

When grappling with your emotions, try to communicate honestly. Don't try to veil your feelings in order to protect your partner. Recognize that individuals use different coping mechanisms and that their reactions most probably are not synchronized. They can't share the same feelings at the same time, but they can express them honestly. "If you are in a relationship and you're being honest, you can't protect each other," explains Dr. Shrednick. "Support means being honest next to each other, not hiding."

Isolation and secrecy.   For a variety of reasons, couples often find it too painful to discuss their fertility problems with others; perhaps they feel unworthy, embarrassed, or stigmatized. Perhaps they don't wish to provoke well-meant but agonizing remarks like "You're not trying hard enough" and "You just need to relax." The result is that they are cut off from potential sources of support.

"We couldn't talk to our families, because they were pressuring us to have children; and we couldn't talk to our friends, because it was just too painful. And we wouldn't talk to each other."

Alienation.   So painful is the inability to conceive that couples may find it impossible to associate, or even come in contact, with women who are pregnant or with other couples with young children. Thus, they avoid their friends, even family members with children, and increase the distance between themselves and others. To prevent alienation, try to accept your feelings and communicate them.

Withdrawal, isolation, and alienation are often just the beginning of an evolution of emotional repercussions associated with infertility, not unlike the grieving process. When the struggle to achieve pregnancy is prolonged, and when the desired outcome seems more elusive than ever, couples find themselves going through the grieving process, acknowledging their feelings of loss and moving toward acceptance and resolution. It allows them to reevaluate their goals concerning childbearing, to explore their options. The grieving process is discussed in the following chapter; resolution is addressed in Chapter 16.

As with so many other complicated issues relative to endometriosis, there are no easy answers, no simple strategies for coping with the feelings, misunderstandings, and practical difficulties aroused by infertility. Information and support are vital. Again, read as much as possible, and encourage your family to read as well. They need to understand the challenges you are facing and the feelings you are struggling with. Take full advantage of the resources available to you; to decrease isolation, to learn how others cope, attend support group meetings. (If there is no support group in your area Resolve or the Endometriosis Association will supply information on how to start your own.) Finally, don't be ashamed to ask for help. A trained infertility counselor can guide you in facing your feelings, communicating with your partner, coping with the reactions of others, and determining your priorities.

SEXUAL DIFFICULTIES

All chronic conditions take their toll on sexual relationships, but most often it is an indirect process. Pain, fatigue, and disability of any kind lead to loss of sexual interest or at least discomfort during intercourse. In addition, endometriosis exerts a more direct and devastating blow—dyspareunia—pain with intercourse—caused by trauma to endometriotic implants during penile penetration. At a time when a woman most needs support, affection, and intimacy, endometriosis puts a wedge between her and her partner.

Dyspareunia

"We don't have sex any more. I think that loss hurts almost more than penetration. We are both very loving to each other, but that part of our lives is missing."

"The last time my lover and I had intercourse was five months ago. Afterward, he had to take me to the hospital for an injection of Demerol because I was in so much pain I couldn't sit up."

"I either avoid intercourse or participate and grit my teeth. I have come to accept that it is not enjoyable for me, just a necessity for our relationship. I am working at becoming a more responsive partner."

Dyspareunia, a common symptom of endometriosis, is, according to psychologist Wanda Wigfall-Williams, particularly devastating. "Women who are supposed to be in the prime of their sexual lives can't enjoy the expression of their sexuality. The mere act of penetration will send them around the bend—not in delight." Dyspareunia not only destroys relationships but a woman's self-image and self-esteem as well. It is particularly tragic because, in almost all cases, say sex therapists, women with endometriosis could eliminate, or at least considerably reduce, their sexual difficulties. But they lack the information with which to do so. Consequently, many relationships do not survive dyspareunia. Couples break up or remain only superficially intact. That is, they stay together, but there is a breakdown of communication and intimacy. The husband may have affairs, seeking sexual gratification outside the marriage. Seldom, however, are couples able to maintain affection and intimacy when sexual difficulties are not eliminated or relieved. Consider three ways women respond to dyspareunia and three ways their partners react.

Grin and bear it.   It is not uncommon for a woman to suffer silently. She fears her partner will reject her or will feel rejected himself. She feels she should not deprive him of sexual satisfaction and so feels guilty when she does so.

"The past few months the pain has been so bad we have hardly had a sex life. But I put up with sex, even though it hurts, because my husband has been extremely understanding and helpful, and it's not fair for him to suffer."

"I try to satisfy my husband so he won't stray."

Another reason women typically "grin and bear it" is because they want to become pregnant—at any cost. In addition to the emotional devastation and the stress of infertility, dyspareunia is a particularly brutal insult to those desperately trying to conceive.

"He won't have sex if he knows it hurts. We are trying to have a child, so I don't want him to know. If I did not want to have another child, I would have no desire for intercourse."

Anticipation and avoidance.   The anticipation of pain is as destructive as the pain itself. It inhibits sexual arousal which prevents lubrication, making the pain worse. As the cycle of pain, fear, and more pain continues, a woman may avoid intercourse altogether.

"I'm scared to have intercourse because I can ache for days afterward. I have become almost asexual, although I do hide my fears one or two days each month to preserve my husband's feelings. He has gone through so much with me that I feel it's necessary. At first, we would argue a lot. He was frustrated and nervous. For a while, in the beginning, I thought we were headed for a divorce."

"When my husband tries to penetrate me, he tries to help me relax, but that only helps a little. I dread going to bed at night and try to go at a different time than my husband."

Vaginismus.   When a woman is experiencing pain with intercourse, her anticipation of the pain may lead to vaginismus—the involuntary and powerful spasm of the vaginal muscles in response to attempted penile penetration. When this response is severe, penetration cannot occur, for the muscles act as a barrier.

Misunderstanding.   Without a thorough knowledge of endometriosis and of female anatomy, it may be difficult for a woman's partner to understand her pain and her fear of pain. This is especially true when a woman who has not yet been diagnosed is experiencing the painful symptoms of endometriosis. Without a "legitimate" reason for pain, misunderstanding abounds. The man feels confused, rejected, and angry.

"Before diagnosis, it came close to ending our relationship, since my husband thought it was an act—to avoid intercourse. Now that we both know why there is pain, we are better able to deal with it."

"Only when he understood that the pain would go away after surgery did he begin to feel that we had a happy future together and that it was worth staying together."

"Our relationship was really falling apart. I wouldn't let him touch me because even arousal was painful. Putting in the diaphragm was painful. So I avoided sex altogether. He accepted my growing disinterest in sex for a while, but then he began to feel like I was rejecting him."

"I would concentrate on a song while we were making love, to distract me from the pain. I'm sure my husband knew I wasn't getting anything out of the act, but I couldn't talk to him about it."

Protectiveness and avoidance. When a man senses—or suspects—that his partner is experiencing pain, he may avoid sexual advances. He may not discuss his reasons for doing so, leaving his partner feeling confused and rejected.

"At first I thought he wasn't interested, and then I found out that he was afraid he was causing me pain."

"My partner is afraid I won't tell him when it hurts, so our sex life is almost nonexistent for part of the month."

Impotence. Guilt—or feelings of rejection or frustration—may lead to sexual dysfunction in the partner of a woman experiencing dyspareunia or vaginismus. His inability to achieve or maintain an erection is misinterpreted by his partner as rejection or disinterest. She may feel rejected and guilty.

Effects of Treatment

In addition to the loss or decrease of sexual desire resulting from dyspareunia or vaginismus, a woman's libido may be decreased by hormonal treatments. Levels of sexual desire may change throughout the course of therapy. Unaware that the change is due to the drugs, a woman is often puzzled and disturbed by her sudden disinterest in sex. Like other sexual difficulties, changes in libido may affect her self-image and disrupt her concept of her sexuality.

Problems with Relationships

Erosion of sexual self-esteem. Individuals with chronic illness often feel different from others. They feel that they are defective in some way. Sexual difficulties compound these feelings of unworthiness, eroding a woman's already diminished self-esteem. In light of her sexual problems, she may reappraise her body image, believing now that she is less attractive, less desirable, and less feminine than other women. Her sexual confidence withers away, and she finds it difficult either to initiate sexual activity or to respond, even when she feels well.

"I felt I wasn't holding up my part of the bargain. I was afraid he felt sorry for me, and that reminded me that I had a problem."

"I have completely avoided being with him. I don't feel I can be intimate, or show him any affection, because I don't feel good about myself. I don't feel capable of loving anyone else, either."

"If I were single right now, I don't think any man would want me."

Breakdown of communication.   Often, when sexual difficulties arise, it's hard for couples to discuss their feelings. This silence leads to myriad misunderstandings. The frustration of being unable to express sexual feelings is compounded by the inability to discuss those frustrations.

Erosion of romance.   An erosion of romance and affection follows a communication breakdown. When intercourse is impossible, many couples typically cease all physical intimacy. Rather than seeking alternative pleasures and reassuring each other of continuing affection, couples refrain from touching, kissing, and verbally expressing affection altogether.

Preexisting problems with relationships.   According to sex therapists, when couples passively accept loss of intimacy—when they stay together but do not communicate, make love, or express affection—they are probably hiding other relationship problems. Endometriosis and dyspareunia give them an excuse to focus on sexual pain as the cause of their deteriorating relationship. They blame everything on it, and they do not look at the other dynamics in their relationship. And, although dyspareunia is usually caused by physical problems, not by fear or dislike of sex, there are women who use it as a convenient excuse to relinquish sexual activity.

"I don't think my pain and discomfort during intercourse comes from endometriosis. I think it is because I don't like sex. But I won't tell my husband that."

"Sometimes, with endometriosis, I think I finally get away with saying and meaning no to sex with men."

ELIMINATING OR DIMINISHING SEXUAL DIFFICULTIES

Much emotional devastation is wrought by dyspareunia, vaginismus, and loss of libido. But it can be eliminated, or significantly decreased. For example, couples can face their sexual difficulties squarely, increase their communication, experiment with positions that do not involve deep penetration, and explore other satisfying sexual activities. In addition, sex therapy can be extremely helpful for most couples who are willing to make the effort. Couples must work together: it is a problem for both. When these steps fail to bring relief, couples should explore the possibility that other problems in their relationship are standing in the way of a mutually satisfying sex life.

Improving Communication

Much of the difficulty associated with dyspareunia results from poor communication. For example, "If a woman tells me she doesn't want to let her partner know that intercourse is painful because she is afraid he will feel rejected," says Dr. Elizabeth Herz of the George Washington University Medical Center, "that tells me that this couple is not communicating."

"The partner needs to be aware of the fact that intercourse is painful and that it is not a rejection of him," says Catherine Tuerk. "It's important for the woman to be honest about it. If she just stops wanting to have intercourse because it hurts, and she doesn't tell him, it's going to be a pretty big strain on the relationship."

Similarly, men need to be more open and honest about their reactions. "Protectiveness, although well-meant," says Dr. Herz, "is not a good approach for the man to take, because it isolates the two. They are no longer sharing their feelings about the whole situation and so each of them starts to cope with their own feelings. Then, they are not really relating any more, and this leads to the breakdown in communications."

Share your feelings. Your partner needs to know why you cannot respond. If he knows you will tell him when you experience pain, he won't be afraid to approach you sexually, and he won't feel rejected or guilty. Share your feelings of sadness at the loss of intimacy and communicate your willingness to work on the situation. If you cannot, seek the help of a sex therapist.

Experimenting with Positions That Reduce Deep Penetration

Sexual pain is often relieved by preventing deep penetration without sacrificing satisfaction. First, says Dr. Herz, "it's important that there is enough foreplay so that the woman will become lubricated and can stay in a state of sexual arousal, which, to a certain extent, can blot out much sexual pain." Next, she explains, you must experiment with different positions that reduce or prevent deep penetration. A woman may find it helpful to straddle her partner so that she can control the depth of penetration.

Dr. Andrea Shrednick recommends the bridge maneuver, a position described by Dr. Helen Kaplan Singer in her *Illustrated Manual of Sex. Therapy* (see Appendix C).[4] Either the man and woman lay side by side, or the woman straddles her partner. Following enough foreplay to provide sufficient lubrication, the man enters and thrusts "with just enough rhythm and depth to maintain an erection." At the same time, either partner can stimulate the woman's clitoris with the fingers. "It's a position," says Dr. Shrednick, "that allows for mutual feelings, mutual satisfaction, touch, and closeness, but not the deep penetration that causes pain." You may find, through experimentation, that other positions will also decrease discomfort.

Finding Alternative Methods of Sexual Satisfaction

Intercourse may still be painful. There are avenues to sexual satisfaction that do not involve penetration: manual stimulation, mutual masturbation, oral stimulation, and femoral intercourse (thrusting the penis between the woman's closed thighs). Finally, sexual activity needn't always lead to intercourse, or even orgasm. Couples can focus on stroking, hugging, kissing, and massage to increase intimacy and enhance their relationship.

Increasing Desire

When diminished sexual desire results from hormones and other medications, women may find that fantasy and erotic books and films increase arousal. Helpful books include *The Joy of Sex, For Each Other: Sharing Sexual Intimacy,* and *My Secret Garden: Women's Sexual Fantasies* (see Appendix C).

Seeking Therapy

Many couples find it too difficult or embarrassing to seek help for sexual problems. However, therapists can help couples increase their knowledge of sexual positions and practices that reduce pain, increase their communication, and maintain their intimacy. They can also help distinguish problems arising from endometriosis from other relationship problems. (For more information on therapy, see Chapter 16.)

Sex and the Single Woman

Sexual pain also presents special difficulties for single women, particularly those who are not involved in a long-term relationship. With each new encounter, they may be fearful of rejection. Perhaps, they feel, others will see them as less feminine, less desirable, once the subject of painful intercourse is raised. Frequently these feelings are too hurtful, so women avoid new relationships.

"I cannot put myself through the turmoil of dating. Someone extremely kind and patient would have to come along before I'll even think about having a relationship."

"I felt I couldn't handle it if I told someone about the endometriosis and sexual pain and was rejected. Not many people understand. Men sometimes think I am using it as an excuse. Some did try to be understanding and were very sympathetic, but that did not make the pain go away."

Therapy may help single women come to terms with their fears and feelings.

Sex and the Adolescent

Young women may be particularly reluctant to discuss dyspareunia with anyone, even their doctors. They may be embarrassed, confused, they may fear disapproval, or they may lack the vocabulary or experience they need to present their problems. If intercourse has been painful from early on, young women may not realize that pain is not the norm. An early painful sexual experience may negatively affect sexual development and body image, so it's important that young women be encouraged to discuss these issues with a sympathetic physician or trained counselor.

15

Tallying the Losses: The Road to Resolution

"I was an individual with two degrees, a wonderful professional life, and plans to go to medical school. I am happily married and have a beautiful child, but this disease has prevented my career from advancing, stressed my marriage to the limit, and left my son with a bedridden mother."

When pain, menstrual irregularities, infertility, or sexual difficulties persist after repeated treatment, you may become increasingly aware of how your life and the lives of those close to you have become organized around, and overtaken by, your illness. When you realize that most of your daily activities, interactions with others, and plans continue to be shadowed and shaped by considerations relative to endometriosis, you will probably also begin to ask yourself how long you can go on that way. Will the treatment carousel ever come to a halt?

You may feel that you are at a crossroads. There are three avenues you can take. One, you can continue your life "on hold." Two, you can accept endometriosis as chronic, acknowledging, perhaps, the *possibility* that you may never get pregnant, yet resolving to live with the disease and/or infertility, actively working to minimize the impact on your life and your emotions. Three, you can choose to have a hysterectomy, and learn to accept the feelings and changes that may accompany surgery. Most women reach this crossroads only when they realize that what once appeared to be a temporary disruption, now threatens to become a permanent loss.

The loss has many parts, both concrete and symbolic.

companionship, romance, intimacy
control
employment, income or its potential, job security
goals (education, career, relationships, family)

independence
physical abilities, vitality, strength, energy
predictability, normalcy, flexibility
pride, dignity
privacy
productivity
self-esteem, self-image, body image, sexuality, notions of femininity
social role, status, and support
time spent with partners, children, family

GRIEVING: WORKING THROUGH THE EMOTIONAL TOLL

Whichever avenue you choose, it's crucial that you grieve for your loss. Grieving is the bridge to resolution—the stage of adaptation. If you decide to live with the disease, you must grieve for the losses you have incurred and those you are likely to incur. If you are resolving issues of infertility, you must mourn the loss of your childbearing abilities, along with other goals and dreams you once had. If you elect to have a hysterectomy, or definitive surgery, you must grieve for all of the above, as well as for the actual loss of your reproductive organs.

Grief is the way individuals process loss. It is a normal and necessary acknowledgment of, and reaction to, an extremely painful reality. The initial response to loss is to repress overpoweringly negative feelings. Grief occurs when individuals confront, accept, and let go of these feelings. It is a cathartic experience. Individuals usually emerge from it capable of moving on, filling the void, and restoring balance in their lives.

The Components of the Grief Cycle

Elisabeth Kübler-Ross is a physician and a psychiatrist renowned for her work with dying patients. In her book, *On Death and Dying*, she delineates the stages of grief experienced by dying patients and their families. Since 1969, when her book was published, the stages it describes—denial and isolation, bargaining, anger and guilt, depression and acceptance—have come to be viewed as a pattern of response to any major loss. They are prerequisite to acceptance of that which at first seems unacceptable. Chronic illness produces many major losses, so you are likely to go through these stages more than once. The more familiar you are with the feelings they generate, the more you realize they are vital to adaptation, the less isolated and confused you will be throughout the grief cycle. Remember, you may not go through all of the stages, and not everyone goes through them in the same order. There is no typical time frame within which individuals grieve. Support and counseling facilitate the grieving process, but, ultimately, you will grieve at your own pace. You may go back and forth between stages, or you may get "stuck" in one before you move on to resolution.

Denial and isolation. Chapter 12 explored the denial that typically follows the diagnosis of a chronic illness. Individuals commonly react with disbelief to what is happening. You may begin the grief cycle by retreating once again into denial—the inability to believe what has *already* happened. As you begin to acknowledge your losses and find the process overwhelmingly painful, you feel sorry for yourself, wishing you could return to your life as it was before your illness. At this stage you may try to "bargain away" your illness, fantasizing that good behavior will bring relief or a cure. You may regret past decisions— delayed childbearing, an abortion—which you imagine may have caused your current problems. You retreat emotionally, denying the reality of the situation. In this stage, you shun treatment, reject support, and take no steps at all toward coping, because you want to believe there really is no problem.

Denial provides time to face facts at your own pace and to bolster yourself for acceptance. Some women remain in denial, continuing to live their lives "on hold." Many move back and forth between denial and awareness before moving on. Denial, although useful in coping with a situation that cannot be changed, becomes an obstacle to adaptation if prolonged. It leaves individuals isolated in their invalidism.

Anger and guilt. Emergence from denial into the next response occurs when symptoms continue with no end in sight and you become fully aware of your loss. The typical response to acknowledgment is anger. Women are often surprised and ashamed to find themselves feeling angry. But individuals with chronic conditions have much to be angry about. They are angry that they seem to have been selected to suffer. They are angry that others don't understand. Anger is real and rational and, like grief, a normal response to loss and a necessary step in the mourning process.

Anger, however, can be appropriate or inappropriate, motivating or immobilizing. Anger may impel you to seek answers or to make changes and is therefore a necessary part of the coping process. But it may also become misdirected, a tool for blame. This redirects energy away from coping. Anger misdirected at doctors, lovers, and friends is destructive because it cuts you off from sources of support. At the same time, unexpressed anger can simmer as resentment.

Anger misdirected toward oneself may lead to guilt. Many women with endometriosis feel guilty, not only for having the illness in the first place (see Chapter 12) and for its effects—the loss of time with family and friends, the loss of ability to be emotionally responsive to others, the loss of ability to meet responsibilities or the demands and expectations of family members or employers. The fact that others must watch you suffer and must suffer with you adds to your guilt.

Women who are infertile experience an added measure of guilt. They feel they have let their parents as well as their mates down by not being able to have a child. A mother may feel responsible for not giving her child a brother or a sister. A woman may feel guilty over a past abortion or prior use of birth control. The erroneous notion that endometriosis is the "career woman's disease," a penalty imposed by delayed childbearing, contributes strongly to guilt.

Finally, many women feel both guilty and inadequate because they think only they are unable to cope, or that others cope better. With no reference points, their own difficulties are seen as personal failure. "The person who had a low self-esteem to begin with, can also easily divert this anger against herself and find another proof that she is not really as good or as worthy as other women," says Dr. Herz.

Guilt is often easier to accept than anger. It is more difficult for some women to admit to being angry, to feel justified for having such a harsh and seemingly ugly emotion. It may not be productive to deny your anger or to try to eliminate it. Instead, recognize it, accept it, be aware of how you focus it, and determine if it is appropriate. Sometimes it's helpful to try to find appropriate outlets instead of spending time and energy worrying about being angry.

Next, try to determine more precisely *why* you are angry. The reasons may be clear: "I'm angry I have a disease, I'm angry I couldn't go to work. I'm angry at the limitations my body is imposing upon my life. I'm angry that others don't understand. I'm angry at the demands others place on me." Or the reasons may be vague, difficult to pinpoint; but as you begin to pay more attention to moments when you feel your anger surface, you may also begin to see a pattern. This will help you understand the underlying source of your feelings.

Examine your angry feelings. Talk about them in an appropriate environment—in a support group or in therapy. Your anger will seem less frightening, less overwhelming. Use relaxation techniques to help defuse the intensity of your feelings. Don't just verbalize your anger. Keep a journal. Turn on the shower and yell. Pummel a punching bag. Once you begin to express your feelings, your anger may then be channeled into positive, creative, constructive acts.

Look at how you direct your anger. It's easy to make your doctor, or your husband, for example, the scapegoat for all your difficulties, the target of your rage. Try to redirect your feelings in a more constructive manner. Is your anger at a particular person or thing rational? Is it justified? If so, work toward solving the problem. If not, try to determine just what it is that is making you angry and try to redirect that anger.

It's extremely important to express your anger and attempt to discover its source. Unexpressed anger and guilt (anger turned inward) can fuel depression. This is because outright expression of anger is often perceived as hostility, which is viewed as socially unacceptable. It is particularly difficult for women who have been socialized to repress their anger to vent their feelings. They feel particularly frightened and uncomfortable when angry. They sense that these feelings are somehow wrong, or selfish. Depression typically occurs when there is no outlet for such powerful feelings.

Depression and acceptance.   Typically, the stage before acceptance is depression. In Chapter 14 depression was discussed in relation to the pain cycle. As stated there, it ranges from mild to severe. You may simply feel sad or helpless, or you may be overwhelmed by despair. Depression that accompanies diagnosis or treatment tends to inhibit your ability to cope. Depression associated with grief, however, is a necessary and appropriate component of the grief cycle. It results from an accurate appraisal of a very real loss.

This stage is characterized by feelings of sadness, crying, apathy, inertia, and the loss of a variety of emotions (see symptoms of depression listed at the beginning of Chapter 14). While Chapter 14 offered strategies for overcoming depression, they are only partially effective for the more profound depression that accompanies grief.

The final stage, acceptance, comes when individuals allow themselves to feel—and express—their sadness over their loss. Friends and family can help by listening and understanding, rather than trying to coax you out of your depression. Support groups and therapy provide outlets for feelings of depression.

PART 4

Resolution: Moving On

If you suspect endometriosis, or have recently been diagnosed, some practical strategies will help you avoid many of the difficulties explored in Part 3 and to cope with those that do arise. We tend to think that certain problems will not happen to us—or that we can postpone worrying about them until they do. Coping with endometriosis is easier if you take action *now*.

If you have had endometriosis for some time, and if you feel your life has already been "derailed," it may be more difficult to accept the fact that you are neither helpless nor hopeless. Perhaps you are resigned to a life "on hold," to a passive acceptance, waiting for the discovery that will bring you relief or make it possible for you to conceive.

It is not too late to learn some techniques that will increase your comfort and control over your life. The thought of starting over, of embarking on a new approach, may be disconcerting. It will take a lot of effort, but it may save you considerable stress in the long run.

You need to confront the realities of living with endometriosis, whatever stage you are in—undiagnosed, only recently diagnosed, struggling to conceive, or considering hysterectomy.

Having faced your feelings and allowed yourself to grieve, accepted the chronicity of your disease, and resolved to take steps to minimize its impact, the next step is accepting responsibility for your own decisions and for managing your own health care. This is the focus of Part 4. To do this, prepare yourself physically and emotionally. As noted earlier, decision making is often hampered by feeling overwhelmed, by passivity, and by a lack of information, but also by pain, stress, fatigue, anxiety, depression, and poor self-esteem, all of which lead to a lack of assertiveness and an inability to trust one's own judgment. Moving on, then, will involve the following steps:

- Developing assertiveness
- Gathering information: learning to collect medical information and to make use of available resources
- Getting the best possible medical care: learning how to choose a doctor and improve the doctor-patient relationship
- Improving your general health: attending to diet, exercise, and rest
- Reducing pain and stress: learning relaxation techniques
- Increasing decision-making abilities
- Restoring emotional equilibrium: learning to help yourself, tapping into support systems, and asking for professional help
- Exploring alternative therapies: looking into nontraditional treatments such as homeopathy, osteopathy, chiropractic, naturopathy, herbalism, and diet and nutrition
- Resolving your feelings about actual or potential infertility
- Identifying your goals and exploring your options: pregnancy, adoption, surrogate motherhood, or childfree living
- Determining when to stop treatment

Remember, none of the above guarantees freedom from pain, or the achievement of your childbearing goals. However, completing the steps above will assure you that you have done everything in your power to make the best of your situation. Women who take these steps, yet continue to live with unacceptable pain and a severely diminished quality of life, may opt for definitive surgery—they will then need to resolve an additional set of issues and losses.

16

Taking Control: Some Practical Strategies

It's important to remember that many of the emotional problems explored in Part 3 arise from an inability to accept the fact that endometriosis is a chronic disease. All too frequently women pursue a cure to the exclusion of all other means of management. Certainly you should pursue treatments that increase comfort or that might bring about remission, but don't neglect other avenues of relief and the other parts of your life. Chasing a cure provides only a superficial sense of control. It actually leaves you feeling dependent, helpless, and—paradoxically—totally *out* of control.

ACCEPTING RESPONSIBILITY: DECISION MAKING

The first step is to recognize that *you* are the one who must decide. To abdicate your decision-making power strips you of control. You feel helpless, and your sense of self-esteem suffers.

Consider your doctor's advice, but determine your own goals and priorities, communicate them, and evaluate his recommendations *in light of your needs*. Consider what others have to say, but don't let their input obscure your own values, needs, and judgment.

"Everyone thinks they want to be told what to do," says Catherine Tuerk, "but in the long run, people need to make their own decisions. You know yourself best, and you are going to have to live with the decisions." Mary Lou Ballweg adds, "When you are dealing with endometriosis, you will be making decisions that deal with the essence of you, relating to your life plan with respect to children, marriage, sexual relationships, careers, feelings about being a woman, and your self-image. You can't let others make such vital decisions."

FOCUSING

You begin in a state of disorder and confusion. It's difficult for you to select and focus clearly on the problems that require your immediate attention. You really don't know where to begin. Anxious, and under considerable stress, it's almost impossible to gather information, establish priorities, make decisions, and set realistic goals. Trying to solve all your problems at once is an approach that usually leads to frustration, defeat, and an increased sense of loss of control.

For example, many women act on the advice of the first doctor they see, hastily making decisions that will affect them for the rest of their lives. They don't take time to fully investigate their options and determine their priorities.

Slow down, but don't procrastinate, either. The following advice will help you make appropriate and informed decisions.

GATHERING INFORMATION

Coping and information go hand in hand. You can't make decisions or set goals without adequate, accurate, and up-to-date information. Being well informed gives you perspective, strength, and confidence. Numerous studies show that patients who are well informed about their condition and knowledgeable about treatment procedures fare better. They are less anxious, and their recovery is more rapid. Information will help you regain a sense of control and make you less dependent on others.

Insurance

Financial worries only add to your stress. If uninsured, investigate and apply for medical coverage *before* you make further attempts at diagnosis. (If your condition is severe, however, don't wait for insurance.) Insurance carriers are reluctant to insure individuals with preexisting conditions, particularly diseases such as endometriosis that likely involve ongoing, expensive treatment. If you are diagnosed before you apply, your illness will be considered a preexisting condition. It may preclude you from acceptance into a medical plan, raise your insurance premiums, or seriously restrict your benefits. If you have medical insurance, talk with your agent. Learn what treatments are covered and what your own financial responsibilities will be.

If you require hospitalization but are unable to finance it, you may be eligible for assistance from the Hill-Burton Free Hospital Care Program. In 1946 Congress passed a law that gave hospitals and other health facilities money for construction and modernization. In return, these facilities agreed to give a certain amount of free care to persons unable to pay. The program covers hospital costs only at participating facilities. (See Appendix B for sources of information about insurance.)

Organizations

The Endometriosis Association, the Endometriosis Society, Resolve, and Chronic Pain Outreach can provide you with a wealth of information while you search for medical care and make treatment decisions. These groups can give you tips on doctors in your area, a perspective on the pros and cons of various treatments, and coping strategies that others have found useful. Most important, they put you in touch with others in similar circumstances. The experience of these women and their perspective on endometriosis are invaluable sources of support. (See Appendix B.)

The Endometriosis Association.   This is an organization of women with endometriosis and others interested in exchanging information about the disease. Headquartered in Milwaukee, the association has chapters throughout the United States and Canada. Chapters offer informal support groups as well as lectures and presentations by experts on endometriosis, infertility, psychology, and related self-care issues. Its goals are to support and help those affected, to educate the public and the medical community about the needs of its members, and to promote further research. Members receive a newsletter six times a year and have access to formal and informal crisis-call listening/counseling services. In addition, the association provides literature on many aspects of endometriosis.

The Endometriosis Society.   Headquartered in London, with chapters throughout England, the society sponsors workshops by specialists, sends members bimonthly newsletters, and offers a range of fact sheets on a wide variety of subjects, including many alternative and adjunctive therapies.

Resolve.   Resolve is a national organization dedicated to the support of infertile individuals. It provides information on all aspects of infertility, both medical and emotional. It offers an extensive bibliography; publishes fact sheets and national and chapter newsletters; provides referrals to infertility specialists, therapists, and other resources; and sponsors workshops, symposia, and other events.

Chronic Pain Outreach.   Chronic Pain Outreach is a national network of self-help chapters offering emotional support, practical help, and information to individuals with chronic pain and their families. It provides advocacy, works to increase public awareness, offers a national newsletter, and serves as a clearinghouse for information about chronic pain. Chapter members work to encourage positive attitudes, promote family understanding, and help pain sufferers regain control over their lives. Chapters offer support group meetings, special programs and workshops, follow-up and support for graduates of pain management programs, library resource materials, and crisis intervention.

Scientific Literature

For details about endometriosis, and to stay abreast of research, consult the medical literature. It is the best source of current information, the same source your doctor uses. Don't be intimidated by technical material. Some will be difficult to understand at first, but you will be surprised how quickly you can learn the jargon. Armed with a good medical dictionary you will be able to grasp the fundamentals before you turn to your doctor for details and clarification. You will also be able to ask intelligent questions.

Start with a basic gynecological textbook. Remember, all that is written is not gospel. Textbooks may contain material that is dated or debatable. Use a basic textbook only to get an overview and to understand the fundamentals and the different opinions about endometriosis. Medical journals, on the other hand, contain reports on the latest findings of medical research.

Whatever the source, critically evaluate the nature of any medical information upon which you will base treatment decisions. You may not be able to assess medical opinion, but you can, and should, distinguish opinion from fact. Recognize advice based on impression and advice based on solid research. When gathering information, look for research and statistics that support claims. Ask about the facts upon which the opinions are based.

Textbooks and journals (see Appendix D) are available at most medical school libraries and many hospital and university libraries. If they are unavailable in your area, contact the National Library of Medicine in Bethesda, Maryland. It has an information network of more than 3000 health science libraries and information centers, coordinated through seven regional medical libraries. Services include reference, interlibrary loan, and access to MEDLARS (Medical Literature Analysis and Retrieval System), a computerized database referencing medical books and journals. Approximately 1800 network libraries provide access to MEDLARS. In addition, the National Library of Medicine offers computer literature searches that provide citations for medical articles on any subject. The fee, usually modest, depends on the comprehensiveness of the search. (For example, a recent search for citations for all articles and available abstracts on endometriosis in the last twenty years— several thousand listings—cost $75.)

GETTING THE BEST POSSIBLE MEDICAL CARE: CHOOSING A DOCTOR

In a recent study consumers indicated that they spent more time selecting supermarkets and clothing stores than doctors. Like every other commodity or professional service, medical care varies in quality, competency, and cost. To find the best possible care, take the approach of an informed consumer.

Many women turn first to their family practitioner or internist for help. Many general practitioners can detect and treat endometriosis, but it makes more sense to seek out those individuals who are best trained and most familiar with endometriosis—gynecologists and reproductive endocrinologists.

Evaluate Credentials

A gynecologist must complete a four-year residency in obstetrics and gynecology upon graduation from medical school. After residency, a gynecologist is free to practice. But practice does not indicate competence, skill, or conformance to standards. To find the best doctor possible, look beyond the title and investigate the physician's credentials.

After residency and two or more years of practice, a gynecologist is eligible for certification by the board of the American College of Obstetricians and Gynecologists. Certification is awarded to those who have passed written and oral examinations administered by the board and who have had all of their hospital cases reviewed by the board. A further distinction bestowed by the board is the title of Fellow of the American College of Obstetricians and Gynecologists (FACOG). It indicates that a board-certified doctor has practiced for five or more years. Such an individual should be able to treat endometriosis. However, since symptoms and diagnosis can be difficult, and are so often vague, many experts suggest consulting a reproductive endocrinologist—a gynecologist who has had two additional years of training in the subspecialty of endocrine and reproductive disorders.

To find a gynecologist or a reproductive endocrinologist, ask your internist or family practitioner for a referral or call your county medical society or local hospital with an obstetrics and gynecology department. Ask other women for recommendations, but investigate the doctors they suggest. See if he is board certified by consulting the *Directory of Medical Specialists*, available at many libraries, or call your local or state health department or medical society. The American College of Obstetricians and Gynecologists will send you a list of its members in your area. Beyond board certification, there are other questions to ask when evaluating a doctor.

1. Where did he serve his residency? In general, doctors who serve residencies in university medical schools are widely considered to be both better trained and more experienced.
2. How long was his residency? It stands to reason that the longer one's residency, the greater one's practical experience and exposure to a wide variety of cases.
3. Where does he have hospital privileges? It is often advantageous to be under the care of a physician with staff privileges at a hospital associated with a university medical school.
4. To what professional societies does he belong? Membership in the American Fertility Society or the American College of Obstetricians and Gynecologists increases the likelihood that he participates in continuing education activities, conferences, and symposia where he is kept informed about current developments in the field.

5. Is he a member of a group practice? Some experts suggest that physicians who are part of a group practice provide better care as a result of the exchange of information and perspective among doctors.

Evaluate Abilities

Learn as much as possible about surgical experience and expertise, in addition to general qualifications. Experience and expertise will influence treatment recommendations. For example, if you have severe endometriosis involving the bowel, a surgeon capable of performing an extensive and complicated bowel resection may advise you to undergo conservative surgery. A less skilled surgeon, adept at hysterectomy but less confident about a bowel resection, may advise hysterectomy. Similarly, when it comes to laser surgery, you want the surgeon to be highly trained. Ask your doctor the following questions about laser laparoscopy or laser laparotomy:

1. Have you taken a course in laser surgery?
2. Have you served a preceptorship (an intensive study with an instructor), including hands-on training with patients?
3. Were you trained in intra-abdominal (more extensive training) or extra-abdominal laser surgery?
4. Have you done more than twenty laser surgeries?

For more information on how to determine a doctor's competence with laser technology, contact the American Society for Laser Medicine and Surgery (see Appendix B).

Male or Female

Would you be more comfortable with a female physician? Some women find it easier to talk openly with another woman. They feel that a woman more easily relates to their problems. If you prefer a female gynecologist, contact the American Medical Women's Association for a referral. You can also contact local chapters of women's organizations (for example, NOW).

Interest and Rapport

When choosing a doctor, remember that ability to communicate with and relate to patients is just as important as training, credentials, and hospital affiliation. Without good rapport, sterling qualifications are useless. Women in particular—and especially those who are afflicted by endometriosis or infertility—need to find physicians who will spend some time with them. When evaluating a doctor, consider whether or not he appears interested in you as an individual, in the difficulties the disease is posing for you and for your lifestyle, and in helping you to help yourself.

Research indicates that patients of doctors who demonstrate such interest are more satisfied, are more willing to comply with recommendations, and experience greater and longer-lasting relief of symptoms than patients of disinterested doctors. Investigate credentials and abilities. But also spend time and effort in finding an individual who

communicates well in words you understand

takes you seriously

displays sympathy, understanding, comfort, and a nonjudgmental attitude

does not paternalize, patronize, or condescend

explains your options thoroughly

mobilizes and motivates you to take part in managing your illness

shows concern with your general well-being, not just your pelvic pain or your inability to become pregnant

encourages your questions and answers them completely

The Doctor-Patient Relationship

The doctor-patient relationship is most productive when both doctor and patient recognize the need to develop a true partnership based on mutual respect and consideration. Some patients place their physicians on a pedestal, granting them complete control, believing doctors have divine power. Such an attitude is unfair and dehumanizing to patients and doctors alike. Similarly, some doctors recognize the importance of the patient's role; others confuse authority with arrogance. Recognize the importance of your role in the doctor-patient relationship and communicate your understanding of that role to your doctor. If you want advice and guidance, yet want to make your own decisions, say so. Be as informed as possible. Let your doctor *know* you are informed. Dr. Thomas Preston, in *The Clay Pedestal*, writes, "Insist on being an equal partner in all decisions, using the doctor's knowledge and skills, but not giving him control over you." Furthermore, he advises, "Let your doctor know you respect his opinion, but that you want the facts as well, and that you can tell the difference."[1]

Although this is excellent advice, it is often difficult for women to put it into practice. Many women find it hard to act assertively on their own behalf (see below). It can be done without hostility or arrogance if you negotiate in advance the terms of the relationship. Many doctors are prepared to accept your terms if you state them clearly. Should your doctor be unwilling to recognize your role in managing your care, find one who is.

To work more effectively with your doctor, learn as much as you can about the ways doctors practice and about the doctor-patient relationship itself. (See Appendix C for the names of several excellent books that explore the dynamics of the doctor-patient interaction.)

Communication

The doctor-patient relationship, like any other, requires open communication, give and take. To improve communication, and to eliminate misunderstanding, let your doctor know your expectations. Different patients have different needs. If you are having emotional difficulties, let him know about it. Some patients expect their doctors to provide medical treatment only. Others expect a more holistic approach.

Don't expect your doctor to read your mind. He can't anticipate all of your concerns. State your needs as clearly as you can. Speak up and ask questions. Some patients hesitate to bring up certain problems. If, for example, you have back pain or dyspareunia, you may not mention it. You wait instead for the doctor to question you. Similarly, his failure to ask about something doesn't mean it's unimportant. Don't withhold any information. It's probably important, and the benefits are twofold: you become better informed, and you are more motivated to comply with instructions.

Write questions down beforehand, and add new ones that occur during consultation. Take notes on his replies as well. Even if you listen carefully, you probably won't recall everything the doctor says. If you think you don't understand, repeat back to him what you believe your understanding to be. Don't be intimidated by jargon. Ask for information in language you can understand. You may find it useful to keep a notebook to record doctor visits, his recommendations, and so on. It's also helpful and calming to have someone else with you—a friend, partner, or family member—during consultations. Finally, be sure to report positive results. If your doctor helps you, let him know. He will want to know what has been useful to you.

Anger and Frustration

So much uncertainty surrounds endometriosis, and treatments can be so frustrating, that it is not uncommon for a woman to get angry with her doctor. When this happens, she may adopt a defensive or an adversarial role. If anger is intruding in the relationship, step back for a moment. Look at your feelings, try to see what it was that provoked them, and try to find a solution. Sort out the anger that is reasonable from the anger that is simply frustration.

Some doctors are not well informed about endometriosis and its treatment. Their judgment, therefore, negatively affects your treatment. Some doctors arrogantly allow their own values and judgments to shape their decisions in regard to your future. Some hold tightly to chauvinistic beliefs and attempt to impose those beliefs on you. These doctors will provoke in you a *reasonable* anger.

Faced with such a doctor, you may begin to invest all of your energy in a combative relationship. Instead, if you believe your anger is a reasonable response to an action, omission, or attitude on the part of your doctor, and you believe the situation can be changed, discuss it. Don't let it simmer. Some differences cannot be resolved. For example, a long-standing attitude based on chauvinistic beliefs is not likely to change. If the relationship is unproductive, expressing anger will not improve it. At this point it would be wise to end the relationship and put more effort into finding a well-informed physician with whom you are comfortable.

Some women with endometriosis are quick to criticize their own doctors and doctors in general: "Why don't they know more about the disease? Why isn't there a cure? Why isn't there more research?" When you suffer from endometriosis it seems irrelevant that medical science is equally confounded by numerous other diseases that are also mysterious and intractable: cancer, lupus, AIDS, herpes, and colitis. We tend to believe that doctors can solve *any* problem—if only they would try harder.

Sometimes doctors *are* less informed than they should be. But sometimes a woman's frustration with her doctor is a displacement of the anger she feels toward having a chronic disease about which little is known. Ask yourself how much of your anger is properly targeted. Are you responding to the care you are getting? Or are you angry because you have a chronic disease and there is so much uncertainty about it?

You may feel frustrated when your doctor cannot answer all of your questions. You may think he is being evasive. However, remember that much about endometriosis is unknown. Sometimes "I don't know" is an honest response to questions like "Will endometriosis progress?" or "What happens if I don't get treatment?" or "Can I get pregnant?" But there is no excuse for a doctor who cannot, or will not, answer questions concerning side effects of medication or risks of surgery.

Above all, realize that arrogance, ignorance, and chauvinism exist in medicine as well as in any other profession. You may encounter these qualities in both male and female physicians. But once you find the right doctor, remember, he is not your enemy. Blaming him will be counterproductive. Having a chronic disease is already stressful. The doctor-patient relationship should not add to your stress.

Getting a Second Opinion

A doctor may advise minor or major surgery, traditional or laser. Ask why the recommended procedure is necessary, ask about the predicted outcome and alternatives, and *always* ask for a second opinion, especially if a hysterectomy or hysterectomy with bilateral salpingo-oophorectomy is recommended. Even a third opinion is sometimes appropriate. A second opinion is important not only for your peace of mind, but also because it may be a prerequisite for insurance reimbursement. It should come from an individual who, like your first doctor, is well versed in the treatment of endometriosis and who is in no way associated with him. Consult a doctor practicing in a different hospital, even a different town. If you need help, contact the National Second Surgical Opinion Program (see Appendix B).

"Doctor-Shopping"

"Doctor-shopping" is a common practice among individuals with chronic conditions who want a different diagnosis or a better prognosis. Women trail from one doctor to another, always looking for a magic cure. Switch doctors if you are being treated poorly, or if you are unable to develop a productive relationship; but think twice about abandoning your doctor simply because he cannot eradicate the disease.

IMPROVING YOUR GENERAL HEALTH

Making any decision requires energy and clear thinking. If you are run down, you will feel your symptoms more intensely, and you will have less strength to face the challenges ahead. Pain, fatigue, and stress cloud one's judgment, interfering with wise decision making. Whatever decision you make, remember that all forms of treatment, particularly surgery, are easier when you are in the best possible health. In emergencies, decisions cannot be deferred. Otherwise, take time to improve your physical and emotional health before deciding on treatment.

While gathering information, take an inventory of your health habits. Determine where improvements can be made. Your symptoms, and the anxiety they create, may encourage or provoke unhealthful habits. If you smoke, tension may cause you to smoke more. If you are in pain, you may have difficulty sleeping. If you are not sleeping well, you may find it hard to stay alert during the day. You may compensate by drinking more coffee or snacking on sugary foods to boost your energy. To dull pain, help you sleep, or calm your nerves, you may drink more alcohol. Too tired to shop or cook, you may get careless with your diet. Finally, if you are tired and in pain, you have probably given up regular exercise. Your concern about your health has doubtless caused you a great deal of stress. That stress leads to a number of physiological changes, principally muscle tension, which exacerbates your pain.

It's not easy to change habits under the best of circumstances, and it's doubly difficult when you are feeling unwell. Therefore, don't try to change all your habits at once. Begin slowly. Each small change encourages another and bolsters motivation. Change what you can when you can. Each accomplishment will allow you to feel more in control, and not so helpless. Don't think of improving your health habits as just one more chore; think of it as indulging yourself.

The best place to begin is to learn techniques for managing pain and stress. Many women wait until they are stressed beyond their limits before they even think about stress management. To conquer pain, they depend entirely on medical treatment, which is seldom fully effective or long lasting. Learn relaxation techniques at the outset. You can defuse stressful situations and ameliorate pain and also begin to increase control and reduce help-lessness. See Chapter 17 for an explanation of these methods.

Next, after checking with your doctor, begin a program of regular exercise to increase flexibility, stamina, and cardiovascular health and to help dispel anxiety and depression. It's difficult to think about exercise when you are in pain. Many women with endometriosis say they cannot exercise at all. For some, strenuous exercise is impossible. But anyone can do some form of mild exercise. Start very slowly with exercises that are not jarring. Don't overdo. Once you get going, though, you will discover that you can do much more than you imagined. Begin, for example, by walking for at least five minutes each day. Soon, increase your walk to ten minutes, then fifteen. Chapter 17 offers some additional suggestions for gentle exercise well suited to women with endometriosis.

If you smoke, now is a good time to quit or at least cut down. Apart from its obvious risks, smoking depletes necessary vitamins and contributes to hazards and complications during pregnancy or surgery. It may seem particularly difficult to give up cigarettes when you are so nervous and anxious. Consider participating in programs that are designed to help you quit, such as hypnosis or Smoke-Enders (see Appendix B for more information). Or ask your doctor to prescribe nicotine gum which may be a helpful way to reduce your nicotine dependency.

Pay special attention to your diet. Start by making small changes. Begin reading about nutrition. Work to cut down—or eliminate—salt, sugar, caffeine, red meats, and fatty, refined, and processed foods. You may find it useful to consult a dietician or nutritionist who can help you devise a more practical plan for a healthful diet (see Appendix B).

Get plenty of rest. Fatigue exacerbates pain and weakens your decision-making abilities. Individuals with chronic illness often won't allow themselves to slow down. Instead, they push themselves even harder. *Give yourself permission to take time out.* Regular exercise, relaxation techniques and less caffeine should all help you sleep.

Finally, schedule time for pleasurable activities. Leisure and hobbies are often the first casualties when chronic illness strikes. But their importance to your overall well-being cannot be overstated.

DEVELOPING ASSERTIVENESS

As noted earlier, women have been socialized to believe that dissension and hostility on their part are socially unacceptable. They equate assertiveness with hostility and so have problems developing their own assertiveness. Assertiveness simply means standing up for yourself. You will need to be assertive throughout the course of your illness. For example, you must be assertive when you communicate with friends, family, and employers who make unreasonable demands you feel you must meet, despite your limitations.

Assertiveness is achieved by identifying goals and needs, taking steps to meet them, and communicating them clearly to others. Being assertive means determining how you want to be treated; and it means ensuring, to the best of your ability, that others understand and respect your feelings. Apart from its obvious benefits (it gets results), assertiveness helps you to avoid frustration, resentment, and misunderstanding and to combat powerlessness, depression, and negative self-esteem.

If you are under the influence of pain and stress, it may be difficult to muster the energy you need to stand up for yourself and to express your feelings. You may be easily intimidated. Participation in support groups is sometimes helpful. You feel that you are part of a larger group working for the same goals. Often, however, developing assertiveness skills requires more direct guidance. Therapists can often be helpful in increasing one's ability to be assertive (see below). In addition, consider taking an assertiveness-training course at a local college or community adult education center. Perhaps you think you have too many other things to worry about right now; lack of assertiveness is the least of your problems. But before you dismiss the idea, reconsider it. You may realize that it is your number-one problem.

IMPROVING DECISION-MAKING TECHNIQUES

Whatever the nature of your dilemma, you are now prepared to get down to the business of deciding. But first, consider the following. They are important steps in the decision-making process.

Think about the problems you solved in the past. According to Dr. Kames, the way one makes decisions is strongly influenced by one's personality. "Some people, for example, have to have things very structured and detailed and make lists. Others need to work on their gut reactions." Therefore, approach decisions in the manner that works best for you. Use the following suggestions as guidelines that you can modify, based on your own style of decision making.

Look at *all* the options. Sometimes, women dismiss certain options without really considering them. Initial reactions are often negative. But consider all angles. Try making one list of all your options and another list of the pros and cons of each.

Determine your goals and priorities. After looking at your options, reconsider your needs. Try writing down your thoughts, thinking first about your ideal goals; then determine which among them are the most important.

Weigh your options against your priorities. Recognize that decision making implies that you may have to give something up. It's often the most difficult part of the process. "The desire to realize all options blocks the process by making true choice impossible," writes Dr. Theodore Isaac Rubin in his book, *Overcoming Indecisiveness.*[2] Accepting the confines of choice, on the other hand, allows you to look fully at your options. Try on each option, imagine the outcome, and see if it fits your needs and lifestyles. Then let your thoughts percolate.

Decide. Commit yourself to your decision, and take the necessary steps to bring about the best possible outcome. Sometimes you have little problem reaching a decision, but you are then unable to fully act on it because you are still considering other possibilities. Once you make a reasoned decision, put other options out of mind and give full energy to the choice you have made.

If you can't come to a decision, seek help. Indecisiveness is often a sign that you cannot accept the fact that you may have to give something up or that you are unable to fully determine priorities. You may need help in improving your decision-making skills or in looking at your options objectively. Skilled therapists can help you to see things more clearly and to broaden your perspective.

RESTORING EMOTIONAL EQUILIBRIUM: GETTING HELP

Endometriosis may persist, or it may recur following treatment. If so, don't wait to see if the next round of treatment is going to be more successful. Instead, take steps to minimize the disruption and disorder your illness is causing you. This involves four general areas:

- managing pain and stress (Chapter 17)
- coping with infertility (Chapters 13 and 14)
- facing sexual difficulties (Chapter 14)
- dealing with your emotions—anger, guilt, anxiety, depression, and feelings of isolation, helplessness, and hopelessness (Chapter 14 and below)

Strategies discussed in the chapters indicated are not always sufficient. The most beneficial, yet perhaps the most difficult, step you can take is acknowledging that, despite your best efforts, there may be limitations to your ability to cope on your own. The most important coping mechanism is knowing when and where to look for help.

Some doctors will provide enough guidance. Sometimes a mate, friend, or family member offers enough support to help you prevent—or manage—serious emotional repercussions. The experience and knowledge of others who have been through it can be invaluable. Most women need such support, but sometimes it's not enough. A professional therapist, particularly one specializing in illness-related issues, can often provide you with an objective viewpoint, help you gain perspective and clarity, and guide you in developing and utilizing your own strategies for coping.

Support Groups

"I felt like an oddball, and I felt very alone. But in a support group you see other people who are functioning and some who aren't. Looking at others in the group, I saw them not as sick, but as whole people, coping with their conditions. And I respected them and related to them, which helped me rediscover my self-respect. Nothing means as much as talking to someone who's been there."

"When I was in pain, when I was confused, when I didn't know what choices to make, I turned to the Endometriosis Association. No one else but those who knew what I was going through could help—not a friend, not doctors, not a lover."

When you are in emotional pain, it's natural to turn exclusively to the person closest to you for support. However, there are several things wrong with this approach.

First, your mate, lover, friend, or parent has problems of their own, unrelated to your illness. They have other responsibilities and demands on their time and energy. They can't always be available to answer your needs. Moreover, they are unfamiliar with the challenges you are facing, so they don't know how to provide the help, support, and perspective you need. Finally, coping with your illness may be a problem for them, so they can't be objective about it. Keep in mind that they are often profoundly affected by the consequences of endometriosis, just as you are, but they don't react in the same way, or at the same time, as you do. No matter how loving, how dedicated, there are natural limits to the support they can provide.

Where do you turn, then, when those around you are unavailable, unsupportive, or at the end of their rope?

Many women find solace in the company of others who are facing the same problems and challenges. Without such contact, these women who suffer from chronic illness feel isolated, alone, and incapable of coping. These feelings are very damaging to one's self-esteem.

Support groups such as the Endometriosis Association, Resolve, and Chronic Pain Outreach put you in contact with others who both reflect and validate your feelings. They provide empathy and sympathy. There is real therapeutic value in discovering that your symptoms and reactions are normal, that you are not overreacting to—or imagining—the pain you are feeling. Knowing that others feel as you do helps break the isolation, the stigma, that so often occur as a result of chronic illness.

In addition, support groups provide an atmosphere of acceptance. You can vent your feelings without the risk of alienating those close to you. You can express your thoughts there when others have tired of listening to you. There is a give and take of information, experience, and tips on coping. You may also want to encourage your mate or other family members and friends to attend support group meetings. They may wish to develop their own groups to help them deal with difficulties arising from your illness. If there are no support groups in your area, contact those listed in Appendix B for information about starting your own.

Whether or not a support group helps depends largely on the leadership and nature of the group. Groups can be counterproductive, especially if they emphasize the negative experiences of the illness and treatment. If the group becomes just a gripe session, it can increase fear, anger, mistrust of doctors, and feelings of helplessness, particularly in women who are underinformed or just beginning to deal with their disease. Negative feelings may be justified, but there is little purpose in instigating and airing them without also sharing effective coping mechanisms. A support group must be more than just a place to express anger and frustration. To get the most out of it, communicate your needs to the leader. Perhaps there are ways the meetings can be more constructive. Look for ways to temper negative experiences by providing guidance for positive action. For example, sessions can be divided into two periods—for sharing stories and feelings and for raising suggestions and solutions.

In the crisis stage, when you have discovered you have a chronic disease, you information. You need need assurance that others too are struggling and coping successfully. Then, a support group is extremely beneficial. Past the crisis stage, when you are coping with the effects of the disease, it is sometimes unproductive to remain in the group. To do so may simply be increasing your identification with the disease, a constant reminder of the problems you have worked so hard to put behind you. Many women now want to help others who are just beginning to struggle. This is satisfying, but it also adds to identification with the disease. Women who want to help can contribute in other ways than by participating in support groups. For example, most self-help groups and associations continually need practical help with fundraising and public relations. Volunteering for such tasks can satisfy your need to stay involved, without keeping you focused on the struggles you have already resolved.

Psychotherapy

While few people feel ashamed to ask for help with physical ailments, many feel it is a sign of weakness to ask for help with emotional troubles. They believe they should solve their own problems. Clearly it is *not* a sign of weakness, nor is it an abdication of personal control. Asking for help is actually a sign of maturity and responsibility.

Perhaps you were told at some point that your symptoms were all in your head. If you seek a therapist, does that validate that belief? Seeking help does not imply that your problems are merely psychological. It simply acknowledges that your illness has brought on emotional problems you can't cope with. Furthermore, your emotions affect your physical illness, compounding its intensity and sometimes standing in the way of recovery. A competent therapist can help you

work through fears and feelings when you learn you have a chronic illness
face facts and retreat from denial and wish-fulfillment fantasies
cope with guilt and self-pity
learn ways to control anger, anxiety, and depression
develop strategies for managing pain and stress
become aware of the unconscious gains and rewards of the sick role
increase your control and decrease helplessness and isolation
restore battered relationships and show others how to help you
improve self-esteem and self-image
reduce the stress of the infertility workup and make decisions relative to infertility
diminish or eliminate sexual difficulties
develop assertiveness
determine priorities
improve decision-making skills
develop goals
cope with loss and grief

Selecting a therapist.   Psychotherapy is practiced by individuals from a variety of disciplines: clinical psychologists, psychiatrists, psychoanalysts, social workers, and psychiatric nurses. These therapists may work with individuals, groups, couples, and families. Psychoanalysts work within a strict theoretical framework; the others may base work on any one of a number of theoretical orientations. Each approach has much to offer. Individuals suffering from chronic illness, however, are most likely to be helped by therapists with training and experience in issues related to physical illness and by those who use behavioral and cognitive techniques. Behavioral techniques substitute adaptive for maladaptive behaviors. Cognitive techniques strive to correct faulty thinking and distorted perception.

When dealing with emotional issues, first determine your priorities. You need to tackle problems one at a time, so start with the most troublesome. According to Dr. Herz, "The patient has to evaluate what creates the greatest problem for her. If it is dyspareunia, a sex therapist may be the most urgent need, while if infertility is the most pressing concern, infertility counseling should be sought first. If it is the cumulative effect of the stresses and strains of the disease upon a couple, a marriage and family therapist may be helpful." The patient, she adds, has to evaluate what is the core and focus of her problems and then pursue treatment accordingly.

When dealing with issues related to endometriosis and infertility, find a therapist experienced in helping individuals with chronic illness or infertility. Ask about the therapist's experience in these specific areas, and try to learn more about his or her approach and techniques. Ask the psychology department of a university medical school for a referral to a therapist trained in the psychology of illness. (For more information on standards and on locating practitioners, see Appendix B.) To find a therapist trained to help with issues of infertility in particular, contact Resolve, the American Fertility Society, or your nearest university medical school's department of reproductive endocrinology. To locate a sex therapist, call a university medical school or hospital or ask your physician or therapist. For more information on finding or evaluating a sex therapist, contact the American Association of Sex Educators, Counselors and Therapists; the Sex Information Council of the United States; or the Society for the Scientific Study of Sex (see also Appendix B).

Criteria for the selection of a therapist are much the same as those for selecting a doctor. Once you have a referral, call for more information. Ask where the therapist was trained and how long the training lasted. Ask about licensing, credentials, and certification. Find out if the therapist is a member of a professional association such as the American Psychological Association. Ask if the therapist has worked with others with problems similar to yours. Ask about fees, schedules, and insurance coverage. Set up an appointment for an initial consultation. During this session, you can ask some preliminary questions: What can be achieved? How long will it take? Determine the quality of rapport. Does the therapist listen carefully? Does he seem sincerely interested? Do you feel comfortable?

Results don't come overnight. It may take more than one or two sessions to determine if the therapist you choose is right for you. Allow enough time either to feel secure in your decision or to determine whether you need to select another therapist. For more information about psychotherapy and advice on selecting a therapist, see Appendix B. A useful book is *The Psychotherapy Maze: A Consumer's Guide to the Ins and Outs of Therapy*. This and other publications are listed in Appendix C.

Financing mental health care.   Numerous studies have shown that mental health care significantly cuts the cost of physical health care for individuals with chronic conditions.

Individuals who learn to cope with the emotional consequences of physical illness experience fewer additional minor illnesses, recover from them more quickly, rely less on medication, and use the health care system less frequently. As a result, many health insurance companies cover a significant portion of the expense of therapy, particularly when it is recommended by a physician. Many companies will pay half of a therapist's fees, others as much as 80 percent. Often there is a limit to the number of sessions covered per year. During the initial consultation, ask about fees and coverage and check with your own insurance carrier as well.

If you have no medical insurance or mental health coverage or if you simply cannot afford the full cost of a therapist, contact your local community health center. There fees are based on a sliding scale, determined by your income and ability to pay.

INFERTILITY ISSUES: PREGNANCY OR PARENTHOOD

Once you have done everything possible to have children, realized that you may never be able to, and grieved over that loss, it's time to reevaluate your goals and your approach. Is pregnancy or parenthood your goal? Reexamine your reasons for wanting children. What are the limits of your ability to cope with infertility treatment? If you are married, you may need to look at the nature of your relationship with your husband. If you conclude, for whatever reason, that pregnancy is as important to you as parenthood, that you would not be satisfied or fulfilled raising a child you did not give birth to, you may continue on your present course or explore a life without children. If you decide to continue treatment, at some point you must decide how much is too much: how much are you willing to struggle to attain pregnancy and for how long? If you by now feel overwhelmed by the demands of treatment, can no longer take the heartache and the disruption, you may choose to stop for a while, or you may decide to stop permanently. There are no rules regarding these choices. You must make your own decisions in your own time and for your own reasons. "The quality of time you spend in infertility treatment is more important than the quantity of time," Dr. Shrednick says. "You must be able to honestly evaluate if you are benefiting from these energies or suffering from them." Some couples continue with infertility treatment to the detriment of all other aspects of life; they have invested so much time and energy that to stop feels like total defeat. According to Dr. Shrednick, however, "Taking this step may actually signal that you have been successful and comfortable with your own limitations and priorities. You have recognized the need to go on with other aspects of your life and you have rewarded yourself with taking action to meet that end. This does not mean to say that you are not sad, angry, or disappointed, but you are not a failure if you have not achieved a pregnancy after one, five, or twenty years of trying."[3]

All of these feelings are very complex, very painful. Most couples need a lot of information and support in appraising their situation and arriving at a conclusion. Self-help groups, support groups, and infertility counseling are immensely helpful as couples pass through this stage.

If, on the other hand, your goal is parenthood, you can pursue two other avenues: adoption and surrogate motherhood.

Adoption.   When infertility treatment is unsuccessful, many couples will consider adoption—a route to parenthood that requires extensive information-gathering, financial security, considerable deliberation and soul-searching—as well as a huge reservoir of determination.

In earlier times couples had relatively few choices concerning adoption. Adoptions were handled by social workers through social service agencies. Young, unwed pregnant women traditionally bore their children and gave them up for adoption. Adoptable babies were plentiful. Anonymity was guaranteed to all parties—adoptive parents, children, and birthparents—through closed records, a system devised to protect the rights and welfare of the children and their biological and adoptive parents. It seemed the perfect solution to a variety of society's problems.

Today, however, birth control is widely available, and there is a trend for young, unwed mothers to raise their own babies. The result is a shortage of adoptable babies—or, more accurately, a shortage of healthy, Caucasian infants. At the same time, an increasingly outspoken adoption report movement has been forged by many birthmothers and adopted children who are fighting for the right to open the records.

These changes have resulted in new adoption laws, new choices, and some complex issues. Today, faced with long waiting lists, eager couples need to consider whether or not they would be comfortable raising a child of a different race, religion, or nationality. Are they equipped emotionally and financially to raise a disabled child, for example, who requires a lifetime of special care? Would an older child satisfy their nurturing needs? Is it imperative that they adopt an infant? In some states records are not sealed; communication is allowed among all parties involved. Should couples explore this "open adoption"? If, on the other hand, they choose the traditional closed record adoption, how will they feel if their adopted child begins to search for his or her birthparents, or vice versa?

Adoption is not a solution to infertility. The couple is still infertile and must still resolve certain issues. For example, although they become parents, they must still grieve for—and come to terms with—their inability to procreate. They need continuing support in their efforts to cope with infertility.

The difficult decision to adopt or not, often made in the midst of the crisis of infertility, is just the first step. Beyond it are issues, choices, and challenges too numerous and too complex to address here. Decisions concerning adoption require that you learn all of your options. Explore both their practical and their emotional consequences. Talk with adoptive parents or other prospective adoptive parents and with adopted children and birthparents. A counselor trained in issues of infertility and adoption can help you examine your options, needs, and feelings. (Appendixes B and C provide numerous resources.)

Surrogate motherhood.   If you cannot conceive or sustain a pregnancy, one option is surrogate motherhood. A surrogate can be hired to receive your husband's sperm, carry the pregnancy to term, and relinquish the child to you and your husband at birth. Surrogates have been bearing children for infertile couples in increasing numbers since the 1970s, yet the practice is beset by controversy. Myriad problems include ill-defined standards, unresolved legal issues, and complex ethical considerations. (For more information about surrogate motherhood, contact Resolve, and see also Appendixes B and C.)

DEFINITIVE SURGERY

If you have put into practice all of these strategies, yet you continue to live with an unacceptable level of pain and disruption, you may be willing to consider a more radical approach—hysterectomy or definitive surgery. "There is a group of women caught between the strong desire for fertility and the misery of living every day with the pain and the disability," says Dr. Metzger. "They are torn between wanting to conceive, or simply not wanting to relinquish their organs, and wanting a cure so that they can get on with their lives." These women, she says, "usually don't have the surgery done until they have worked it out in their minds that this is the right thing to do. They have looked at all of their desires, they have determined their priorities, and have reached the point where they feel that they must go on with their lives."

But even deciding to think about hysterectomy is difficult for many women. According to Mary Lou Ballweg, it is helpful to set limits on how much pain or disruption you will suffer before you take steps toward definitive surgery, then resolve not to go beyond those limits. "Women must ask themselves at what point they will feel that the quality of their lives has deteriorated to the degree that they can't or won't take it any more." Limits vary. Your limit may be one week of pain each month. Or you may decide that even one twenty-four-hour period of pain per month is unacceptable. But wherever one draws the line, she explains, "Setting limits gives women the feeling that there is a light at the end of the tunnel." If you can't decide, are unable to set such a limit, or find yourself continually stretching your limit, seek professional guidance. It will help you clarify or reorder your priorities.

Women's feelings following hysterectomy or definitive surgery vary. Some are filled with regret. They are unable to shake off the sense that they made a terrible mistake. Others are immeasurably relieved. The consistent characteristic of the latter is that *they* were the ones who made the decision, and they had done so only after gathering enough information to ease their fears and concerns. They adjusted more easily to hysterectomy because they learned about all of the medical and emotional repercussions ahead of time. There were fewer surprises so they had fewer occasions to regret their decisions.

If you are ready to think about hysterectomy, make sure you don't consent to surgery until you have all the medical facts, have talked with other women who have taken similar steps, and have thoroughly explored your feelings about the operation. Take time to learn about the procedure, adjust to the idea, and get yourself into the best possible physical and emotional shape. Find out about the symptoms of surgical menopause and their treatments and alternative remedies. Consider the medical risks and complications as well as your fears about surgery itself. They may be based on the myth that you will look old, be depressed, and no longer enjoy a satisfying sex life. Explore your feelings concerning loss. How does the loss of your womb and your childbearing ability affect your self-esteem, sexuality, and body image? How do you feel about the reaction of your partner and your family and friends?

To help you consider all of these issues, take advantage of as many resources as possible. Contact organizations and associations concerned with women's health. They can provide you with much useful information (see Appendix B). Read as much as possible. Appendix C lists numerous books that will guide you in exploring your feelings. They provide useful information to help you make decisions and cope with the physical and emotional consequences of surgery. Contact Resolve and the Endometriosis Association to learn about hysterectomy and support groups. Consider preoperative counseling as well.

17

Managing Pain and Stress

Acute pain is time limited. It serves a purpose: to warn of injury, to caution against further damage, and to alert us to the need for medical intervention. It is typically responsive to painkilling medications and treatments that address its underlying causes. While acute pain may arouse anxiety, its effects are felt for only a relatively short period of time. Daily activities, lifestyle, and immediate goals are only temporarily disrupted. You know that an end is in sight. "People are sympathetic to acute pain," says Dr. Elyse Singer, neurologist at the National Institutes of Health Pain Research Facility in Bethesda, Maryland. "You get tender loving care. It's socially acceptable."[1]

Chronic pain, on the other hand, is pain that has outlasted its usefulness. In the case of endometriosis, it may initially alert you to the presence of the disease. But if treatments are ineffective, or only temporarily effective, continuing pain serves no useful purpose. It becomes a relentless encroachment on all facets of life, a detriment to your well being. As a result, it is likely to produce not just transient anxiety but prolonged stress, depression, and despair. Those around you may not be entirely understanding of and sympathetic to pain that comes and goes lasting for only a few days a month. You may try to dismiss the pain, pretending it's not there, until it gets so bad you can no longer ignore it. Then, perhaps, you turn to pain medication. But drugs bring little relief. Nevertheless, you may still be hesitant or unwilling to investigate a pain management program because you are still looking for a cure.

"It is only when women have changed their whole lives because of pain," explains Dr. Deborah Metzger, "that they may finally reach the point where they want something done about it, regardless of the costs or the consequences." For many women with endometriosis, this point arrives after repeated hormonal therapies, with their side effects and risks, or following surgery upon surgery, with their risks, costs, complications, and painful and unproductive recovery periods. When efforts to cope with increasing and more persistent

211

pain have failed, taking all of a woman's physical and psychic energies, blotting out much of her life's pleasures and satisfactions, she may opt for definitive surgery *before* she explores other avenues of pain management.

Investigate pain management techniques first. Pain cannot always be completely eliminated. You can, however, through comprehensive pain management, learn to decrease its domination over your life.

Chronic pain is more than the perception of painful stimuli. It is enlarged by your reaction to it. It reverberates—affecting your mood, relationships, sex life, career, and family responsibilities. It diminishes the quantity and quality of your leisure pleasures, reduces your physical activity, and interferes with sleep. All these effects can lead to anxiety, depression, despair, and hopelessness. Hurting is seldom confined to a particular organ or body part. Pain management, therefore, must not be limited to specific points of pain but must address pain's total effect on your life.

"We all have a certain model of pain and illness that we grow up with—an acute care model," explains Dr. Linda Kames. "Everyone shares it, including doctors. What happens is that when you get sick or have an injury and go to a doctor, he tells you what is wrong and gives you medication. You go to bed, get as much tender loving care as you can, and in a little while you are better. When you have an illness that doesn't respond to this model— either you don't get an accurate diagnosis or the illness doesn't go away after a certain amount of time—doctors continue to treat patients with the acute care model over and over again, and patients respond in the same ways over and over again. It is completely ineffective. All of the treatments that are effective and good for an acute illness, like the flu or breaking your leg, are exactly wrong. They are either ineffective or actually harmful for chronic illness, and one of those is drugs."

The medications used to treat acute pain become less and less effective against chronic pain in the long run: analgesics cause organ damage; with prolonged daily use, narcotic or tranquilizing medications actually make pain worse. They cloud the higher brain centers that help you deal with both emotional and physical pain. Patients can end up with a drug dependency problem as well. "Almost any kind of drug that you use for pain is good for a two or three-week period. With longer use it starts to cause more trouble than it is worth," says Dr. Kames.

By replacing an acute pain approach with a comprehensive approach—geared specifically to problems associated with chronic pain—you begin to control pain and its effects.

COMPREHENSIVE PAIN MANAGEMENT: THE PAIN CLINIC

A comprehensive approach to the management of chronic pain is multidisciplinary. It requires the skills of a variety of practitioners who work together to treat pain as both a physical and a psychosocial problem. To address each aspect of the pain experience, they provide somatic treatment for specific physical symptoms and behavioral counseling. Patients learn to alter their perception of pain and substitute adaptive for maladaptive behaviors. The team may include anesthesiologists, physiatrists, neurologists, psychiatrists, psychologists, acupuncturists, biofeedback technicians, nurses, physical and occupational therapists, and other specialists.

The ideal resource for such an approach is a pain center. Here you find all, or many, of these practitioners. A program can be tailored to your specific needs. Anesthesiologists developed the first multidisciplinary pain centers. Now there are hundreds of pain clinics across the United States, operating on either an outpatient or an inpatient basis. Residential programs usually last for six weeks. Whether inpatient or outpatient, the first step is to evaluate your physical condition, your psychological state, and your behavioral approach to pain. First, the source of pain is investigated. Then, a treatment is developed. It may include any combination of the following:

acupuncture
biofeedback
hypnosis
electrical stimulation
physical and occupational therapy
psychological counseling
behavior modification
stress management training

These techniques are described below.

To completely eradicate pain is often an unrealistic goal. The purpose of the pain clinic's comprehensive approach is to reduce pain as much as possible. Women can then function more effectively with the pain that remains. Its goals are

- to administer medication on schedule (time-contingent rather than pain-contingent); and to wean patients off narcotics and tranquilizers
- to eliminate physical symptoms through acupuncture, electric nerve stimulation, physical therapy, etc.
- to make you aware of how thoughts, attitudes, and behaviors affect pain
- to alter your perception of pain and thus lessen its impact
- to teach behavioral methods to promote relaxation
- to break the cycle of pain, stress, depression, and despair that arises from the pain lifestyle
- to teach you to recognize secondary gains from the pain lifestyle; and to replace maladaptive pain behaviors with adaptive behaviors
- to teach you to alter cognitions (change your thinking) to reduce negative thoughts and feelings
- to reactivate patients gradually through physical and occupational therapy, exercise, and recreation

- to improve relationships affected by pain and pain behaviors
- to provide marital, family, and sex therapy
- to improve decision making and goal setting

The UCLA Pelvic Pain Program

The approach of the six-week, outpatient Pelvic Pain Program at the UCLA Pain Management Center, says Dr. Kames, is "to look at endometriosis not as a disease that is going to have an immediate cure, but as a chronic illness that needs to be managed by learning how to deal with and prevent pain. The goal of the program is to give the patient responsibility for and control of her health care and restore her to normal functioning."

First, a complete medical, gynecological, and pain history is taken. Patients are evaluated by a gynecologist, usually by a neurologist or an anesthesiologist, and a psychologist. In many cases, women who enter the program have already been diagnosed. If not, a laparoscopy is performed to rule out other possibilities and confirm the presence and extent of endometriosis. "We also want to find out if there is other musculoskeletal or soft tissue involvement as well as the disease," says Dr. Kames. "A lot of times women with endometriosis have trigger points, which greatly contribute to the amount of pain they are experiencing." Trigger points are irritable knots within muscles. They arise as a result of constriction of blood flow to muscle areas that are tensed against pain.

Psychological testing to determine the need for psychological treatment is in addition to treatment of symptoms. A woman's personality and the way she copes with illness and pain make a big difference in how she will likely respond to treatment. Psychological testing looks for symptoms of stress. It seeks to determine in what ways, if any, individuals are benefiting from their pain. They may be receiving secondary gains they are not aware of.

Following evaluation, patients get comprehensive medical treatment, behavior modification, relaxation training, and instruction in the development of coping skills. The mainstay of the physical treatment is acupuncture. Patients may also get TENS (transcutaneous electrical nerve stimulation), physical therapy, and injections of local anesthetics to ease the pain associated with trigger points. But all facets of treatment are applied simultaneously, not sequentially, with communication among various team practitioners.

It's sometimes necessary to give antidepressants. "People often become very depressed from having this disease and from having pain for a long time," notes Dr. Kames. "When you become extremely depressed, you really don't perceive things accurately and you will not be able to tell whether or not you are improving. If it looks as if depression has reached the point at which it is going to interfere with the treatment process, we may use an antidepressant. Soon, patients have learned other techniques and skills, so they don't feel as depressed anymore and no longer require these medications." Also, some of the chemicals involved in pain are involved in depression; thus, antidepressants have some analgesic effect, which increases the effectiveness of the treatments.

A vital component of the program is behavior therapy. Patients learn self-control procedures and generalized coping skills. Behavior therapy restores to patients a sense of control. It teaches them how to plan for pain and how to deal with stressors. Participants learn progressive relaxation, which reduces muscle tension that contributes to pain. They also learn self-hypnosis and biofeedback. The goal is to teach individuals to alter their responses to pain. An important element is *response substitution*—replacing a negative response with a positive one. "We talk through the panic and the thoughts that pain gives rise to," says Dr. Kames, "and we talk through different situations that can occur." Rather than panicking when pain strikes, patients are taught to do something else, such as controlled breathing exercises or relaxation techniques.

The UCLA team teaches problem solving and decision making and works to improve women's self-esteem and self-image. "The goal is to help them change their attitude toward illness and to see themselves as functioning, creative people, even though they have a chronic illness," explains Dr. Kames. "People come in with the idea that there is something wrong with them that has to be fixed. If you can make them see that they have a chronic illness that can't be cured but can be managed, then they no longer have to see themselves as maimed."

Patients' lives have often been put "on hold" by endometriosis. The program reactivates them gradually. They get back to work, school, or exercise at a comfortable pace.

How others respond to your pain and to your behavior affects your level and perception of pain. It can also contribute to or impede your adaptation. Good pain management programs involve spouses and family members and deal with relationship issues.

"At the end of the six-week program, the pain is usually alleviated and the patient has learned to cope effectively and is able to return to a normal level of physical and psychosocial activity," says Dr. Kames. Patients are given audiocassette tapes to help them continue to practice their newly developed skills. "We then see the patients in follow-up at one month, three months, six months, and a year. They get a booster treatment of acupuncture at six months. By this time, they have learned to handle things by themselves. They know how to monitor pain so that it never has to get as bad as it was to begin with. They are able to take care of pain problems at an earlier point."

Finding a Pain Clinic

A good pain clinic offers a variety of treatment modalities. Some, particularly inpatient clinics, are primarily behavioral. They offer less direct treatment of physical symptoms. It's important to find a program that addresses both the physical and the emotional aspects of pain. To find a clinic in your area, ask your doctor, county medical association, hospital, or medical school, or contact the American Association of Anesthesiologists (see Appendix B).

DEVISING YOUR OWN COMPREHENSIVE APPROACH

Many women cannot attend pain clinics. The programs are usually very costly and prohibitive without medical insurance. Some have long waiting lists. If you live in a rural area there may be none nearby.

For those of you unable to participate in a pain management program, the pain management methods in the next section will be useful. Taught and practiced by individual therapists and practitioners, they are widely considered most effective when tailored to individual needs. Each is only one component of a total pain management strategy, and will be more effective when combined with counseling. A behavioral psychologist or a psychologist experienced in gynecological problems and skilled in health psychology or behavioral medicine is preferable. For further information, see Appendixes B, C, and E.

The techniques described below are divided into four categories: pain management techniques, general body work, relaxation techniques, and behavior therapy. The techniques in *all* categories help alleviate pain, but only those used directly and exclusively for pain relief are grouped under pain management techniques.

Pain Management Techniques

Acupuncture.   The ancient Chinese art of acupuncture—the insertion of thin needles at various points in the skin—brings significant relief to many women suffering from dysmenorrhea, endometriosis, and postoperative pain, as well as related disorders and discomforts.

In the ancient Chinese system of medicine, Ch'i (or Qi)—the vital life force—is believed to course through the body in more than two dozen meridians or conduits, passing over 800 points associated with specific organs or body functions. Ch'i regulates the nerves, organs, and circulation. Health, according to the Chinese philosophy, results from a balance and a free flow of Ch'i through the meridians, while illness is a manifestation of an imbalance, a stagnation, or an obstruction of Ch'i in a meridian. An imbalance at one point or in one organ is believed to affect other points and the functioning of their corresponding organs. The placement of acupuncture needles on the various points linked by the meridians (acupoints) is believed to restore the balance and flow of Ch'i and thereby eliminate associated symptoms and prevent disease.

After taking a detailed case history, the acupuncturist locates the acupoints corresponding to your symptoms and inserts and manipulates the needles. You will feel a pinprick and a tingling sensation. Most patients describe the treatment as painless. The depth of the needle penetration, the number of acupoints stimulated, and the duration of treatment will depend upon your particular symptoms.

In one study patients undergoing hysterectomy or hysterectomy with bilateral salpingo-oophorectomy were treated with acupuncture in the recovery room before awakening from anesthesia and once a day for two days following surgery. They had a shorter hospital stay, less postoperative gastrointestinal distress, and a decreased need for pain medication than those not treated.

Acupuncture is not readily available in all parts of the country. In some states, acupuncturists are licensed after passing state examinations; in others, the practice can only be performed by a physician, dentist, chiropractor, or individual working under the guidance of a physician. Check with your doctor or state medical association about local laws regulating acupuncture. Contact your insurance representative to see if acupuncture is covered under your policy. To locate an acupuncturist, ask your doctor, your local or state medical association, or a nearby medical school or hospital for a referral to an individual practitioner or to a pain management program using this technique.

Acupressure.   Acupressure, an ancient Chinese first aid technique, is based on the same theoretical principles as acupuncture, but acupoints are stimulated by the application of pressure rather than needles. Varieties of acupressure include Do-In, Jin Shin Do, Tsubo Therapy, and G-Jo, all of which strive to balance the vital life force through different pressure techniques. Once the technique has been demonstrated, it can be performed for you by a friend or relative. To locate a practitioner, contact a local holistic health center or consult the *Directory of Holistic Medicine and Alternative Health Care Service in the United States* (see Appendix C).

Electrotherapy.   Transcutaneous electrical nerve stimulation (TENS) is a pain control technique by which a small, battery-powered machine conducts an alternating electric current through electrode pads placed upon painful areas or upon nerve networks corresponding to those areas. Although TENS doesn't work for everyone, when it does work, pain relief is often swift. One of its advantages is that individuals may purchase the portable units and use them whenever pain strikes.

Subcutaneous nerve stimulation (SCNS), sometimes called electroacupuncture, is similar to TENS, except that the electrical current is introduced under the skin through a pair of needles. In a study of women with endometriosis undergoing treatment with SCNS, a single session produced temporary alleviation of menstrual cramps, and consecutive daily treatments produced long-term suppression of gynecological pain. The patients experiencing pain, despite conservative medical and surgical intervention, were treated with needles attached to an electrical output one hour daily for one and a half months. All subjects reported 30 to 50 percent pain relief at the end of the first week and 60 to 80 percent relief by the end of twenty treatments. Patients followed for three to five years reported themselves to be pain free and without need of further medical or surgical treatment.[2]

Heat.   Most women with menstrual pain have discovered that heat brings a measure of relief. A hot bath, shower, sauna, or whirlpool is often helpful. For more sustained relief, you can repeatedly apply hot compresses—towels soaked in hot water or steam-heated—to the abdominal area or other areas where muscle tension occurs. An electrical heating pad is very effective. Heat not only works directly on the nerves that transmit pain but relaxes the muscles and is mentally soothing as well.

Trigger point myotherapy.   As observed earlier, trigger points are particularly sensitive areas caused by muscle tension. Myotherapy is a muscle pressure technique used to relieve the spasm and pain in trigger points and to prevent the development of additional points. Myotherapy can help relieve headaches, back pain, menstrual cramps, and leg and foot cramps resulting from endometriosis as well as from hormone treatment. To locate a trained practitioner, ask your doctor, call the department of anesthesiology at a local hospital or medical school, or contact a pain treatment center for suggestions or a referral (see Appendix E).

Body Work to Relieve Pain and Stress

Massage.   Massage, whether by a professional or a friend, should become a regular habit for any woman with endometriosis. Both a relaxer and a stimulant, it is exceptionally effective in relieving the muscle tension that accumulates from daily stress and from bracing against anticipated pain. There are a wide variety of techniques. To learn more about them, and for information on finding and evaluating a massage therapist, see Appendixes B and C.

Shiatsu.   Similar to both acupressure and massage, shiatsu is a Japanese finger-pressure technique used in the treatment of pain. Shiatsu, like acupuncture and acupressure, stimulates Ch'i (Ki in Japanese), so regular practice is believed to prevent disease as well. On your first visit to a shiatsu therapist, a case history will be taken. The therapist, with thumbs, fingers, palm or heel of the hand, elbows, or feet, will manipulate various points of your body corresponding with meridians and acupoints. The therapist may also prescribe exercises and may train another individual—a friend or family member—to use shiatsu techniques with you. To learn more about shiatsu and to locate a practitioner, contact the Shiatsu Therapy Center (see Appendix B).

Foot reflexology (zone therapy).   Also similar to acupressure is foot reflexology, or zone therapy. Derived from Oriental medicine, it is based on the premise that discomfort and disease arise from obstructions of the body's vital energy. Points in the foot are said to correspond to various zones and organs of the body. Massage and manipulation of the various points results in a stimulation of the energy in the affected zones and a corresponding relief of pain. More likely, pressure on various areas of the soles of the feet stimulate nerve endings connected to various parts of the body. To learn more, see Appendix B. Consult as well the *Directory of Holistic Medicine and Alternative Health Care Service in the United States* (Appendix C).

Alexander Technique.   In the late nineteenth century an actor named F. Matthias Alexander began to lose his voice during performances. He discovered that his posture was to blame: he had a habit of moving his head backward and downward, which adversely affected his voice. Alexander researched the ways faulty posture profoundly affects an individual's well being and devised a system of postural reconditioning to correct inappropriate movements and postures.

Since faulty posture contributes to muscle tension and pain, the technique is very helpful for women with endometriosis. It helps avoid problems that arise from bracing against pain.

It also relieves headache, low back pain, and gastrointestinal difficulties that result from postural abuses.

The Alexander Technique is geared to suit the individual's own postural problems. It cannot be self-taught. An instructor will teach you beneficial ways to stand, sit, walk, and lift. To learn more, and to locate a qualified practitioner, contact the American Center for the Alexander Technique (see Appendix B).

Feldenkrais method. Another system designed to correct postural abuses that contribute to pain is the Feldenkrais method, designed by Dr. Moshe Feldenkrais, an engineer and physicist. There are two components to the Feldenkrais method, "awareness through movement"—movement and postural training courses taught to large groups, and "functional integration"—individual hands-on demonstration by a Feldenkrais trainer. To learn more about the Feldenkrais method, and to locate courses and practitioners, refer to Appendixes B and C.

Exercise. Exercise provides obvious benefits such as weight reduction or control and improved cardiovascular health. It is also a stress fighter, a pain reliever, and a demonstrated depression reducer. Women with pain resulting from endometriosis often think they cannot exercise. Try to find exercises that are going to be the least difficult and start slowly. Most women find they can swim or walk. If it hurts too much to swim or walk for twenty minutes, start with five minutes and build up. Swimming is an excellent nonjarring aerobic exercise for women with endometriosis. However, it offers no protection against osteoporosis so should not be used as a sole form of exercise. Combine it whenever possible with other weight-bearing forms of exercise such as walking. Avoid jarring exercises, like jogging, or very rigorous aerobics, particularly if you have significant adhesions. If you are having difficulty exercising, it may help to have your doctor or a physical therapist help you design an exercise program tailored to your individual needs and abilities.

Yoga. An ancient Indian philosophical system, yoga is many things to many people: a form of exercise, a superior relaxation technique, and a healing art. Yoga means to yoke, or unite. It is a multifaceted discipline practiced to achieve unity and harmony of body, mind, and spirit. There are many different varieties of yoga, but the most familiar form in the West is Hatha Yoga, a branch that employs physical postures (asanas) and breathing exercises to replace tension with tranquility and to increase mental and physical stamina, flexibility, agility, and relaxation.

Yoga can be learned from illustrated manuals, but instruction from an experienced trainer is better. A trainer can monitor your mastery of breathing and meditative techniques and guide you in the proper alignment of your body during postures. A trainer also can help you devise a program that best suits your needs.

A routine part of most Hatha Yoga programs is the inverted posture such as the head or shoulder stand. It may be wise not to perform inverted positions during menstruation, considering the theory of retrograde menstruation as a possible cause of endometriosis. Generally, though, many yoga exercises are effective in relieving menstrual cramps.

T'ai Chi Ch'uan.   Another gentle form of exercise, often combined with relaxation training, is T'ai Chi Ch'uan, a Chinese system of movement that blends elements of dance and martial arts techniques. Those who practice T'ai Chi describe it as seemingly effortless, thoroughly absorbing, and relaxing. Proponents claim that the slow, nonstrenuous, fluid turning, stretching, and bending movements stimulate and massage the internal organs. To find a T'ai Chi trainer, contact a local martial arts school for a referral, or consult an adult education center.

Stress Reduction: Relaxation Techniques

Everyone experiences stress from time to time, but the challenges of endometriosis compound the normal stresses of daily life. They introduce a complex of stressors that aggravate symptoms, erode emotional well being, and contribute to the development of additional disorders.

Stress might be described as any situation that taxes one's ability to cope. It is perceived as a threat: the brain sends a message to the body to thwart danger—fight or flee—inappropriate and ineffective responses today.

Imagine, for example, that several days before your period you feel the first indication of pain. Anticipating what is to come, your jaws clench, your neck muscles tighten, your breathing becomes shallow, your heart begins to pound, and your chest becomes tight. You can neither fight nor flee; yet the brain's messengers signal a release of hormones that cause your heart rate and blood pressure to rise, your metabolism to accelerate, your breathing to become rapid and shallow, and your muscles to contract. The reaction is useless, yet it sets the stage for tension and pain. Soon, your neck is stiff and your head is throbbing. Throughout the day you are tense and irritable. Your cramps have worsened. In the morning, your joints are stiff and painful.

Relaxation training produces opposing physiological changes: it slows the heart rate, increases respiration, relaxes the muscles, and quiets the mind. In addition, it boosts production of natural painkillers—morphinelike substances called beta-endorphins. By learning to tap into your body's own healing and quieting reflexes, you effectively reduce and prevent stress.

The first step is to become more attuned to the role stress plays in your life. Identify your individual stress triggers. Once stress becomes habitual, it's often difficult to recognize its presence and its harmful effects. It's important to realize that each woman responds to stress in her own way. What is stressful to one may not be to another. Pay attention to feelings and events that create anxiety or tension. Common signs of stress include

insomnia	sleep disorders
loss of appetite	frequent colds

irritability   gastrointestinal disorders
panic   headaches
muscle aches   fatigue
cold hands or feet   unusual behavior
rapid heartbeat   depression
inability to breathe deeply   indifference
difficulty concentrating

Once you become aware of these situations and circumstances that are stressful for you, you can predict, and perhaps prevent, stress reactions. Work on eliminating stressful events. Lessen their impact by modifying your habits or your lifestyle. Through relaxation training you can learn to alter your reaction to those stress-provoking circumstances over which you have little or no control. It becomes possible to diminish their effects.

Some of the relaxation techniques described below can be learned in minutes. They require no expense, equipment, or formal training. Others must be performed or taught by a qualified practitioner. In many cases health insurance will cover a portion of the expense of training, particularly when you are referred to a stress management professional by your physician. None of these techniques has any serious negative consequences or medical contraindications; still, discuss them with your doctor or therapist to determine the best method for you.

But none will cure endometriosis either. What they do is relieve pain, by reducing stress. In addition, they afford you a degree of personal control over your emotions and your physical responses. They help you alter your perception of pain. The most important feature of each technique is self-mastery. It is not the device or the therapist that do the work and bring about change—it is you.

Breathing control.   The simplest relaxation technique is breathing control. By paying attention to the depth, rhythm, and manner of breathing, you can bring about physiological changes that decrease tension. You also provide distraction from pain.

Breath control is well known to women who undergo natural childbirth with the aid of the Lamaze method. It can be effectively used to relieve menstrual cramps as well. When in pain, make a conscious effort to slow your breathing rhythm. Breathe deeply through your nose. Use your diaphragm, not just your chest, to completely fill your lungs. This increases oxygen to the blood and lowers the heart rate. In addition, the stimulation of the tissue of the nostrils has been demonstrated to relieve menstrual cramps.

Biofeedback.   Through biofeedback, individuals learn to alter normally unconscious body processes such as heart rate, muscle activity, skin temperature, and brain wave activity. Biofeedback basically involves any device or system that provides information about your body that you can use to measure specific changes. If, for example, you step on a scale, that scale feeds back information. When you change your eating habits to lose weight, the scale registers and feeds back new information—graphic evidence of physiological change which reinforces new behavior.

Electrodes attached to the skin convert minute physiological, chemical, or electrical changes into auditory or visual signals. There are different types of devices. The electro-myograph (EMG) monitors muscle tension by recording muscle contractions. As the machine registers electrical activity in the muscles, and feeds back this information through a tone or a flashing light on a monitor, you hear or see evidence of the contrast in muscle tension levels during stress and during relaxation.

Thermal biofeedback measures changes in skin temperature. Equipment may be as simple as a hand-held strip of material to indicate skin temperature. Electroencephalogram (EEG) biofeedback monitors electrical brain wave activity; and galvanic skin response (GSR) biofeedback monitors the electrical resistance of the skin.

In biofeedback, you work to alter physiological responses by manipulating the signals provided by the biofeedback devices. You are taught to relax and visualize changes in muscle tension or skin temperature; the signals let you know when you have achieved the desired results. After considerable practice with the apparatus, you can achieve awareness and control of muscle tension and skin temperature without the use of the equipment.

When using biofeedback specifically for dysmenorrhea, you can concentrate on improving blood flow to the uterine muscle, which reduces spasm and pain. In addition to learning how to relax the uterine muscles, you can also work to create a sensation of warmth in the uterine and vaginal areas. Usually you are first taught to control the temperature of your hands and feet, then to apply a similar technique to any part of the body in pain. Biofeedback techniques are also used by women experiencing painful intercourse, and by postmenopausal women to lessen hot flashes and to counter symptoms of vaginal atrophy.

It's important to remember that biofeedback is not a treatment. The devices themselves do nothing more than provide information. You do the work. The knowledge that you are, in fact, capable of effectively controlling your body increases your overall sense of control, esteem, motivation, and energy. Like acupuncture and other techniques, biofeedback is most effective when combined with other relaxation methods and behavior therapy. To find a therapist, ask your doctor or contact your local mental health center or medical society. You may also get in touch with the psychiatry department at a university or medical school, the Biofeedback Society of America, or the American Association of Biofeedback Clinicians (see Appendix B).

Meditation. Meditation is a catch-all for a variety of techniques based on ancient Eastern religious and philosophical practices. Although all forms share a common goal—to quiet the mind by transcending thought—there are many ways to meditate. The best known of these is .Transcendental Meditation. TM was introduced to the United States by Maharishi Mahesh Yogi in the 1960s.

To practice TM, sit in a quiet, comfortable room and mentally repeat a mantra (a word or phrase) to keep distracting thoughts from entering the mind. Individuals can control heart rate this way, slow respiration, alter brain waves and skin temperature, decrease muscle tension, reduce oxygen consumption, increase circulation, lower production of carbon dioxide, and reduce blood concentrations of lactate. High levels of lactate are associated with anxiety.

Harvard Medical School professor Dr. Herbert Benson calls these physiological responses the "relaxation response." It can be achieved through other forms of meditation as well. Attention is focused either on a specific sound, as in TM, or on a single spot or object (such as a candle flame). All that is required is a quiet environment, a mental device to control attention, a passive attitude, and a comfortable position.[3] To learn more about meditation, refer to the resources in Appendixes B and C.

Progressive relaxation.   Developed early in this century by Dr. Edmund Jacobson, progressive relaxation is a simple technique for achieving deep muscle relaxation. In the 1920s Dr. Jacobson conducted various experiments. These revealed that, when individuals imagine themselves to be running, the muscles involved in running respond with small contractions. Similarly, when people think verbally, the muscles involved in speech are tensed. Muscles contract, reasoned Dr. Jacobson, in response to stressful mental imagery.

He observed that tense hospital patients did not recuperate as readily as other patients and devised for them a series of relaxation exercises. These exercises require no formal training and take only a few minutes twice a day. Regular practice helps make you aware of the most minute amounts of unnecessary muscle tension. You learn what situations provoke these muscular responses. Progressive relaxation is especially helpful when you feel yourself bracing against anticipated pain.

To practice, stretch out on your back in a quiet, comfortable room. Slowly tighten your fist muscles and feel the tension in your hand. Clench harder, then relax. Notice the contrasting sensations. Continue with the other hand, and repeat these steps, working through the various muscle groups in your body, paying special attention to the muscles in your shoulders, neck, and face.

Imagery.   The power of mental images to induce physiological change is alluded to in earlier discussions of biofeedback, progressive relaxation, and hypnosis (below). It is effectively used alone as well.

Through techniques known as imagineering, active imagination, visualization, and mental imagery, you learn to create mental images that can eliminate or blot out painful stimuli and stressful thoughts. "Images are the language of the unconscious mind, and when properly programmed, they are able to mobilize to a remarkable degree the body's intrinsic ability to heal itself," explains Dr. David Bresler in his book, *Free Yourself From Pain.* "The language of imagery directly accesses the autonomic nervous system which regulates breathing, the heartbeat, blood chemistry, digestion, tissue degeneration and repair, immune and inflammatory responses and many other bodily functions essential to life."[4]

Like hypnosis, imagery is used to transform a painful stimulus into a different kind of stimulus, to create a stimulus that competes with pain, or to move pain to different and less bothersome locations or out of the body altogether.

It also helps reinforce self-esteem: you visualize yourself as healthy and in control of your body and your emotions.

Therapists can develop your ability to harness your imagination in the relief of pain. Contact the American Imagery Institute (Appendix B). For guidance in your own exploration of imagery, refer to publications in Appendix C.

Hypnosis and self-hypnosis.   Pain involves both a physical sensation and an emotional reaction to that sensation. Through hypnosis, it is possible to alter both the physical sensation and the emotional response.

A variety of hypnotic techniques can be used. Symptom suppression trains you to change the way you perceive painful sensations. Symptom substitution trains you to move pain to another part of the body where it is less distressing. Eventually you learn to move it out of the body altogether.

Dr. Milton V. Kline is director of the Institute for Research in Hypnosis and Psychotherapy in New York. He says, "One can use a process of cognitive orientation, which involves visualizing or imagining that part of the body that is in distress. If you visualize a muscle group as being stretched out, rather than cramped or in spasm, those muscle groups tend to respond to images and the suggestions that the individuals are given or give themselves."[5]

Another hypnotic method commonly used is the "handwarming technique." You envision yourself becoming more and more relaxed and focus on your hands growing warm. When your hands get warm, a vasomotor change has occurred—the blood vessels dilate to increase circulation. "You can do the same thing with any part of the body," says Dr. Kline. "If there is abdominal or pelvic cramping, once you are in hypnosis you can both visualize and think about that part of the body growing nice and warm, which will increase circulation around that area and reduce spasm and pain. At the same time you can visualize that part of the anatomy growing very calm and relaxed."

Hypnotic directions or suggestions are particularly effective when they involve reinforcement via images and visual metaphors. When you think, for example, of your abdomen being relaxed, think of it as a calm, clear lake which is smooth and has no ripples in it.

The beneficial effects have been well documented. "In experimental studies in which electromyography has been used on muscle groups that are in spasm, individuals exposed to hypnosis or self-hypnosis report that their cramping has disappeared, but the electromyographic tracings also indicate that there is no longer any electrical stimulation coming from that cramped muscle group," says Dr. Kline.

These techniques are effective not only for dysmenorrhea but for PMS symptoms, menopausal symptoms, dyspareunia, and vaginismus as well. They can be used not only to counteract, but to prevent, these complaints. By learning to use self-hypnotic procedures, you can induce hypnosis prior to the onset of your menstrual period to eliminate or minimize symptoms. In addition, hypnotic techniques control preoperative anxiety as well as postoperative pain.

According to Dr. Kline, approximately eight sessions are needed to reduce pain and to learn self-hypnosis techniques. Pain relief can last from five to seven hours after each session with a therapist or each period of self-hypnotic practice. Of course, once you learn the techniques, you have continual access to pain relief through autosuggestion. In addition, many hypnotherapists make audiotapes for clients. If necessary, these can be used continuously. "Endless" tapes can also be made; hypnotic suggestion throughout the night prevents pain from interrupting sleep.

For best results, consult a highly trained hypnotist or, preferably, a psychologist, psychiatrist, or psychiatric social worker. To locate a qualified hypnotherapist, contact the organizations listed in Appendix B.

Autogenic training.   Autogenic training is a relaxation method that blends elements of yoga, meditation, hypnosis, deep breathing, and imagery. It was developed in the 1930s by German neurologist Johannes Schultz, who observed that his patients who underwent hypnosis experienced sensations of body warmth and heaviness in their limbs. Dr. Schultz believed that individuals could achieve the same results by placing themselves in a state of passive concentration (similar to self-hypnosis), using mantras to suggest physiological changes.

To this end, he devised a series of six exercises that can be practiced for about twenty minutes two or three times a day. The exercises focus on creating a heavy, warm feeling in the limbs, a calm and regular heartbeat, deep and relaxed breathing, warmth in the abdomen, and coolness in the forehead. After inducing deep relaxation and entering a state of passive concentration, you will repeat suggestions to yourself, such as "my right arm is warm," until you feel the sensation of warmth in your arm. More advanced autogenic training emphasizes meditative techniques and guided imagery to relax the mind. For autogenic therapy to be effective, it should be learned under the guidance of a professional. Consult the *Directory of Holistic Medicine and Alternative Health Care in the United States* (Appendix C).

Relaxation tapes.   For those who are unable to participate in relaxation training or therapy, and who find it difficult to learn relaxation procedures on their own, a variety of useful, commercially prepared audiocassette tapes are available. Check your local record or book shops, or look in Appendix C under Holistic Health.

Distraction—increasing pleasurable activities.   Many pain and stress control techniques operate on the principle of distraction. When individuals are in pain, they tend to avoid pleasurable activities or pastimes that provide distraction. You might say, for example, that you cannot go to a party because you are in pain. Staying home won't eliminate your pain. It will, however, isolate you, providing no distraction from pain. You can stay home and concentrate on your pain, or you can make the effort to focus your attention on a pleasurable distraction. Resist the temptation to retreat to your sickbed. Make a point of incorporating activities that bring pleasure or satisfaction into each day, especially the worst days. If your hobbies and interests are too physically taxing, be flexible. Expand your interests; develop new activities that can be incorporated into your life despite physical limitations. If you must rest, try to find a quiet activity to occupy your thoughts. It takes discipline, but, with the help of relaxation techniques, you can begin to take control of your thoughts, feelings, and physiological responses.

All of the techniques described above require patience and discipline. Above all they demand practice. For relaxation training to be effective, it must be done daily. Exercise must be done regularly. Once a self-improvement measure is learned, individuals commonly become complacent. You forego it one day and suddenly one day stretches into two, then three. Soon, you forget or you continue to let it slide. After a while, you lose the benefits gained and it's a great effort to begin again.

To benefit from self-care techniques, incorporate them into your lifestyle. Use them consistently, not only when you are in severe pain. There is no guarantee that these practices will totally eliminate your pain and stress. They will, however, if done regularly, vastly increase your comfort, your outlook, and your control over your own well being.

A Psychological Approach

A psychological approach to comprehensive pain management will tap and expand upon your own inner resources for pain control. You can alter your perception of pain as well as your reactions to it. With psychological methods, therapists can teach you to use your mind to combat stresses and emotional strains that compound pain.

Psychological methods bolster your own inherent ability to manage pain and thereby decrease feelings of helplessness and increase a sense of control. In addition to helping alleviate pain, this increases self-esteem.

Behavior therapy (behavior modification).   Behavior therapy is based on the principle that disorders are learned behaviors and that behavior can be modified by re-learning—that is, by substituting adaptive behaviors for maladaptive behaviors.

With regard to pain behaviors, behavior modification seeks to alter your perception of pain, or the role of pain in your life, by teaching you to alter your behavior. Many pain management techniques such as biofeedback, relaxation training, and hypnosis are actually some form of behavior modification. Although pain management techniques produce physiological changes that directly or indirectly reduce pain, they also change your behavior, your way of looking at pain. Thus, behavior therapy emphasizes self-control procedures and generalized coping skills to deal more effectively with pain and illness.

The two most widely used behavioral techniques in pain management are relaxation training and operant conditioning.

Relaxation training, achieved through methods described above, is based on the concept of reciprocal inhibition. A therapist can inhibit a certain behavior in a client by training that individual to substitute another behavior that is incompatible with the original behavior. For example, relaxation and anxiety cannot coexist. One is incompatible with the other. By training an individual to elicit a state of relaxation, the therapist blocks anxiety behaviors.

Operant conditioning is based on the premise that the results of our behaviors influence subsequent behavior. We are likely to repeat behaviors for which we receive positive reinforcement (reward), and we are less likely to repeat behaviors for which we receive either no reward or negative reinforcement.

For some, pain leads to secondary gains: attention, affection, or release from difficult or unpleasant situations, responsibilities, or realities of life. This is not to suggest that pain is a contrivance to achieve these ends. It is very real, but reinforcements unconsciously add to it.

Pain gets reinforced directly. People pay more attention to you when you are sick. It also gets reinforced indirectly. It is a way to avoid difficult things. This is not deliberate; it is an unconscious, learned response. (See Chapter 14 for a more detailed discussion of the pain lifestyle.)

Operant conditioning strives to modify behavior by eliminating positive reinforcement for maladaptive behaviors and offering rewards only for adaptive behaviors. It works on the premise that this unconscious, learned response can be unlearned. A therapist will look at a person's situation and environment and determine to what degree pain behaviors are learned responses that are being reinforced. He or she will then work to "condition" that response by teaching the patient to substitute a new response. Since pain behaviors are often unwittingly encouraged by those around you, effective operant conditioning must involve your mate and your family and teach them to respond differently to your behavior.

You are taught first to recognize secondary gains; second, to substitute "well" behaviors for pain behaviors. Rewards in the form of attention, for example, are offered for adaptive, productive, goal-oriented behaviors such as getting physical exercise. Pain behaviors, such as inappropriate complaining or avoidance of tasks, are ignored.

Other ways therapists can help.   Psychiatrists, psychologists, social workers, and other trained mental health professionals from a variety of theoretical perspectives, and with a range of different techniques and approaches, all can help you recognize and diminish the effect of pain upon your life. Psychological counseling can be especially helpful in working with issues of decreased self-image and self-esteem resulting from chronic pain. Therapists can improve your ability to separate yourself from your pain, to say "I may have pain, but I am not my pain." Therapists can also help you to

understand the grieving process related to pain
develop coping mechanisms for dealing with episodes of pain
pay attention to the control you do have over pain
focus on parts of the body that are not having pain
reduce pain compounders such as anxiety or stress
understand the ways in which pain affects your relationships

For information on selecting a therapist, see Chapter 16.

18

Beyond the Medical Mainstream: Exploring Alternative Therapies

It is unlikely that your physician will recommend any of the alternative healing methods in this chapter. There are no significant studies that scientifically verify their effectiveness. Some women, however, credit these therapies with having significantly relieved the pain and other symptoms of endometriosis. Symptoms of PMS, menopause, emotional strain, and even infertility have, they say, been affected as well.

Biofeedback, acupuncture, and hypnosis are considered by many to be "alternative" methods of treatment. A more accurate adjective, however, would be "adjunctive." That is, these practices, discussed in Chapter 17, follow, or complement, traditional medical methods. Their proponents and practitioners do not claim they cure disease, or even affect the underlying disease process. They merely maintain that they help relieve symptoms. Often, practitioners work in association with, or through referrals by, conventional (allopathic) physicians, who, to a certain extent, look upon them favorably.

By definition, an "alternative" treatment is one that offers options *other than*, rather than *in addition to*, conventional treatment. With the exception of chiropractic and osteopathy, alternative therapies are meant to replace conventional treatment. The practices described below, therefore, are not so much specific healing therapies as alternative systems or philosophies of medicine. Each defines disease in its own way, and each has a unique approach toward healing. Often, these definitions and approaches are at odds with traditional concepts and practices. For this reason, and because they have been subject to only meager scientific scrutiny, these alternative methods are usually not accepted by medical doctors. As mentioned, chiropractic and osteopathy are the exceptions. They are often used along with traditional approaches.

Most alternative medical systems are holistic: they treat the whole patient rather than a specific ailment or body part. They aim to prevent not only disease but dis-ease as well. The greatest advantage of a holistic approach is that it encourages individuals to take a more active role in their own health care. Self-care measures and attitudes are stressed. Holistic therapies recognize that all illness has an impact upon one's emotional well being. Treatment, to be truly effective, must address all of the ways individuals are affected by illness. This is a particularly welcome approach for women with endometriosis.

The alternative therapies and techniques described below are not harmful in and of themselves; there are, however, some dangers for women with endometriosis. Undiagnosed women who merely suspect endometriosis may find the idea of alternative treatment more appealing than diagnostic laparoscopy and medical or surgical treatment. However, because endometriosis can occasionally result in life-threatening complications, alternative approaches should be considered only *after* diagnosis and when serious health threats (ectopic pregnancy, ruptured ovarian endometrioma, bowel obstruction, ureteral obstruction) are not an issue. In addition, undiagnosed women should make sure they do not have other conditions with similar symptoms. Cancer, for example, requires immediate, traditional medical intervention, although some alternative practitioners would argue the point.

Disabled, and in pain, many individuals seek any type of treatment that offers promise of relief or cure. Like doctor-shopping and doctor-hopping, indiscriminate experimentation keeps you from dealing with the issues at hand. To hope that an alternative therapy will ultimately cure endometriosis is unrealistic. It diverts you from developing the important coping abilities you need to face the tasks ahead.

By investigating alternatives you may have much to gain, but you may lose as well. First, alternative therapies are expensive and insurance coverage is inconsistent. Second, they are time consuming. If explored precipitously, they may cause patients to lose a considerable amount of valuable time during which conventional treatment could probably provide relief. Unrealistic expectations can then put you right back on the treatment carousel chasing after an elusive cure.

As mentioned before, the scientific data are sparse. Moreover, standards on practice and training are vague and ill-defined. The world of alternative medicine is rife with charlatanism. Alongside a corps of dedicated, well-trained practitioners parade legions of lesser or totally untrained hucksters, eager to cash in on the increasing acceptance, indeed, the popularity, of holistic medicine.

Some holistic practices have been endorsed by a number of traditional physicians, but many doctors remain skeptical. Nevertheless, if you think an alternative therapy may offer you some promise, then by all means explore your options. But approach them as a vigilant consumer would, and be sure your expectations are realistic. Beware of practitioners who speak in terms of cure. Investigate both methods and practitioners carefully, and ask the following questions: How does the therapy work? What is its scientific rationale? How does it support its claims for success? How long does it take? What results can I anticipate? What will it cost? Is it covered by medical insurance? Will I have to give up other forms of treatment and medications? Read all you can on alternative methods and specific techniques (see Appendix C).

Interview practitioners carefully. Ask if a particular therapy was used for other women with problems like yours. Get the names of such patients and talk to them about their experiences. Above all, talk to other women who have endometriosis and who have used nontraditional methods. To learn more, contact the Endometriosis Association or the Endometriosis Society. The latter, headquartered in England, reports frequently on members' experiences with alternative approaches in its newsletter. Other organizations are listed in Appendix B.

A final caution: Most holistic practitioners stress the role of the patient in his or her own health care. And it *is* very important to take responsibility for finding the best medical care and for doing everything possible to improve your well being. Be aware, though, that some holistic practitioners, in encouraging such responsibility, may be encouraging patients to take the blame for being unwell. There is a fine line to be drawn here. You are responsible for coping as best you can, but you are not responsible for your illness. Scrupulously avoid any practice or practitioner who uses "blame-the-victim" tactics.

HOMEOPATHY

Homeopathy, developed in the early nineteenth century, aims, like other holistic systems, to treat the whole person, not merely specific diseases. Like the Chinese philosophies on which acupuncture is based, homeopathy is rooted in the belief that illness results from an imbalance in the body's vital force, that all illness involves the body, the mind, and the spirit.

Homeopaths, like naturopaths (see below), are more widely accepted in Europe than in the United States. They believe that symptoms reflect the mobilization of the body's own healing mechanisms against a threat to health. When those healing mechanisms are inadequate, homeopaths aim to stimulate and bolster them through minute doses of natural remedies that would, in healthy persons, produce the symptoms of the disease being treated (*homeo*—like; *pathy*—suffering). "Like cures like."

Homeopathic doctors are fully trained medical doctors who have studied homeopathy as a postgraduate medical specialty. They take detailed patient histories and, based on symptoms, select a single remedy. Homeopathic remedies are believed to minimize side effects and increase the "energy" of the remedy. The patient is then followed for a period of time so that the effects of the preparation can be determined.

OSTEOPATHY

The principles and techniques of osteopathic medicine were developed and first described in 1876 by Dr. Andrew Taylor Still, a physician and engineer. Osteopathic medicine stresses the interaction between the musculoskeletal system, which accounts for more than 60 percent of the body's mass, and all other organs and body systems. The basic premise is that aberrations in the musculoskeletal system resulting from illness, injury, and inefficient or faulty posture restrict circulation, produce inappropriate reflexes, and affect the nervous system. These produce changes in the functions of other body systems or are affected by them.

Osteopaths seek to relieve and prevent disorders arising from misalignment due to misuse or injury or circulatory or nerve problems. They, like doctors of medicine, are physicians and surgeons fully trained and licensed to provide complete health care. Like M.D.s, D.O.s work in specialized fields such as obstetrics and gynecology, internal medicine, and pediatrics. They use the entire repertoire of traditional diagnostic techniques and medical and surgical therapies; but they also are trained to correct structural problems through manipulation of the muscles, ligaments, and bones.

In the case of endometriosis, says Dr. J. Polsinelli, D.O., executive director of the American College of Osteopathic Obstetricians and Gynecologists, a woman may suffer from secondary low back problems as a result of aberrations of the autonomic nervous system. "Using osteopathic manipulative therapy (OMT) in conjunction with all other modalities in the treatment of endometriosis—such as hormones, anti-inflammatories and surgery—the osteopathic obstetrician/gynecologist is in a position to provide more complete treatment for the patient."[1]

CHIROPRACTIC

Chiropractic is a Greek word for manual medicine or practice. It is a nonchemical, nonsurgical mode of prevention and treatment that aims to enhance the body's own healing capacities. Like osteopaths, chiropractors emphasize the integrity of the spinal column as prerequisite for health. They too attempt to treat patients holistically.

Although osteopathy and chiropractic are similar, osteopaths believe disability and disease are aggravated by or result from nervous system disturbance due to circulation disorders caused by constricted blood vessels. Chiropractors, on the other hand, maintain that partial dislocations in the musculoskeletal system (subluxations) cause the disturbances of the nervous system and can cause or aggravate disease. Furthermore, they maintain, disorder in any organ or tissue disturbs the function of other organs and tissues.

A chiropractor will take a case history, perform neurological, physical, breast, and pelvic examinations, and take x-rays and blood and urine analyses. Spine and joints are examined and reflexes tested. Therapeutic techniques include massage, manipulation of the spine and joints, and skeletal balancing. Some chiropractors (known as "straights") rely exclusively on spinal adjustment. Others (known as "mixers") manipulate other joints as well, calling on a wider repertoire of techniques including vitamin therapy, nutritional counseling, massage, hydrotherapy, ultrasound, traction, exercise, ultraviolet and infrared light, colonic irrigation (high-pressure enemas), acupuncture, and psychotherapy.

Doctors of chiropractic (D.C.s) are not medical doctors. They do not claim the title of physician. Osteopaths' training is essentially equivalent to that of medical doctors. They are equipped to provide comprehensive medical care. Chiropractors, however, are less rigorously, less broadly trained. Nevertheless, to practice, they must pass stringent state licensing exams. All fifty states grant chiropractic licenses.

HERBALISM

Herbalism is one of the oldest of all the healing arts; it has been used by all cultures throughout time. Today, herbal remedies are viewed by some as natural and therefore inherently superior to any pharmaceutical treatment. Others see it as an old-fashioned method based on superstition.

Herbal medicines are prepared from the flowers, roots, leaves, stems, seeds, and bark of plants. They are inhaled, applied to the skin as a salve, lotion, or ointment, inserted as a suppository, or ingested as a tea or tablet. Often, different herbs are combined for maximum therapeutic effect. Among the herbs said to be helpful for symptoms of endometriosis are Vitex Agnus Cashtus, Thyme, and Motherwort.

Herbalism, thought to be harmless, is frequently dabbled in carelessly. Herbs are natural, but, like many other natural substances, certain herbs and combinations of herbs can be extremely toxic. And, like other medicinal substances, they do produce side effects. If you find the idea of herbal treatments appealing, resist the temptation to experiment with word-of-mouth remedies and self-made concoctions. Thoroughly investigate the remedy first, and consult your doctor.

Despite a lengthy tradition, the practice of herbalism is illegal in the United States: there is no standardized training or certification. Nevertheless, it *is* practiced, not only by some naturopaths, homeopaths, and chiropractors, but by untrained individuals as well.

NATUROPATHY

Naturopathy, or nature cure, refers to a holistic practice based solely on natural methods of healing. It borrows from homeopathy, nutrition therapy, herbalism, and manipulative therapies. Like the alternative therapies above, it is based on the belief that the physical, emotional, and spiritual are intertwined and balanced by a vital life force—the body's innate healing power. Illness results from an imbalance of this force. Natural healing methods, individualized for each patient, are used to mobilize the body's own healing ability.

The naturopath will generally elicit a detailed medical and personal history, perform a physical examination, and schedule laboratory tests. He or she will then individualize treatment methods and educate the patient on techniques to cleanse the body, eradicate toxins, and bolster the body's strength. Among these techniques (often used in combination) are fasting, vitamin and mineral therapy, color therapy, colonic irrigation, hydrotherapy, herbal remedies, breathing exercises, relaxation techniques, mud packs, exercise, massage, joint manipulation, irridology, acupuncture, biofeedback, electrical stimulation, and psychotherapy. Licensed naturopathic physicians may also perform minor surgery.

There is one technique naturopaths use that women with endometriosis find particularly helpful: the sitz bath. To take a sitz bath, sit for two minutes in a bathtub filled with enough hot water to cover the pelvic area. Then sit in cold water for one minute. Massage the pelvic area and the lower back while soaking. Alternating hot and cold wet compresses are helpful, too.

Like general practitioners, naturopathic physicians are trained in scientific treatment methods. In addition, they are trained in natural methods. Yet, unlike homeopaths, osteopaths, and chiropractors, they are not uniformly accorded legal status as medical specialists. Although some naturopathic training programs resemble the four-year programs of medical students, there are no well-defined standards for education. (At several schools it is even possible to get a diploma from a correspondence course.[2]) As a result, naturopathic physicians are prohibited from practicing in some states. In other states they may practice under common law. Orthodox medicine mistrusts naturopathic methods, yet many practitioners are currently licensed—in Arizona, Connecticut, Florida, Hawaii, Nevada, Oregon, Washington, and the District of Columbia.[3] Unlike osteopathy and chiropractic, naturopathy is seldom covered by medical insurance.

DIET, NUTRITION, AND VITAMIN SUPPLEMENTS

Many women claim they get considerable relief from symptoms of endometriosis as a result of dietary changes and vitamin and mineral supplements. Unfortunately, there is little scientific evidence to support or refute these claims. Researchers generally have paid little attention to the role of nutrition in relief of pain resulting from endometriosis. Good nutrition may decrease pain, but without scientific study there are no guidelines for planning a nutritional program specifically for the needs of women with endometriosis.

Among the nutritional changes believed to be helpful are reduced consumption of red meat, refined and processed foods, sugar, and caffeine; supplementation of the nutritional amino acid phenylalanine (DLPA); and increased consumption of calcium, foods rich in protein, and B vitamins. The following vitamin and mineral supplements are said to bring relief: vitamins A, B- complex, C, and E; Selenium Ace, which is a combination of selenium and vitamins A, C, and E; biochemic tissue salts; magnesium; and zinc.

In addition, some women report dramatic relief through the use of macrobiotics. Macrobiotics is a nutritional philosophy, developed early in this century, that seeks to balance the forces of yin and yang in the body. According to this system, various foods have either yin or yang characteristics. Advocates of macrobiotics believe that illness arises from an imbalance of these forces.

The staples of the macrobiotic diet are cooked vegetables, miso soup (a paste made from fermented soya beans, sea salt, and grain), cooked grains, and a limited amount of raw vegetables and fruits. Critics argue that the diet may lead to a deficiency of certain vitamins and an excessive consumption of salt. Another drawback is that the diet is extremely demanding. It requires serious commitment.

The philosophy of macrobiotics, and the art of planning and sustaining a macrobiotic diet, are best learned from qualified teachers. Before undergoing any major dietary changes, contact your doctor or a trained nutritionist or dietician (see Appendix B).

Another nutritional remedy is evening primrose oil. The subject of considerable research, it has proved promising in relief of symptoms associated with endometriosis and PMS. With the exception of mother's milk, evening primrose oil is the only natural source of gammalinolenic acid, an essential fatty acid which affects the production of prostaglandins. Preliminary findings of ongoing studies indicate that women given a combination of 80 percent evening primrose oil and 20 percent eicosapentaenoic acid, which is derived from fish oil, experience significant relief from pain. For more information about evening primrose oil (manufactured as Efamol), contact the manufacturer, Efamol House, Woodbridge Meadows, Guildford, Surry, GU1 1BA, England.

Both the Endometriosis Association and the Endometriosis Society have collected information from members concerning their experiences with and recommendations about alternative therapies. To learn more, request fact sheets from these organizations and see Appendixes B and C.

APPENDIX A

Glossary of Diagnostic and Therapeutic Procedures

The following are brief descriptions of the tests and procedures you may face during diagnosis and treatment of endometriosis. (Fortunately, most women will undergo only several.) Many of the procedures outlined below detect and treat other disorders, but are discussed here only as they apply to endometriosis and related conditions, or as they are used to differentiate endometriosis from other diseases and disorders. Lab tests of blood and urine and routine office procedures, such as wet mount smears and pap tests, are not included.

Gather details before undergoing *any* procedure. Ask why the procedure is necessary, what findings you can expect, and whether or not there is an alternative. Tests and procedures are less frightening if you know *in advance* what to expect. Similarly, recovery will be easier if you know what precautions are necessary and are familiar with signs of complications. Ask the physician, nurse, or technician where the procedure will be performed, what it entails, what it will feel like, and how you will feel afterward. Ask about side effects, risks and complications, precautions, preparation, and recovery. Ask also about the risks and complications of anesthesia. Ask what the procedure costs, and check with your insurance agent to see if it is covered. Finally, if you are anxious, talk with other women who have been through it and can share their experience with you.

Anesthesia.　Many of the procedures outlined below require either local or general anesthesia. It is helpful to understand anesthesia and its effects.

A local anesthetic is relatively risk-free. It numbs the site of the procedure, generally by injection, allowing you to remain fully awake. You may be given a sedative beforehand, a pill, injection, or intravenous drip, to relax you or help prevent tension and reflexes that might interfere. Or, less commonly, you may be given a spinal block: an anesthetic injected into the spinal canal to numb the lower portion of the body.

General anesthesia renders you unconscious for the duration of the procedure. It is administered by an anesthesiologist. Patients usually meet the anesthesiologist the evening before to discuss their medical history, allergies, and prior experiences with anesthesia. Most risks associated with surgery are related to anesthesia. So it is important to relate your medical history accurately and precisely, and to ask questions to calm any fears you have. You will be told to abstain from food and drink for eight to twelve hours beforehand. This is to prevent vomiting. You will probably be sedated before you are brought to the operating room. At this time, or possibly when you are on the operating table, an intravenous (IV) tube will be inserted into your arm or hand. In addition, a blood pressure cuff will be wrapped on your arm, and electrodes will be placed on your arm and chest so that your vital signs can be monitored throughout the operation. The anesthetic may be administered through a gas mask in place of, or in addition to, the IV. Once you are unconscious, a tube may be placed through your mouth into your windpipe. When you wake up in the recovery room you will still be groggy for an hour or two. Some feel nauseated and may vomit. You may feel achy and tired for days, or the endotracheal tube may cause your throat to be sore.

A variety of publications provide details about both anesthesia and the procedures below, including their minor and major risks. See Appendix C.

Anoscopy.   See **Sigmoidoscopy.**

Barium enema.   See **Lower GI (LGI) series.**

Breast self-examination.   This procedure should be performed monthly just after the menstrual period by all women. This is especially important for women taking hormones. Stand in front of a mirror, holding your arms at your sides. Become familiar with the normal appearance of your breasts, so you can check their shape, size, skin texture, and coloring. Note the appearance of veins and the angle of the nipples. Put your hands on your hips and tighten your pectoral muscles. Look for dimpling or puckering in the skin and symmetry in the breasts and the contracting muscles. Repeat this with your arms clasped chest high in front of you, and again with your arms behind your head. Then, squeeze each nipple, checking for any discharge. Lying on your back, place your left hand behind your neck; with your right hand examine your left breast (follow the same procedure to examine your right breast). With your fingers together, palpate the breast in a circular motion. Begin at the outside and work methodically in a spiral toward the nipple, being careful to examine the entire breast. Also palpate the armpit and the area between it and the breast. Report any lumps, thickenings, discolorations, bulges, skin changes, discharges, or abnormalities to your physician or gynecologist. For a more complete description, write the Office of Cancer Communications, The National Cancer Institute, The National Institutes of Health, Building 31, Room 10A18, Bethesda, MD 20815.

Cervical biopsy.   Performed in the gynecologist's office, a cervical biopsy involves the removal of samples of growths on the cervix with small forceps. The tissue is examined under a microscope to determine the nature of the growth and rule out a malignancy. A small instrument may also be used to scrape the inside surface of the cervix. You may feel a pinching sensation when the biopsy is taken, and minor bleeding, cramping, and a slight vaginal discharge may follow. The doctor will usually perform the biopsy with the aid of a colposcope. (See colposcopy.)

Cervical conization (Cone biopsy).   Removal of a small cone of tissue of the cervix for microscopic examination to detect cell changes. Performed by a physician in a hospital, with general anesthesia, conization is both a diagnostic (cervical cancer) and therapeutic (cervical dysplasia and carcinoma in situ) procedure. It is often used when **colposcopy** reveals no abnormalities following an abnormal Pap test. The patient, under general anesthesia, lies on the examining table with feet in stirrups. After the doctor inserts the speculum into the vagina, he washes the cervix and vagina with an antiseptic. A cone-shaped incision is made in the cervix to remove the tissue. The incision is then stitched. Bleeding may occur following the procedure.

Chest x-ray.   An x-ray of the chest is used to detect pleural endometriosis and rule out the possibility of cancer in a pulmonary nodule. The x-ray, which is painless, is performed by a nurse or x-ray technician (in your doctor's office, in a hospital x-ray department, or in the office of a radiologist) as a routine part of a physical exam or in preparation for surgery.

Colonoscopy.   Usually performed in the doctor's office by a gastroenterologist, this procedure allows the large intestine (the colon) to be seen; a biopsy can be performed at the same time to rule out a malignancy or to determine the location and extent of endometriosis in the colon. It is also used to evaluate abdominal pain, blood in the stool, diarrhea, and constipation. For three days the patient drinks only clear liquids and takes laxatives. On the evening prior to and the morning of the test, the patient may be asked to take an enema. The physician inserts a colonoscope (a large, flexible tube) into the rectum, manipulating it until it extends the length of the colon. This allows visualization of the inner wall of the colon. Since the test can be painful, the patient is sedated. See also **Sigmoidoscopy.**

Colposcopy.   Visualization of the vagina and cervix. This is a simple, painless diagnostic procedure performed in an office by a gynecologist to help determine the nature of a lesion on the vagina or cervix and to rule out a malignancy. It is also used to facilitate **cervical conization.** It may be performed to investigate pain or bleeding caused by intercourse. The patient lies on the examining table with her feet in stirrups. The physician places a speculum in the vagina, washes the vagina with acetic acid to reveal abnormal areas, and places a magnifying instrument (colposcope) in front of the vagina. (The colposcope does not touch the body.) Through the lens, the doctor can see a magnified image of the vaginal and cervical lining. He may take photographs to compare with the results of subsequent examinations.

Conization.   See **Cervical conization.**

CT (CAT) Scan.   Computer-analyzed x-ray examination of a specific level or plane of body tissue (CT stands for computerized tomography). Performed by a radiologist and an x-ray technician in a hospital x-ray department or specially equipped radiology office, a CT scan is a diagnostic procedure used to help locate lesions, determine their size, and differentiate masses of endometriosis from other growths. It may also detect collected blood or fluid in the pleural cavity, a symptom of pleural endometriosis. The CT scanner scans the body, taking x- rays of cross-sections from different angles. These views are displayed on a monitor and analyzed by computer. The patient reclines on an x-ray table which slides into the scanner—a large hollow rotating cylinder. Sometimes the process is repeated, following administration of contrast dyes to highlight and differentiate body parts. Dyes may be administered orally, by enema, or by injection. The CT scan itself is painless, but the contrast dyes may produce a warm sensation when injected. Nausea, vomiting, and headaches are rare.

Culdocentesis.   Aspiration of fluid from the pelvic cavity for microscopic examination. This diagnostic procedure is performed in an office by a physician and an assistant to determine whether or not there is unusual fluid in the pelvic cavity when a woman complains of lower abdominal pain, a ruptured ovarian cyst, or an ectopic pregnancy. Patients first walk or sit to cause fluids to sink to the bottom of the pelvis, then lie on the examining table with feet in stirrups. Patients are usually sedated, rarely anesthetized. Inserting a speculum, the doctor uses a tenaculum to slightly raise the cervix. He then inserts a needle through the vaginal wall into the cul-de-sac. Fluid found there is suctioned into a syringe. The test may involve several attempts to aspirate fluid. If no fluid is found, a **laparoscopy** or **ultrasound** may be required to determine the cause of the abdominal pain. If the patient has not been sedated, the manipulation of the cervix with the tenaculum may cause an unpleasant sensation, and the insertion of the needle may be painful.

Cystoscopy (Cystourethroscopy).   Visualization of the urinary tract. Performed by a urologist and at least one assistant in a hospital, physician's office, or radiology office, this diagnostic procedure allows the physician to view the lining of the urethra, ureters, and bladder through a thin fiberoptic tube inserted through the urethra and manipulated into the bladder. Cystoscopy may be ordered for patients with recurrent urinary tract infections, urinary urgency or frequency, pain or burning upon urination, or blood in the urine, in order to differentiate urinary tract endometriosis from other conditions producing similar symptoms. The patient, who may be sedated, lies on the examining table with feet in stirrups. Local, general, or spinal anesthesia may be used. If general anesthesia is used, no food or drink is allowed for eight to twelve hours prior to the procedure. If a general anesthesia is not used, a local anesthetic is administered. A lubricated scope is placed through the urethra into the bladder. A liquid is introduced through the scope to distend the bladder so that the doctor can inspect the bladder and posterior urethra. If a biopsy is necessary, small instruments inserted through the scope collect small amounts of urine and tissue. If you are awake during the procedure, the solution to distend your bladder may feel cool and produce a bloated feeling and a feeling of a need to urinate. The withdrawal of the instruments from the urethra may cause a burning sensation. If the ureters and kidney are to be viewed, a **pyelography** may be done. Urinary burning and frequency may occur for a few days after cystoscopy. The patient may be instructed to take an antibiotic before and after the test to avoid infection.

D & C (Dilation and curettage).   Dilation of the cervix followed by a scraping of the uterine lining. Both a diagnostic and therapeutic procedure, a D & C is performed in a hospital, either on an inpatient or an outpatient basis, by a gynecologist or general practitioner. A D & C is done for a variety of reasons: to diagnose or treat unusual or irregular bleeding; to clean the uterus after a spontaneous abortion; before a laparoscopy to dilate the cervix and facilitate administration of instruments into the cervical canal and uterus; to diagnose fibroids, polyps, endometrial hyperplasia, and uterine cancer; and to contribute to the diagnosis of cervical cancer. In the operating room the patient is given a sedative and usually put under general anesthesia, although a local anesthetic can be used. The external genital area and the vagina and cervix are washed with an antiseptic, and the pubic hair may be shaved. Following pelvic examination, the doctor inserts a speculum and grasps and steadies the cervix with a tenaculum. A thin metal probe is used to gauge the depth of the uterus. The cervical opening is then stretched (by the insertion and manipulation of tapered dilators of increasing diameters) to about an inch; the cervix can then accept the introduction of a curette into the uterus. A spoon-shaped scraping instrument, the curette is used to scrape away the endometrium. A sample of this uterine tissue is later examined under a microscope. You may need to stay in the hospital for several days, and, during that time, you may feel the aftereffects of the general anesthesia. There may be some bleeding, passing of blood clots, cramping, and mild backaches following the D & C. The next menstrual period is often late, and periods are often heavier for a month or two.

Endometrial biopsy.   Removal of tissue from the uterus for microscopic examination. Performed in the hospital on an inpatient or outpatient basis by a general practitioner or gynecologist, an endometrial biopsy generally has one of three purposes: to determine the cause of heavy or irregular menstrual periods; to determine if the endometrium of a woman undergoing infertility investigation is prepared to sustain and nourish the fertilized egg; or to test for uterine cancer before or during the use of estrogen replacement therapy. Following blood and urine tests, and sometimes after the administration of a local anesthetic, the doctor will place a speculum in the vagina and grasp the cervix with a tenaculum. A cannula is inserted into the uterus through the cervical opening, through which a small sample of the endometrium is suctioned out. There may be some cramping afterward.

GI Series.   See **Lower GI (LGI) series; Upper GI (UGI) series.**

Huhner test.   See **Postcoital test.**

Hysterectomy.   Excision of the uterus and cervix. Hysterectomy is performed in a hospital by a gynecologist or other surgeon on a patient under general anesthesia. Prior to surgery, usually the evening before, the patient relates her medical history to the anesthesiologist and discusses the upcoming procedure. Blood and urine tests and a chest x-ray are taken. Following a clear diet for twenty-four hours, one or more enemas are given, and the abdominal and pelvic areas shaved and cleaned. The patient may be instructed to douche. In the operating room, (sometimes before) an intravenous line is inserted into the hand or arm for the administration of medications or anesthesia. Throughout the operation vital signs are monitored. After surgery the incision, which may be vertical or horizontal, is sutured or closed with staples. Vital signs will continue to be monitored in the recovery room. The hospital stay is generally seven to ten days, and pain is likely to last for several days following surgery. During this time there may be some brown vaginal bleeding. Bowel function may be disrupted. After a few days the patient is able to walk about. Recovery is usually four to nine weeks, although many women say full recovery takes as long as a year. Normal activities can be resumed in four to six weeks, but strenuous activities must be increased gradually. Fatigue is very common following surgery, as are mild urinary tract problems. Although menopausal symptoms are rare (the ovaries remain intact), hot flashes may occur for a brief time after surgery in some women because of a disruption in the blood supply. If they continue, the blood supply was probably impaired. Some women experience depression, but it is usually transient. Some report decreased sexual pleasure; others claim the opposite. Some women find that orgasmic intensity is lessened. (During arousal the uterus fills with blood, which is dispersed upon orgasm, contributing to the vibratory feeling some women experience during orgasm. When the uterus is gone, orgasm may be less intense. Many women are never keenly aware of the vibrations, so their absence often goes unnoticed.) See also **Hysterectomy with bilateral salpingo-oophorectomy.**

Hysterectomy with bilateral salpingo-oophorectomy.   Excision of the fallopian tubes and ovaries in addition to the uterus and cervix. Preparation, basic procedures, and recovery period are identical to those for hysterectomy (see **hysterectomy**). This surgery usually leads to the development of menopausal symptoms such as hot flashes, vaginal atrophy, and osteoporosis in women who are not given replacement estrogen, and it may increase the risk of heart disease. In addition, less intense orgasm, as well as decreased sexual interest and comfort may ensue. These changes are due in part to changing hormonal levels; more directly to irritation caused by changes in the texture of the vaginal lining.

Hysterosalpingography (Uterotubography).   X-ray examination of the uterus and fallopian tubes involving the injection of contrast dye. Performed in a hospital radiology department by a gynecologist or radiologist and a technician or assistant, this diagnostic procedure is usually performed as part of the infertility workup to determine whether or not the fallopian tubes are obstructed, to view the inside of the uterus, and to investigate the cause of spontaneous abortion. Patients fast for one to three days before the test and may be given a sedative beforehand. The patient then lies on the examining table with feet in stirrups. The doctor inserts a speculum into the vagina and grasps the cervix with a tenaculum. He then washes the cervix and inserts a cannula into the cervical opening. On a video monitor the doctor will watch to see if the contrast dye passes through the fallopian tubes, indicating that the tubes are unobstructed. At the same time x-rays are taken. The injection of the contrast material is sometimes quite painful; more often it produces mild or moderate cramping. After the test, there may be a vaginal discharge or leakage of the dye.

Hysteroscopy. Visualization of the uterus. This diagnostic procedure is performed in a physician's office or in the hospital, on an outpatient basis, under either local or general anesthesia. It allows the physician to view the interior of the uterus in order to locate growths such as polyps, fibroids, adhesions, or nodules caused by adenomyosis. Under local anesthesia, patients are usually sedated and given an analgesic. The patient then reclines on the examining table. After the cervix is dilated, a tube is inserted through the cervix and into the uterus through which a liquid or carbon dioxide gas is introduced to inflate the uterine cavity. Then, a lighted scope is inserted through the cervix into the cavity to allow visualization. Visible growths can be removed with special instruments. The test can be quite painful and is usually done under general anesthesia.

Laparoscopy. Visualization of the interior of the abdomen (see Figure 11). Performed in a hospital, on an inpatient or outpatient basis, by a gynecologist or other surgeon, usually with general anesthesia, this diagnostic procedure is used to determine the cause or causes of abdominal and pelvic pain, to help pinpoint the causes of infertility, and for sterilization. (It may also be used therapeutically—see Chapter 8.) The test is typically scheduled to take place before ovulation. The laparoscope—a thin, lighted, viewing instrument fitted with a telescopic lens—is introduced into the abdominal cavity through a small incision (puncture) in the abdominal wall. Through it the surgeon can view the exterior of the abdominal and pelvic organs; the intestines, liver, spleen, cul-de-sac, uterus, uterine ligaments, fallopian tubes, and ovaries. In preparation for laparoscopy, blood and urine tests are taken, as well as a cervical culture to rule out pelvic infection. Patients are instructed not to eat for eight to twelve hours prior to surgery and may be sedated before the operation. First, pubic hair is shaved; then, the abdominal and pelvic area washed with an antiseptic. In the operating room electrodes attached to an electrocardiogram monitor are placed on the chest and arm to monitor heart function. The anesthesia is administered intravenously and the patient slowly loses consciousness. The anesthesiologist then inserts an endotracheal tube through the mouth into the windpipe, through which oxygen and anesthetics are pumped into the lungs. As he monitors your vital signs, the anesthesiologist will control the flow of oxygen and anesthesia. A cannula is inserted into the cervical opening to manipulate the uterus and to enable the surgeon to later inject dye to test the patency of the tubes. Although the patient will have urinated before surgery, a catheter is inserted into the urethra to drain urine. A full bladder would obscure the surgeon's view. Once the bladder is empty, the catheter is removed. The operating table is tilted so that the head is lower than the feet. The surgeon makes a small incision (usually about an inch) into the abdominal wall near the navel, into which a needle is inserted. Through the needle, carbon dioxide gas fills the abdominal cavity to lift and separate the organs. This allows the laparoscope to be inserted through the puncture so that the surgeon can easily view the organs. One or two smaller incisions may be made near the pubic hairline through which a probe or cannula is inserted to manipulate the organs and improve visibility. To determine if the tubes are occluded, the surgeon injects a blue water-based dye through a cannula (inserted into the vagina and cervical opening) to the uterus and the fallopian tubes, watching for pools of dye or any impediment to the passage of dye. If the surgeon decides to treat endometriosis during laparoscopy—to remove adhesions or growths—another small puncture is made, through which tools are inserted and manipulated. These instruments may also be used, through this puncture, to collect biopsy samples or to aspirate fluid. A D & C may be performed at this time as well (see D & C). After the surgeon has viewed the organs and performed any necessary therapeutic procedures, the laparoscope and other instruments are withdrawn, and the abdomen is allowed to deflate. The incision is closed, usually with a Band-Aid, adhesive tape, or several dissolvable stitches. A scar, if visible at all, is minor. After the procedure patients are taken to the recovery room and allowed to awaken gradually. Once on their feet—usually within three hours, providing there are no complications—they may leave the hospital. The recovery period generally lasts only a day or two, during which time the patient may feel the aftereffects of the general anesthesia—abdominal bloating, shoulder pain (resulting from the accumulation of gas when tilted backward on the operating table), and pain and discoloration at the site of the punctures. The skin and the muscles in the abdomen may be sore from the inflation caused by the gas. Strenuous activity usually can be resumed within two weeks. For women who are obese, or for those who have had prior abdominal surgery, a procedure known as open laparoscopy may be used, in which a somewhat larger and deeper incision is made. See also **Videolaseroscopy.**

Laparotomy.   Major abdominal surgery. Usually performed by a gynecologist or other surgeon prior to ovulation, laparotomy is both a diagnostic and therapeutic procedure requiring general anesthesia. It may be used to remove implants, cysts, and adhesions, to test tubal patency, and to correct the pelvic anatomy. After admission to the hospital, the patient is given a number of routine tests, including an electrocardiogram, to monitor heart function, and blood and urine tests. The evening before surgery the patient is given an enema to empty the large intestines and a douche to clean the vagina. The top of the pubic hair is shaved. For the rest of the evening, and until surgery, no food or liquids may be taken. In the morning an IV line is placed in the hand or arm, through which fluids and nutrients flow and, perhaps, steroids and antihistamines to prevent the formation of scar tissue. Before the operation (sometimes the night before), the anesthesiologist discusses the medical history and answers any questions the patient may have. At this time the patient may be given a sedative. In the operating room electrodes attached to an electrocardiogram device monitor the heartbeat. The general anesthetic is delivered through the IV and the patient slowly loses consciousness. The anesthesiologist inserts an endotracheal tube into the windpipe to administer oxygen and anesthesia to the lungs. He also monitors vital signs throughout the operation and controls the flow of oxygen and anesthesia. After a pelvic examination, the surgeon places a catheter into the urethra to drain the bladder. He then makes a crescent-shaped incision above the pubic hair through the abdominal muscle into the abdominal cavity. The skin is then clamped open and the intestines and bladder moved aside to allow the surgeon to see the reproductive organs. He then searches the pelvis for endometriosis and will cauterize, vaporize, or excise lesions, nodules, and cysts. If necessary, he will perform a tuboplasty to open the fallopian tubes. At this time he may also perform such procedures as appendectomy, uterine suspension, oophorectomy, ovarian wedge resection, presacral or uterosacral neurectomy, or myomectomy (see the Glossary). When all the necessary procedures are completed, all layers of the abdominal wall are stitched with dissolvable sutures or stapled. The endotracheal tube is removed and the patient is taken to the recovery room where vital signs are monitored until stable. Once in her room, the patient will slowly awaken. At this time her throat may be sore from the tube and she may bleed vaginally. The patient likely will be given painkillers and catheterized for the remainder of the day as she sleeps. The hospital stay lasts approximately five days, during which time activity level is gradually increased and diet normalized as the patient's gastrointestinal function slowly returns. Recovery requires an additional two-week period of rest at home, during which time strenuous activity is to be avoided. During this period the patient may experience pain as well as numbness in the abdomen and vaginal bleeding. After two weeks moderate activity and sexual intercourse may be resumed. Complete recovery normally takes about six weeks.

Lower GI (LGI) Series (Barium enema).   Insertion of barium into the intestines for the purpose of x-ray examination. This diagnostic procedure is performed by a radiologist and an x-ray technician, either in the x-ray department of a hospital or in the office of a gastroenterologist or radiologist. In patients who complain of rectal bleeding, constipation, or diarrhea, it may be performed to rule out a malignancy or a benign condition such as colitis. In preparation, a rigorous bowel cleaning involves a liquid diet followed by repeated enemas. Barium, a contrast material, is inserted into the colon through a tube in the rectum. X-rays are taken, and additional x-rays (introducing air in the colon to contrast with barium) may also be taken. The preparation can cause fatigue, discomfort, and soreness in the anal area. The introduction of barium and air may cause some cramping. See also **Upper GI (UGI) series.**

Lung biopsy.   Removal of lung tissue for examination. This diagnostic procedure is performed in a hospital by a surgeon. The patient is under either local or general anesthesia. The small piece of tissue is collected through a needle inserted between the ribs; by an instrument inserted down the throat, through either the mouth or nose (bronchoscopy); or surgically through an incision in the chest (open biopsy). Before the procedure a chest x-ray and blood tests are taken. A needle biopsy is usually done on an outpatient basis in a hospital radiology department. The patient, who may be sedated before the test, sits in a chair, crossing her arms on a table. X-rays are taken to pinpoint the growth or lesion, and the skin is marked at the corresponding location. After the skin is washed with an antiseptic, a local anesthetic is injected, and the needle is inserted. The doctor then makes a small incision with a scalpel. While the patient is holding her breath, he puts the needle through the incision and into the lung. The procedure may be painful. A sample is collected through the needle before the needle is withdrawn, and a dressing is applied over the incision. If there are no complications within two to four hours, the patient may be released. Recovery may take a day or two, and strenuous activities should be curtailed for several more days. An *open biopsy* requires general anesthesia and is usually performed on an inpatient basis by a surgeon. After a sedative and anesthesia are administered, an incision is made in the chest to allow the removal of a wedge of lung tissue. The chest wall muscles and the skin are then stitched closed. A chest x-ray is taken. For one or two days after surgery a tube stretched from the lung through the incision prevents the lung from collapsing. During this time the incision site may be sore and may itch.

Lymph node biopsy.   Removal of lymph node tissue for microscopic examination. This diagnostic procedure, performed by a physician in a hospital, is generally painless, although the injection for the local anesthetic may sting, and the site may be sore for a couple of days. A sample of lymph node tissue is collected through a needle inserted in the node after the administration of the anesthetic. An entire node may be surgically removed while the patient is under general anesthesia.

Mammography.   X-ray of the breast. This diagnostic procedure is performed by an x-ray technician in a radiologist's office or in a hospital radiology department. The x-ray is evaluated by the radiologist. A mammogram is used to investigate breast disorders and to detect cancer. It is also a prerequisite for hormone replacement therapy, both to detect incipient cancer and to provide a baseline for future tests. The patient sits, stands, or reclines, depending on the equipment. Each breast is placed between a plate containing the x-ray film and a device that flattens the breast. The patient is instructed to raise her arm out of the way and hold her breath. Often, two films are taken of each breast. Apart from the discomfort caused by compression, the procedure is painless.

Oophorectomy (Ovariectomy).   Removal of one (unilateral oophorectomy) or both ovaries (bilateral oophorectomy). If the fallopian tube or tubes are also removed, it is called a **salpingo-oophorectomy.** After a unilateral oophorectomy the patient retains her childbearing potential and is not at risk for the development of the symptoms of surgical menopause. The procedure is usually part of a laparotomy. (See **Laparotomy** for a description of the general conditions under which it is performed.)

Ovariectomy.   See **Oophorectomy.**

Pelvic ultrasound (Ultrasonography).   Translates sound waves into a video image. This diagnostic procedure is performed by a radiologist or gynecologist in a hospital or doctor's office. It is painless, so no anesthesia is necessary. In ultrasound, which is essentially radar, an instrument called a transducer sends high-frequency sound waves back and forth across the abdominal or pelvic area. The sound waves, bouncing off the pelvic organs, are recorded by a microphone and displayed on a video monitor. Ultrasound of the uterus, ovaries, or fallopian tubes is done to investigate abnormal growths; dysmenorrhea, pelvic pain, abnormal bleeding, and other menstrual irregularities; and urinary tract disorders. It may also be done after treatment to see if growths have regressed or to check for recurrence; and it is used to view the fetus during pregnancy. Several glasses of water about an hour before the test fill the bladder. The patient cannot urinate until after the test—approximately twenty to thirty minutes—and the pressure on the bladder can be quite uncomfortable. The patient reclines on a table; a gel is applied to the abdomen to help conduct the sound waves; and the doctor or technician slides the transducer across the abdomen vertically and horizontally. Waves are viewed on the video monitor and photographs taken.

Pleural fluid analysis, Pleural tap, Pleurocentesis.   See **Thoracentesis.**

Postcoital test (Huhner test).   Analysis of vaginal and cervical secretions performed within twelve hours of intercourse. This procedure evaluates the quality of the cervical mucus; that is, the ability of sperm to penetrate, bypass, and survive it. It is usually done by a reproductive endocrinologist as part of an infertility investigation. The patient is instructed to have intercourse just before ovulation (and within twelve hours of the appointment with the infertility specialist) and not to bathe or douche. The doctor takes a sample of cervical mucus with a swab in order to examine under the microscope the number and motility of the sperm cells. The test may be repeated the following month to ensure that it is done prior to ovulation since the characteristics of the mucus will naturally change during each month.

Proctoscopy. See **Sigmoidoscopy.**

Pyelography (Urography).   X-ray of the kidney and the ureters, involving injection of contrast dye. This diagnostic procedure is performed by a radiologist and an x-ray technician in a radiologist's office or, on an outpatient basis, in a hospital radiology department. It is commonly referred to as intravenous pyelography (IVP). That is, the contrast dye is injected intravenously and passes quickly into the urine. It is used to investigate such symptoms as frequent urinary tract infections, blood in the urine, and flank pain—all of which may indicate endometriosis of the urinary tract. The procedure varies, depending on the doctor and the purpose for it. The afternoon before the IVP, the patient takes a laxative to clean the intestines. Diet may be restricted for the remainder of that evening. Before the test the patient is told to urinate, then lie still on the x-ray table while a plain x-ray is taken. After the film is developed and analyzed, a contrast material is injected through a needle into the arm and transmitted by the blood into the kidneys and through the urinary tract. (In retrograde pyelography, the contrast dye is injected through a catheter into the ureters.) The contrast material may produce a burning sensation, which may radiate to other parts of the body and may leave a strange taste in the patient's mouth. Several films are taken at intervals, usually five minutes, to watch the progress of the contrast material through the urinary tract. Between the first and second film, the patient may be fitted with a beltlike device that prevents the contrast dye from entering the ureters. After the next film, the device is removed. The patient may then be asked to urinate again, and another film is taken. Occasionally the test causes nausea, vomiting, headaches, dizziness, numbness, or weakness. In addition, it sometimes produces nasal symptoms, such as a runny nose or sneezing.

Rectosigmoidoscopy. See **Sigmoidoscopy.**

Renography (Renal scan, Renal scintigraphy, Kidney scan).   X-ray examination of the kidney. This diagnostic procedure, which involves the injection of radioactive materials, is performed by a nuclear medicine physician and a technician in a hospital radiology or nuclear medicine department, usually on an outpatient basis. The test is used to evaluate flank pain and kidney function, or when damage to the kidney may have been caused by endometriosis. The patient sits or lies still. The skin on the inside of the elbow is cleaned with an antiseptic and a small amount of radioactive material is injected into a vein. It progresses through the bloodstream to the kidneys, through the kidney's circulating system to the ureter and bladder, all tracked by a camera. A different radioactive material is then injected and a number of x-rays taken during a half-hour period. Sometimes additional films are necessary several hours later, but normally the patient is released after voiding the bladder. To reduce additional exposure to radioactive waste, the patient is advised to flush the toilet immediately after urination for a twenty-four-hour period. Apart from the prick of the needle, the test is painless.

Rubin's insufflation test.   Diagnostic test to determine tubal patency. This test, performed in the gynecologist's office, has been largely replaced by **hysterosalpingography.** Carbon dioxide gas is inserted slowly into the uterine cavity through a pressure tube connected to a measuring device. If the tubes are open, some gas will leak out of the tubes into the abdominal cavity, irritating the diaphragm and causing shoulder pain. Open tubes are also indicated when the measuring device shows that gas pressure is not building rapidly in the uterine cavity. The test is seldom used now because it provides far less information than the hysterosalpingogram. It does not indicate the shape of the uterine cavity, nor does it allow the physician to know if the tubes are only partially open, which tube is obstructed, if both tubes are obstructed, or where the obstruction is located. If the test reveals any obstruction, a hysterosalpingogram is necessary. The Rubin's test is often uncomfortable.

Salpingo-oophorectomy.   See **Oophorectomy.**

Sigmoidoscopy (anoscopy, proctoscopy, Rectosigmoidoscopy) and biopsy.   Visualization of the lower colon. This diagnostic procedure is performed by a physician in his office or in a hospital room. The lower gastrointestinal tract, including the sigmoid colon, the rectum, and the anus, is visualized to detect abnormal growths or lesions and to determine the cause of symptoms such as rectal pain, bleeding, blood in the stools, diarrhea, and constipation. It is also used to further investigate abnormalities revealed through a **Barium enema.** The bowels must be cleaned in preparation for the test, but the method varies from doctor to doctor. Sometimes a liquid diet is ordered for several days before the test and one or more enemas required. The tests are awkward, somewhat uncomfortable, and often embarrassing for patients who lie on a table in a fetal position or are positioned on their hands and knees, which may cause some pressure in the head and face. The doctor inserts a lubricated, gloved finger into the anus to feel for abnormalities. Then, a lubricated anoscope—a short, lighted, hollow tube—is gently inserted to view the anal canal, the outermost several inches of the colon. Bearing down as if having a bowel movement facilitates entry of the tube. The tube is then taken out slowly. To view the rectum, a longer tube, a proctoscope, is used. Then, a sigmoidoscope, a still longer tube, is used to view the rectosigmoid and the sigmoid—the longer, curved, lower part of the large intestine. There are two types of sigmoidoscopes. A rigid sigmoidoscope is approximately one foot long and one inch in diameter; a flexible fiberoptic sigmoidoscope is a lighted tube two feet long threaded with fiberglass. It allows the surgeon to bend the source of light around curves. Air may be blown through the sigmoidoscope and stool, blood, or mucus may be suctioned to allow a clear view. Small growths can be removed with small instruments introduced through the sigmoidoscope for biopsy. After the scope has been manipulated as far into the colon as it can go, it is slowly withdrawn. Insertion and manipulation of the tubes may cause some discomfort, gas pains, and a need to defecate. When the last scope is removed the patient rests for a few minutes to avoid dizziness. Mild gas pain and passing gas is common. Biopsies may cause slightly bloody stools. See also **Colonoscopy.**

Skin biopsy.   A skin biopsy, performed by a physician in his office, is a microscopic examination of a nodule or lesion to determine if it is composed of endometriotic tissue. The biopsy may be done in three ways. All require a local anesthetic. For a punch biopsy, the doctor uses an instrument resembling a hole punch to free a small circular sample of tissue, which is then removed with a needle or forceps. If the sample is large, a couple of stitches may be necessary. For a shave biopsy, the doctor shaves off the growth with a scalpel. For an excisional biopsy, the growth is excised with a scalpel and closed with stitches. A large area will be covered by a skin graft. Although the procedure is painless, the anesthetic may sting.

Thoracentesis and Pleural biopsy.   Withdrawal of fluid from the pleural cavity for microscopic examination. This diagnostic procedure involves blood tests and a chest x-ray. The patient is given medication to prevent coughing. A local anesthetic is administered and a needle inserted into the chest wall between the ribs through which fluid from the pleural cavity is aspirated with a syringe. If a biopsy is performed, an instrument is inserted into the needle in order to collect a small sample of the fluid and the pleura. After the procedure a technician may take an x-ray to be certain the lung was not punctured.

Ultrasound. See **Pelvic ultrasound.**

Upper GI (UGI) Series. X-ray of the upper gastrointestinal tract. This diagnostic procedure is performed by a radiologist and an x-ray technician in an office or the radiology department of a hospital to evaluate patients with diarrhea, abdominal pain, heartburn, or gastrointestinal bleeding. Patients abstain from food, liquids, cigarettes, and gum for twelve hours. The procedure begins with a thick, chalky barium "milkshake" (usually flavored) in an amount specified by the technician. The barium flows through the digestive tract—the esophagus, stomach, and the duodenum (the first part of the small intestine). It is tracked by the radiologist on a fluoroscope, an x-ray tube connected to a video monitor. X-rays are taken at different intervals. The table to which the patient is strapped tilts to allow the barium to flow in a certain way. Pressure to the abdomen does the same thing. In a double-contrast study, the patient drinks the barium through a punctured straw, or is given pills, to introduce air into the stomach. Air in the stomach highlights the stomach and the intestines so they can be viewed more clearly. A small bowel follow-through may then be performed. The radiologist watches the passage of another barium "milkshake" through the entire small intestine. The test takes as long as four hours; x-rays are taken at thirty-minute intervals. Stools are whitened by the barium for several days after the test. See also **Lower GI (LGI) series (Barium enema).**

Urography. See **Pyelography**

Uterotubography. See **Hysterosalpingography.**

Videolaseroscopy. This therapeutic procedure is the same as laser laparoscopy (described in Chapter 8), except that the laparoscope is fitted with a miniature video camera with a zoom lens. Rather than bend over the eyepiece of the laparoscope, the doctor views an image of the interior of the abdominal cavity on a video monitor. The procedure has three advantages over laparoscopy. First, it is a more comfortable and less fatiguing operation for the surgeon to perform. Second, the surgeon can magnify surfaces within the pelvic cavity in order to differentiate areas of endometriosis that may not be visible through the laparoscope alone. Finally, a videotape of the operation can be used for future reference. This may reduce the necessity in some cases of a second laparoscopy. Often, for example, when a patient consults a second doctor, that physician may want to perform another laparoscopy because he does not want to rely on the judgment of the surgeon who performed the initial laparoscopy. If videolaseroscopy is used, a videotape may serve the same purpose. See also **Laparoscopy.**

APPENDIX B

Resources: Organizations

Many of the organizations listed below provide information, publications, courses, or referrals to practitioners. For more information, call or write asking about complete services. Include a self-addressed, stamped envelope with your request.

ACUPUNCTURE/ACUPRESSURE

The G-Jo Institute
P.O. Box 8060
Hollywood, Florida 33084
(305) 524–0318

ADOPTION

Concerned United Birthparents
595 Central Avenue
Dover, New Hampshire 03820
(603) 749–3744

Committee for Single Adoptive Parents
P.O. Box 4074
Chevy Chase, Maryland 20815
(202) 966–6367

Latin American Parents Association (LAPA)
National Headquarters
P.O. Box 72
Seaford, New York 11783
(516) 752–0086

National Adoption Exchange
1218 Chestnut Street
Philadelphia, Pennsylvania 19107
(215) 925–0200

National Adoption Resource Exchange
(NARE)
67 Irving Place
New York, New York 10003
(212) 254–7410

National Committee for Adoption
3146 Connecticut Avenue, N.W., Suite 326
Washington, D.C. 20036
(202) 463–7559

Open Adoption Resources
3035 Alden Street
Eugene, Oregon 97405
(503) 343–4825

Organization for a United Response (OURS)
3148 Humboldt Avenue, South
Minneapolis, Minnesota 55408
(612) 535–4829

ALEXANDER TECHNIQUE

American Center for the Alexander Technique
142 West End Avenue
New York, New York 10023
(212) 799–0468

American Center for the Alexander Technique
9359 Olympic Boulevard
Beverly Hills, California 90211
(213) 470–2672

BIOFEEDBACK

American Association of Biofeedback Clinicians
2424 South Dempster Avenue
Des Plaines, Illinois 60016
(312) 827–0440

Biofeedback Society of America
10200 West 44th Avenue, #304
Wheat Ridge, Colorado 80033
(303) 422–8436

CHIROPRACTIC

American Chiropractic Association
1091 Wilson Boulevard
Arlington, Virginia 22201
(703) 276–8800

International Chiropractors Association
1901 L Street, N.W., Suite 800
Washington, D.C. 20036
(202) 659–6476

ELECTRIC NERVE STIMULATION

Pain Control Network
(800) 833–9911

Walker Pain Institute
1964 Westwood Boulevard
Second Floor, Suite 2043
Los Angeles, California 90015
(213) 475–6766

ENDOMETRIOSIS

The Endometriosis Association
U.S.–Canadian Headquarters
P.O. Box 92187
Milwaukee, Wisconsin 53202
(414) 962–8972
(800) 992–ENDO

The Endometriosis Society
65 Holmdene Avenue
Herne Hill
London SE24 9LD
England
(01) 737–4764

FELDENKRAIS TECHNIQUE

Feldenkrais Guild
P.O. Box 1145
San Francisco, California 94101
(415) 440–8708

GAMETE INTRAFALLOPIAN TRANSFER

Texas Health Science Center
San Antonio, Texas
(512) 567–7000

University of Minnesota Medical School
Minneapolis, Minnesota 55455
(612) 873–8725

HEALTH CARE (GENERAL)

Health Research Group
2000 P Street, N.W.
Washington, D.C. 20036
(202) 872–0320

National Health Information Clearinghouse
P.O. Box 1133
Washington, D.C. 20013-1133
(703) 522–2590

The National Self-Help Clearinghouse
33 West 42nd Street
New York, New York 10036
(212) 840–1259

HEALTH CARE FOR WOMEN

American College of Obstetricians and
Gynecologists
600 Maryland Avenue, S.W.
Washington, D.C. 10014
(202) 638–5577

American Medical Women's Association
465 Grand Street
New York, New York 10002
(212) 533–5104

Coalition for the Medical Rights of Women
2845 24th Street
San Francisco, California 94110
(415) 826–4401

Feminist Women's Health Center
6411 Hollywood Boulevard
Los Angeles, California 90028
(213) 469–4844

Health/PAC (Health Policy Advisory Center)
17 Murray Street
New York, New York 10007
(212) 267–8890

National Women's Health Network
224 Seventh Street, S.E.
Washington, D.C. 20003
(202) 543–9222

HOLISTIC HEALTH

American Holistic Medical Association
2727 Fairview Avenue East #D
Seattle, Washington 98102
(206) 322–6842

International Association of Holistic Health
Practitioners
3419 Thom Boulevard
Las Vegas, Nevada 89106
(702) 873–4542

People's Medical Society
14 East Minor Street
Emmaus, Pennsylvania 18049
(215) 967–2136

For audio and videotaped instruction on various
holistic disciplines, contact:

Bromiley Resource Training
P.O. Box 222278
Carmel, California 93922

Yes! Bookshop
1035 31st Street N.W.
Washington, D.C. 20007-4482
(202) 338–7874
(800) 252–3433

HOMEOPATHY

Homeopathic Educational Services
2124 Kittridge Street
Berkeley, California 94704
(415) 693–9270 (2–6 p.m., M–F, Pacific
Standard Time)

International Foundation for Homeopathy
2366 Eastlake Avenue East, 301
Seattle, Washington 98102
(206) 324–8230

National Center for Homeopathy
1500 Massachusetts Avenue, N.W.
Washington, D.C. 20005
(202) 223–6182

HYPNOSIS

American Association of Professional
Hypnotherapists
P.O. Box 731
McLean, Virginia 22101
(703) 448–9623

American Society of Clinical Hypnosis
2250 East Devon Avenue, Suite 336
Des Plaines, Illinois 60018
(312) 297–3317

International Society for Professional Hypnosis
124 South Main Street
Coopersburg, Pennsylvania 18036
(215) 866–8418

Society for Clinical and Experimental Hypnosis
129-A Kings Park Drive
Liverpool, New York 13090
(315) 652–7299

HYSTERECTOMY/SURGICAL MENOPAUSE

Center for Climacteric Studies
University of Florida
901 N.W. Eighth Avenue, Suite B-5
Gainesville, Florida 32601
(904) 391–7172

IMAGERY

American Imagery Institute
P.O. Box 13453
Milwaukee, Wisconsin 53213
(414) 781–4045

INFERTILITY

American Fertility Society
2131 Magnolia Avenue, Suite 201
Birmingham, Alabama 35256-6199
(205) 251-9764

Center for Communications in Infertility
P.O. Box 516
Yorktown Heights, New York 10598
(914) 962-7140

The Infertility Center of New York
14 East 60th Street
New York, New York 10022
(212) 371-0811

Resolve, Inc.
P.O. Box 474
Belmont, Massachusetts 02178
(617) 484-2424

INFORMATION GATHERING

For information about MEDLARS: The
Computerized Literature Retrieval Services of
the National Library of Medicine, The
National Library of Medicine's Public Search
Service, Regional Medical Libraries or
Interlibrary Loan policies, contact:

Office of Inquiries and Publications
Management
8600 Rockville Pike
Bethesda, Maryland 20209

IN VITRO FERTILIZATION

For information about centers performing IFV/
ET, contact:

Resolve, Inc.
P.O. Box 474
Belmont, Massachusetts 02178
(617) 484-2424

MACROBIOTICS

East West Foundation
17 Station Street
P.O. Box 850
Brookline, Massachusetts 02147
(617) 783-0045

The George Ohsawa Macrobiotic Foundation
1511 Robinson Street
Oroville, California 95965
(916) 533-7702

The Kushi Institute
17 Station Street
P.O. Box 1100
Brookline, Massachusetts 02147
(617) 738-0045

Macrobiotic Educational Association
4905 Del Ray Avenue, Suite 400
Bethesda, Maryland 20814
(301) 656-6545

MASSAGE

The Alliance of Students and Practitioners of
Medical Massage and Related Therapy
c/o The Swedish Institute
875 Avenue of the Americas
New York, New York 10001
(212) 695-3964

American Massage Therapy Association
P.O. Box 1270
Kingsport, Tennessee 37662
(615) 245-8071

MEDICAL INSURANCE

Group Health Association of America
Department NHIC
624 Ninth Street, N.W., Suite 700
Washington, D.C. 20001
(202) 429-0741

Health Insurance Association of America
1850 K Street, N.W.
Washington, D.C. 20006
(202) 862–4000

Hill-Burton Free Hospital Care Program
(800) 638–0742; in Maryland, (800) 492–
0359

National Insurance Consumer Organization
344 Commerce Street
Alexandria, Virginia 22314
(703) 549–8050

Office of Health Maintenance Organizations
Division of Private Sector Liaison
Parklawn Building, Room 17A-55
5600 Fishers Lane
Rockville, Maryland 20857

People's Medical Society
14 East Minor Street
Emmaus, Pennsylvania 18049
(215) 967–2136

MEDICAL TESTING AND SURGERY

American Association of Gynecological
Laparoscopists
11239 South Lakewood Boulevard
Downey, California 90241
(213) 862–8181

American Institute of Ultrasound in Medicine
4405 East-West Highway, Suite 504
Bethesda, Maryland 20814
(301) 656–6117

American Society of Anesthesiologists
515 Busse Highway
Park Ridge, Illinois 60068
(312) 825–5586

American Society for Laser Medicine and
Surgery, Inc.
813 Second Street, Suite 200
Wausau, Wisconsin 54401
(715) 845–9283

National Second Surgical Opinion Program
(800) 638–6833; in Maryland, (800) 492–
6603
Provides help with obtaining a physician to
provide a second opinion for individuals advised
to undergo nonemergency surgery.

MEDITATION

Continental Capital of the Age of the
Enlightenment, North America
1111 H Street
Washington, D.C. 20005
(202) 783–8181

MENSTRUATION

PMS Access
Box 9326
Madison, Wisconsin 53715
(800) 222–4PMS; in Wisconsin, (608) 833–
4PMS

MISCARRIAGE

For a listing of organizations concerned with
miscarriage, see *Surviving Pregnancy Loss* by
R. Friedman and B. Gradstein, or contact
Resolve.

NATUROPATHY

National Association of Naturopathic
Physicians
2613 N. Stevens
Tacoma, Washington 98407
(206) 752–2555

National College of Naturopathic Medicine
11231 South East Market Street
Portland, Oregon 97216
(503) 255–4860

NUTRITION

American Dietetic Association
430 North Michigan Avenue
Chicago, Illinois 60611
(312) 280–5000

Center for Science in the Public Interest
1755 S Street, N.W.
Washington, D.C. 20009
(202) 332–9110

Hippocrates Health Institute
25 Exeter Street
Boston, Massachusetts 02116
(617) 267–9295

Vegetarian Association of America
P.O. Box 547
South Orange, New Jersey 07079
(201) 731–4901

OSTEOPATHY

American College of Osteopathic Obstetricians
and Gynecologists
900 Auburn Road
Pontiac, Michigan 48057
(313) 332–6360

American Osteopathic Association
212 East Ohio Street
Chicago, Illinois 60611
(312) 280–5800

OSTEOPOROSIS

American Brittle Bone Society
1256 Merrill Dr.
Marshalton, Pennsylvania 19380
(215) 692–6248

PAIN

American Society of Anesthesiologists
515 Busse Parkway
Park Ridge, Illinois 60068
(312) 825–5586

American Pain Society
70 West Hubbard, Suite 202
Chicago, Illinois 60610
(312) 644–2623

Commission on Accreditation of Rehabilitation
Facilities (CARF)
2500 North Pantano Road
Tucson, Arizona 85715
(602) 886–8575

National Chronic Pain Outreach Association
822 Wycliffe Court
Manassas, Virginia 22110
(703) 368–8884

PSYCHOTHERAPY

American Association for the Advancement of
Behavior Therapy
420 Lexington Ave.
New York, New York 10170
(212) 682–0065

American Association for Marriage and Family
Therapy
1717 K Street, N.W.
Washington, D.C. 20006
(202) 429–1825

American Family Therapy Association
2550 M Street, N.W., Suite 275
Washington, D.C. 20037
(202) 463–8510

American Mental Health Counselor's
Association
5999 Stevenson Avenue
Alexandria, Virginia 22304
(800) 354–2008

American Psychiatric Association
1700 18th Street, N.W.
Washington, D.C. 20009
(202) 797–4900

American Psychological Association
1200 17th Street, N.W.
Washington, D.C. 20036
(202) 833–7600

Association for Short-Term Psychotherapy
103 East 86th Street
New York, New York 10028
(212) 722-5521

Family Service Association of America
11700 West Lake Park Drive
Milwaukee, Wisconsin
(414) 359-2110

Mental Health Association
1800 North Kent Street
Rosslyn, Virginia 22209
(703) 528-6405

National Association of Community Health
Centers
1625 I Street, N.W., Suite 420
Washington, D.C. 20006
(202) 833-9280

National Association of Social Workers
1425 H Street, N.W., Suite 600
Washington, D.C. 20005
(202) 628-6200

National Association of Social Workers, Inc.
7981 Eastern Avenue
Silver Spring, Maryland 20910
(301) 565-0333

National Mental Health Association
1021 Prince Street
Alexandria, Virginia 22314
(703) 684-7722

National Clearinghouse for Mental Health
Information
Public Inquiries Section
5600 Fishers Lane, Room 11A-21
Rockville, Maryland 20857
(301) 443-4513

SEX

American Association of Sex Educators,
Counselors and Therapists
11 Dupont Circle
Washington, D.C. 20036
(202) 462-1171

Sex Information Council of the United States
80 Fifth Avenue, Suite 801
New York, New York 10011
(212) 673-3850

Society for the Scientific Study of Sex
P.O. Box 29795
Philadelphia, Pennsylvania 19117
(215) 782-1430

SHIATSU

Ohasi Institute
52 West 55th Street
New York, New York 10019
(212) 684-4190

Shiatsu Therapy Center
924 29th Street
Sacramento, California 95816
(916) 453-1770

SMOKING

American Lung Association
11740 Broadway
New York, New York 10019
(212) 245-8000

Office of Smoking and Health
Room 116, Parklawn Building
5600 Fishers Lane
Rockville, Maryland 20857

STRESS

The American Institute of Stress
124 Park Avenue
Yonkers, New York 10703
(914) 963-1200

Institute for Stress Management
United States International University
10455 Pomerado Road
San Diego, California 92131
(619) 693-4753

SURGEONS

American Board of Surgery
1617 John F. Kennedy Boulevard
Philadelphia, Pennsylvania 19103
(215) 568-4000

American College of Surgeons
55 East Erie Street
Chicago, Illinois 60611
(312) 664-4050

APPENDIX C

Resources: Publications

ACUPUNCTURE

Chang, S.T. *The Complete Book of Acupuncture*. Berkeley, CA: Celestial Arts, 1976.

ADOPTION

Bolles, E.B. *The Penguin Adoption Handbook*. New York: Penguin Books, 1984.

Gilman, L. *The Adoption Resource Book*. New York: Harper & Row, 1984.

Krementz, J. *How It Feels to Be Adopted*. New York: Alfred A. Knopf, 1982.

Martin, C.D. *Beating the Adoption Game*. La Jolla, CA: Oak Tree Publications, 1980.

McNamara, J. *The Adoption Advisor*. New York: Hawthorne Books, 1975.

Plumez, J.H. *Successful Adoption: A Guide to Finding a Child and Raising a Family*. New York: Crown, 1982.

Smith, J., and F. Miroff. *Your Own Child: A Social Psychological Approach to Adoption*. Boston, MA: University Press of America, 1981.

Sorosky, A.D., A. Baron, and R. Pannor. *The Adoption Triangle*. New York: Anchor Press/ Doubleday, 1978.

ALEXANDER TECHNIQUE

Stransky, J. and R.S. Stowe. *The Alexander Technique*. New York: Beaufort Books, 1981.

ALTERNATIVE THERAPIES (GENERAL)

Campbell, A., ed. *Natural Health Handbook*. Secaucus, NJ: Chartwell Books, 1984.

Hafen, B.Q., and K.J. Frandsen. *From Acupuncture to Yoga: Alternative Methods of Healing*. Englewood Cliffs, NJ: Prentice- Hall, 1983.

Hulke, M., ed. *The Encyclopedia of Alternative Medicine and Self- Help*. New York: Schocken Books, 1979.

Inglis, B., and R. West. *The Alternative Health Guide*. New York: Alfred A. Knopf, 1983.

Moore, M.C., and L.J. Moore. *The Complete Book of Holistic Health*. Englewood Cliffs, NJ: Prentice-Hall, 1983.

ANGER

Tavris, C. *Anger: The Misunderstood Emotion*. New York: Simon & Schuster, A Touchstone Book, 1982.

ASSERTIVENESS TRAINING

Bowers, S.A., and G.H. Bowers. *Asserting Yourself.* Reading, MA: Addison-Wesley, 1976.

Butler, P.E. *Self-Assertion for Women: A Guide to Becoming Androgenous.* San Francisco, CA: Canfield Press, 1976.

AUTOGENIC TRAINING

Schultz, J.H., and W. Luthe. *Autogenic Therapy* (vol. 1). New York: Grune and Stratton, 1969.

BIOFEEDBACK

Brown, B.B. *Stress and the Art of Biofeedback.* New York: Bantam Books, 1981.

CHILDBEARING: DECISION MAKING

Bombardieri, M. *The Baby Decision: How to Make the Most Important Choice of Your Life.* New York: Rawson, Wade, 1981.

Faux, M. *Childless by Choice: Choosing Childlessness in the Eighties.* New York: Doubleday, 1984.

Shealy, N.C., and M.C. Shealy. *To Parent or Not?* Virginia Beach, VA: Donning, 1981.

Whelan, E.M. *A Baby?....Maybe.* New York: Bobbs-Merrill Co., 1975.

CHIROPRACTIC

Langone, J. *Chiropractors.* Reading, MA: Addison-Wesley, 1982.

Schafer, R.C. *Chiropractic State of the Art.* Des Moines, IA: American Chiropractic Association, 1976.

COPING WITH CHRONIC ILLNESS

Cousins, N. *Anatomy of an Illness.* New York: Bantam Books, 1981.

Pitzele, S.K. *We Are Not Alone: Learning to Live with Chronic Illness.* Minneapolis, MN: Thompson & Co., 1985.

DEPRESSION

Emery, J. *A New Beginning: How You Can Change Your Life through Cognitive Therapy.* New York: Simon and Schuster, 1984.

DOCTORS

Belsky, M.S., and L. Gross. *Beyond the Medical Mystique: How to Choose and Use Your Doctor.* New York: Arbor House, 1975.

Cassell, E.J. *The Healer's Art.* Cambridge, MA: The MIT Press, 1985.

Cornacchia, H.J., and S. Barrett. *Shopping for Health Care: The Essential Guide to Products and Services.* New York: New American Library, 1982.

Freese, A.S., *Managing Your Doctor.* New York: Stein and Day, 1975.

Preston, T. *The Clay Pedestal: A Re-examination of the Doctor-Patient Relationship*. Seattle, WA: Madrona, 1981.

Scully, D. *Men Who Control Women's Health: The Education of Obstetricians and Gynecologists*. Boston: Houghton Mifflin, 1980.

DRUGS

Bressler, R., D. Bogdonoff, and G.J. Subak-Sharpe, eds. *The Physician's Drug Manual*. Garden City, NY: Biomedical Information Corp./Doubleday, 1981.

Graedon, J. *The People's Pharmacy-2*. Dresden, TN: Avon Books, 1980.

Griffith, H.W. *Complete Guide to Prescription and Non-Prescription Drugs*. Tucson, AZ: HP Books, 1983.

Long, J.W. *The Essential Guide to Prescription Drugs*. New York: Harper & Row, 1982.

Physician's Desk Reference. Oradell, NJ: Medical Economics Co., annual.

Physicians' Desk Reference for Nonprescription Drugs. Oradell, NJ: Medical Economics Co., annual.

Stern, E.L. *Prescription Drugs and Their Side Effects*. (7th ed.). New York: Putnam Publishing Group, 1984.

Zimmerman, D.R. *The Essential Guide to Non-Prescription Drugs*. New York: Harper & Row, 1983.

ENDOMETRIOSIS

Older, J. *Endometriosis*. New York: Scribner, 1984.

THE FELDENKRAIS METHOD

Rywerant, Y. *The Feldenkrais Method: Teaching by Handling*. San Francisco, CA: Harper & Row, 1983.

HERBALISM

Fulder, S. *About Ginseng*. Wellingborough, England: Thorsons, 1976.

Lust, J. *The Herb Book*. Sun Valley, CA: Lust Publications, 1974.

HOLISTIC HEALTH (BOOKS)

Bliss, S., ed. *The New Holistic Health Handbook: Living Well in a New Age*. Berkeley: The Stephen Greene Press, 1985.

Ferguson, T. *Medical Self-Care: Access to Health Tools*. New York: Summit Books, 1980.

Linde, S., and D.J. Carrow. *Directory of Holistic Medicine and Alternative Health Care Service in the United States*. Phoenix, AZ: Health Plus, 1986.

Moore, M.C., and L.J. Moore. *The Complete Handbook of Holistic Health*. Englewood Cliffs, NJ: Prentice-Hall, 1983.

Weill, A. *Health and Healing*. Boston: Houghton Mifflin, 1983.

HOLISTIC HEALTH (PERIODICALS)

Journal of Holistic Medicine

Co-Evolution Quarterly

East West Journal

Holistic Life Magazine

Holistic Health Review

Journal of Health Science

Let's Live

Medical Self Care Magazine

New Age Journal

Prevention

Well Being

Vegetarian Times

Whole Life Times

Wholistic Living News

HOMEOPATHY

Cummings, S., and D. Ullman. *Everybody's Guide to Homeopathic Medicine.* Los Angeles: J.D. Tarcher, 1984.

Vithoulkas, G. *Homeopathy: Medicine of the New Man.* New York: Arco, 1979.

THE HOSPITAL EXPERIENCE

Gots, R., and A. Kaufman. *The People's Hospital Book.* New York: Crown, 1978.

Huttman, B. *The Patient's Advocate: The Complete Book of Patient's Rights.* Harmondsworth, England: Penguin Books, 1981.

Inlander, C.B., and E. Weiner, *Take This Book to the Hospital with You: A Consumer's Guide to Surviving Your Hospital Stay.* Emmaus, PA: Rodale Press, 1985.

Nierenberg, J., and F. Janovic. *The Hospital Experience: A Guide for Patients and Their Families.* New York: Berkley Books, 1985.

HYPNOSIS

Hilgard, R., and J.R. Hilgard. *Hypnosis in the Relief of Pain.* Los Altos, CA: W. Kaufmann, 1983.

Kelly, S.F., and R.J. Kelly. *Hypnosis: Understanding How It Can Work for You.* Reading, MA: Addison-Wesley, 1985.

HYSTERECTOMY/MENOPAUSE/SURGICAL MENOPAUSE

Budoff, P.W. *No More Hot Flashes and Other Good News*. New York: G.P. Putnam, 1983.

Cutler, W.B., C.R. Garcia, and D.A. Edwards. *Menopause: A Guide for Women and the Men Who Love Them*. New York: W.W. Norton, 1983.

Fonda, J., with M. McCarthy. *Women Coming of Age*. New York: Simon & Schuster, 1984.

Greenwood, S. *Menopause Naturally*. San Francisco, CA: Volcano Press, 1984.

Morgan, S. *Coping with a Hysterectomy*. New York: Dial Press, 1982.

Reitz, R. *Menopause: A Positive Approach*. Harmondsworth, England: Penguin Books, 1983.

Seaman, B., and G. Seaman. *Women and the Crisis in Sex Hormones*. New York: Bantam Books, 1981.

Wigfall-Williams, W. *Hysterectomy: Learning the Facts, Coping with the Feelings, Facing the Future*. New York: Michael Kesend, 1986.

IMAGERY

Achterberg, J. *Imagery in Healing: Shamanism and Modern Medicine*. Boston: New Science Library, Shambhala, 1985.

Block, N. *Imagery*. Cambridge, MA: MIT Press, 1981.

Fry, A. *Visualization: Directing the Movies of Your Mind*. New York: Barnes & Noble Books, 1978.

Samuels, M., and N. Samuels. *Seeing with the Mind's Eye*. New York: Random House/Bookworks, 1983.

Singer, J.L., and E. Switzer. *Mind-Play: The Creative Uses of Fantasy*. Englewood Cliffs, NJ: Prentice-Hall, 1980.

INFERTILITY

For an extensive bibliography of books on all aspects of infertility (including miscarriage and adoption), contact Resolve. (See Appendix B.)

Amelar, R.D., L. Dubin, and P.C. Walsh. *Male Infertility*. Philadelphia: W.B. Saunders, 1977.

Andrews, L.B. *New Conceptions: A Consumer's Guide to the Newest Infertility Treatments*. New York: St. Martin's Press, 1984.

Bellina, J.H., and J. Wilson. *You Can Have a Baby*. New York: Crown, 1985.

Burgwyn, D. *Marriage Without Children*. New York: Harper & Row, 1981.

Corson, S.L., *Conquering Infertility*. East Norwalk, CT: Appleton-Century-Crofts, 1983.

Friedman, R., and B. Gradstein. *Surviving Pregnancy Loss*. Boston: Little, Brown, 1982.

Keane, N.P. *The Surrogate Mother*. New York: Everest House, 1981.

Menning, B.E. *Infertility: A Guide for Childless Couples*. Englewood Cliffs, NJ: Prentice-Hall, 1977.

Mitchard, J.M. *Mother Less Child*. New York: W.W. Norton, 1985.

Peck, E., and J. Senderowitz. *Pronatalism: The Myth of Mom and Apple Pie*. New York: Thomas Y. Crowell, 1974.

Stangel, J.J. *Fertility and Conception: An Essential Guide for Childless Couples*. New York: New American Library, 1979.

LOSS AND GRIEF

Kushner, H. *When Bad Things Happen to Good People*. New York: Schocken Books, 1981.

Ramsay, R.W., and R. Noorbergen. *Living With Loss*. New York: William Morrow, 1981.

Tatelbaum, J. *The Courage to Grieve*. New York: Harper & Row, 1980.

MACROBIOTICS (BOOKS)

Kushi, M. *Natural Healing Through Macrobiotics*. Tokyo: Japan Publications, 1978.

Kushi, M., and C. Millman. *Infertility and Reproductive Disorders*. Tokyo: Japan Publications, 1986.

MACROBIOTICS (PERIODICALS)

East West Journal, published by the East West Foundation

Macrobiotics Today, published by the George Ohsawa Foundation

Macromuse, published by the Macrobiotic Education Association

MASSAGE

Downing, G. *The Massage Book*. New York: Random House/Bodyworks, 1972.

Downing, G. *Massage and Meditation*. New York: Random House, 1974.

MEDICAL TESTING AND SURGERY

Curtis, L.R., G.B. Curtis, and M.K. Beard. *My Body-My Decision: What You Should Know About the Most Common Female Surgeries*. Tucson, AZ: HP Books, 1986.

Denny, M.K. *Second Opinion*. New York: Grosset & Dunlap, 1979.

Galton, L. *The Patient's Guide to Surgery*. New York: Hearst Books, 1976.

Fox, M.L., and T.G. Schnabel. *It's Your Body: Know What the Doctor Ordered!* Bowie, MD: The Charles Press, 1979.

Isenberg, S., and L.M. Elting. *The Consumer's Guide to Successful Surgery*. New York: St. Martin's Press, 1976.

Klein, A.E. *Medical Tests and You*. New York: Grosset and Dunlap, 1978.

McDonald, J.A. *Facing the Scalpel*. Englewood Cliffs, NJ: Prentice-Hall, 1981.

Moskowitz, M.A., and M.E. Osband. *The Book of Medical Tests*. New York: W.W. Norton, 1984.

Sobel, D.S., and T. Ferguson. *The People's Book of Medical Tests*. New York: Summit Books, A Medical Self-Care Book, 1985.

MEDITATION

Benson, H., and M.S. Klipper. *The Relaxation Response.* New York: Avon Books, 1976.

Bloomfield, H., M. Cains, and D. Jaffe. *TM: Discovering Inner Energy and Overcoming Stress.* New York: Delacorte, 1975.

LeShan, L. *How to Meditate.* New York: Bantam Books, 1984.

MENSTRUATION

Delaney, J., M.J. Lupton, and E. Toth. *The Curse: A Cultural History of Menstruation.* New York: New American Library, A Mentor Book, 1977.

Harrison, M. *Self-Help for Premenstrual Syndrome.* New York: Random House, 1982.

Schrotenboer, K., and G.J. Subak-Sharpe. *Freedom from Menstrual Cramps.* New York: Pocket Books, 1981.

Weideger, P. *Menstruation and Menopause: The Physiology and Psychology, the Myth and the Reality.* New York: Alfred A. Knopf, 1976.

MISCARRIAGE

Berezin, N. *After a Loss in Pregnancy.* New York: Simon and Schuster, 1982.

Borg, S., and J. Lasker. *When Pregnancy Fails: Families Coping with Miscarriage, Stillbirth, and Infant Death.* Boston: Beacon Press, 1981.

Friedman, R., and B. Gradstein. *Surviving Pregnancy Loss.* Boston: Little, Brown, 1982.

Panuthos, C., and C. Romeo. *Ended Beginnings: Healing Childbearing Losses.* South Hadley, MA: Bergin and Garvey, 1984.

NATUROPATHY

Turner, R.N. *Naturopathic Medicine: Treating the Whole Person.* Wellingborough, England: Thorsons, 1984.

NUTRITION

Airola, P. *Every Woman's Book.* Phoenix, AZ: Health Plus, 1979.

Brody, J. *Jane Brody's Nutrition Book.* New York: Bantam, 1987.

Lappe, F.M. *Diet for a Small Planet.* New York: Ballantine, 1982.

Passwater, R.A. *Selenium as Food and Medicine.* New Canaan, CT: Keats Publishing, 1980.

OSTEOPATHY

Chaitow, L., N.D., D.O. *Osteopathy: Head-to-Toe Health Through Manipulation.* Wellingborough, England: Thorsons, 1974.

OSTEOPOROSIS

Notelowitz, M., and M. Ware. *Stand Tall! Every Woman's Guide to Preventing Osteoporosis.* Gainesville, FL: Triad Publishing, 1982.

Smith, W., and S.H. Cohn. *Osteoporosis: How to Prevent the Brittle Bone Disease.* New York: Simon & Schuster, 1985.

PAIN

Bresler, D.E., and R. Trubo. *Free Yourself From Pain.* New York: Simon & Schuster, A Wallaby Book, 1979.

Bogen, M. *The Path to Pain Control.* Boston, MA: Houghton Mifflin, 1982.

Shealy, C.N. *The Pain Game.* Berkeley, CA: Celestial Arts, 1976.

Smoller, B., and B. Schulman. *Pain Control: The Bethesda Program.* Garden City, NY: Doubleday, 1982.

Whitbread, J. *Stop Hurting! Start Living! The Pain Control Book.* New York: Dell, A Delta Book, 1981.

REFLEXOLOGY

Canter, M. *Helping Yourself With Foot Reflexology.* Parker Publishing, 1969.

Kunz, K. and B. Kunz. *The Complete Guide to Foot Reflexology.* Englewood Cliffs, NJ: Prentice-Hall, 1980.

Rick, S. *The Reflexology Workout.* New York: Crown, 1986.

RELAXATION TRAINING (AUDIOCASSETTES)

For audiocassettes and other resources concerning relaxation training, contact:

Yes! Bookshop
1035 31st Street, N.W.
Washington, D.C. 20007
(202) 338-2727

"Laura Hitchcock's Deep Muscle Relaxation for Surgery Patients," an audiocassette, is available from
Dr. Laura Hitchcock
7802 Marion Lane
Bethesda, Maryland 20808

SELF-ESTEEM

Sanford, L.T., and M. Donovan. *Women and Self-Esteem: Understanding and Improving the Way We Think and Feel About Ourselves.* Garden City, NY: Anchor Press/Doubleday, 1984.

SEX

Barbach, L. *For Each Other: Sharing Sexual Intimacy.* Garden City, NY: Anchor Books/Doubleday, 1983.

Barbach, L. *For Yourself: The Fulfillment of Female Sexuality.* New York: Doubleday, 1975.

Broderick, C. *Couples: How to Confront Problems and Maintain Loving Relationships.* New York: Simon & Schuster, 1979.

Comfort, A. *The Joy of Sex.* New York: Crown, 1972.

Friday, N. *My Secret Garden: Women's Sexual Fantasies.* New York: Pocket Books, 1973.

Hite, S. *The Hite Report.* New York: Dell, 1981.

Kaplan, H.S. *Illustrated Manual of Sex Therapy.* New York: Quadrangle/New York Times, 1975.

Kaplan, H. *The New Sex Therapy.* New York: Bruner/Mazel, 1974.

Masters, W.H., and V.E. Johnson. *Human Sexual Response.* New York: Bantam Books, 1981.

Masters, W.H., V.E. Johnson, and R. Kolodny. *Masters and Johnson on Sex and Human Loving.* Boston: Little, Brown, 1986.

McCarthy, B., and E. McCarthy. *Sexual Awareness: Enhancing Sexual Pleasure.* New York: Carroll and Graf, 1984.

STRESS

Benson, H. *Beyond the Relaxation Response.* New York: Berkley Books, 1985.

Benson, H., and M.Z. Klipper. *The Relaxation Response.* New York: Avon Books, 1976.

Brown, B.B. *Between Health and Illness.* Boston: Houghton Mifflin, 1984. Reprinted by Bantam Books, 1985.

Greenberg, J.S. *Managing Stress: A Personal Guide.* Dubuque, IA: William C. Brown, 1984.

Pelletier, K.R. *Mind as Healer, Mind as Slayer: A Holistic Approach to Preventing Stress Disorders.* New York: Dell, A Delta Book, 1977.

Selye, H. *Stress Without Distress.* New York: Harper & Row, 1974. Reprinted by Signet, New American Library, 1975.

Selye, H. *The Stress of Life* (rev. ed.). New York: McGraw-Hill, 1978.

THERAPY AND THERAPEUTIC TECHNIQUES

Adams, S., and R. Orgel. *Through the Mental Health Maze.* Washington, DC: Health Research Group, 2000 P Street, N.W., Washington, DC 20036.

Ehrenberg, O., and M. Ehrenberg. *The Psychotherapy Maze: A Consumer's Guide to the Ins and Outs of Therapy.* New York: Holt, Rinehart and Winston, 1977.

Emery, G. *A New Beginning: How You Can Change Your Life Through Cognitive Therapy.* New York: Simon & Schuster, A Touchstone Book, 1981.

Emery, G., and J. Campbell. *Rapid Relief from Emotional Distress.* New York: Rawson Associates, 1986.

Fisch, S.C. *Choosing a Psychotherapist: A Consumer's Guide to Mental Health Treatment.* Waterford, MI: Minerva Press,

Kovel, J. *A Complete Guide to Therapy: From Psychoanalysis to Behavior Modification.* New York: Pantheon Books, 1976.

Quinnett, P. *The Troubled People Book.* New York: Continuum, 1982.

Rathus, S.A., and J.S. Nevid. *Behavior Therapy: Strategies for Solving Problems in Living.* New York: Signet, New American Library, 1977.

Rubin, T.I. *Overcoming Indecisiveness: The Eight Stages of Effective Decision-Making.* New York: Avon Books, 1985.

U.S. Department of Health and Human Services. *A Consumer's Guide to Mental Health Services.* Publication Number (adm) 80–214. Rockville, MD: National Institute of Mental Health.

TRIGGER POINT MYOTHERAPY

Prudden, B. *Myotherapy.* Garden City, NY: Dial Press, Doubleday, 1981.

YOGA

Sivananda Yoga Center. *The Sivananda Companion to Yoga.* New York: Simon & Schuster, 1985.

Yoga Journal

APPENDIX D

Resources: Scientific Literature

ENDOMETRIOSIS

Chalmers, J.A. *Endometriosis*. London: Butterworth, 1975.

Goodall, J.R. *A Study of Endometriosis*. Philadelphia: J.B. Lippincott, 1943.

Raynaud, J.P., L. Martini, and T. Ojasoo, eds. *Medical Management of Endometriosis*. New York: Raven Press, 1984.

GYNECOLOGY AND FERTILITY (TEXTBOOKS)

Aiman, J., ed. *Infertility: Diagnosis and Management*. New York: Springer-Verlag, 1984.

Buttram, V.C., Jr., and R.C. Reiter. *Surgical Treatment of the Infertile Female*. Baltimore: Williams & Wilkins, 1985.

Jones, H., and G.S. Jones. *Novak's Textbook of Gynecology*. 3rd student ed. Baltimore: Williams and Wilkins, 1981.

Kistner, R.W. *Gynecology: Principles and Practices*. Chicago: Year Book, 1986.

Mishell, D., and V. Davajan, eds. *Reproductive Endocrinology, Infertility and Contraception*. Philadelphia: F.A. Davis, 1979.

Wilson, J.R., and E.R. Carrington. *Obstetrics and Gynecology*. St. Louis: C.V. Mosby, 1979.

OBSTETRICS AND GYNECOLOGY (PERIODICALS)

American Journal of Obstetrics and Gynecology

Biology of Reproduction

British Journal of Obstetrics and Gynecology

Contemporary Obstetrics and Gynecology

Clinical Obstetrics and Gynecology

Clinics in Obstetrics and Gynecology

Current Problems in Obstetrics and Gynecology

Endocrinology

Fertility and Sterility

Journal of Gynecology and Reproductive Biology
Journal of Obstetrical, Gynecological, and Neonatal Nursing
Journal of Reproductive Medicine
Obstetrical and Gynecological Survey
Obstetrics and Gynecology
Seminars in Reproductive Endocrinology

APPENDIX E

Pain Management Centers

There are hundreds of pain centers in the United States. To locate a pain center, ask your doctor, your county medical association, hospital, or medical school, the American Association of Anesthesiologists, or the Commission on Accreditation of Rehabilitation Facilities. Below is a sampling of pain management centers.

Boston Pain Center
Massachusetts Rehabilitation Hospital
125 Nashua Street
Boston, Massachusetts 12114
(617) 523–1818

Columbia-Presbyterian Medical Center Pain Treatment Service
622 West 168th Street
New York, New York 10032
(202) 694–7114

Duke Pain Clinic
Duke University Medical Center
Durham, North Carolina 27710
(919) 684–6542

Emory Pain Control Center
1441 Clifton Road, N.E.
Atlanta, Georgia 30322
(404) 329–5492

Georgetown University Medical Center Pain Clinic
3800 Reservoir Road
Washington, D.C. 20007
(202) 625–7163

The Johns Hopkins Hospital Pain Treatment Center
Meyer Building, Room 279
Baltimore, Maryland 21205
(301) 955–3270

Mayo Clinic Pain Management Center
St. Mary's Hospital
5-D East
Rochester, Minnesota 55902
(507) 284–8311

Mercy Hospital Center for Chronic Pain and Disability Rehabilitation
301 North Jefferson Davis Parkway
New Orleans, Louisiana 70119
(504) 486–7361, ext. 350

Mt. Sinai Medical Center
The Pain Center
4300 Alton Road
Miami Beach, Florida 33140
(305) 674–2070

Nebraska Pain Management Center
University of Nebraska Hospital
42nd Street and Dewey Avenue
Omaha, Nebraska 68105
(402) 559–4000

New York University Medical Center
Comprehensive Pain Center
550 First Avenue
New York, New York 10016
(212) 340–7316

Northwest Pain Center
10615 South East Cherry Blossom Drive
Portland, Oregon 97216
(503) 256–1930

Rush Pain Center
Rush-Presbyterian Hospital
1725 West Harrison Street, Suite 162
Chicago, Illinois 60612
(312) 942–6631

Scripps Clinic and Research Foundation Pain Treatment Center
La Jolla, California 92037
(714) 455–9100

Temple University Hospital Pain Control Center

3401 North Broad Street
Philadelphia, Pennsylvania 19140
(215) 221–2100

University of Texas Pain Service
Hermann Professional Building
Suite 712
Houston, Texas 77030
(713) 792–5761

University of Virginia Pain Center
University of Virginia Medical Center
Charlottesville, Virginia 22908
(804) 924–6681

University of Wisconsin Clinical Science Center Pain Clinic
600 Highland Avenue
Madison, Wisconsin 53792
(608) 263–8094

UCLA Pain Management Center
Pelvic Pain Program
Department of Anesthesiology
UCLA School of Medicine
10833 Le Conte
Los Angeles, CA 90024
(213) 825-4291

APPENDIX F

Tracking the Symptoms of Endometriosis: Sample Charts

Place a number from one to four for each symptom (see key below) in the box corresponding to the date on which symptoms occur. Use the spaces at the bottom of the chart to indicate symptoms not listed and to add any additional comments. If you take medication for symptoms, note type of medication and indicate, in the space for comments, whether or not it is effective.

1 mild (light)
2 moderate (medium)
3 severe (heavy)
4 incapacitating (i.e., disrupts work, sleep, or interferes with mobility)

MONTH _____

DATE	1	2	3	4	5	6	7	8	9	10	11	12	13	14	15	16	17	18	19	20	21	22	23	24	25	26	27	28	29	30	31
SYMPTOMS																															
Menstruation																															
Cramps																															
Pelvic pain																															
Dyspareunia																															
Pain in area of ovary																															

Backache

Breast
discharge

Nausea

Vomiting

Rectal pain

Rectal
bleeding

Gastrointestinal
pain or cramps

Diarrhea

Constipation

Urgency to
defecate

Straining with
defecation

Blood in stools

Pain near
naval

Sharp gas
pains

Abdominal bloating																
Pain upon urination																
Burning upon urination																
Pus or blood in urine																
Urinary frequency																
Urinary urgency																
Urinary retention																
Pain in side																
Pain in groin																
Fever in degrees																
Headache																
Tenderness around kidneys																
Extreme fatigue																
Coughing of blood																

Chest pain

Shoulder pain

Shortness of
breath

Pain in hip,
leg, or thigh

Other symptoms
(Specify)

Comments

Notes

PART 1 INTRODUCTION

1. John M. Leventhal, in foreword to Ronald Batt and John D. Naples, "Endometriosis," *Current Problems in Obstetrics and Gynecology* 6 (1982):5.

2. Robert B. Greenblatt, ed., in foreword to *Recent Advances in Endometriosis*, International Congress, Serial No. 638 (New York: Elsevier, 1976).

3. Neal E. Krupp, "Adaptation to chronic illness," *Postgraduate Medicine* 60 (1978):124.

CHAPTER 1

1. *The Tampax Report* (Lake Success, NY: Tambrands, 1981), 5.

2. Barbara Ehrenreich and Deirdre English, *For Her Own Good: 150 Years of Expert Advice to Women* (Garden City, NY: Anchor Press/Doubleday, Anchor Books Edition, 1979), 211.

3. William S. Kroger and S. C. Freed, *Psychosomatic Gynecology* (Philadelphia: W.B. Saunders, 1951), 237.

4. Ibid.

5. Janet Delaney, Mary Jane Lupton, and Emily Toth, *The Curse* (New York: E.P. Dutton, 1976), 106.

6. *The Tampax Report*, 2–5.

7. Robert W. Kistner, *Gynecology: Principles and Practices* (Chicago: Year Book Publishers, 1979), 630.

8. James Walker, Ian MacGillivray, and Malcolm C. MacNaughton, *Combined Textbook of Obstetrics and Gynecology*, 9th ed. (Edinburgh: Churchill Livingstone, 1976), 596, 666.

9. Delaney, Lupton, and Toth, *The Curse*, 2–7.

10. Gena Corea, *The Hidden Malpractice: How American Medicine Mistreats Women*, rev. ed. (New York: Harper & Row, Colophon Books, 1985), 268.

11. Charles K. Wright, in discussion of James R. Dingfelder, "Primary dysmenorrhea treatment with prostaglandin inhibitors: A review," *American Journal of Obstetrics and Gynecology* 140 (1981): 878.

12. Lynda Madaras and Jane Patterson, *Womancare*.(New York: Avon, 1984), 611.

13. M. Yusoff Dawood, "Etiology and treatment of dysmenorrhea," *Seminars in Reproductive Endocrinology* 3 (1985):287.

14. Ibid.

15. Mason C. Andrews, in discussion of James R. Dingfelder, "Primary dysmenorrhea treatment with prostaglandin inhibitors: A review," *American Journal of Obstetrics and Gynecology* 140 (1981):877.

CHAPTER 2

1. Robert W. Kistner, *Gynecology: Principles and Practices*, 4th ed. (Chicago: Year Book, 1979), 398.

2. Ibid., 395.

3. *Important Facts about Endometriosis* (Washington, DC: American College of Obstetricians and Gynecologists, 1981), 6.

4. Daniel R. Mishell and Val Davajan, *Reproductive Endocrinology, Infertility, and Contraception* (Philadelphia: F.A. Davis, 1979), 432.

5. Kistner, *Gynecology*, 444.

6. Jean-Pierre Raynaud, Luciano Martini, and Tiiu Ojasoo, eds., *Medical Management of Endometriosis* (New York: Raven Press, 1984), 27

7. *Vital and Health Statistics: Patterns of Ambulatory Care in Obstetrics and Gynecology* (Hyattsville, MD: U.S. Department of Health and Human Services, 1984), 32.

8. The lower figure is cited in W. Paul Dmowski and Ewa Radwanska, "Current concepts on pathology, histogenesis and etiology of endometriosis," *Acta Obstet Gynecol Scand* (Suppl.) 123 (1984):73; the higher figure is cited in Veasy C. Buttram, Jr., and John W. Betts, "Endometriosis," *Current Problems in Obstetrics and Gynecology* 2 (1979):5.

9. U.S. Department of Commerce, Bureau of Census, *Statistical Abstract of the United States*, 106 ed., 24.

10. David W. Cramer et al., "The relationship of endometriosis to menstrual characteristics, smoking, and exercise," *The Journal of the American Medical Association* 244 (1986): 1904.

11. S. Jenkins, David L. Olive, and Arthur F. Haney, "Endometriosis: Pathogenetic implications of the anatomic distribution," *Obstetrics and Gynecology* 67 (1986): 335.

12. Jouko Halme et al., "Retrograde menstruation in healthy women and in patients with endometriosis," *Obstetrics and Gynecology* 64 (1984): 151.

13. David Redwine, telephone conversation with author, March 1986.

14. Dmowski and Radwanska, "Current concepts," 32.

15. Ibid.

16. George T. Schneider discussing L. Russell Malinak et al., "Heritable aspects of endometriosis II: Clinical characteristics of familial endometriosis," *American Journal of Obstetrics and Gynecology* 137 (1980): 335.

17. Julia Older, *Endometriosis* (New York: Charles Scribner's Sons, 1984), 121.

18. Claudia Wallis, "The career woman's disease?" in *Time*, April 28, 1986, p. 62.

19. David Redwine, poster presentation at the American Fertility Society annual meeting, Chicago, September–October 1985.

20. Brooks Ranney, "The prevention, inhibition, palliation, and treatment of endometriosis," *American Journal of Obstetrics and Gynecology* 123 (December 1975): 780.

21. Veasy C. Buttram, Jr., "Cyclic use of combination oral contraceptives and the severity of endometriosis," *Fertility and Sterility* 31 (1979): 348.

22. David L. Cramer, et al. "Association of endometriosis with oral contraceptive use," American Fertility Society annual meeting, Abstract No. 328, September 1986.

23. David L. Cramer et al., "The relationship of endometriosis to menstrual characteristics, smoking, and exercise." *Journal of the American Medical Association* 224 (14): 1906.

24. Kistner, *Gynecology*, 402.

25. James Robert Goodall, *A study of endometriosis, endosalpingiosis, endocervicosis, and peritoneo-ovarian sclerosis* (Philadelphia: J. B. Lippincott, 1943), 134.

26. Joe Vincent Meigs, "Endometriosis: Etiologic role of marriage, age, and parity; conservative treatment," *Obstetrics and Gynecology* 2 (1953): 47. (Read before the American College of Surgeons, New York, September 23, 1952.)

27. Charles F. Cobb, "Endometriosis in the general surgical patient," *Surgical Rounds* 8 (1985): 69.

CHAPTER 3

1. Veasy C. Buttram, Jr., and John W. Betts, "Endometriosis," *Current Problems in Obstetrics and Gynecology* 2 (1979): 8.

2. M. Yusoff Dawood, *Dysmenorrhea* (Baltimore: Williams & Wilkins, 1981), 132.

3. Nicole Jonys, John H. Boutselis, and Anthony S. Neri, "Endometriosis," in *Gynecologic Endocrinology*, eds. Jay T. Gold and John B. Josimovich (Hagerstown: Harper & Row, 1980), 434.

4. Cecilia L. Schmidt, presentation at the Endometriosis Symposium, New York University Postgraduate Medical School, October 18, 1985.

5. Edward R. Samper, Gene W. Slagle, and Albert M. Hand, "Colonic endometriosis: its clinical spectrum," Southern Medical Journal 77 (1984): 912.

6. Claire Kane and Pierre Drouin, "Obstructive uropathy associated with endometriosis," *American Journal of Obstetrics and Gynecology* 151 (1985): 207.

7. Cecilia Schmidt, Endometriosis Symposium, New York University Postgraduate Medical School, October 18, 1985.

8. Kane and Drouin, "Obstructive uropathy," 207.

CHAPTER 4

1. Jaroslav F. Hulka, *Textbook of Laparoscopy* (New York: Grune and Stratton, 1985), 103.

2. Veasy C. Buttram, Jr., and Robert C. Reiter, *Surgical Treatment of the Infertile Female* (Baltimore: Williams & Wilkins, 1985), 98.

3. James Aiman, ed., *Infertility: Diagnosis and Management* (New York: Springer-Verlag, 1981) 257.

4. Veasy C. Buttram, Jr., "Conservative surgery for endometriosis in the infertile female: A study of 106 patients with implications for both medical and surgical therapy," *Fertility and Sterility* 31 (1979): 12.

5. Aiman, *Infertility*, 257.

6. Donald P. Goldstein, Corrine De Cholnoky, and S. Jean Emans, "Adolescent endometriosis," *Journal of Adolescent Health Care* 1 (1980): 37.

7. David Redwine, poster presentation at the American Fertility Society annual meeting, Chicago, September–October, 1985.

8. Dr. Charles W. Hohler, vice-president of the American Institute of Ultrasound in Medicine, Bethesda, Maryland, in letter to author, November 3, 1985.

9. Robert L. Barbieri, "CA-125 in patients with endometriosis," *Fertility and Sterility* 45 (1986): 768

CHAPTER 5

1. Roger W. Miller, "Doctors, patients don't communicate," *FDA Consumer*, July–August 1983. (reprint).

2. Antti Kauppila and Lars Ronnberg, "Naproxen sodium in dysmenorrhea secondary to endometriosis," *Obstetrics and Gynecology* 65 (1985): 379.

3. Buttram, "Cyclic use of oral contraceptives," 348.

CHAPTER 6

1. Buttram and Reiter, *Surgical Treatment*, 105.

2. James Aiman, *Infertility*, 261.

3. Schmidt, "Endometriosis: A reappraisal," 163.

4. Robert L. Barbieri and Robert W. Kistner, "Hormonal therapy of endometriosis," in *Medical Management of Endometriosis*, ed. Jean-Pierre Raynaud et al. (New York: Raven Press, 1984), 31.

5. W. Paul Dmowski, presentation at the American Fertility Society annual meeting, Chicago, September–October 1985.

6. Aiman, *Infertility*, 261.

7. Schmidt, "Endometriosis: A reappraisal," 163.

8. Robert B. Greenblatt et al., "Clinical studies with an antigonadotropin—Danazol," *Fertility and Sterility* 22 (1971): 102.

9. W. Paul Dmowski, in interview with author, March 1986.

10. Dmowski and Radwanska, "Current concepts," 76.

11. Raynaud et al., *Medical Management of Endometriosis*, 33.

12. W. Paul Dmowski, in presentation at the American Fertility Society annual meeting, Chicago, September–October 1985.

13. Ibid.

14. Ibid.

15. Aiman, *Infertility*, 262.

16. Brooks Ranney, "Operative treatment of endometriosis," in *Reid's Controversy in Obstetrics and Gynecology*, ed. F. P. Zuspan and C. D. Christian (Philadelphia: W. B. Saunders, 1983), 548.

17. Dmowski and Radwanska, "Endometriosis and infertility," *Acta Obstet Gynecol Scand*, Suppl. 123 (1984):76.

18. W. Paul Dmowski, presentation at the American Fertility Society annual meeting, Chicago, September–October 1985.

19. Ibid.

20. Ibid.

21. Buttram and Reiter, *Surgical Treatment*, 108.

22. David Meldrum, "Management of endometriosis with gonadotropin-releasing hormone agonists," *Fertility and Sterility* 44 (1985):581.

23. Schmidt, "Endometriosis: A reappraisal," 167.

CHAPTER 7

1. Janet W. McArthur and Howard Ulfelder, "The effect of pregnancy upon endometriosis," *Obstetrics and Gynecology Survey* 20 (1965):709.

2. Ibid.

3. Goodall, *A study of endometriosis*, 134.

4. Meigs, "Endometriosis: Etiologic role," 46.

5. McArthur and Ulfelder, "The effect of pregnancy," 719.

6. Leslie A. Walton, "A reexamination of endometriosis after pregnancy," *Journal of Reproductive Medicine* 19 (1977):341.

7. Brooks Ranney, "The prevention...of Endometriosis," 779.

8. Brooks Ranney, "Endometriosis: Pathogenesis, symptoms, and findings," *Clinical Obstetrics and Gynecology* 23 (1980):878.

9. Walker et al. *Combined Textbook*, 769.

CHAPTER 8

1. Brooks Ranney, "Operative treatment of endometriosis," in *Reid's Controversy in Obstetrics and Gynecology*, 556.

2. Veasy C. Buttram, Jr., presentation at the American Fertility Society annual meeting, Chicago, September–October 1985.

3. Ibid.

4. Ibid.

5. Donald E. Pittaway, "Appendectomy in the surgical treatment of endometriosis," *Obstetrics and Gynecology* 61 (1983):421.

6. Aiman, *Infertility*, 261.

7. Aiman, *Infertility*, 265.

8. Aiman, *Infertility*, 264.

9. Schmidt, "Endometriosis: A reappraisal," 168.

10. Aiman, *Infertility*, 264–265.

11. Schmidt, "Endometriosis: A reappraisal," 168.

12. James M. Wheeler and L. Russell Malinak, "Recurrent endometriosis: Incidence, management, and prognosis," *American Journal of Obstetrics and Gynecology* 146 (1983):247.

13. Buttram and Reiter, *Surgical Treatment*, 116.

14. James M. Wheeler and L. Russell Malinak, paper presented at the American Fertility Society annual meeting, Chicago, September–October 1985.

15. Aiman, *Infertility*, 265.

16. Wheeler and Malinak, paper presented at the American Fertility Society annual meeting, Chicago, September–October 1985.

17. Ibid.

18. *Endometriosis Association Newsletter* (October 1983), 9.

19. Aiman, *Infertility*, 265.

20. Buttram and Reiter, *Surgical Treatment*, 130.

CHAPTER 9

1. Charles B. Hammond and Wayne S. Maxson, "Current status of estrogen replacement therapy for the menopause," *Fertility and Sterility* 37 (1982): 5.

2. Ibid, 11.

3. Firaud V. Foster, Howard A. Zacur, and John A. Rock, "Hot flashes in postmenopausal women ameliorated by danazol," *Fertility and Sterility* 43 (1985): 404.

4. D.H. Richards, "A post-hysterectomy syndrome," *The Lancet* (October 26, 1974): 983–985.

5. Morris Notelovitz and Marsha Ware, *Stand Tall!: Every Woman's Guide to Preventing Osteoporosis* (Toronto: Bantam Books, 1985): 17, 55.

6. Mishell and Davajan, *Reproductive Endocrinology*, 475.

7. Wendy Smith, in consultation with Dr. Stanton H. Cohn, *Osteoporosis: How to Prevent the Brittle-Bone Disease* (New York: Simon & Schuster, 1985), 19.

8. Barbara Seaman and Gideon Seaman, *Women and the Crisis in Sex Hormones* (New York: Bantam Books, 1981), 351.

9. Ibid., 351.

10. Ibid., 355.

11. Dr. Margaret Davis, interview with author, March 1986.

12. R. Don Gambrell, Jr., "The menopause: Benefits and risks of estrogen-progestogen replacement therapy," *Fertility and Sterility* 37 (April 1982): 470.

13. Mishell and Davajan, *Reproductive Endocrinology*, 475.

14. Valerie Miller, assistant professor at George Washington University Medical Center, quoted in George Washington University news release, September 4, 1984.

15. Mishell and Davajan, *Reproductive Endocrinology*, 475.

16. Gambrell, "The menopause," 469.

CHAPTER 10

1. Rafael Jewelewicz, presentation at Endometriosis Symposium, New York University Postgraduate Medical School, October 18, 1985.

2. Deborah Metzger et al., "Association of endometriosis and spontaneous abortion: Effect of control group selection," *Fertility and Sterility* 45 (January 1986): 18.

PART 3 INTRODUCTION

1. Eric J. Cassell, *The Healer's Art* (Cambridge, MA: MIT Press, 1985), 26.

CHAPTER 12

1. Dr. Linda Kames, interview with author, March 1986.

2. Dr. Elizabeth Herz, interview with author, March 1986.

CHAPTER 14

1. Robert H. Dworkin, et al., "Predicting treatment response in depressed and non-depressed pain patients," *Pain* 24 (1986):343–351.

2. Patricia Mahlstedt, "The psychological component of infertility," *Fertility and Sterility* 43 (March 1985): 343.

3. Helen Kaplan Singer, *Illustrated Manual of Sex Therapy* (New York: Quadrangle/New York Times, 1975), 99.

CHAPTER 16

1. Thomas Preston, *The Clay Pedestal: A Re-examination of the Doctor-Patient Relationship* (Seattle: Madrona, 1981), 211.

2. Theodore Isaac Rubin, *Overcoming Indecisiveness: The Eight Stages of Effective Decision-Making* (New York: Avon, 1985), 448.

3. Andrea Shrednick, "The emotional outlet," *Perspectives on Infertility* 2 (Yorktown Heights, New York: The Center for Communications in Infertility, November/December 1983), 8.

CHAPTER 17

1. Elyse Singer, in presentation to the Washington, D.C., Chapter of the Endometriosis Association, November 1985.

2. Judith B. Walker and Ronald L. Katz, "Peripheral nerve stimulation in the management of dysmenorrhea," *Pain* 11 (1981): 355–356.

3. Herbert Benson, *The Relaxation Response* (New York: Avon, 1976), 159–160.

4. David Bresler and Richard Trubo, *Free Yourself From Pain* (New York: Simon & Schuster, A Wallaby Book, 1979), 189.

5. Milton V. Kline, interview with author, March 1986.

CHAPTER 18

1. J. Polsinelli, executive director of the American College of Osteopathic Obstetricians and Gynecologists, letter to author, November 26, 1985.

2. Bruce Miller, "Natural healing through naturopathy," *East West Journal* (December 1985), 57.

3. Ibid., 58.

Glossary

Adenomyosis. A condition similar to endometriosis, previously called *endometriosis interna*, in which the endometrium invades the uterine musculature.

Adhesions. Bands of fibrous tissue that adhere abnormally to adjacent membranes, sometimes causing the binding of organs that normally are separate (see Figure 10).

Adrenal gland. A body above each kidney that produces hormones.

Amenorrhea (primary). The complete absence of menstruation following puberty.

Amenorrhea (secondary). Cessation of menstrual periods.

Amniocentesis. Aspiration of amniotic fluid for analysis, to assess the condition of the fetus.

Analgesic. Pain-relieving medication.

Anaphylaxis. A violent response to a foreign substance.

Androgens. Hormones produced in greater amounts by men, smaller amounts by women, responsible for secondary masculine characteristics such as facial hair.

Anoscopy. Visualization of the anus through a scope. *See also* in Appendix A.

Anovulation. Failure to ovulate.

Anterior. In front of, or the front part of, a structure.

Anteflexed. Bent forward.

Anteverted. Tilted forward.

Antibody. A substance that fights or interacts with only the antigen that caused its formation, or with a closely related antigen.

Antigen. Any substance that can cause the formation of, and react to, antibodies.

Appendectomy. Removal of the appendix.

283

Appendicitis.   Inflammation of the appendix.

Artificial insemination.   The insertion of sperm into the vagina.

Aspiration.   The suctioning of fluid from the body for analysis.

Atresia.   Absence or closure of an orifice or organ.

Atrophy.   Wasting away or decreasing in size.

Autoimmunity.   An immune reaction against components of the body's tissues.

Barium enema.   Insertion of barium into the intestines for the purpose of x-ray examination. *See also* in Appendix A.

Basal body temperature.   The lowest body temperature, recorded (orally or rectally) upon awakening in the morning to detect ovulation.

Benign.   Not malignant.

Biopsy.   The removal and analysis of tissue for diagnosis.

Candidiasis.   An infection caused by Candida albicans, a yeastlike fungus.

Cannula.   A hollow tube inserted into an incision or cavity during a surgical procedure.

Carcinogenic.   Able to produce a carcinoma (malignant or cancerous tumor).

Carpal tunnel syndrome.   A compression of the median nerve in the carpal tunnel of the wrist, resulting in pain, burning, or tingling in the fingers, hand, and arm.

Castration.   Removal of the sex glands (in the female, bilateral oophorectomy).

Cautery.   The fusion or destruction of tissue with heat.

Cervix.   The lowest part of the uterus (see Figure 1).

Cesarean section.   Surgical delivery of the fetus through the abdominal wall.

Cilia.   Hairlike projections.

Clomiphene citrate (Serophene or Clomid).   An estrogen analogue used to induce ovulation.

Coccyx.   The lower end of the spine—the tailbone.

Coelom.   The body cavity of the embryo.

Colonoscopy.   Visualization of the colon (large intestine) through a scope. *See also* in Appendix A.

Colostomy.   The surgical creation of an opening to the colon on the surface of the body.

Colposcopy.   Visualization of the vagina and cervix through a magnifying device. *See also* in Appendix A.

Congenital.   Existing at or before birth.

Conization.   The removal of a small cone of tissue for microscopic examination. *See also* in Appendix A.

Corpus luteum.   A yellow glandular mass on the ovary formed from the ovarian follicle that has matured and expelled its ovum. The corpus luteum produces progesterone during the second half of the normal menstrual cycle.

Cryosurgery.   Destruction of tissue by freezing.

CT (CAT) scan.   Computer-analyzed x-ray examination of a layer of tissue. CT stands for computerized tomography.

Cul-de-sac (Pouch of Douglas).   Pouch between the uterus and rectum (see Figure 3).

Culdocentesis.   Aspiration of fluid from the pelvic cavity for microscopic examination. *See also* in Appendix A.

Cyst.   A closed cavity or sac, possibly containing a liquid or semisolid substance.

Cystoscopy.   Visualization of the urinary tract through a scope. *See also* in Appendix A.

D & C (dilation and curettage).   Dilation of the cervix followed by a scraping of the uterine lining. *See also* in Appendix A.

Diethylstilbestrol (DES).   Synthetic estrogen used in the past to prevent miscarriage, as a "morning-after pill," and as treatment for endometriosis. Shown to produce abnormalities in offspring of women who took it.

Dissect.   To cut apart or separate.

Diverticulitis.   Inflammation of diverticula—small herniations (pouches) in the muscular wall of the colon.

Dysmenorrhea.   Painful or difficult menstruation. *Primary:* without underlying organic pathology. *Secondary:* due to an organic disorder.

Dyspareunia.   Painful or difficult intercourse.

Dysplasia.   Abnormality of development of cells.

Dysuria.   Painful or difficult urination.

Excise.   To cut off or out.

Ectopic.   Misplaced. In an ectopic pregnancy, the fertilized egg implants outside the uterine cavity, usually in a fallopian tube.

Endometrial biopsy.   The examination of tissue sample from the uterus. *See also* in Appendix A.

Endometrioma.   A cyst containing endometriotic tissue.

Endometrium.   Inner lining of the uterus which develops and is shed each month at menstruation.

Episiotomy.   The incision of vulvar tissue to facilitate childbirth.

Epithelium.   The lining of internal and external body surfaces.

Estrogens.   Female sex hormones, produced primarily in the ovaries between puberty and menopause.

Etiology.   Cause.

Fallopian tubes.   Tubes that transport the ovum from the ovary to the uterus (see Figure 1).

FSH.   See **Follicle stimulating hormone.**

Fibroid tumor (leiomyoma).   Benign fibrous growth in the muscle of the uterus.

Fimbria.   One fingerlike projection of a fringed edge. Fimbriated ends are the flared outer ends of the fallopian tubes.

Flank.   Area between the ribs and the hips.

Follicle.   Part of the ovary that contains, nurtures, and releases the egg.

Follicle stimulating hormone (FSH).   Hormone produced in the pituitary gland which, with the luteinizing hormone, stimulates the ovary to mature a follicle for ovulation.

Genitourinary. Genital-urinary.

GI. Gastrointestinal.

GnRH. See **Gonadotropin releasing hormone.**

Gonadotropin. Hormones produced by the pituitary gland that stimulate the testicles or ovaries.

Gonadotropin releasing hormone (GnRH). Substance produced in the hypothalamus that directs the pituitary to release the follicle stimulating hormone and luteinizing hormone.

Gonorrhea. Infectious disease of the cervix, rectum, and urethra, usually transmitted through sexual contact.

HCG. See **Human chorionic gonadotropin.**

Hernia. Protrusion of a structure or organ through an abnormal opening.

Hormones. Chemical substances produced by the endocrine glands which regulate various body processes.

Huhner test. See **Postcoital test.**

Human chorionic gonadotropin (HCG). Hormone secreted by the placenta during pregnancy which maintains the corpus luteum and preserves the pregnancy.

Human menopausal gonadotropins (HMG). An extract of menopausal urine rich in FSH and LH, used to correct anovulation.

Hypermenorrhea. Increased menstrual flow. Intervals and periods are of normal duration.

Hyperplasia. Abnormal multiplication of normal cells.

Hyperprolactinemia. Excessive production of prolactin.

Hypertension. Persistently elevated arterial blood pressure.

Hypomenorrhea. Decreased menstrual flow. Intervals and periods are of normal duration.

Hypoprolactinemia. Diminished production of prolactin.

Hypothalamus. Area of the brain that directs the integration of the autonomic nervous system, the endocrine system, and other functions.

Hysterectomy. Excision of the uterus and cervix. *See also* in Appendix A.

Hysterosalpingography.   X-ray involving the injection of contrast dye into the uterus to assess whether or not the fallopian tubes are obstructed. *See also* in Appendix A.

Hysteroscopy.   Visualization of the interior of the uterus through a scope. *See also* in Appendix A.

Iatrogenic.   Caused by physicians; condition resulting from medical treatment.

Ileum.   Portion of the small intestine (see Figure 5).

Ileus.   Blockage of the intestines.

Ilium.   Hipbone.

Inflammatory bowel disease (IBD).   Inflammation of the small or large bowel. The term refers to both ulcerative colitis and Crohn's disease.

Inguinal canal.   Canal in the abdominal wall that contains the uterine round ligaments.

In situ.   In natural or original position.

Intrauterine.   In the uterus.

In vitro fertilization (IVF, test tube fertilization).   Procedure in which an ovum is removed from the follicle, fertilized outside the body, and replaced in the uterus.

Irritable bowel syndrome.   A condition characterized by involuntary spasms of the colon.

IVP.   Intravenous pyelography. See also **Pyelography.**

Labia.   Folds of tissue at the entrance of the vagina.

Laparoscopy.   Visualization of the interior of the abdomen through a scope. *See also* in Appendix A.

Laparotomy.   Major abdominal surgery. *See also* in Appendix A.

Leiomyoma.   See **Fibroid tumor.**

LH.   See **Luteinizing hormone.**

Ligaments.   Bands of elastic and muscle tissue which hold abdominal organs in place.

Luteal phase.   The last fourteen days of the menstrual cycle, from ovulation to the onset of menstruation, during which the corpus luteum is formed and secretes progesterone. See also **Corpus**

luteum. A luteal phase defect is inadequate progesterone production by the corpus luteum which hinders implantation of the fertilized ovum in the uterus.

Luteinization. Process by which the ovarian follicle becomes a corpus luteum.

Luteinizing hormone (LH). Hormone secreted by the pituitary gland throughout the menstrual cycle which stimulates maturation of an ovarian follicle and release of the ovum. LH-RH is a luteinizing hormone-releasing hormone.

Luteinizing unruptured follicle (LUF) syndrome. The absence of ovulation despite clinical evidence that ovulation has taken place.

Malignant. Becoming progressively worse and resulting in death.

Mammography. X-ray of the breast. *See also* in Appendix A.

Menarche. The onset of menstruation.

Menopause. The cessation of menstruation.

Menorrhagia. Excessive and prolonged menstrual flow.

Menorrhalgia. Difficulty during menstruation, including premenstrual distress, pelvic pain, and dysmenorrhea.

Menstruation (menses). The monthly shedding of the endometrium.

Metaplasia. Abnormal change in adult tissue cells.

Metastasis. The transfer of disease from one organ or part to another not directly connected with it. Transfer may be of cells or pathogenic microorganisms.

Metrorrhagia. Bleeding between periods or at irregular intervals.

Mittelschmerz. Pain at ovulation (literally, middle pain).

Motility. Ability to move.

Mucosa. A mucus membrane.

Myomectomy. Surgical removal of a fibroid tumor.

Myometrium. Smooth muscle of the uterus.

Neoplasia. Formation of new and abnormal cell growth.

Neurectomy.   Removal of part of a nerve.

Nodule.   Small lump.

Nulliparous.   Having never given birth to a live infant.

Oophorectomy.   Removal of the ovary or ovaries. *See also* in Appendix A.

Osteoporosis.   Excessive loss of bone density.

Ovarian wedge resection.   Partial removal of the ovary.

Ovariectomy.   Removal of the ovary or ovaries. *See also* in Appendix A.

Ovaries.   Female sex glands that produce eggs (ova) and manufacture estrogens and progesterone.

Ovulation.   Expulsion of a ripened egg, usually occurring at the middle of the menstrual cycle.

Ovum (ova).   Egg(s).

Pap test.   A staining technique used to detect abnormal cells.

Patent.   Unobstructed.

Pelvic inflammatory disease (PID, Salpingitis).   Infection of the fallopian tubes, the cervix, uterus, and ovaries, often caused by sexually transmitted diseases and the use of the intrauterine devices.

Perineum.   The space between the vaginal opening and the anus.

Peritoneum.   Membrane lining of the abdominal walls.

Peritonitis.   Inflammation of the peritoneum.

PID.   See **Pelvic inflammatory disease.**

Pituitary gland.   Gland located at the base of the brain which secretes hormones.

Placenta.   The organ or structure by which mother and fetus are joined, through which the fetus is nourished.

Pleura.   The membrane surrounding the lungs and lining the chest cavity (see Figure 6). Pleural: pertaining to the pleura.

Pneumothorax.   The accumulation of air or gas in the chest cavity.

Polymenorrhea. Menstrual cycles shorter than three weeks.

Polyp. Protruding growth from a mucous membrane.

Postcoital test. Analysis of vaginal and cervical secretions performed within a few hours of intercourse. *See also* in Appendix A.

Posterior. In back of, or the back part of, a structure.

Pouch of Douglas. See **Cul-de-sac.**

Proctoscopy. Visualization of the rectum through a scope. *See also* in Appendix A.

Progestational agents. Natural or synthetic hormones that contribute to the development of the endometrium. Also known as progesterone, progestins, and progestogens.

Progesterone. See **Progestational agents.** Responsible for preparing the endometrium to nourish a fertilized ovum.

Prolactin. Hormone that stimulates the production of milk.

Prostaglandins. Naturally occurring hormonelike fatty acids which stimulate contraction of uterine muscle.

Pseudomenopause. The chemical simulation of the hormonal environment of menopause for the treatment of endometriosis.

Pseudopregnancy. The chemical simulation of the hormonal environment of pregnancy for the treatment of endometriosis.

Psychogenic. Originating in the mind.

Pulmonary. Pertaining to the lungs.

Pyelography. X-ray examination of the kidney and the ureters. *See also* in Appendix A.

Rectum. The lowest part of the large intestine (see Figure 5).

Rectosigmoid. Part of the large intestine above the rectum (see Figure 4).

Rectosigmoidoscopy. Visualization of the rectosigmoid through a scope. *See also* in Appendix A.

Rectovaginal septum. A wall of membrane separating the rectum and the vagina (see Figure 4).

Refractory.   Resistant to treatment or cure.

Renography.   X-ray examination of the kidney. *See also* in Appendix A.

Resect.   To excise part of an organ.

Retrograde menstruation.   The backward flow of menstrual fluid through the fallopian tubes and into the pelvic cavity.

Retroflexed.   Bent backward.

Retroverted.   Tilted backward.

Round ligament.   One of eight uterine ligaments.

Rubin's insufflation test.   Diagnostic test to determine tubal patency. *See also* in Appendix A.

Sacral.   Pertaining to the sacrum.

Sacrum.   Curved portion of the lower spine.

Salpingectomy.   Removal of the fallopian tube.

Salpingo-oophorectomy.   Removal of the fallopian tube and ovary or ovaries. *See also* in Appendix A.

Salpingitis.   See **Pelvic inflammatory disease.**

Salpingitis isthmica nodosa.   Nodular thickening of the fallopian tubes.

Sciatic nerve.   Nerve running from the hipbone through the thigh.

Septum.   A division or partition.

Sigmoid colon.   Lower part of the large intestine.

Sigmoidoscopy.   Visualization of the lower colon through a scope. *See also* in Appendix A.

Spasm.   A sudden, involuntary contraction.

Speculum.   An appliance for opening to view a passage or cavity of the body.

Spontaneous abortion.   Miscarriage.

Stenosis.   Narrowing.

Tenaculum.   A hooklike instrument for seizing and holding body parts.

Testosterone.   Male sex hormone produced in the testicles.

Thoracentesis.   Aspiration of fluid from the pleural cavity for microscopic analysis. *See also* in Appendix A.

Thorax.   The chest cavity (see Figure 6).

Thromboembolism.   Blocked blood vessel formed by a blood clot carried from its place of origin to another blood vessel through the bloodstream.

Thrombosis.   Formation of a blood clot.

Tomography.   X-ray examination of a specific plane, or layer, of body tissue. See also **CT (CAT) Scan.**

Transverse colon.   The part of the intestine that stretches across the upper part of the abdomen.

Ultrasound.   Translation of sound waves into a video image. *See also* Appendix A.

Umbilicus.   The navel.

Ureter.   Tube that carries urine from the kidney to the bladder (see Figure 5).

Urethra.   Tube that carries urine out of the bladder (see Figure 5).

Urography.   See **Pyelography.**

Uterine suspension.   Shortening and repositioning the uterine ligaments to hold the uterus up and out of the cul-de-sac—to prevent the formation of adhesions.

Uterosacral ligament.   Uterine ligament.

Uterotubography.   See **Hysterosalpingography.**

Uterus.   Pear-shaped, muscular organ which maintains the fetus during pregnancy (see Figure 1).

Vagina.   Canal between external genitalia and the uterus (see Figure 1).

Vaginal atrophy.   A drying and thinning of vaginal tissues.

Vaginal fornix.   The area of the vagina that meets the cervix (see Figure 1).

Vaginismus.   Muscle spasm at the opening of the vagina hindering penetration during sexual intercourse.

Vulva.   External female genitalia.

Wedge resection.   Removal of a triangular wedge of tissue.

Selected Bibliography

In addition to the books and journals listed in appendixes C and D, the following research materials were used in the preparation of this book.

Aiman, J., ed. *Infertility: Diagnosis and Management*. New York: Springer-Verlag, 1984.

Aitkan, C. Psychosocial aspects of disease and their management. *Psychother. Psychosom.* 42:52–55 (1984).

American College of Obstetricians and Gynecologists. Estrogen replacement therapy. *Technical Bulletin*, no. 70 (June 1983).

Ananth, J. Hysterectomy and sexual counseling. *Psychiatric Journal of the University of Ottawa* 8(4):213–217 (December 1983).

Anthony, C.P., and G.A. Thibodeu. *Textbook of Anatomy & Physiology* (11th ed.). St. Louis: C.V. Mosby, 1983.

Badawy, S.Z., V. Cuenca, A. Stitzel, R.D. Jacobs, and R.H. Tomar. Autoimmune phenomena in infertile patients with endometriosis. *Obstetrics and Gynecology* 63(3):271–275 (March 1984).

Barbieri, R.L. CA-125 in patients with endometriosis. *Fertility and Sterility* 45(6):767–769 (June 1986).

Barbieri, R.L., S. Evans, and R.W. Kistner. Danazol in the treatment of endometriosis: Analysis of 100 cases with a four-year follow-up. *Fertility and Sterility* 37:737–746 (June 1982).

Barbieri, R.L., and R.W. Kistner. Hormonal therapy of endometriosis. In *Medical Management of Endometriosis*, edited by J.P. Raynaud, et al. New York: Raven Press, 1984, pp. 27–39.

Batt, R., and J.D. Naples. Endometriosis. *Current Problems in Obstetrics and Gynecology* 6(1):1–98 (September 1982).

Beggs, J.R. Endometriosis: A male perspective. Unpublished article, 1985.

Berkow, R., ed. *The Merck Manual of Diagnosis and Therapy*, 14th ed. Rahway, NJ: Merck Sharpe and Dohme Laboratories, 1982.

Biberoglu, K.D., and S.J. Behrman. Dosage aspects of danazol therapy in endometriosis: Short-term and long-term effectiveness. *American Journal of Obstetrics and Gynecology* 139(6):645–654 (March 1981).

Block, A.R. An investigation of the response of the spouse to chronic pain behavior. *Psychosomatic Medicine* 43(5):415–422 (October 1981).

Block, A.R., and S.L. Boyer. The spouse's adjustment to chronic pain: Cognitive and emotional factors. *Social Science Medicine* 19(12):1313–1317 (1984).

Boyd, M.E. Endometriosis. *Canadian Journal of Surgery* 28(6):471-473 (November 1984).

Bresnick, E., and M.L. Taymor. The role of counseling in infertility. *Fertility and Sterility* 32(2):154–156 (August 1979).

Broome, A., and L. Wallace, eds. *Psychology and Gynaecological Problems*. London: Tavistock, 1984.

Buchanan, D.C. Group therapy for chronic physically ill patients. *Psychosomatics* 19(7):425–431 (July 1978).

Buttram, V.C., Jr., Conservative surgery for endometriosis in the infertile female: A study of 206 patients with implications for both medical and surgical therapy. *Fertility and Sterility* 31:117–123 (February 1979).

Buttram, V.C., Jr., Cyclic use of combination oral contraceptives and the severity of endometriosis. *Fertility and Sterility* 31(3):347–348 (March 1979).

Buttram, V.C., Jr., Evolution of the revised American fertility society classification of endometriosis. *Fertility and Sterility* 43(3):347–350 (March 1985).

Buttram, V.C., Jr., and J.W. Betts. Endometriosis. *Current Problems in Obstetrics and Gynecology* 2(11):1–58 (July 1979).

Buttram, V.C., Jr., and R.C. Reiter. *Surgical Treatment of the Infertile Female*. Baltimore: Williams & Wilkins, 1985.

Buttram, V.C., Jr., and R.C. Reiter. Treatment of endometriosis with danazol—second interim report. *Fertility and Sterility* 41(2):375.

Buttram, V.C., Jr., R.C. Reiter, and S. Ward. Treatment of endometriosis with danazol: Report of a 6-year prospective study. *Fertility and Sterility* 43(3):353–360 (March 1985).

Carney, M.W.P. Menstrual disturbances: A psychogenic disorder? *Clinics in Obstetrics and Gynecology* 8(1):103–108 (April 1981).

Cassell, E.J. *The Healer's Art*. Cambridge, MA: The MIT Press, 1985.

Chadwick, M. *The Psychological Effects of Menstruation*. New York: Nervous and Mental Disease Publishing Co., 1932.

Chalmers, J.A. *Endometriosis*. London: Butterworth, 1975.

Chapman, R.C. New directions in the understanding and management of pain. *Social Science Medicine* 19(12):1261–1277 (1984).

Chatman, D.L., and A.B. Ward. Endometriosis in adolescents. *Journal of Reproductive Medicine* 27(3):156–160 (March 1982).

Chong, A.P., and M.S. Baggish. Management of pelvic endometriosis by means of intraabdominal carbon dioxide laser. *Fertility and Sterility* 41(1):14–19 (January 1984).

Ciccone, D.S., and R.C. Grzesiak. Cognitive dimensions of chronic pain. *Social Science Medicine* 19(12):1339–1345 (1984).

Cobb, C.F. Endometriosis in the general surgical patient. *Surgical Rounds* 8(7):66–82 (July 1985).

Corea, G. *The Hidden Malpractice: How American Medicine Mistreats Women* (rev. ed.). New York: Harper & Row, Harper Colophon Books, 1985.

Cousins, N. *Anatomy of an Illness*. New York: Bantam Books, 1981.

Cousins, N. *The Healing Heart*. New York: Avon Books, 1983.

Covino, N.A., G.F. Dirks, R.I. Fisch, and J.V. Seidel. Characteristics of depression of chronically ill medical patients. *Psychother. Psychosom*. 39:10–22 (1983).

Crain, J.L., and A.A. Luciano. Fluid evaluation in infertility. *Obstetrics and Gynecology* 61(2):159–164 (February 1983).

Cramer, D.W., E. Wilson, R. Stillman, et al. Association of endometriosis with oral contraception use. Abstract 328, American Fertility Society annual meeting in Toronto, September 1986, p. 113.

Cramer, D.W., E. Wilson, R. Stillman, et al. The relation of endometriosis to menstrual characteristics, smoking, and exercise. *Journal of the American Medical Association* 244(14):1904–1908 (April 11, 1986).

Croom, R.D., M.L. Donovan, and W.H. Schwesinger. Intestinal endometriosis. *American Journal of Surgery* 148(5):660–667 (November 1984).

Cutler, G.B., Jr., A.R. Hoffman, R.S. Swerdloff, R.J. Santen, D.R. Meldrum, and F. Comite. Therapeutic applications of luteinizing hormone-releasing hormone and its analogs. *Annals of Internal Medicine* 102(5):643–657 (May 1985).

Dawood, M.Y. *Dysmenorrhea*. Baltimore: Williams & Wilkins, 1981.

Dawood, M.Y. Etiology and treatment of dysmenorrhea. *Seminars in Reproductive Endocrinology* 3(3):283–294 (August 1985).

Dawood, M.Y., F.S. Kahn-Dawood, and L. Wilson, Jr. Peritoneal fluid prostaglandins and prostanoids in women with endometriosis. *American Journal of Obstetrics and Gynecology* 148(4):391–394 (February 15, 1984).

Dawood, M.Y., J.L. McGuire, and L.M. Demers. *Premenstrual Syndrome and Dysmenorrhea*. Baltimore: Urban and Schwarzenberg, 1984.

Delaney, J., M.J. Lupton, and E. Toth. *The Curse*. New York: E.P. Dutton, 1976.

DeVaul, R.A., and S. Zisook. Chronic pain: The psychiatrist's role. *Psychosomatics* 19(7):417–421 (July 1978).

Dewhurst, Sir John. *Integrated Obstetrics and Gynaecology for Postgraduates*. (3d ed.). Oxford: Blackwell Scientific Publications, 1981.

Dingfelder, J.R. Primary dysmenorrhea treatment with prostaglandin inhibitors: A review. *American Journal of Obstetrics and Gynecologists* 140(8):874–879 (August 15, 1981).

Dmowski, W.P. Pitfalls in clinical, laparoscopic and histological diagnosis of endometriosis. *Acta Obstet Gynecol Scand* (Supp.) 123:61–66 (1984).

Dmowski, W.P., E. Kapetanakis, and A. Scommegna. Variable effects of danazol on endometriosis at 4 low-dose levels. *Obstetrics and Gynecology* 59(4):408–415 (April 1982).

Dmowski, W.P., and E. Radwanska. Current concepts on pathology, histogenesis and etiology of endometriosis. *Acta Obstet Gynecol Scand* (Supp.) 123:29–33 (1984).

Dmowski, W.P., R. Rao, and A. Scommegna. The luteinized unruptured follicle syndrome and endometriosis. *Fertility and Sterility* 33(1):30–34 (January 1980).

Dmowski, W.P., R.W. Steele, and G.F. Baker. Deficient cellular immunity in endometriosis. *American Journal of Obstetrics and Gynecology* 141:377–383 (1981).

Doberl, A., et al. Regression of endometriosis following shorter treatment with, or lower dosage of, danazol. *Acta Obstet Gynecol Scand* (Supp.) 123:51–58 (1984).

Doctors, patients don't communicate. *FDA Consumer*, July–August 1983.

Dworkin, R.H. et al. Predicting treatment response in depressed and non-depressed chronic pain patients. *Pain* 24 (1986) 343–353.

Ehrenreich, B., and D. English. *Complaints and Disorders: The Sexual Politics of Sickness*. Old Westbury, NY: The Feminist Press, 1973.

Ehrenreich, B., and D. English. *For Her Own Good: 150 Years of the Experts' Advice to Women*. Garden City, NJ: Anchor Press/Doubleday, Anchor Books, 1979.

Elliot, D.L., A.F. Barker, and L.M. Dixon. Catamenial hemoptysis: New methods of diagnosis and therapy. *Chest* 87(5):687–688 (May 1985).

Endometriosis can be "silent killer" of kidney. *Ob/Gyn News*, October 1–14, 1982.

Endometriosis is a common cause of infertility in women, but often it is misdiagnosed, an expert warns. *People*, October 28, 1985.

Engel, G.L. A life setting conducive to illness: The giving-up—given-up complex. *Annals of Internal Medicine* 69(2):293–300 (August 1968).

Engelbart, H.J., and M.A.E. Vrancken. Chronic pain from the perspective of health: A view based on systems theory. *Social Science Medicine* 19(12):1383–1392 (1984).

Felton, B.J., T.A. Revenson, and G.A. Hinrichsen. Stress and coping in the explanation of psychological adjustment among chronically ill adults. *Social Science Medicine* 18(10):889–898 (1984).

Feste, J.R. Laser laparoscopy: A new modality. *Journal of Reproductive Medicine* 30(5):413–417 (May 1985).

Fletcher, D.J. Coping with stress. *Postgraduate Medicine* 77(4):93–100 (March 1985).

Foster, G.V., H.A. Zacur, and J.A. Rock. Hot flashes in postmenopausal women ameliorated by danazol. *Fertility and Sterility* 43(3):401–404 (March 1985).

Gambrell, R.D., Jr. The menopause: Benefits and risks of estrogen-progestogen replacement therapy. *Fertility and Sterility* 37(4):457–474 (April 1982).

Garcia, C., and W.B. Cutler. Preservation of the ovary: A reevaluation. *Fertility and Sterility* 42(4):510–514 (October 1984).

Garcia, C.R., L. Mastroianni, Jr., R.D. Amelan, and L. Dubin. *Current Therapy of Infertility, 1982–83*. Trenton, NJ: B.C. Decker, 1982.

Gastrell, B., J. Cornoni-Huntley, and J.A. Brody. Estrogen use and postmenopausal women: A basis for informed decisions. *Journal of Family Practice* 11(6):841–860 (1980).

Gold, J.J., and J. Josimovich. *Gynecologic Endocrinology* (3d ed.). Hagerstown, MD: Harper & Row, 1980.

Goldstein, D.P., C. De Cholnoky, and S.J. Emans. Adolescent endometriosis. *Journal of Adolescent Health Care* 1(1):37–41 (September 1980).

Gompel, C., and S.G. Silverberg. *Pathology in Gynecology and Obstetrics* (3d ed.). Philadelphia: J.B. Lippincott, 1985.

Goodall, J.R. *A Study of Endometriosis*. Philadelphia: J.B. Lippincott, 1943.

Green, J.A. The mind-body hyphen. *Social Policy*, March 1974.

Greenblatt, R.B., ed. *Recent Advances in Endometriosis*. New York: Elsevier, 1976. International Congress, Serial No. 638. Symposium in Atlanta, Georgia, 1975.

Greenwood, S. Hot flashes: How to cope when the heat is on. *Ms.*, May 1985.

Groll, M. Endometriosis and spontaneous abortion. *Fertility and Sterility* 41(6):933–935 (June 1984).

Guck, T.P., F.M. Skultety, P.W. Meilman, and E.T. Dowd. Multidisciplinary pain center follow-up study: Evaluation with a no-treatment control group. *Pain* 21:295–306 (1985).

Guzick, D.S., and J.A. Rock. A comparison of danazol and conservative surgery for the treatment of infertility due to mild or moderate endometriosis. *Fertility and Sterility* 40(5):580–584 (November 1983).

Halme, J., S. Becker, and R. Wing. Accentuated cyclic activation of peritoneal macrophages in patients with endometriosis. *American Journal of Obstetrics and Gynecology* 148(1):85–90 (January 1984).

Halme, J., M.G. Hammond, J.F. Hulka, S.G. Raj, and L.M. Talbert. Retrograde menstruation in healthy women and in patients with endometriosis. *Obstetrics and Gynecology* 64(2):151–154 (August 1984).

Hammond, C.B., and W.S. Maxson. Current status of estrogen replacement therapy for the menopause. *Fertility and Sterility* 37(1):5–20 (January 1982).

Handy, L.C. Nursing management of the woman with osteoporosis. *Journal of Obstetrical, Gynecological and Neonatal Nursing* 14(2):107–111 (March–April 1985).

Haney, A.F., M.A. Misukonis, and J.B. Weinberg. Macrophages and infertility: Oviductal macrophages as potential mediators of infertility. *Fertility and Sterility* 39(3):310–315 (March 1983).

Harrison, M. *Self-Help for Premenstrual Syndrome*. New York: Random House, 1982.

Harrison, M. *A Woman in Residence*. Harmondsworth, England: Penguin Books, 1983.

Hartman, L.M. The interface between sexual dysfunction and marital conflict. *American Journal of Psychiatry* 137(5):576–579 (May 1980).

Henderson, B.E., R.K. Ross, A. Paganini-Hill, and T.M. Mack. Estrogen use and cardiovascular disease. *American Journal of Obstetrics and Gynecology* 154(6):1181–1186 (June 1986).

Hiatt, R.A., R. Bawol, G.D. Friedman, et al. Exogenous estrogen and breast cancer after bilateral oophorectomy. *Cancer* 54:139–144 (July 1984).

Hibbard, L.T., W.R. Schumann, and G.E. Goldstein. Thoracic endometriosis: A review and report of two cases. *American Journal of Obstetrics and Gynecology* 140(2):227–232 May 15, 1981).

Hirschowitz, J.S., N.G. Soler, and J. Wortsman. The galactorrhoea-endometriosis syndrome. *The Lancet*, April 29, 1978, pp. 896–898.

Hollender, M.H. Hysterectomy and feelings of femininity. *Medical Aspects of Human Sexuality* 111(7):6–15 (July 1969).

Houston, D.E. Evidence for the risk of pelvic endometriosis by age, race and socioeconomic status. *Epidemiological Reviews* 6:167–191 (1984).

Hulka, J.F. *Textbook of Laparoscopy.* New York: Grune and Stratton, 1985.

Israel, L.S. *Diagnosis and Treatment of Menstrual Disorders and Sterility* (5th ed.). New York: Harper & Row, 1967.

Jenkins, S., D.L. Olive, and A.F. Haney. Endometriosis: Pathogenetic implications of the anatomic distribution. *Obstetrics and Gynecology* 67(3):335–338 (March 1986).

Jones, H.W., Jr., and J.A. Rock. *Reparative and Reconstructive Surgery of the Female Reproductive Tract.* Baltimore: Williams & Wilkins, 1983.

Kane, C., and P. Drouin. Obstructive uropathy associated with endometriosis. *American Journal of Obstetrics and Gynecology* 151(2):207–211 (January 15, 1985).

Kauppila, A., and L. Ronnberg. Naproxen sodium in dysmenorrhea secondary to endometriosis. *Obstetrics and Gynecology* 65(3):379–383 (March 1985).

Kelly, R.W., and D.K. Roberts. CO2 laser laparoscopy. *Journal of Reproductive Medicine* 28(10):638–640 (October 1983).

Keye, W.R., Jr. Female sexual activity, satisfaction and function in infertile women. *Infertility* 5(4):275–285 (1982–83).

Keye, W.R., Jr. Psychosexual responses to infertility. *Clinical Obstetrics and Gynecology* 27(3):760–776 (September 1984).

Keye, W.R., Jr. *Laser Surgery in Gynecology and Obstetrics.* Boston: G.K. Hall, 1985.

Kistner, R.W. Endometriosis. In *Reproductive Endocrinology, Infertility and Contraception,* edited by Daniel Mishell and Val Davajan. Philadelphia: F.A. Davis, 1979.

Kistner, R.W. *Gynecology: Principles and Practice* (3d ed.). Chicago: Year Book, 1979.

Kistner, R.W. Endometriosis. In *Current Therapy in Obstetrics and Gynecology 2,* edited by Edward T. Quilligan. Philadelphia: W.B. Saunders, 1983.

Kistner, R.W. *Gynecology: Principles and Practice* (4th ed.). Chicago: Year Book, 1986.

Klonoff, E.A. Use of behavior therapy in obstetrics and gynecology. *Advances in Psychosomatic Medicine* 12:150–165 (1985).

Kodadek, S.M. Working with the chronically ill. *Nurse Practitioner,* March 1985.

Koninckx, P.R., P. Ide, W. Vandenbroucke, and I.A. Brosens. New aspects of the pathophysiology of endometriosis and associated infertility. *Journal of Reproductive Medicine* 24(6):257–260 (June 1980).

Koskimies, A.I., B. Meyer, and O. Widholm. Treatment of vaginal endometriosis with danazol. *Acta Obstet Gynecol Scand* (Supp.) 123:67–68 (1984).

Kraaimaat, F.W., and A.T. Veeninga. Life stress and hysterectomy-oophorectomy. *Maturitas* 6:319–325 (1984).

Kroger, W.S., and S.C. Freed. *Psychosomatic Gynecology*. Philadelphia: W.B. Saunders, 1951.

Krupp, N.E. Adaptation to chronic illness. *Postgraduate Medicine* 60(5):122–125 (November 1978).

Kübler-Ross, E. *On Death and Dying*. New York: Macmillan, Collier Books, 1969.

Lalinec-Michaud, M., and F. Engelsmann. Anxiety, fears and depression related to hysterectomy. *Canadian Journal of Psychiatry* 30(1):44–47 (February 1985).

Lamb, K., and N. Berg. Tampon use in women with endometriosis. *Journal of Community Health* 10(4):215–225 (Winter 1985).

Lamb, K., R.G. Hoffmann, and T.R. Nichols. Family trait analysis: A case-control study of 13 women with endometriosis and their best friends. *American Journal of Obstetrics and Gynecology* 154(3):596–601 (March 1986).

Langmade, C.F. Pelvic endometriosis and ureteral obstruction. *American Journal of Obstetrics and Gynecology* 122(4):476–484 (June 1975).

Lawrence, S.A., and R.M. Lawrence. A model of adaptation to the stress of chronic illness. *Nursing Forum* 18(1):33–42 (1979).

Lemay A., R. Maheux, N. Faure, C. Jean, and A.T. Fazekas. Reversible hypogonadism induced by a luteinizing hormone-releasing hormone (LH-RH) agonist (buserelin) as a new therapeutic approach for endometriosis. *Fertility and Sterility* 41(6):863–871 (June 1984).

Lemay, A., and G. Quesnel. Potential new treatment of endometriosis: Reversible inhibition of pituitary-ovarian function by chronic intranasal administration of a luteinizing hormone-releasing hormone (LH-RH) agonist. *Fertility and Sterility* 38(8):376–379 (September 1982).

Levy, N.B. The chronically ill patient. *Psychiatric Quarterly* 51(3):189–197 (Fall 1979).

Lichtendorf, S.S. *Eve's Journey: The Physical Experience of Being Female*. New York: Berkley Books, 1983.

Lipowski, Z.J. Psychosocial reactions to physical illness. *Canadian Medical Association Journal* 128:1069–1072 (May 1, 1983).

Lobb, M.L., et al. A behavioral technique for recovery from the psychological trauma of hysterectomy. *Perceptual and Motor Skills* 59:677–678 (1984).

Low, R.A., A.D. Roberts, and D.A. Lees. A comparative study of various doses of danazol in the treatment of endometriosis. *British Journal of Obstetrics and Gynaecology*. 91(2):167–171 (February 1984).

Macek, C. Neurological deficits, back pain tied to endometriosis. *Journal of the American Medical Association* 249(6):686 (February 11, 1983).

Madaras, L. and J. Patterson. *Womancare*. New York: Avon Books, 1984.

Mahlstedt, P.P. The psychological component of infertility. *Fertility and Sterility* 43(3):335–346 (March 1985).

Malinak, L.R., V.C. Buttram, Jr., S. Elias, and J.L. Simpson. Heritable aspects of endometriosis II. Clinical characteristics of familial endometriosis. *American Journal of Obstetrics and Gynecology* 137(3):332–337 (June 1980).

Malinak, L.R., and J.M. Wheeler. Endometriosis. In *Infertility: Diagnosis and Management*, edited by James Aiman. New York: Springer-Verlag, 1984.

Martin, D.C. CO2 laser laparoscopy for the treatment of endometriosis associated with infertility. *Journal of Reproductive Medicine* 30(5):409–412 (May 1985).

Matteucci, B.M., C.H. McGrory, and R.J. Dehoratius. Drug therapy for osteoporosis. *American Family Physician* 32(1):177–179 (July 1985).

McArthur, J.W., and H. Ulfelder. The effect of pregnancy upon endometriosis. *Obstetrics and Gynecology Survey* 20(5):709–733 (October 1965).

McPherson, A., and A. Anderson. The "ectomies." In *Women's Problems in General Practice*, edited by Ann McPherson and Anne Anderson. Oxford General Practice Series 4. Oxford: Oxford University Press, 1983.

Mechanic, D. Illness behavior, social adaptation, and the management of illness. *Journal of Nervous and Mental Disease* 165(2):79–87 (August 1977).

Meigs, J.V. Endometriosis: Etiologic role of marriage age and parity; conservative treatment. *Obstetrics and Gynecology* 2(1):46–53 (July 1953).

Meldrum, D.R. Management of endometriosis with gonadotropin-releasing hormone agonists. *Fertility and Sterility* 44(5):581–582 (November 1985).

Meldrum, D.R., R.J. Chang, J. Lu, W. Vale, J. Rivier, and H.L. Judd. "Medical oophorectomy" using a long-acting GnRH agonist—a possible new approach to the treatment of endometriosis. *Journal of Clinical Endocrinology and Metabolism* 54(5):1081–1083 (May 1982).

Meldrum, D.R., W.M. Pardridge, W.G. Karow, J. Rivier, W. Vale, and H.L. Judd. Hormonal effects of danazol and medical oophorectomy in endometriosis. *Obstetrics and Gynecology* 62(4):480–485 (October 1983).

Menges, L.J. Pain: still an intriguing puzzle. *Social Science Medicine* 19(12):1257–1260 (1984).

Menning, B.E. The emotional needs of infertile couples. *Fertility and Sterility* 34(4):313–319 (October 1980).

Michols, V., J.G. Boutselis, and A.S. Neri. Endometriosis. In *Gynecologic Endocrinology* (3d. ed.). Hagerstown, MD: Harper & Row, 1980.

Miller, B.W. Natural healing through naturopathy. *East West Journal*, December 1985, pp. 55–59.

Miller, J.F. *Coping with Chronic Illness: Overcoming Powerlessness*. Philadelphia: F.A. Davis, 1985.

Mishell, D.R., Jr., and P.F. Brenner. *Management of Common Problems in Obstetrics and Gynecology*. Oradell, NJ: Medical Economics Co., 1983.

Mishell, D.R., and V. Davajan. *Reproductive Endocrinology, Infertility and Contraception*. Philadelphia: F.A. Davis, 1979.

Miyazawa, K. Incidence of endometriosis among Japanese women. *Obstetrics and Gynecology* 48(4):407–409 (October 1974).

Moore, E.E., J.H. Harger, J.A. Rock, and D.F. Archer. Management of pelvic endometriosis with low-dose danazol. *Fertility and Sterility* 36(1):15–19 (July 1981).

Muldoon, T.G., V.B. Mahesh, and B. Perez-Ballester, eds. *Recent Advances in Fertility Research. Part B, Developments in the Management of Reproductive Disorders.* International Symposium in Buenos Aires. New York: Alan R. Liss, 1982.

Myscato, J.J., A.F. Haney, and J.B. Weinberg. Sperm phagocytosis by human peritoneal macrophages: A possible cause of infertility in endometriosis. *American Journal of Obstetrics and Gynecology* 144(5):503–510 (November 1, 1982).

Neurological deficits, back pain tied to endometriosis. *Journal of the American Medical Association* 249(6):686 (February 11, 1983).

Nezhat, C., S.R. Crowgey, and C.P. Garrison. Surgical treatment of endometriosis via laser laparoscopy. *Fertility and Sterility* 45(6):778–783 (June 1986).

Nikkanen V., and R. Punnonen. External endometriosis in 801 operated patients. *Acta Obstet Gynecol Scand* 63(8):699–701 (1984).

Noble, A.D., and A.T. Letchworth. Treatment of endometriosis: A study of medical management. *British Journal of Obstetrics and Gynaecology* 87(8):726–728 (August 1980).

Nordenskjold, F., and S. Fex. Vocal effects of danazol therapy. *Acta Obstet Gynecol Scand* (Supp.) 123:131–132 (1984).

Ohlgisser, M., Y. Sorokin, and M. Heitfetz. Gynecologic laparoscopy: A review article. *Obstetrical and Gynecological Survey* 40(7):385–395 (July 1985).

Older, J. *Endometriosis.* New York: Scribner, 1984.

Olson, M., and N.J. Alexander. *In-Vitro Fertilization Embryo Transfer.* Portland, OR: Oregon Health Sciences University, n.d.

Ory, S.J. Clinical uses of luteinizing hormone-releasing hormone. *Fertility and Sterility* 39(5):577–587 (May 1983).

Peaper, R.E., and P.A. Schwartz. Effect of danazol on vocal pitch: A case study. *Obstetrics and Gynecology* 65(1):131–135 (January 1985).

Peterson, H.B., N.C. Lee, and G.L. Rubin. ERT: What are the cancer risks? *Contemporary Obstetrics and Gynecology*, October 1985, pp. 55–82.

Pittaway, D.E. Appendectomy in the surgical treatment of endometriosis. *Obstetrics and Gynecology* 61(4):421–424 (April 1983).

Polon, M.L. Endometriosis. *Seminars in Reproductive Endocrinology* 2(2):186–196 (May 1984).

Portuondo, J.A., A.D. Echanojauregui, C. Herran, and I. Alijarte. Early conception in patients with untreated mild endometriosis. *Fertility and Sterility* 39(1):22–25 (January 1983).

Pratt, J.H., and T.J. Williams. Indications for complete pelvic operations and more radical procedures in the treatment of severe or extensive endometriosis. *Clinical Obstetrics and Gynecology* 23(3):937–950 (September 1980).

Ranney, B. Endometriosis: Pathogenesis, symptoms, and findings. *Clinical Obstetrics and Gynecology* 23(3):865–873 (September 1980).

Ranney, B. The prevention, inhibition, palliation, and treatment of endometriosis. *American Journal of Obstetrics and Gynecology* 123(3):423–426 (December 1975).

Raynaud, J.P., L. Martini, and T. Ojasoo, eds. *Medical Management of Endometriosis.* New York: Raven Press, 1984.

Reiser, M.F. Biopsychosocial model of research. *Psychosomatic Medicine* (Supp.) 42(1:11):145–151 (1980).

Renaer, M. Reflections of pain in gynecologic practice. *European Journal of Gynecology and Reproductive Biology* 18:245–254 (1984).

Richards, A. A post-hysterectomy syndrome. *The Lancet*, October 26, 1974, pp. 989–985.

Robinson, A.G. Endometriosis and the anterior coccyx—observations on five cases. *Research Forum* 1(4):120–122 (Summer 1985).

Rodin, J. A sense of control. *Psychology Today*, December 1984, p. 45.

Rogers, S.F., E.C. Lotze, and G.M. Grunert. Endometriosis then and now: Evolution of surgical techniques and treatment. *Journal of Reproductive Medicine* 29(8):613–620 (August 1984).

Rosenfeld, D.L., and E. Mitchell. Treating the emotional aspects of infertility: Counseling services in an infertility clinic. *American Journal of Obstetrical Gynecology* 135(2):177–179 (September 15, 1979).

Roth, D.L., and D.S. Holmes. Influence of physical fitness in determining the impact of stressful life events on physical and psychologic health. *Psychosomatic Medicine* 47(2):164–173 (March–April 1985).

Runck, B. *Biofeedback: Issues in Treatment Assessment.* National Institute of Mental Health Science Reports. DHHS Publication No. (ADM) 80–1032. Rockville, MD: U.S. Department of Health and Human Services, 1980.

Runnels, G.O. Sick—a way of life. *Journal of the Mississippi State Medical Association* 24:301–304 (November 1983).

Russman, F., G. D'Ablaing, III, and R.P. Marrs. Pregnancy complicated by ruptured endometrioma. *Obstetrics and Gynecology* 62(4):519–521 (October 1983).

Salter, J.R. Gynaecological symptoms and psychological distress in potential hysterectomy patients. *Journal of Psychosomatic Research* 29(2):155–159 (1985).

Samper, E.R., G.W. Slagle, and A.M. Hand. Colonic endometriosis: Its clinical spectrum. *Southern Medical Journal* 77(7):912–914 (July 1984). ,

Sanford, L.T., and M.E. Donovan. *Women & Self-Esteem: Understanding & Improving the Way We Think & Feel About Ourselves.* Garden City, NY: Anchor Press/Doubleday, 1984.

Schenken, R.S., and L.R. Malinak. Reoperation after initial treatment of endometriosis with conservative surgery. *American Journal of Obstetrics and Gynecology* 131(4):416–424 (June 15, 1978).

Schenken, R.S., and L.R. Malinak. Postoperative danazol therapy in infertility patients with severe endometriosis. *Fertility and Sterility* 36:460–463 (October 1981).

Schenken, R.S., and L.R. Malinak. Conservative surgery versus expectant management for the infertile patient with mild endometriosis. *Fertility and Sterility* 37(2):183–186 (February 1982).

Schenken, R.S., and L.R. Malinak. Recurrent endometriosis: Incidence, management, and prognosis. *American Journal of Obstetrics and Gynecology* 146(3):247–253 (June 1983).

Schmidt, C.L. Endometriosis: A reappraisal of pathogenesis and treatment. *Fertility and Sterility* 44(2):157–173 (August 1985).

Schriock, E., S.E. Monroe, H. Henzl, and R.B. Jaffe. Treatment of endometriosis with a potent agonist of gonadotropin-releasing hormone (nafarelin). *Fertility and Sterility* 44(5):583–588 (November 1985).

Schrotenboer, K., and G.J. Subak-Sharpe. *Freedom From Menstrual Cramps*. New York: Pocket Books, 1981.

Seibel, M.M., M.J. Berger, F.G. Weinstein, and M.L. Taymor. The effectiveness of danazol on subsequent fertility in minimal endometriosis. *Fertility and Sterility* 38(5):534–537 (November 1982).

Seibel, M.M., and M.M. Taymor. Emotional aspects of infertility. *Fertility and Sterility* 37(2):137–145 (February 1982).

Semmens, J.P., C.C. Tsai, E.C. Semmens, and C.B. Loadholt. Effects of estrogen therapy on vaginal physiology during menopause. *Obstetrics and Gynecology* 66(1):15–18 (July 1985).

Seyfer, A.E., L.A. Mologne, R.L. Morris, and J.R. Clark. Endometriosis causing acute small bowel obstruction: Report of a case and review of the literature. *American Surgeon* 41(3):168–171 (March 1975).

Shaw, R.W., H.M. Fraser, and H. Boyle. Intranasal treatment with luteinizing hormone-releasing hormone agonist in women with endometriosis. *British Medical Journal* 287:1667–1669 (December 3, 1983).

Sherwin, B.B., M.M. Gelfand, and W. Brender. Androgen enhances sexual motivation in females: A prospective, crossover study of sex steroid administration in the surgical menopause. *Psychosomatic Medicine* 47:339–351 (July–August 1985).

Simpson, R.L., S. Elias, L.R. Malinak, and V.C. Buttram, Jr. Heritable aspects of endometriosis. I. Genetic Studies. *American Journal of Obstetrics and Gynecology* 137(3):327–331 (June 1980).

Sloane, E. *Biology of Women*, 2nd ed. New York: Wiley, 1985.

Soderberg, C.H., and E.H. Dahlquist. Catamenial pneumothorax. *Surgery* 79(02):236–239 (February 1976).

Speroff, L., moderator. Symposium: Adding progestogens to ERT. *Contemporary Obstetrics and Gynecology*, September 1985, pp. 225–241.

Spronk, V.R.A., and N.E. Warmenhoven. Patient education in general practice: Opinions of general practitioners. *Patient Education and Counseling* 5(2):68–75 (1983).

Steege, J.F. Dyspareunia and Vaginismus. *Clinical Obstetrics and Gynecology* 27(3):750–759 (September 1984).

Steele, R.W., W.P. Dmowski, and D.J. Marmer. Immunologic aspects of human endometriosis. *American Journal of Reproductive Immunology* 6(1):33–36 (July–August 1984).

Stewart, M., and C.W. Buck. Physicians' knowledge of and response to patients' problems. *Medical Care* 15(7):578–585 (July 1977).

Stretcher, V.J. Improving physician-patient interactions: A review. *Patient Counseling and Health Education* 4(3):129–136 (1983).

Suginami, H., K. Hamada, and K. Yano. A case of endometriosis of the lung treated with danazol. *Obstetrics and Gynecology* (Supp.) 66(3):68S–71S (September 1985).

Sulewski, J.M., F.D. Curcio, C. Bronitsky, and V.G. Stenger. The treatment of endometriosis at laparoscopy for infertility. *American Journal of Obstetrics and Gynecology* 138(2):128–132 (September 1980).

Tambrands, Inc. *The Tampax Report*. Lake Success, NY: 1981.

Tavris, C. *Anger: The Misunderstood Emotion*. New York: Simon & Schuster, A Touchstone Book, 1984.

Techniques tips for doctor-patient communication: A roundtable. *Patient Care* 15(21):106–110 (December 15, 1981).

Townell, N.H., and J.D. Vanderwalt. Intestinal endometriosis. *Postgraduate Medical Journal* 60(706):514–517 (August 1984).

Townell, N.H., J.D. Vanderwalt, and G.M. Jagger. Intestinal endometriosis: Diagnosis and management. *British Journal of Surgery* 71(8):629–630 (August 1984).

Tsoi, M.M., P.C. Ho, and R.S.M. Poon. Pre-operation indicators and post-hysterectomy outcome. *British Journal of Clinical Psychology* 23:151–152 (1984).

Tsuei, J.J. Acupuncture treatment in modern practice of obstetrics and gynecology. *Journal of Chinese Medicine* 1(2):37–41 (June 1984).

U.S. Department of Health and Human Services. *Vital and Health Statistics: Patterns of Ambulatory Care in Obstetrics and Gynecology*. Hyattsville, MD: February 1984.

Walker, J., I. MacGillivray, and M. MacNaughton. *Combined Textbook of Obstetrics and Gynaecology* (9th ed.). Edinburgh: Churchill Livingstone, 1976.

Walker, J.B., and R. L. Katz. Peripheral nerve stimulation in the management of dysmenorrhea. *Pain* 11:355–361 (1981).

Wallis, C. The career woman's disease? *Time*, April 28, 1986, p. 62.

Walton, L.A. A reexamination of endometriosis after pregnancy. *Journal of Reproductive Medicine* 19(6):341–344 (December 1977).

Watters, W.W., J. Askwith, M. Cohen, and J.A. Lamont. An assessment approach to couples with sexual problems. *Canadian Journal of Psychiatry* 30(1):2–11 (February 1985).

Weaver, M.T. Acupressure: An overview of theory and application. *Nurse Practitioner* 10(8):38–42 (August 1985).

Wedell, M.A., P. Billings, and J.A. Fayez. Endometriosis and the infertile patient. *Journal of Obstetrical, Gynecological and Neonatal Nursing* 14(4)280–283 (July–August 1985).

Weed, J.C. Prostaglandins as related to endometriosis. *Clinical Obstetrics and Gynecology* 23(3):895–899 (September 1980).

Weed, J.C., and P.C. Arquembourg. Endometriosis: Can it produce an autoimmune response resulting in infertility? *Clinical Obstetrics and Gynecology* 23(3):885–893 (September 1980).

Weideger, P. *Menstruation and Menopause: The Physiology and Psychology, the Myth and the Reality.* New York: Alfred A. Knopf, 1976.

Weiner, H. An integrative model of health, illness, and disease. *Health Social Worker* 9:253–260 (Fall 1984).

Wheeler, J.M., B.M. Johnston, and L.R. Malinak. The relationship of endometriosis to spontaneous abortion. *Fertility and Sterility* 39(5):656–660 (May 1983).

Wheeler, J.M., and L. R. Malinak. Postoperative danazol therapy in infertility patients with severe endometriosis. *Fertility and Sterility* 36(4):460–463 (October 1981).

Wheeler, J.M., and L.R. Malinak. Recurrent endometriosis: Incidence, management, and prognosis. *American Journal of Obstetrics and Gynecology* 146(3):247–253 (June 1, 1983).

Wilson, J.R., and E.R. Carrington. *Obstetrics and Gynecology.* St. Louis: C.V. Mosby, 1979.

Wingo, P.A., et al. The mortality risk associated with hysterectomy, Part 1. *American Journal of Obstetrics and Gynecology* 152(7):803–808 (August 1, 1985).

Wise, T.N. Sexual dysfunctions following diseases of the reproductive organs. *Advances in Psychosomatic Medicine* 12:136–149 (1985).

Youngs, D.D., and A.A. Ahrhardt. *Psychosomatic Obstetrics and Gynecology.* New York: Appleton-Century-Crofts, 1980.

Zuspan, F.P., and C.D. Christian. *Reid's Controversy in Obstetrics and Gynecology.* Philadelphia: W.B. Saunders, 1983.

Index